Women Reveal What They Fear Most

Tame your FEARS

& Transform Them into Faith, Confidence & Action

CAROL KENT

NAVPRESS
BRINGING TRUTH TO LIFE
NavPress Publishing Group
P.O. Box 35001, Colorado Springs, Colorado 80935

The Navigators is an international Christian organization. Jesus Christ gave His followers the Great
Commission to go and make disciples (Matthew
28:19). The aim of The Navigators is to help fulfill
that commission by multiplying laborers for Christ in
every nation.

NavPress is the publishing ministry of The Navigators.
NavPress publications are tools to help Christians grow.
Although publications alone cannot make disciples
or change lives, they can help believers learn biblical
discipleship, and apply what they learn to their lives
and ministries.

Third printing, 1994

Some of the anecdotal illustrations in this book are
true to life and are included with the permission of the
persons involved. In some cases, names and identifying
details have been changed to protect the privacy of the
people involved. All other illustrations are composites
of real situations, and any resemblance to people living
or dead is coincidental.

Unless otherwise identified, all Scripture quotations in
this publication are taken from the *HOLY BIBLE: NEW
INTERNATIONAL VERSION®* (NIV®). Copyright © 1973,
1978, 1984 by International Bible Society. Used by
permission of Zondervan Publishing House. All rights
reserved. Other versions used include: the *New King
James Version* (NKJV), copyright © 1979, 1980, 1982, 1990,
Thomas Nelson Inc., Publishers; *The Living Bible* (TLB) ©
1971, used by permission of Tyndale House Publishers,
Inc., Wheaton, IL 60189, all rights reserved; and the
King James Version (KJV).

Kent, Carol, 1947-
    Tame your fears : and transform them into faith,
confidence, and action / Carol Kent.
        p.   cm.
    ISBN 0-89109-760-0
    1. Christian women—Religious life.   2. Fear—
Religious aspects—Christianity.   I. Title.
BV4527.K453   1993
248.8'43—dc20

FOR A FREE CATALOG OF
NAVPRESS BOOKS & BIBLE STUDIES,
CALL 1-800-366-7788 (USA)
or 1-416-499-4615 (CANADA)

Contents

✤

This book is lovingly dedicated to my son,
Jason Paul Kent

❖

Dear J.P.,

Yesterday I attended your induction into the United States Naval Academy. My heart is filled with a paradoxical mixture of passionate pride and terrorizing fear.

As I watched you march in formation, I realized my days of hands on parenting are over and you are entering adulthood. In his address, Rear Admiral Lynch said,

> Your children are the cream of the crop. They competed against thousands of applicants for the place they secured as incoming midshipmen, and they are winners! We will train them to be the future military and political leaders of the country. You have given us your most prized possessions and we do not take that lightly. Your child will only ever return home again as a visitor.

While his words reverberated in my ears, the Navy jets flew overhead and the ceremony ended as abruptly as it began. I saw you briefly, and awkwardly said goodbye. I watched you walk away in a sailor's uniform in an unfamiliar place with a whole new life ahead of you. Tears clouded my vision as I turned to your father and said, "Have we taught him everything he needs to know?"

Son, you have brought me more joy and pride than I can describe. You are surrounded by prayer. In the middle of "in your face" harassment, never lose your sense of humor. Be a man of courage, integrity, honesty, and deep faith. In letting go of you, I am learning that the opposite of fear is faith. Endure "plebe summer" as a good soldier of Jesus Christ. He is grooming you for a unique place in His Kingdom!

I love you,
Mom

AVAILABLE FOR GROUPS:
Tame Your Fears Study Guide

Acknowledgments

Some authors are "writers who occasionally speak." I am a speaker who occasionally writes. In practical terms, that means the time it takes to write a book is not scheduled on my daily calendar. Several support people have come alongside at precisely the right moments to enable me to roll a manuscript off the computer (almost) on time and turn in a finished project.

I am indebted to these incredible people:

My editor, Traci Mullins—I am convinced that a mediocre editor explains; a good editor guides; a superior editor encourages during the process of explaining and guiding; and a great editor inspires and confronts, while giving confidence to an author. Traci is a rare gem as an editor. Her creative genius is woven throughout this project, and her ability to combine professionalism and friendship made the writing process a pleasure!

My husband, Gene Kent—This man lives out the true meaning of what Christian marriage is supposed to be. He envelops me with respect, humor, friendship, and passion. He frees me to meet deadlines without guilt and brings me chocolate candy bars when I'm brain dead.

My sisters—Jennie Dimkoff, Paula Afman, Bonnie Emmorey, and

Joy Carlson—I never get tired of the question, "Are all of those girls really in your family?" Growing up with so many women was a wonderful experience. Each of my sisters has overcome paralyzing fear to become the woman of influence she is today. Thanks to each of you for loving me intensely and for encouraging me along the way.

My administrative assistant, Shelly Aldrich—One day I took a step of faith and hired this woman to answer correspondence, handle phone calls, order office supplies, deal with interruptions, run errands, and feed my cat in my absence. (What a job description!) She makes me look better than I deserve and has freed me to do what God called me to do without getting trapped in paperwork.

My friends and prayer supporters—I am indebted to Sherrie Eldridge, Janet Johnson Fleck, Rhua Bliss, and Anne-Louise Denmark for sharing their personal journeys as illustrations in this book; Ginger Sisson, Deborah K. Jones, Kathe Wunnenberg, and Barbara Owlsley spent hours researching the topic of fear and provided me with countless numbers of computer printouts and copies of articles and illustrations that were invaluable during the writing process; Tommy Olmstead sent side-splitting cards filled with tasteless, hilarious humor to keep me encouraged; Linda Neff sent inspiring quotations to keep me motivated; Mama Afman prayed without ceasing, along with so many of those already listed above.

This book is a tribute to the combined efforts of each of you!

PART ONE

HOPE ... WHEN LIFE GETS LIFE GETS SCARY

"If I'm Such a Great Christian, Why Do I Have This Problem?"

DISCOVERING WE ARE NOT ALONE

✣

Have you ever thought how infectious fear can be?
It spreads from one person to another more quickly and certainly
than any of the fevers we know so well.

AMY CARMICHAEL
You Are My Hiding Place

"I can't do this! I don't want to do this! I don't want to be here! I think it is totally irrational to spend all this money to terrorize myself and risk possible injury that could keep me from functioning properly for weeks to come!" My words tumbled out frantically, mingled with stifled sobs.

My husband worked quietly, but steadily, as he continued to tighten my rented ski boots in preparation for what I knew was the inevitable experience just ahead. Then, with uncharacteristic candor, he looked me in the eyes and said, "You're afraid. So what? What's the worst thing that could happen? You might fall down and you'd have to get up again."

Now I was angry. He didn't understand. Fear was a subject I knew too well. A virus I had transferred to others. An emotion I loathed. A bed-partner I slept with. A paralyzing emotion I sometimes denied but always had to face. *Why couldn't he understand the depth of my fear? Why was he pushing me to do something I had no desire to do?*

We had lived in Michigan for years, within easy driving distance of numerous ski resorts. Every winter it always turned cold and snowy . . . and every winter I went into hibernation until the first breath of spring.

Skiing was for yuppies who lived "on the edge," I convinced myself. It was a sport for people who did not value straight noses and unbroken bones. It was for those who thrived on adrenaline for stimulation—instead of honest work in a legitimate vocation.

But our teenage son had requested downhill skis for Christmas, and we decided to treat him to a New Year's weekend at Shanty Creek Ski Lodge. From the moment he took his first trip down the hill, he was hooked. By the second day his skis were gliding down Schuss Mountain with precise accuracy, and it was hard to get him to take breaks for meals. He had discovered *his* sport!

Halfway through the weekend my husband, Gene, said, "Honey, Jason loves skiing. He's our only child. He will probably marry a woman who likes this sport. We may spend many future vacation weekends in ski lodges. If you want to spend time with your family, you have a choice: You can sit in the lodge drinking hot chocolate by the fire for the rest of your life, or you can conquer this phobia."

He was right. I hate it when he's right, especially when I have to admit it. Besides, I had already gained my seven extra Christmas pounds, and the prospects of that hot chocolate increasing the diameter of my thighs while *they* were getting exercise did not create a desirable image. I reluctantly yielded to his suggestion and registered for a ski lesson from one of the experts at the lodge.

Gene finished tightening my boots, then he carefully helped me balance as I moved in the direction of the bunny hill. I found myself wondering how many people had died on that hill—or worse yet, how many were permanently maimed?

He softened a bit. "Carol, I heard a speaker recently who said, 'There are only two fears we are born with: *falling* and *loud noises*. All the rest are learned or acquired.' I know you can conquer this fear!"

THE PROBLEM DEFINED

I was afraid of falling, all right. But my fear went deeper than that. His words reverberated in my mind "all the rest are *learned* or *acquired*." Where did fear come from? How did it get so powerful? Why did it immobilize so many people? What was the origin of this monster anyway? And most of all, *why* did it continue to plague *me*? After all, I had been a Christian for many years. I was a leader. A speaker. An author.

A wife. A mom. An educated, hard-working woman who believed the Bible and loved God. *Why did I still have this problem?*

Fear is one of our oldest and deadliest enemies. It causes illness, stifles creativity, prevents love, destroys families, depletes energy, feeds addictions, and holds people in bondage. For many women, fear is often an unwanted constant companion that will not leave. In the middle of watching the destructive force of fear, sometimes we forget there's a positive side to fear as well.

Webster tells us fear is any one of several responses: "(1) anxiety and agitation caused by the presence of danger, evil, or pain; dread, fright; (2) awe, reverence; (3) a feeling of uneasiness, anxiety, concern."[1]

That definition is helpful, but even more insight comes when we investigate fear as a verb: "(1) to be afraid of, to dread" (I can identify with that!); "(2) to feel reverence or awe for" (I certainly *fear* God in that way!); "(3) to expect with misgiving . . . to *feel* fear . . . to be uneasy or anxious."[2] (*Now that's a definition I can relate to.*) And that's what this book is all about!

UNDERSTANDING THE UNDERLYING TYPES OF FEAR

There are basically three types of fear: "holy" fear, "self-preserving" fear, and "slavish" fear. The first comes from our reverence for and awe of the God who created us and loves us. To investigate that type of fear fully would take a full-length book all by itself. The second has everything to do with the God-given instinct to run from danger, avert an accident, or protect ourselves and those we love. This "wise" form of fear causes us to take responsibility for ourselves and others. It provides the motivation to teach our children to look both ways before crossing the street and to use caution on a bicycle.

This book, however, is about "slavish" fear—the negative type that kills expressions of love, plugs lines of communication, imprisons victims of abuse, taunts with ridiculous phobias, controls by manipulation, and erodes all confidence and security. *Wise, self-preserving fear shifts into slavish fear when it becomes obsessive and controlling.* When a child reaches an age of maturity and a parent prevents the development of natural independence by immobilizing him or her with fears that are not based on reality, slavish fear takes over. When a sport as regulated and exhilarating as downhill snow skiing paralyzes me because of a twenty-year-old memory of one bad experience, I am allowing myself to be victimized by fear.

Boiled down to the bottom line, the negative aspect of fear is a problem of (1) *focus* and (2) *self-reliance*. It all began in the Garden of Eden. Adam and Eve had known a perfect relationship with God. They knew Him as their creator, companion, teacher, and friend. At that time in history the only fear present was absolutely holy. There was purity in God's relationship with Adam and Eve.

After Adam and Eve disobeyed God, a change occurred. With no instruction, Adam had an instant awareness of slavish fear. When God called, Adam responded, "I heard you in the garden, and I was afraid because I was naked; so I hid" (Genesis 3:10). Instead of rushing to be with his best friend, Adam is now doubting his position, fearful of not being accepted, and hiding in the bushes.

The false roots of Adam's fear are still with us today. God had always been there for him, but self-reliance kept him from asking for help:

- Adam feared abandonment, yet he chose to abandon the One he needed the most.
- He was ashamed of revealing who he really was, yet needed to be honest with God to learn how to live in a sinful world.
- He made himself lonely because he feared rejection.
- He gave in to temptation and felt unforgiven and afraid.

When sin entered the human race, Adam's *focus* was taken off God. *Self-reliance* (and let's add *self-preservation*) kicked in, and Adam was running and hiding. (Okay. I admit it. Eve had the problem too.) And today we're still doing the same thing—running and hiding! Adam's response is a lot like mine.

Slavish fear is a natural consequence of self-reliance. Sometimes "helping myself out and doing my best in the middle of my fears" keeps me from admitting that *sin and self-reliance are the same thing*. Trusting in "self" as Adam did leads to shame, slavery, obsessive, controlling behavior, and to thick walls of self-protection. It becomes a learned cycle that is hard to break.

Running. Hiding. Protecting myself. As Proverbs tells us, "The wicked man flees though no one pursues, but the righteous are as bold as a lion" (28:1). All this sometimes seems complicated to me, because when I'm afraid and choosing "run and hide" type behavior, I'm usually not telling myself, "Well, I'm emotionally running away from God right now, so that's why I'm feeling this overwhelming terror. It's just a problem of focus and self-reliance that I learned from Adam and Eve. I'll just change my direction."

When God asked Adam whether or not he had eaten from the forbidden tree, Adam immediately began to hurl blame in Eve's direction—a tactic I often use myself! When I'm afraid, I want to blame someone else for the problem. "The man said, 'The woman you put here with me—she gave me some fruit from the tree, and I ate it'" (Genesis 3:12).

When we are afraid and we're looking for someone to blame, our self-preservation kicks in and we often hurl (as Adam did) in a variety of ways.

J. Grant Howard put it this way:

We act as judge and jury and condemn others. We project our problems on those who live with us. We ridicule. We dominate. We are dogmatic. We are sarcastic, obnoxious, overbearing. We pronounce the final word, when we have no reason nor right to. We cut a person down neatly with a word of criticism. To his face. Or behind his back. We nitpick at someone else's behavior patterns and often fail to acknowledge our own weaknesses. We say, "You never do anything right. You always forget." "Never" and "always" are super-sharp, expertly-barbed arrows from the hurler's communication quiver. We blame God. We blame others. We even blame ourselves.[3]

Fear is complicated. Like Adam and Eve, sometimes we hurl blame and other times we emotionally run from God by conveniently "forgetting" past abuse that so deeply needs His healing. Or we lose ourselves in perfectionism. Perhaps we form codependent relationships with friends or relatives. Our running keeps us from revealing our doubts about God's love . . . or at times, the very *existence* of God. We dismiss prison-like phobias as "little hang-ups." We rarely reveal the true magnitude of our fear to other human beings. They might think we are weak.

Most of us have never thought much about where our fear came from or how it developed. What we *do* know is that it's a monster we live with, an emotion that's sometimes out of control. Our fear is an undesired and uninvited guest that invades the inner sanctums of our lives and establishes residency.

When fear invades, it comes with a customized wardrobe of disguises. So, for many of us, *recognizing* fear in its many forms is a lifetime struggle. *Dealing* with that fear once we've recognized it is a much greater challenge.

Fear is subtle and has many hidden forms. Attractive forms. Productive aspects. Admirable faces. Like someone dressing up for a costume party, fear can appear glamorous; the outside looks flawless, but the inside is rotting. Hurting. Hidden. Sick. Running. Dishonest. The person is masquerading as "healthy," but beneath her facade she is terminally ill.

If you picked up this book because the title caught your eye, that person might be you. Or it could be your friend, your sister, your mother, your neighbor, or your coworker. One thing you can't escape: You *do* know this person. And therefore you alone are responsible to do *something*. But what?

A POSITIVE SIDE TO FEAR?

Until recently, I never saw any personal benefits connected to fear. The disadvantages always seemed so obvious. I know women who are trapped in a web of spine-weakening and spirit-breaking fears. At times, I am one of those women. Some of the negative conditions fear produces are apprehension, anxiety, low productivity, loss of vitality and serenity, intimidation, paralysis, resentment, rage, and obsessive self-protection.

The plus side of all of this is that there are positive conditions fear can lead us to: awe, adrenaline, humility, a shift of focus from finite to infinite power. When I give myself permission to see the positive aspects of fear, I get a totally new focus on the potential of this powerful emotion. Fear is often viewed as a roadblock to happiness, an insurmountable obstacle on the road to success and fulfillment. In this book we will learn techniques for taming fear, for turning it into appropriate power, positive action, and love.

Peter McWilliams' words remind us of the benefit of fear:

Fear provides the energy to do your best in a new situation. When you're afraid, your senses sharpen, your eyes narrow, you have more adrenaline, more precise focus, more energy. You are more aware.

If you're afraid to do something, do it despite the fear. As time goes by, you will realize that the fear is actually working to your advantage.[4]

FIVE FORMS OF FEAR

Before we talk about the solution, we need to identify slavish fear in its many forms. During the past two years, I have been absorbed in this topic. Certain fears have at times paralyzed me, so I began asking women all over the United States and Canada what their fears were. Their answers convinced me that geographical location, economic background, educational credentials, denominational affiliation, and strength of personality made very little difference in the intensity of fear.

All of us have experienced the paralyzing grip of this emotion we would rather live without! The comforting factor I discovered is that we are not alone. Here are the catagories of fear that women have described to me repeatedly.

THE FEAR OF THINGS THAT HAVEN'T HAPPENED . . . YET!

Fear 1: Paralyzing Phobias

Cheryl was a "basket case." She was afraid of everything. If someone shook her hand, she knew she'd get a disease. If we were in a crowded room, she couldn't breathe. If we were at the beach, she didn't swim—the water was too cold, or she'd forgotten her swimming suit. There was always an excuse, but we knew she was afraid of the water. She had phobias to go along with situations most people never dreamed could happen. Irrational panic was her constant companion—and Cheryl seemed to need a baby-sitter more than a friend.

Fear 2: Potential Disasters

Diana's husband was an hour late for dinner. With every passing minute her anxiety increased. There had been layoffs at his plant. At first factory positions were cut, and now the management team was being streamlined. Her husband had called earlier in the day asking her to pray. A meeting was set up for that afternoon and more cuts would be discussed. What if he lost his job? With the economy so uncertain, where would he go? How could they pay the mortgage payment? And what about the children's college tuition? What would they do? As the clock continued to record the passing of time, she was *sure* he had received a pink slip. Her head pounded with the start of a migraine. Much of Diana's life was consumed with what she knew were "legitimate" fears of negative things that might happen to someone in her family.

THE FEAR OF BEING VULNERABLE

Fear 3: Losing Control

Kathy was greatly respected. She was the hardest working committee member on the retreat staff. When she accepted a job, it was done correctly and quickly. Her motto seemed to be, "If it's worth doing, it's worth doing right!" In fact, Kathy was about as close to perfect as a human being could get. Her house was immaculate. Her children were clean and well-behaved. She was almost too perfect.

It was hard to get close to Kathy, because you always felt as if you were interrupting her well-planned life and her carefully scheduled day. Although her outside image was enviable, Kathy was miserable. Her family was miserable. Even their dog was miserable. Kathy's controlling personality and manipulation of family members were making life inside the "white picket fence" unbearable. Kathy was afraid of being vulnerable and sought to mask her fears in a prison of her own making. Her fear of losing control was itself controlling; everyone around her felt as if they were behind bars too!

Fear 4: Revealing Who I Really Am

Cindy was embarrassed by her background. Her father was an alcoholic, and her mother raised four children on welfare and part-time work. Cindy's greatest desire was to get an education and lift herself out of that lifestyle of gloom. A school counselor took interest in Cindy and helped her get a scholarship to an accredited university.

Life changed drastically for the young woman who had experienced poverty and the inner city. She married a dynamic, compassionate man who loved her without reservation. But Cindy was filled with fear at her husband's family reunions. Anxiety plagued her when she faced his business dinners or had to make small talk with her middle-class neighbors. Cindy's fear of self-disclosure and her shame regarding her background kept her caught in a web of insecurity. A life that had all the markings of happiness was stained with fear.

THE FEAR OF ABANDONMENT

Fear 5: Disappointing People
"Where are you?" The voice calling the car phone was rough. Domineering. Authoritative. Parental. Kay's husband was checking up on her again. "I'm home from work early. I'm hungry and I want dinner on the table *now*! I told you it was okay for you to work as long as you took care of your responsibilities in this house first! If you're too busy to pay attention to the most important person in your life, I'll find someone who can!" He hung up.

For seventeen years of marriage it was the same old story. Kay was miserably unhappy. When Steve was successful in business and able to finance his personal pleasures, he was fun to be with. When he was drinking and/or feeling financial strain, he was abusive, controlling, and obnoxious. Kay was dependent on Steve for a roof over her head, support for their son, and for proving to her parents that she had made the right choice in a husband they had questions about. She was afraid he might leave her penniless and homeless, but she was more afraid of disappointing and alienating her strict Christian mother and father who did not approve of divorce under *any* circumstances. In a warped way she was deeply emotionally attached to this man and she *did* love him. The fear of being abandoned by him and by her parents simultaneously was more than she could endure.

Fear 6: Being Rejected
Joanne pulled the blankets up over her head. She was discouraged, depressed, and afraid. A few months ago she and her husband had a major communication breakdown. But they were Christians, so she thought they would work out their problems.

But last night he had dispassionately told her he had filed for divorce—"irreconcilable differences," the paper stated. His unemotional approach to ending the marriage was incomprehensible. They shared *three* children. She was being rejected by the man she always thought loved her. What if her children chose *his* side in the divorce? What if the people at church blamed *her* for not being a better wife? What if she was unable to get a job that would adequately care for her children's needs? What if she was alone for the rest of her life?

The sobering fear of abandonment obliterated her ability to function in a normal fashion. She was constantly on the verge of tears. Simple tasks felt like impossible feats. This was unfair—cruel and unusual punishment for a woman who had devoted her whole adult life to being a good wife and mother.

THE FEAR OF TRUTH

Fear 7: Facing My Past

The letter came from an old friend. Victoria is the kind of person I always wanted to be like—immensely talented, attractive, vivacious. But beneath her energy was a deep sadness. For as long as I had known her, I sensed something was haunting her. But what?

I read, "Sometime I would like to talk with you about what I've been learning in counseling. It has been wonderful/horrible, emotional, and very informative. I am finally finding out some of the reasons why I have been rather joyless. I am in awe of what our minds are able to do—what our emotions remember but our minds forget—and I'm in greater awe of how God protects us but is still ready to help us by revealing our pain.

"I have wondered why I *couldn't* have the joy that sometimes sounds rather easy to get. . . . I'm on the verge of remembering (and exposing) some frightening things. Until that happens I can't put a lot of relationships in my life in proper perspective."

My heart is heavy for Victoria. She is afraid to face the past, but she knows there is no other way to get on with the future.

Fear 8: Losing My Faith

Joyce waited until I was alone. We were in an exquisite retreat setting in the mountains with a large group of women from her dynamic young church. I had spotted her in the background waiting to talk to me. When the time came, her eyes flooded with tears and she strained to get the words out.

"Carol, I have no one to talk to. All these women think I'm one of their leaders, but I'm not sure I even believe in God anymore. The doubts I have make me ashamed, and if my husband and children knew what I'm telling you, it would destroy them. But I'm so afraid I have lost my faith completely. *Who* is God? *Where* is He? My mother just died of cancer, and my dad has heart problems. My prayers have gone unanswered. *Why* does He let innocent people suffer? I know I'm not supposed to question Him, but I don't believe anymore. How can I be a Christian and feel this way? I'm so afraid, and I can't turn to anyone in my church for help."

Many women share this fear of losing their faith. They have nagging doubts, disbeliefs, and forgiveness issues, when they feel a real Christian should be able to resolve all of this.

THE FEAR OF MAKING WRONG CHOICES

Fear 9: Getting Trapped

Heather was a go-getter. She had married her high school sweetheart at eighteen. She gave birth to two children before her twenty-second birthday. Now she was in her early thirties and feeling a little sad that she hadn't waited for marriage and children until *after* her education was completed. Her husband, Rod, was a nice guy and a good provider, but after working long hours in a local factory, he wasn't too enthusiastic about meeting her emotional or intellectual needs. Heather wanted to pursue a college degree, and Rod was feeling threatened.

Emotion enveloped Heather as she came to grips with her worst fear: being trapped in a dead-end situation. She felt that she would never be able to live up to her potential because of lost opportunity. How could she stay married to a man who held her in intellectual slavery by his own fears that she might "outgrow" him and find companionship with a more educated and refined partner? Actually, that thought rather appealed to Heather, and her imagination played mental videos of the longed-for romance and the exquisite hero who would rescue her from this present bondage.

Fear 10: Achieving Success/Admitting Failure

Carrie *loved* to write. She had kept her thoughts recorded in a journal since junior high. As she matured, Carrie always knew her life would revolve around the publishing world. She obtained a degree in journalism and accepted a position as an editor with a major book publisher. Her editing skills were excellent, and she enjoyed working with the authors.

When a position opened as acquisitions editor for her publisher, she accepted the job with a sense of controlled exhilaration—and very real fear. What if she failed? What if her ideas weren't creative enough to inspire the writers she worked with? What if she pushed a project through that the rest of the editorial staff had questions about and it bombed? It would be her fault! The fear of risking her professional reputation kept her from pursuing exciting projects.

The idea of succeeding was just as threatening to Carrie. If the authors she recommended did well, that might mean an increased workload and higher expectations. Doing well could be more stressful than failing. Carrie was caught in the fear of making a wrong choice.

WHAT DO I DO NEXT?

Identifying our fears and admitting we have a problem is only the beginning. Most of us have struggled for a lifetime with fear at some level. I've been frustrated by an underlying belief that "godly Christian women" aren't supposed to struggle with phobias, fears, and anxieties, because "trusting the Lord" should be more than enough to handle any problem. So I'm a failure. Now what?

The first step to finding a solution is to acknowledge that there *are* times when we question our faith and struggle with fear. Some of us have had fleeting thoughts of suicide. Most often, instead of physical suicide, we experience emotional suicide. Fear becomes "comfortable" because it's familiar. We're used to feeling like powerless subjects in the fear monster's kingdom. Instead of taming the monster and enjoying our lives, we allow ourselves to die slowly by many of the following prescriptions: denial, addictions, withdrawal, control, shame, and self-hatred. Why?

The next chapter will take us a step further by explaining the chain reaction we go through when fear is developed and ultimately defeated. There *is* a way to face this monster squarely, and we have been empowered by God to overcome it and get on with productive and happy lives. But He never forces this on us. He lets us choose.

AN INVITATION

If you have ever asked yourself the following questions, the rest of this book was written for you:

- Are my fears the same as fears faced by other women?
- What *is* fear, and can it be controlled?
- Is my perfectionism actually based in the fear of being vulnerable?
- If I reveal myself to you, will you accept me—or judge me?
- Why am I afraid that the worst-case scenario will happen to me or my family?
- Why am I so afraid of being rejected, abandoned, or lonely?
- If I face the fears of the past and admit the truth, will I cause myself more pain?
- If I make wrong choices in my career or relationships, will the consequences be insurmountable?
- Can I *really* be a Christian if I struggle with fear?
- Is there a positive side to fear that could actually be a springboard to success and happiness?

Overcoming lifelong fear is inconvenient. The process destroys carefully constructed facades. It leaves one feeling naked. Unprotected. Vulnerable. Exposed. It seems odd to speak of fear as "safe," but as with any long-term companion—even a cruel one—saying goodbye is difficult. Henri Nouwen confirms the frightening risk involved in the process:

> We are afraid that the God who says He loves us will prove in the end to be more demanding than loving. I am convinced that the real reason we pray so little is fear: fear of facing God, fear also of facing our own and others' brokenness. I think our fearful hearts are saying: "Can I really trust God? Will He really show me His love when I don't keep anything hidden from Him—neither my own pain nor the pain of the world—or will I be crushed by His anger and lose the little bit of freedom I have so carefully carved out for myself?"[5]

Facing our fear head on can feel intensely risky. But it can be a stepping stone to humble faith, renewed confidence, appropriate power and courage, and trusting reverence toward a sovereign, powerful, and loving God. "Perfect love casts out fear."[6] It's in the Bible. And it's true. But how does it work? If you are among the few who dare to embrace change, read on.

"What Happens Inside My Head When I'm Afraid?"

RECOGNIZING AND TAMING YOUR FEARS

*Fear was designed by God to give our bodies the sudden bursts
of strength and speed we need in emergencies.
But when fear becomes a permanent condition, it can paralyze the spirit,
keeping us from taking the risks of generosity,
love, and vulnerability that characterize citizens of God's kingdom.*

DAVID NEFF
"Christians Who Fear Too Much," *Christianity Today*

The long-awaited package was in the mailbox. The professional label with the return address and logo of the company confirmed my suspicions. With hands trembling, I opened the padded envelope and removed the cassette tapes. A decision had to be made. I could listen to them now or prolong the torture.

The call had come a year earlier from a woman asking if I would be willing to speak for their denominational conference. The location sounded exotic to this mother of a preschooler, who rarely got out of town, much less out of state, with private accommodations in a top-of-the-line hotel. Before the woman hung up, she asked if the group could have my presentations professionally recorded so conference participants could purchase tapes of the sessions.

I was *excited*! This was the most important opportunity in ministry that had ever come my way. A stimulating challenge! However, as the date approached, *living through* my commitment was much more taxing than I had anticipated. The preparation for the messages wasn't the problem. I had taught Bible studies for years . . . but being "good enough" for this sophisticated audience was so intimidating I wanted to back out. But it was too late.

I boarded an airplane and flew to meet this sizable group. It was the first time an organization had paid for expensive travel arrangements so that I could be their keynote speaker. Panic gripped my heart as I approached the lectern. Thoughts raced.

"How could I *ever* be professional enough to be worth the amount of money they paid to bring me here?

"What if my mouth gets so dry I am not able to speak a word? Worse yet, what if my brain leaves my body when I stand in front of the audience?

"*Why* did I accept an assignment that is totally out of my realm of potential success?

"I am scared to death! What if my heart quits pumping and I die?

"What if I do such a terrible job that these people tell other groups what a failure I am?" (Well, at least I'd *never* have to speak in public again!)

Three weeks after the event, I realized I *did* live through the experience and now the suspense was killing me. Did I sound as bad as I knew I was? Or by some miracle had God transformed my frayed nerves into supernatural energy? I could bear the uncertainty no longer.

I slipped the tape into the cassette player and pushed "PLAY." The magnetic tape rolled, but the inferior quality of the recording surprised me. With my opening remarks came a loud, unnerving "thump, thump, thump" that reverberated over the recorded message. It was so unrelenting and distracting it was hard to follow the central idea. Then, as the minutes rolled on, there was more air time between thumps, and finally, ten minutes into the talk, all discernable thumping stopped. What was the problem? A reputable company had done the recording.

As I pondered the confusing situation, a piece of paper fluttered to the floor from the padded envelope. It read:

Dear Mrs. Kent,

When we heard the recording of your first talk at the conference we thought our equipment was terribly defective. But the longer we listened, we realized our sensitive microphone was just picking up the sound of your beating heart. Obviously, you relaxed after a while!

DISSECTING THE *REAL* PROBLEM

Fear has so many forms that sometimes a solution seems elusive. On numerous occasions I have tried to "talk myself out of" fearful feelings. It never worked, although it *did* make me feel like I was doing *something*. Whether the problem is as basic as the fear of public speaking or as psychologically deep as the fear of abandonment or betrayal, some basic definitions can help us to form a framework for dealing with the problem.

The solution to overcoming fear is *not* positive self-talk or a greater effort to control my own behavior or the behavior of others. *The solution is a broken humility and trust in a sovereign, engaged, and loving God.*

But how does that work? What sounds logical, or even like "the proper spiritual response," on paper is often much more difficult to experience in real-life situations. And it leaves me cold. Wanting to give up.

My friend Nancy has a distorted concept of God due to past damage by an abusive father. If the solution to the fear problem is to let God be the ultimate deliverer and protector, how can she address her fear or rage toward God for His apparent abandonment in the past? Her fears are great. Her rage seems justified. God seems far away and uninvolved in her life—and cruel. Why would a loving God have allowed the abuse to take place? Most days it's easier for her to disguise her problem than to identify her basic fears and deal with them.

We might like to think that only those who have been emotionally devastated struggle with fear, but that's not always true. Paul Moede sheds light on this:

> Fear is not the private domain of the weak. It strikes at the
> best of us. It does not restrict itself to the individual but, like a
> virus, it can be transmitted to others. And its most dangerous
> aspect—especially for the Christian—is its ability to slap hand-
> cuffs and shackles on life, to keep the believer who wears them
> bound up in a prison of frustration and hopelessness. In this
> prison, God can actually become the perceived enemy instead of
> the Deliverer.[1]

How do we get so distorted in our thinking—so brainwashed by the fear monster? We need to take a closer look at those sneaky little human propensities mentioned earlier.

TERROR AT SEA

The setting is the Sea of Galilee.[2] Jesus Christ's public ministry is in its heyday. People have been healed. Demon-possessed men have been delivered. Thousands have been fed with a little boy's lunch. Pretty newsworthy stuff!

Jesus is physically exhausted. Emotionally spent. In need of time with His Father. The disciples get into the boat and go ahead of Him. He dismisses the crowd and goes into the hills for a time of prayer. As evening comes, a storm threatens. The boat is thrashed around by rowdy waves. The wind grows harsh. Jesus walks on the water toward His friends.

The scared-stiff disciples think He's a ghost and scream in terror. Jesus *immediately* responds, "Take courage! It is I. Don't be afraid." Impulsive Peter gets inspired and wants to walk on the water to meet Him. He gets out of the boat, heads in Jesus' direction, recognizes the destructive force of the wind, and panics!

He screams, "Lord, save me!" *Immediately* Jesus reaches out to him, saves him from his worst fear, comforts him, and builds a spiritual lesson out of the whole event.

Peter had the same problem we have: *focus* and *self-reliance*. The whole story is easier to understand when we see ourselves on the page.

1. *Uncertain circumstances*—Almost every time I deal with fear, I face uncertain circumstances—just like the disciples did. My situation seems unfamiliar. My boat is rocking. My favorite Captain does not seem to be on board. My future is unknown.

2. *Wrong conclusions*—In the middle of my panic, I often look at the obvious instead of the supernatural. Instead of seeing Jesus supernaturally at work in the middle of my storm, I see all kinds of ghosts, represented by my personal fears. Sometimes I voice my fears loudly as the disciples did. Other times I feel angry and powerless. "Where is Jesus when I need Him most?"

3. *Impulsive conduct*—Peter's "jump out of the boat" behavior reminds me of myself. Sometimes I cry, "Lord, if You are *really* here,

in the middle of my panic and my frightening situation, prove Yourself supernaturally. I mean, *do* something so I know it's You!"

4. *Desperate call*—When I, like Peter, step out in trust, I sometimes take my eyes off Him and focus on my terrorizing circumstances. The "winds of fear" look much worse than they did before I tried to trust Him. I cry, "Lord, save me!"

5. *Immediate calm—Without delay* He reaches out to me and says, "You of little faith . . . why did you doubt?" And in the security of His compassionate eye contact and warm, affirming grip, my heart begins the measured, careful journey toward accepting His perfect love.

There it is—spelled out in the Bible. Jesus is the solution to the terrors around us. So why do so many of us *not* experience this immediate calming connection with God in the middle of our overwhelming fears? What can we do when Jesus doesn't "fix" our situation? This book will address those questions.

SIX DISGUISES OF FEAR

Many of us have lived behind our disguises for so long we hardly recognize that fear motivates many of our destructive behaviors. I have, at times, starred in all the roles in the play "The Six Disguises of Fear." Sometimes my performances have been worthy of standing ovations. One role could have brought me an Oscar. The beginning of positive change comes when we leave our costumes in the dressing room after admitting to one of the following roles.

1. A *perfectionist* lifestyle: "If I can please all of the people in my life with flawless behavior and control everything and everyone around me, I won't have to admit my deep insecurities and fears."

2. A *possessive* nature: "If I can protect the people I love the most by establishing the borders of their activities and guarding the dimensions of their interactions with other people, I will safeguard them from fearful experiences."

3. A *"picky"* attitude: "If I can criticize someone else, I will look better. I won't have to admit that it makes me feel like a bigger and less fearful person when I put somebody else's personality or methods down in order to secure my own position."

4. A *pretentious* faith: "If I make a list of what *real* Christians do and don't do and show people my saintliness in action, perhaps I can cover

up my fears, which are usually expressed through pride, inflexibility, legalism, and condemnation of 'less godly' people."

5. A *passionate* workaholism: "If I invest my total energy in worthy causes and/or work hard enough to earn the approval of my superiors, I'll be too tired to worry about my fears. If I just keep busy enough with my family responsibilities and personal activities, I won't have to acknowledge the ache inside of me and admit that I don't know how to give or receive love."

6. A *plastic* smile: "If I look like a trusting person, soon I'll feel like a trusting person. When I'm confused and afraid, I just keep smiling, especially at church, because most of those people expect me to be spiritually mature—and they are the *last* people I would admit my fears to!"

PERSONAL INVENTORY

Take a minute to identify any of the disguises mentioned above that you identify with. After you've given that some thought, ask yourself the following questions:

- What is the "ache" in my soul that has never been filled?
- Are my disguises so much a part of who I am that I have never admitted (even to myself) the fears they cover up?
- What (or who) triggers a fearful response in me?
- Do I struggle with guilt over my fears?
- Am I afraid to give and receive love?
- Am I experiencing a sense of hopelessness?
- Do I *want* to change, or am I afraid to leave the paradoxical comfort zone of my fearful disguises?

THE ANATOMY OF FEAR

In simple terms fear can be described as, "Anxiety and agitation caused by the presence of danger, evil, or pain; it is dread, fright, or a feeling of uneasiness, anxiety, or concern; it's to be afraid of somebody or something (real or imagined); it is to expect with misgiving, to be uneasy or anxious."[3] So what really happens inside my head when I'm afraid? When we analyze the whole process, it's easier to understand as a chain reaction.

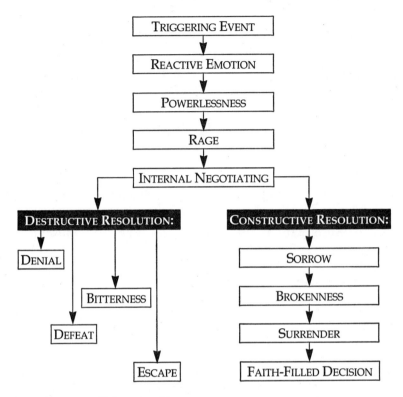

Triggering Event/Situation/Person
Something or someone is always the cause of fear. There is a "trigger point" that makes us aware of danger, evil, or pain. The cause might be from a real or imagined source, but it feels threatening, harmful, and disarming.

Reactive Emotion
Our first honest reaction to the triggering event is virtually involuntary. It might be the emotion of shock, terror, panic, dread, anxiety, horror, hurt, anger, or shame. Depending on our personalities, we have different initial reactions to the same events. For instance, one person might have a panic reaction that is immediately recognizable as fear. Someone else's first response might be anger, which could be displayed by a volatile outburst or by passive, wounded withdrawal. Although the initial reactive emotion may vary, fear is always what's underneath.

Powerlessness

After we have an intense, automatic, emotional response to an event, it doesn't take long to realize that things aren't going according to our plan. We feel alone and unprotected before a scary, powerful person or situation. We are not in control the way we would like to be or thought we were. Things are happening to us—or inside of us—without our permission! This powerless feeling often leads to thoughts of despair. If you have been emotionally or physically abused, you can quickly identify with this stage in the chain reaction.

This is a frightening feeling, and we aren't comfortable staying with it for long. We feel overwhelmed by what is happening, the way Peter felt when he looked around him at the storm. When our focus is on ourselves and our life circumstances, rather than on Christ, we realize we are pretty puny and helpless. If we were sinless, we would immediately turn our focus to Christ's sufficiency, but every human's natural tendency is to try to regain control first. So we move to the next stage.

Rage

The rage response sometimes begins with a feeling of betrayal. "Wait a minute, here. What happened to my safety and security? How can this be happening to me? I can't believe *that person* or *life* or *God* has let me down so completely!" At this point, sometimes unconsciously, we raise our fist in the face of God. We cry, "I hate what is happening here, and *I won't have it!* I refuse to feel helpless and dependent. God, You have let me down by allowing me to experience this situation or emotion, and I can't trust You anymore. I'm determined to find a better way to resolve my feelings."

This rage response may or may not feel like anger, but in essence, it's a posture of defiance (self-reliance) that is based on the fear that God can't be trusted, so we must go it alone in order to have things the way we want them. This is the nature of sin.

Internal Negotiating

Here lies the turning point in the whole chain reaction. The first four steps occur very quickly—almost involuntarily. Sometimes we are not even aware of every step. Once we have (1) *identified a trigger point*, (2) *experienced a reactive emotion*, (3) *felt totally power-*

less, and (4) *responded with overt or subtle rage*, we begin (5) *internal negotiating*.

This is where we thrash around trying to come up with a way to fix our feelings or situation. It's our self-centered, determined effort to escape both our pain/powerlessness and the need to surrender to a Power greater than ourselves. At this pivotal point, we come up with our options: *Will we choose the path of self-reliance or the path of God-reliance?* Depending on our answer, we will "resolve" our fear in either a destructive (God-denying) way or a constructive (God-honoring) way. One of the two following courses of action will be chosen.

Destructive Course of Action

If we choose the destructive route, we'll get stuck in one of four "resolutions." None of these choices solves the problem or takes away the fear. All are rigid, dead-end choices.

Denial: A frequent reaction to fear is to deny there is a problem, person, or painful situation that must be dealt with. Even when our initial reactions to a triggering event are powerful, we are amazingly adept at climbing to the surface of life again where we can pretend we aren't really angry or afraid.

Defeat: Many of us respond to fear with a posture of automatic defeat. We believe negative things have happened to us, causing our fears, and we have no power to change our feelings or life situations. We have no energy or confidence to take action and believe we can't handle our triggering event, situation, or person—so we give up. We play the role of a hopeless victim, squashed by life and by God.

Bitterness: Another popular response to fear is to look around and find someone else to blame—our parents, spouse, friends, coworkers, or even God. If we can point the finger at another person who is responsible for causing our grief, we can "justify" our paralyzing bitterness and delay any positive action toward resolving the fear in a God-honoring way.

Escape: Perhaps the most prevalent of all the destructive resolutions to fear is running away from reality. Many of us have become quite skilled at muffling our troubles in layers of compulsive/addictive behavior so we don't have to admit our feelings or deal with our fears.

This choice denys God a chance to work and leads to perfectionism, legalistic spirituality, workaholism, codependency, or enslavement to a wide variety of mood-altering substances or behaviors.

Constructive Course of Action

On the other hand, if we choose the constructive route, avoiding the four dead-end choices, we allow our rageful, self-reliant thrashing around to bring us to our knees — and into a more honest, substantial relationship with God.

Sorrow

Sometimes we wallow around in a mental pigpen of betrayal, powerlessness, hurt, and anger for a long time. The turning point occurs when we stop trying to "fix" our feelings or situation and begin to grieve honestly and deeply. We live in a "groaning" creation where imperfect people hurt and disappoint us. That's sad. When powerful people abuse their positions and make us fearful, that's sad. When we are abandoned by someone we expected to love us, that's sad. But when we allow the sorrow of a sinful world to penetrate us, something else happens. When we cease playing the blame game and allow ourselves to grieve, we change.

Celebrate the moment! Horrible as it is, sorrow is the first major step toward a real solution. We have been betrayed. That's sad. We have felt powerless. That's sad. We have been profoundly hurt. That's sad. We've been angry and internally consumed with rage. That's sad. We aren't relating to other people and God the way He intended His children to relate. That's sad. But Christ promised that those who mourn will be comforted!

Brokenness

We are needy people. When we acknowledge on a deep level that we are much too impotent and unwise to resolve our problems and fears without help from a Power much greater than ourselves — God the Father — we are on our way to real healing. We can continue to respond with fearful emotions while we're walking on the uncertain waters of life. Or we can recognize the strength of the hand that He is already extending toward us and humbly acknowledge our need. We can say, "Lord, I cannot pick myself up by my own bootstraps. I need

You." A broken heart is a humble heart, and a humble heart isn't too ashamed or self-reliant to ask for help.

Surrender

Surrender is knowing where to turn and doing it. It's crying, "Father, save me! I'm drowning in my circumstances. My fears envelop me. Uncertainties are everywhere. My past is a ghost before me. Father, forgive me for thinking I could solve all this on my own. Take away any false guilt I carry for the honest feelings of hurt or anger I have had or for what others have done to me. Help me to toss my extra baggage overboard. Teach me how to trust You. My boat cannot sail in these rough waters without You."

Surrender can be a hard pill to swallow. It implies giving up my will. My desires. My plan of action. My fearful disguises. Taking off my masks. Revealing my need. Confessing my sin. Admitting that after years of serving Jesus, I still struggle with understanding the perfect love that casts out fear. With my surrender comes a willingness to be taught. To give up the limelight, the excuses. To stop blaming other people and events for my fears and struggles.

As I let go I feel lighter. Less weighed-down. More honest. Less compulsive. *Maybe this new feeling is what Christianity is supposed to feel like.* I hope so.

Faith-Filled Decision

Once I let go of the situation, the person, the deep emotion of fear along with the potential consequences and implications and place it all in God's hands, I can decide to trust Him to take me through whatever lies ahead. I can face my past and accept the truth. I can reveal who I am to others and not be overwhelmed with shame or anxiety. I can live today without sinking in the storms of the past. I can set my sail, even knowing there will be fearful winds ahead and uncertain rocks beneath the surface.

Something is different. It has to do with the mystery of my *fear of God*. He is awesome. He is holy. He is kind. He is good. He loves me. Beneath my meager understanding of Him is the knowledge that *nothing* can happen to me that does not have the potential for transforming me into His likeness and bringing glory to His name. No disgrace, hurt, pain, abuse, shame, embarrassment, or fear needs to be wasted. He can turn it to good.

A PERSONAL CHALLENGE

How can someone believe this assumption of a kind God at work in the middle of life's fears if they have never experienced and don't now know what His "perfect love" is? This book will address that question. The next ten chapters deal with specific fears many women have (or share). I'm among you. A fellow struggler. Maybe you're in bondage to one of them too.

Don't be discouraged. There's hope just ahead. Take a risk. Step out of the boat and walk on the water. It is frightening at first. But when your eyes meet those of the Captain, your fear is diminished. Your confidence grows. Your faith is restored. When He reaches for your hand on the uncertain waters, look to Him, hold tightly, and don't be afraid.

PART TWO

OVERCOMING THE FEAR OF THINGS THAT HAVEN'T HAPPENED...YET!

CHAPTER THREE

"Why Do I Let Irrational Panic Immobilize Me?"
FEAR 1: PARALYZING PHOBIAS

✛

Severe anxiety disorders can exist even in loving Christian homes.
They are often the outcome of strictness, misunderstandings,
or miscommunication, and they result in unexpressed anger and resentment.

KAREN RANDAU
Conquering Fear

Moonlit gravestones. Dark shadows. Eerie sounds. Stray cats. Sadness. Death. Funeral homes. Cars with flags. Somber faces. People crying. The year we moved to the house next to the cemetery produced the worst memories of my childhood. My second-story bedroom window faced the burial grounds, and the scene from that spot would send chills through anyone who struggled with fear. I knew I was a Christian and that Heaven would be my final destination—but the process of dying and getting there always bothered me.

The panoramic view from the window was never pleasant or uplifting, but there were two horrible times to look toward the cemetery: when the moon was bright and when a group of mourners stood by one of those big holes in the ground. I'd pull my shade down, placing a tangible barrier between me and all of those dead bodies outside. But sometimes I had to look. And I was terrorized.

One glance out that window when the moon was full produced hundreds of shiny reflections off the grave markers on that well-used piece of property. And instantly I'd think about all of the decaying bodies in the ground right outside my window.

I had a morbid recurring thought. As a six-year-old who had been taken to church and Sunday school from her earliest days, I was well

39

acquainted with the part in the Bible that says "the dead in Christ will rise first." I prayed Jesus would not return before we moved to a different house. I truly believed my heart would fall out of my body if the Lord came back and I had to see those graves open. If Jesus *did* come for His own while we lived in that house, I hoped it would be during the daylight. Maybe I could handle the situation if I wasn't alone in my bedroom at night.

One evening I was put to bed early. Mom and Dad were entertaining company, and I knew I was not to interrupt the party the adults were having downstairs. I couldn't sleep, and hesitantly, I *dared* to peek out the window. The moon illuminated the entire graveyard and macabre shadows dancing between the trees and the marble stones convinced me that *something* (or *someone*) ghastly and hideous was coming toward my window. My terror was all-consuming. My breathing became erratic, and I thought I could actually hear the sound of my heart beating.

Quickly, I weighed the consequences between my father's wrath if I interrupted the party and my total inability to live with this gripping fear alone. I had a tooth that was slightly loose, but not ready to fall out on its own yet. I knew if the tooth came out, it would earn me the right to go down the steps where there was safety from the grisly scene out my window.

With determined action, I took a piece of string, tied it around my tooth, and secured the other end to the door handle. It took fierce courage to slam that door—but the desired result was forthcoming. My prize tooth and blood-stained pajamas earned me a ticket to the party below. And I was safe for another night from the hideous shadows and reminders of death on the other side of my window.

THE GHOSTS OF TODAY

I have often looked back on that stage of my life with a smile. After all, children are afraid of many imaginary ghosts. Certainly the power of imagination makes their fears far more exaggerated than any potential existing danger. But then I realize there are some days when I deal with fears that are just as debilitating as those I experienced from the bedroom window. Only this time they don't look like eerie shadows. Because I'm older and can actually identify some of the "gruesome goblins" of fear in my life, they are more obvious and, in many ways, more painful and paralyzing. I know I *should* be mature enough and wise enough to deal with my fears as a rational adult should, but I can't.

FOUR IMPORTANT FACTS

"What are you afraid of?" I have asked hundreds of women that question, and the answers range from bugs to unemployment, public speaking, the water, high places or crowded places, to abandonment, intimacy, getting trapped in the wrong marriage or the wrong job, dealing with the past, to failure or success, and back to spiders, flying, the dark, the process of dying and facing death, or the unknown. And the list goes on.

I soon came to the conclusion that (1) *all women fear something.* It took a very short time to realize that (2) *some women fear more than others.* *Nation's Business,* in an article titled "How to Turn Off the Anxiety Alarm," stated:

> One moment you're fine. The next, you're gripped by a terror so overpowering you feel as if you're going to die. In 10 or 15 minutes that sense of impending doom passes, leaving you limp, exhausted, and wondering what happened.
>
> Panic disorder, which affects up to 2 percent of the U.S. population, is characterized by chest pain, shortness of breath, dizziness, sweating, trembling, and a racing heart. The all-consuming anxiety typically causes sufferers to think they are having a heart attack—or going mad.[1]

The article went on to quote the National Institute of Mental Health, saying that "approximately 10 percent of all people will have a panic attack at some time in their lives. But victims of full-blown panic disorder can experience four or more panic attacks every month. One-third may become so enslaved by their affliction that they develop agoraphobia—fear of going into open places."[2]

Thinking back to the panic attacks I occasionally experienced in the bedroom next to the cemetery, I remember feeling momentarily disabled, unable to think rationally, and totally panic-stricken—but I soon realized I would live. When women experience severe panic they are not always convinced they will be able to go on functioning as "normal" human beings.

My next conclusion was that (3) *some women remain frozen in fear for much of their lives.* Then I found an article titled "Phobias, Panic, and Fear—Oh My!" and I discovered how widespread the problem really is.

> If panic fills your heart every time you approach an airplane or a tall building, join the club. Recent studies conducted by the National Institute of Mental Health in Rockville, Maryland, indicate that anxiety disorders are the number-one mental-health problem among American women. If fact, panic, anxiety and phobias interrupt the lives of nearly 20 to 30 million people in the United States.[3]

The more I studied, the more I realized that while totally debilitating panic attacks may affect only 2 percent of the population, more minor versions of paralyzing phobias hit most of us at some time or another. In fact, if we each looked back on the past couple of weeks, we could probably list one or two examples at this very moment.

So what makes the difference between the woman who becomes immobilized by fear and the woman who experiences various forms of panic, anxiety, and worry but is able to remain functional and even productive in her daily life? I finally realized that (4) *each woman can choose a constructive or destructive resolution to her fears.*

For a moment that thought bothered me. What about the woman who when confronted with fear instantly gets negative physical symptoms—a racing heart, sweating, heavy breathing, pain in the chest, trembling, and dizziness? It seemed unfair to suggest that she could choose a different path when her symptoms were so automatic. However, each of us *does* have a choice. Will we remain frozen in a no-win situation, or will we get help and begin understanding and internalizing a constructive way of dealing with the paralyzing phobias of the past?

As I pondered my conclusions, they felt right.

1. *All women fear something.* It's normal and even healthy to have some fears. We are not alone. Millions of women have dealt with some of the same fears we face every day.

2. *Some women fear more than others.* A few of us, due to past issues,

struggle with fear at a much deeper level than others. This does not mean we are strange, unchristian, or in need of institutional care. It's a fact of life.

3. *A few women remain frozen in fear.* Some of you picked up this book because that statement describes you right now. The paralyzing phobias in your life have placed you in a prison of misery and hopelessness. There are days when you are convinced *nothing* can change your current situation and at times you feel like giving up.

4. *Each woman can choose a constructive or a destructive resolution to her fears.* Hope is tied to the belief that a change for the better is in the future. God created us with the ability to choose, and He offers us the opportunity to make important decisions every day. As one person noted, "Though no one can go back and make a new start, anyone can start from now and make a brand new end."[4] It's never too late.

A PEEK IN THE BEDROOM WINDOW

My triggering event/situation/person: Looking back at my crippling panic, I know the event that triggered my fear was the move to the house next to the cemetery—along with the bedroom selected for me by my parents, with a far-reaching view of the gravestones.

My reactive emotion: Even though I knew the process of dying was a normal function, my heart failed me when I thought of bodies in caskets, vaults in the ground outside, and bodies coming out of those graves when Jesus returned for His own. My consuming emotion when I looked out at the dark cemetery was *horror.*

My powerlessness: As a child who wanted to trust God, I had a dilemma. I prayed God would take away the fear. But He didn't. I was the oldest of several children, and there were no extra beds in other rooms. I was stuck in a no-win, paralyzing situation. To leave the room was to be disobedient to my parents. To stay in the room was to face the ghastly fear of whatever was beyond the window. My total focus was on my personal pain and my inability to change the circumstances.

My rage: Sometimes I felt angry. I was sure my father did not understand the deep level of my fear. He thought I was a big baby who had to get used to the new house. My dad was a soldier in World War II and death was a fact of life. Something to be reckoned with as part of growing up. He loved me deeply, but he was also convinced that I would get used to the cemetery and overcome my "silly fear." At that time in my young life, I didn't realize rage was brewing, but it was. I was misunderstood by my father. I was *not* a big baby. I was deeply afraid of the dark, of death, and of unknown monsters on the other side of the windowpane. I was furious!

My internal negotiating: Even at the age of six I had a strong natural bent toward self-reliance. There *had* to be a way to take care of my problem. The fear was more than I could bear. I wondered if anyone had ever *died* from fear. On the specific night I described, my internal negotiating led me to an escape—extracting a tooth—so I could have a legitimate reason to leave the room and run from my paralyzing panic to safety.

My choice: After choosing a dishonest resolution to my fear, I had to face some facts. If I pulled out a tooth every time I needed to escape from my fears, I would soon run out of baby teeth and I would have major dental problems. I needed a more constructive resolution.

My sorrow: I was convinced my mother understood the depth of my fear. In years past I had run to her side of the bed when I awoke in the middle of the night with nightmares. She always put an arm around me and let me fall asleep in her bed before Dad got up and placed me back in my own bed, long after my fears were quieted. One day when we were alone in my room, Mama looked out the scary window with me. With tears in my eyes I admitted how frightened I was. She didn't laugh at me. She grieved with me and felt my sorrow as her own.

My brokenness: When my mother began to realize how debilitating and gripping my fear of the cemetery was, we talked together—and to God—about the panic I was feeling. With deep emotion I told God I couldn't handle it anymore. The fear consumed me, and I felt helpless before it.

My surrender: After I poured out my heart to God, Mama got out "The Promise Box." It was filled with little cards with Scripture verses on them and a "thought for the day." The box was always found on the kitchen table, and every day after our evening meal, one of the six children in our family would have a turn at picking a new promise.

On this day Mother permanently removed one of the promise cards. She read to me, "When I am afraid, I will trust in you" (Psalm 56:3). She talked to me about how fear can be a friend that causes us to reach out to God. She said how difficult it would be to understand what it means to trust God if we never experienced a fearful emotion. That day I surrendered my phobia to God.

Lawrence Richards commented on the same concept Mother taught me that day:

> David saw fear not as an evil, but as an opportunity to trust. . . . Depressed and certain that he would lose his life if he stayed in Israel, David went to the land of the Philistines. There he was recognized and seized. David pretended to be insane and was released. The whole incident is electric with the FEAR that David experienced—fear that caused him to flee in the first place, fear when taken captive, certainly fear as he returned to his homeland still a fugitive. Yet through this terrifying experience David came to see fear as a friend, rather than as an enemy.[5]

My faith-filled decision: On the day I surrendered my fear to God, Mama placed the promise card in my hands and folded my fingers around it. Many times I felt afraid for a while, but I never returned to my former debilitating panic. From that time on, the card was always under my pillow as a reminder that I was not alone. And when the moonlight danced on the marble stones, I held the card—and I felt safe.

Once again Larry Richards describes what I learned:

> How is fear a friend? Fear is a friend because it is only when we are afraid that we plumb the depths of trust. We cannot know what trust means unless we live through experiences in which the Lord is all we have to hold on to. Through his experience of fear, David became able to share a great and wonderful discovery with us,
> When I am afraid,
> I will trust in You.
> In God, whose Word I praise,
> In God I trust; I will not be afraid.
> What can mortal man do to me?[6]

WHEN DOES A FEAR BECOME A PHOBIA?

None of us wants to be paralyzed by a phobia. But it happens. Most of us at some time struggle with fears that are illogical. And if there is a legitimate cause for the fear, we have an ability to magnify the potential problem beyond logical reason. Webster's dictionary defines a phobia as a "morbid and often irrational dread of some specific thing."[7]

An article in a well-known women's magazine, titled "Scare Tactics—Living With Your Secret Fears," stated,

> What are you afraid of? When we asked that question around the *Mademoiselle* office, the replies ran the gamut. . . . In short, everyone's scared of something. Which isn't really a problem—unless it develops into a fear that's irrationally out of proportion to the actual danger and so intense that it starts interfering with your daily life.[8]

That's the best definition of "phobic fear" I've found! I began to think of the women I'd met who experienced varying stages of fear. In the beginning, many of our fears are normal, self-protective emotions. But when our fear gets totally out of proportion to the actual danger—and when we let the fear interfere with our daily schedule—the fear becomes a phobia.

Sometimes paralyzing fears are based on things that *might* happen. In the scenarios that follow, remember that each of us has a choice: Will we stay frozen in fear, allowing our phobia to get out of proportion to the actual danger, or will we move forward?

Losing someone we love: Jenny panics when she thinks of the possibility that her mother will die. Her mom has always been there for her—through an unhappy marriage, financial problems, and a major health crisis. Though her mom is in good health, Jenny is consumed with anxiety about losing her.

Aging: Sharon is afraid of getting older. As a young woman she won several beauty contests, and she feels that her worth is very tied to her appearance. As fine lines appear around her eyes and lips, Sharon is absorbed in irrational worry about her dissipating value to others.

Being raped: Judith is a professional woman who is sometimes paralyzed by the fear of being raped in her apartment building. She finds it difficult to unlock her front door after dark.

War, nuclear holocaust: Brenda is the daughter of a military man.

Her father was her hero and best friend — but he was killed in Vietnam She is unable to watch television news for fear of hearing information about war and international conflict.

Loss of financial security: Jane's husband is an engineer working in the aerospace industry, and she knows there will be layoffs. Her home is exquisite, but there's a high mortgage. And with two children in college, her worst fear is the potential financial devastation that could be just around the corner.

This list could have many additions, but these brief vignettes remind us that many of our fears are tied to things that have not physically touched our lives yet — although they might happen in the future. Some of these fears have not reached the phobia stage yet, but they are beginning to alter our behavior on a daily basis. We start planning ahead to avoid certain places, people, or events. We become paranoid. Sometimes the change in our behavior is so gradual we convince ourselves we do not have a problem. Phobic fears often follow a destructive path, and we wind up (sometimes unconsciously) choosing one of the following false resolutions: (1) denial, (2) defeat, (3) bitterness, or (4) escape into compulsive/addictive behaviors.

FROZEN IN A SEA OF HOPELESSNESS

When a triggering event produces a reactive emotion of fear that develops into an irrational panic, it is easy to feel totally powerless. We then move to rage and on to internal negotiating. We get stuck in beliefs and reactions like these:

- I am totally powerless to change my fearful situation.
- There is nothing I can do to alter my losing reaction to fear.
- I am so angry at the person who triggers this fear in me!
- I am so mad at myself for this embarrassing and emotional reaction.

When we choose to remain frozen in a sea of hopelessness, our internal negotiating often leads to thoughts like these:

- I will have feelings of panic, extreme discomfort, worry, and anxiety until I die. I'm fighting a losing battle.
- I can't handle my fears, so I'm giving up on trying.

- If I had more supportive people in my life, I'd be able to let go of my fears.
- I refuse to admit I have a problem. If I work harder, I'll forget my worries.

In every case, paralyzing phobias lead us to a poor quality of life, a sense of being trapped inside our own skin, and a defeatist attitude that does not make room for wise counsel from friends or professionals or any thought of choosing another path. Simply stated, we say, "I quit!"

Some of us are not at the "I quit" stage, but we do feel more than slightly helpless when it comes to finding a constructive resolution for our fears. Nicky Marone, an educational psychologist and seminar speaker, makes an important point in her book *Women and Risk: How to Master Your Fears and Do What You Never Thought You Could Do*:

Many of us . . . live a secret life, which . . . is kept hidden from others. It is in this secret life that we understand the meaning of helplessness. It is in this secret life that we can be held in the grip of repetitive and destructive behavior patterns. We may hold steadfastly to unhealthy love relationships; we may struggle endlessly with eating disorders or substance abuse; we may panic needlessly at the unforeseen changes in our lives. Depression stalks some of us like a samurai. Many of us scrupulously avoid risk or challenge in any areas but the ones in which we have already succeeded, fearing the process of learning a new task. Even after achieving most of our goals, many of us remain plagued by the secret self-doubts of low self-esteem.[9]

While Marone's book is certainly not theological in its approach to the problem, I agree with her statement, "We bear an unnecessary burden, which undermines our ability to take risks and act in our own best interests. . . . We suffer from a condition shared by many women . . . a condition known as learned helplessness."[10]

Women are not the only people who match this profile, but we tend to assume fearful behaviors are a "gender" response. Instead of learning a constructive way of dealing with our fears and acting on an empowerment that is already ours if we tap into divine resources, we allow ourselves to fall into old patterns. False resolutions to fear often propel us into silence, depression, subservient compliance, and addictions—sometimes in the name of being a "good Christian woman."

LESSONS FROM MOSES

You might disagree with me, but I believe Moses had a phobia when it came to public speaking. God had called him to lead the children of Israel, and his reason for being less than enthusiastic gives us some clues to his apparent fear.[11]

Moses said to God, "Who am I that I should go to Pharaoh, and that I should bring the children of Israel out of Egypt?"

So God said, "I will certainly be with you."

Guess what! Moses was told ahead of time that he would be supernaturally empowered by God Himself for this awesome task. God didn't even use a courier service to give out this information. He told him personally!

Then Moses said, "But suppose they will not believe me or listen to my voice; suppose they say, 'The Lord has not appeared to you'"?

We aren't told in Scripture if Moses' phobia had reached a paralyzing state, but it's easy to envision emotion in his tone. Moses said, "O Lord, I have never been eloquent, neither in the past nor since you have spoken to your servant. I am slow of speech and tongue." Can you *feel* the panic in his voice? He fears the place of leadership, and he is totally convinced his communication skills are the worst!

The Lord said to him, "Who gave man his mouth? Who makes him deaf or dumb? Who gives him sight or makes him blind? Is it not I, the LORD? Now go; I will help you speak and will teach you what to say."

I can almost hear God saying, "Moses, leave your low self-esteem and fear behind. Refuse to accept a resolution of denial, defeat, bitterness, or escape. I will *empower* you beyond any human level to do My work and accomplish your life purpose. My greatest joy would be to see you trust Me enough to make a faith-filled decision to overcome this fear."

Yet, after all that, Moses responds, "O Lord, please send someone else to do it." My "unable to be biblically verified" thought on this response is that Moses was very near a destructive, rigid resolution of total defeat. If we had a tape recording of his thoughts, the playback might sound like this: "Please, Lord, pick my brother for this job. I am totally powerless to change my fearful situation, and Aaron is a much better speaker than I am anyway. It's his gift! There is nothing I can do to alter my reaction to this fear. I will have feelings of panic, extreme discomfort, worry, and anxiety every time I stand before a crowd – or more than two people. I can't handle my fears, so I'm giving up on trying."

Fortunately, Moses' story doesn't end here. In fact, after he accepted the dreaded job of leadership, he became a powerful leader and an empowered, confident communicator. Acts 7 records that Moses was "mighty in words and deeds."

If Moses had chosen the *destructive* path of giving in to this phobia, the chain reaction might have looked like this:

Triggering event: God selects Moses for a huge leadership position.

Reactive emotion: Fear – "Lord, I've never been eloquent."

Sense of powerlessness: "O Lord, please send someone else to do it."

Rage: Moses could have said, "I'm upset! If God wants me to lead, He should have given me different gifts. This is unfair."

Internal negotiating: I wonder if Moses rationalized, "I can handle this situation myself. I'll get my brother to do the talking. He has a flair for putting words together so people understand what he means to say."

Choice of a destructive resolution: Moses could have selected either of the following options: (1) *defeat* – "I give up! I've never been good at speaking and I never will be. I'm defeated and I know it!" (2) *escape* – Moses could have turned to addictive workaholism and perfectionism, trying for a lifetime to make up for giving in to his phobia and turning his back on God's call and God's enabling.

The Bible doesn't tell us in detail what happened at this point, but I believe that the constructive path Moses selected in time made all the difference. The steps are the same in the beginning: *triggering event, reactive emotion, powerlessness,* and *rage.* But his *internal negotiating* might have allowed him to see a more constructive resolution for his fear. Perhaps the scenario went like this:

Internal negotiating: Moses might have said to himself, "From my experience as a believer, I know God never calls people to a task without enabling them to accomplish the mission. I don't know how He'll be able to use me, but I'm willing to try."

Scripture does not outline the emotional stages Moses went through after God showed him miraculous signs and encouraged him by saying, "Now go; I will help you speak and will teach you what to say." What we *do* know is that there came a time when Moses' faith-filled decisions were respected by all and honored by God. That leads me to believe Moses experienced *sorrow*. ("Lord, I wish I could speak with greater conviction and clarity. My fear makes me ill every time I have to talk in front of people. I feel so inadequate as a leader.")

I wonder if Moses then moved to *brokenness*. ("Father, in myself, I can't do the job. I give up trying to manipulate people, situations, and Your will. I can't do it anymore.") This kind of attitude always leads to *surrender*. ("God, it's not my will; it's Yours! I desire to be Your servant in the way You choose to use me. My focus is now on You, and I give my self-reliant will up to You.") This attitude always leads to *faith-filled decisions*.

A LOOK BACK THROUGH THE BEDROOM WINDOW

My greatest childhood phobia had to do with the "death" outside my bedroom window. As I became an adult, I struggled with Moses' problem—public speaking. Throughout our lives there will always be moonbeams dancing on the grave markers of life, reminding us of immobilizing fears. If our focus is not on God, we will feel powerless and full of rage. It will become easy to fall into denial, defeat, bitterness, or some type of escape.

But if we release our self-reliant patterns and learn to choose a constructive resolution for our fears, the benefits will be overwhelming.

Dr. Susan Jeffers reinforces the idea that we need to do something—anything—to keep from being frozen in our paralyzing fears:

> Say yes to life. Participate. Move. Act. Write. Read. Sign up. Take a stand. Or do whatever it takes for you. Get involved in the process. . . . Whatever it takes to get you there, *feel the fear and do it anyway*.[12]

There's something motivating in her words, but I quickly realize that I as a Christian woman have a hidden asset. I am not in the process alone. My human courage or self-empowerment alone would not give me the strength to achieve success.

God has given me a choice—*stay frozen* or *get moving* toward taming my fears. Instead of getting stuck in the process, I can choose to get help. Instead of waiting for assistance to come to me, I can pick up the phone and ask. Instead of blaming my mother, father, siblings, or church members for not giving me more assistance, I can take the initiative.

The surprising result is that a yielded inner spirit always leads me to feel grief for the phobia that has held me in bondage. This sorrow brings me to a brokenness before God. As I yield my will to Him and experience true surrender, I find a strength for my current situation that I never had before. And with that strength I am empowered to make faith-filled decisions.

As an adult, I now look at gravestones with a whole new attitude. Instead of seeing death, I see hope for eternity. Instead of concentrating on the end of this life and the process of dying, I look to my future in a place without fear. Instead of dreading the night, I look to the morning.

An Epitaph to Strive For

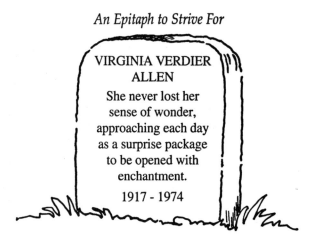

VIRGINIA VERDIER
ALLEN

She never lost her
sense of wonder,
approaching each day
as a surprise package
to be opened with
enchantment.

1917 - 1974

This stone marks the grave of Virginia Allen in Mackinac Island Cemetery. I have a feeling Virginia, who died at the age of fifty-seven, learned how to process her fears in a constructive way, which freed her to look to each new day with hope and anticipation. May we all learn to see with her eyes.

"Why Does the Fear of Things that Might Happen Consume My Mental and Spiritual Energy?"

FEAR 2: POTENTIAL DISASTERS

It ain't no use putting up your umbrella till it rains.

ALICE CALDWELL RICE

T he young mother was frightened. She had waited to talk with me privately after the meeting was over. "Carol, I don't know what to do. I have three children. My husband just lost his job, and we're living on unemployment compensation.

"My oldest son will start kindergarten next fall, and most of the people in our church think the public schools are corrupt and full of drugs and anti-God teaching. We can't afford the tuition at the Christian school in our area, and I know I am not cut out to home-school my children. I just don't have the patience for it! I am so afraid my son will turn away from God if I send him to a public school."

The young mom was like many others I had met—afraid of so many things that haven't happened yet. I thought of my own fears. My child wasn't starting kindergarten, but in a strange way, I identified with this woman. My son was about to enter adulthood. Free to make his own choices. Free to make his own mistakes. And free to follow his own dreams.

A "SUMMIT" EXPERIENCE

As the mother of an only child, I've been a bit on the overprotective side. Sending a sixteen-year-old all the way to Colorado for three weeks of camp seemed like a big step. We had heard of a Christian leadership training camp called Summit Ministries—and it sounded like it provided a unique combination of high adventure and solid teaching. I tried not to be too emotional at the airport as we said our goodbyes. By my standards, Jason seemed too young to be flying by himself.

Fear gripped my heart. What if he couldn't find his connecting gate in Kansas City? What if the camp didn't have transportation at the airport in Colorado Springs and he was left alone? What if he fell in love with a girl who lives on the other side of the country? What if he met older students who influenced him in negative ways?

When our son returned home, he was different. More mature. Less interested in video games. More involved in making plans for his future. He began talking about the importance of having a "Christian worldview" in the midst of our changing society.

Guardedly, he said, "Mom, what would you think if I told you I'm interested in a military career?" I could feel a lump forming in my throat. This child was special. He was intelligent, dynamic, full of fun and adventure, and he had a heart for the Lord. Why would he even think of going in that direction? It could be dangerous! I tried to follow my own advice to others. I listened more than I talked and waited for him to finish his sentences before opening my mouth. He handed me the journal he had written during camp, and my eyes fell on these words:

August 10
I prayed to God today about my future plans. I told Him of all my desires and asked for them within His will. I cried after I prayed because it was so intense. I wish all my prayers were like this.

Leadership was the center of the prayer, and it's my lifelong goal. I would like to lead our nation back to God, try to correct the wrongs, and make God first in all things. God has shown me His influence in every area of life that I see. "Lord, I want to be used by You in the work that You have set apart for me since my birth . . . and with the desires You have placed within me, I believe that You are leading me toward military leadership, or maybe even toward politics."

As I read to the end, my eyes filled with tears. My little boy had become a man. Fear was starting to choke me. Only yesterday I was putting him on the bus for kindergarten.

My silent prayer was more like a desperate plea: "Lord, *please*, he's my *only* son. Don't take him away from me. Change the desires of his heart to something safe, less controversial, and closer to home. Please, God, the military is full of rough language and danger and killing. And politics are corrupted by ambitious zealots and special interest groups. Lord, You know if he goes into politics the media will destroy him for his conservative, biblical views on controversial issues. God, I cannot sacrifice my son in this way. Please change his mind."

Thoughts swirled through my mind. Could it be that *God's* plan for my son might not be *my* plan? Could God's plan involve faraway places and the coarse atmosphere of a military compound? Had my son been unduly influenced by science fiction novels and spell-binding media events? Or could these "desires of his heart" actually have come from God?

He continued, "Mom, I'd like to apply to the U.S. Naval Academy in Annapolis, Maryland. It's one of the finest engineering schools in the country, and I could get the best discipline and training in leadership that I could ever hope for. I want this more than anything."

"WHAT IF . . . ?" — WHAT WOMEN WORRY ABOUT

Most of us spend a portion of every day worrying about the "what ifs." We have an amazing ability to imagine the "worst case scenario," then we convince ourselves it *will* happen to us or to one of our family members or friends. An old Swedish proverb states, "Worry gives a small thing a big shadow." And worry eventually gives way to anxiety.

In a book titled *Conquering Fear*, Karen Randau wrote, "While *fear* focuses on an immediately impending danger (such as a car wreck about to happen), *anxiety* is a constant level of internal tension over something that may or may not occur in the future."[1] (I think I have just heard my own condition described.) Randau went on to quote Dr. Edmund J. Bourne, who said, "[Anxiety] is a vague, distant, or even unrecognized danger . . . about something bad happening."[2] Anxiety brings a sense of apprehension, intense dread, and a dark shadow of uncertainty.

This chapter deals with the fear of "things that *might* happen." In the past ten days I have heard the following comments from women who have struggled with this type of fear/anxiety:

- What if I lose my job? The company is going to lay off more people, and I just know I'll be one of them.
- What if I have a car accident? I just know I'll be maimed or killed. I better not drive. I've had a wreck before, and I know it will happen again.
- What if the economy falls apart? What will happen to our country?
- What if I never get married? I don't have any retirement plan and the Social Security system seems so shaky. I always thought I'd be married and financially secure by now, but I'm not.
- What if I can't get pregnant? I want a child more than anything and every month my disappointment is deeper and I fear the worst—infertility.
- What if I'm a bad mother? How can I ever be sure I'm raising my children properly?
- What if my husband gets interested in another woman? He's so attractive and I'm getting older, and his secretary thinks he's wonderful.
- What if I can't afford to pay for my children's education? People can't make a living in today's world without a degree.
- What if we get transferred to another place? My whole world is wrapped up in this community. My family lives here. I have meaningful fellowship in my church. I just *can't* leave here.

The list could go on and on.

Take a minute to write down all of the anxious thoughts you've had this week involving "things that haven't happened yet—and may never happen." Are you and I normal? Or are our lives unusually shrouded by a curtain of doom? Jane and Robert Handly, in an article titled "Why Can't I Stop Worrying?" state:

You wake up suddenly and look over at the glowing numbers on your alarm clock. It's three a.m. — again — and your mind is spinning with worries. . . . First, those Christmas bills you've got to pay. And what about the diet you're starting tomorrow? And how about your kids, your job, your marriage — the entire global economy? Before long, it's good-bye to sleep and hello to another red-eyed morning.[3]

These authors go on to quote a 1987 study which concluded that women are two to three times more prone to chronic worry than men are. It's true — all of us worry about some things. But how do we compare with other women?

According to a poll by Yankelovich Clancy Shulman, we're more concerned about the following issues than we were in the past: (1) money; (2) jobs; and (3) planning for the future.[4] According to a recent Gallup poll, women are the most worried about (1) the economy; (2) unemployment; (3) drugs; (4) poverty and homelessness.[5]

If these studies are accurate, most of us are very worried about finances, employment/unemployment, and how this affects our future. In Larry Burkett's best-selling book *The Coming Economic Earthquake*, he reminds us of our past:

For those who lived through a decade of depression, there was an indelible imprint that can never be erased. For every available job, there were a hundred applicants. Tens of thousands of homeless people drifted across the country searching for nothing more than enough food to sustain life for one more day. No one had believed the prosperity of the twenties could end so quickly. A few people prospered, but millions lived in despair.[6]

As you and I listen to politicians telling us the deficit is far worse than preliminary figures indicated, we worry. Remembering the past, we wonder about the future.

As I read further in Burkett's book, my anxiety increased:

Spending beyond our means endangers our economic future. Debt prosperity is a fleeting illusion that is impossible to maintain. The use of credit doesn't eliminate a problem. It delays it and makes it worse. The federal government now owes nearly $4 trillion, with virtually no way to repay the debt. By the year 2000, when the debt will be $20 trillion, just the interest alone will consume all the taxes paid by all Americans.

The time is approaching when the government can no longer fund its overspending without destroying the business base of America. When that time comes, there will be few options available other than the printing of more money. Every nation that has gone this route has sparked hyperinflation that eventually wiped out the middle class.[7]

This reminder of what I'd rather forget makes me feel depressed, defeated, worried, anxious, and fearful. For many of us, the fear of "something that might happen" slowly begins to turn into a deeper level of fear, that makes us feel as if our problem has escalated into a total inability to handle life, plan for the future, or provide safety and happiness for our children. If we aren't careful, we can even wind up saying: "I give up. The economic earthquake is coming. I can't do anything to stop it. My future is ruined. My family has no future. Fearful signs are everywhere. I'm going to quit trying!"

FIVE TRUTHS TO CONSIDER

Whenever I'm tempted to feel hopeless, I find it helpful to remember five simple truths.

1. *Life is full of negative things that might happen.* We can't escape bad news. It's on the front page of the paper. It's on the TV screen. It's in the conversations of people who surround us. We live in a fallen, sinful world. The Bible states, "We know that the whole creation has been groaning as in the pains of childbirth right up to the present time."[8] Life *is* hard, and it shouldn't surprise us that a fallen world will provide disappointment, painful losses, unfulfilled expectations, and sadness.

2. *As long as I choose a path of personal growth, I will face fearful situations.* The day nothing happens that makes us feel a little bit afraid, we'd better watch out! We may have quit breathing. Deceased people are the only ones who never worry about the future or concern themselves with job security or financial reversals or their children's welfare.

If you are making any progress at all, you *will* have concerns about what might happen in the future.

3. *Acknowledging my anxieties is a positive first step.* As a Christian woman, I have Someone to share my anxieties with. In the New Testament we are instructed, "Cast all your anxiety on him because he cares for you."[9] I can tell God anything, and He won't be angry or surprised.

It also helps to talk to someone who can give advice in a specific area. In an article titled "How to Feel Better About the Future," Dr. John Norcross, a professor and chairman of psychology at the University of Scranton in Pennsylvania, said, "The first smart response to fear is to face it. . . . Then, measure your fear against the odds of its happening. If you think your job is on the line, for example, ask your company management whether layoffs are likely — and check with personnel about severance packages, just in case. To help put things in perspective, discuss your concerns with your spouse (or a friend)."[10]

4. *An attitude of optimism will make today more enjoyable.* One morning I hurriedly flipped on my radio. Chuck Swindoll was preaching and he quoted comedian Fred Allen: "It isn't good to suppress your laughter because it goes down and spreads your hips." I have no idea what Chuck's sermon was about, but that one comment helped me to forget for a whole day my "real" troubles and the fears over things that "might" happen in the future. Every time I tried to get serious, I laughed out loud.

Barbara Johnson wrote, "Doctors and physical fitness experts tell us that laughter is just plain good for your health. One expert, who travels around staging workshops on how to be fit, says healthy people laugh 100 to 400 times a day. . . . I read about a medical doctor who calls laughter 'internal jogging.' He says that hearty laughter has a beneficial effect on most of your body's major systems — and it's a lot more fun than calisthenics. Laughing 100 times a day works the heart as much as exercising for ten minutes on a rowing machine." Barb goes on to say, "One bumper sticker I saw [stated], 'ONE LAUGH = 3 TBSP. OF OAT BRAN.' . . . The best thing to do when feeling overwhelmed is to take a 'laugh break.' If you're all worn out and feeling defeated, take time out to laugh. It can actually rejuvenate you."[11]

5. *Choosing a faith-filled decision is much less frightening than living*

with the underlying fear that comes from feeling helpless. First, let's consider the bad news. Nicky Marone, a woman who has done extensive work in helping women overcome helplessness, take risks, and master fear wrote, "Learned helplessness ensnares a woman in a tangled web of paralyzing beliefs, emotions, and behaviors. She consistently doubts herself even when she performs at consistently high levels. Superior achievement in one area of her life does not necessarily translate into high self-esteem or promote self-confidence in others areas."[12] It's important to ask ourselves if we have chosen to allow fear to paralyze us. We are in serious trouble when we start believing what we've been saying aloud when panic strikes: "I can't do anything. I can't handle this fear."

Marone continued, "Criticism can so immobilize her with its implication of inferiority (which she already believes anyway) that she may scrupulously avoid new challenges, risks, or changes. . . . Fear and self-doubt short-circuit her attempts at change. . . . She eventually becomes blind to genuine opportunities to transform the areas of her life that make her unhappy. Learned helplessness becomes the grim reaper of her dreams."[13] In my travels I have met numerous women who at first glance look like winners, but after talking to them, I realize they have chosen to be helpless victims of the fear of negative things that might happen.

Choosing a faith-filled decision might seem frightening, risky, impossible, senseless, stretching, gut-wrenching, and unnatural. But it's worth it! Old patterns usually feel safer, even if we've been miserable, than attempting a new method of dealing with fear. Sometimes we lose the approval of significant people—because it's chancy for them to risk losing us if we begin to shed the "helplessness" they still cling to. (We might not want to be in their support group any more.)

IS IT POSSIBLE TO UNLEARN OLD PATTERNS?

I have often wondered where worry came from. Did it begin with Adam and Eve, or is it a highly developed form of fear that we have "perfected" in the twentieth century? Some women believe they learned it at their mother's knee. The authors of an article in the *Ladies' Home Journal* observed, "One woman stated, 'My mother had this great ability to create disastrous scenarios in her mind, and it rubbed off on me.' Some women told us that fretting made them feel they had some control over the dangers in life. By imagining the worst, they believed they could prevent it from happening."[14]

The article also explains that one of the biggest reasons women spend so much time worrying is because we have a "powerful nurturing instinct" that somehow makes us feel responsible for everyone. I think that isn't true of every woman I've met, but I *have* decided a whole book could be written on why we have this problem of worrying about things that might happen. But what I really want to know is: What can I do to change the pattern?

DOES THE BIBLE HAVE ANY ADVICE ON THE SUBJECT?

One of the passages my mother encouraged me to memorize as a young woman was Philippians 4:6-8 (TLB): "Don't worry about anything; instead, pray about everything; tell God your needs and don't forget to thank him for his answers. If you do this you will experience God's peace, which is far more wonderful than the human mind can understand. His peace will keep your thoughts and your hearts quiet and at rest as you trust in Christ Jesus."

It sounds so simple. Kind of like the song Bobby McFerrin made popular a few years ago, "Don't Worry, Be Happy." Pray about everything. Tell God my needs. Thank Him when I get answers. Repeat the pattern until I get peace. I want that! And God's peace will *really* keep my heart and mind quiet and at rest? Even if my son pursues a military career? Even if he lives on the other side of the globe? Even if I have no control over the circumstances? It sounds too simple. I've lived with fear so long I want a more difficult answer. I want to feel like I *earned* an answer to my dilemma. "God, why do I always want to make Your plan more difficult than it is?"

Jesus has more advice on the subject: "Therefore do not worry about tomorrow, for tomorrow will worry about itself. Each day has enough trouble of its own."[15] That must mean that worrying about things that haven't happened yet is a direct act of disobedience. God says every day that comes my way will have plenty of its own trauma, and I'm not to dwell on future "what ifs."

I'm not happy with this instruction. Part of my personality really *enjoys* worrying. In fact, it makes me feel mature to think ahead to all of the negatives in a situation. Who knows? Someone might appreciate my insight. But so far, I haven't met that person.

ONE WOMAN'S STORY

Mary was young. Engaged. In love with a wonderful man. It must have felt like everything was going her way. Until the angel came. That was her triggering event! Joseph was to be her husband. Would the fear of a future event cloud their happiness? Would their carefully made plans be interrupted? Would they be exposed to public embarrassment and ridicule? What really happened?[16]

Triggering event/situation/person: The angel's announcement— "Greetings, you who are highly favored! The Lord is with you."

Reactive emotion: "Mary was greatly troubled at his words and wondered what kind of greeting this might be." I can only imagine the extreme panic Mary must have felt at that moment. Why would a heavenly being pick her out of the crowd for a special announcement? It must have been overwhelming!

Next comes the exciting "find" in the whole scenario! There is an interesting deviation from the chain reaction we have worked through in previous chapters. Most of us, even when following a constructive path for dealing with our fear, go through a feeling of *powerlessness*, followed by *rage*; we do some *internal negotiating*, which can lead us to *sorrow*, *brokenness*, and on to *surrender* and a *faith-filled decision*.

But Mary was different. There is a chance she experienced a moment of *powerlessness*. After all, she was vulnerable, exposed, and unprotected in the face of a startling announcement delivered by a heavenly being. There certainly is a chance she very quickly went through all of the steps internally, but after reading the Scripture carefully, I don't think so.

So what happened? I believe Mary's walk with God was so full of trust and her belief that the Messiah was coming was so strong that she skipped the usual pattern. The angel made the announcement: "Do not be afraid, Mary, you have found favor with God. You will be with child and give birth to a son, and you are to give him the name Jesus."

Mary asked wise questions. How could this happen? A virgin could have a baby? *I will be the baby's mother?*

After the angel's explanation, Mary heard these words, affirming everything she already believed about her Creator: "For nothing is impossible with God."

Surrender: Without hesitation, Mary responded, "I am the Lord's servant." With those words Mary released her own will and the security of her previous way of life and yielded to God's purpose for her.

Faith-filled decision: "May it be to me as you have said." As I try to put myself in this young woman's shoes, I marvel at her lack of "what ifs." She was empowered with an ability to believe and trust, based on past teaching, which she knew to be true, experience, and supernatural confidence. She was embarking on a difficult road with more risks than most of us face in a lifetime—the potential loss of a fiancé who might not understand, friends and family members who might misjudge her, and birthing a son who would die the most painful death invented by mankind. We see no "learned helplessness" here. No second thoughts. No fits of sobbing or "begging off the assignment."

Mary teaches me that I, too, can practice a constructive way of dealing with my own fears and learn the value of "instant surrender" that leads to a positive, faith-filled decision. I'm encouraged to know that a time might come when I don't feel betrayed in the middle of my fear. There could come a day when, instead of choosing denial, defeat, bitterness, or escape, I move to a faith that says, "I trust You for tomorrow, even if the day is filled with uncertainty and trouble."

IT'S EASIER SAID THAN DONE

So how does Mary's story apply to my life today? She had a son. I have a son. One day Jesus was missing and she found Him in the temple, sitting among the teachers, asking questions and interacting with the leaders, amazing them with His responses. She must have been as surprised as I have been to realize that her boy had become a young man. Too soon. Why, just yesterday he was playing in the carpenter's shop.

Jesus was filled with a sense of purpose. His future plans were set. "Didn't you know I had to be in my Father's house?"[17] He was living out the plan God had for Him since birth. A plan different from what Mary would have wanted for her firstborn son.

Years later I look at this story through a mother's eyes and realize that my fears for "tomorrow" are well-intentioned. I want to be a good mother, not a "worryin' woman." I want my son to fulfill God's purpose for his life, but I want it to be an easy path, without too many obstacles in the way. I find myself wanting to negotiate with God about these "desires" He's put in Jason's heart. I'm not good at letting go.

Sue Monk Kidd said it best: "Letting go is like releasing a tight spring at the core of yourself, one you've spent your whole life winding and maintaining. When you let go, you grow still and silent. You learn to sit among the cornstalks and wait with God."[18] I'm not good at releasing. I'm terrible at waiting. I'm even worse at trusting God for the "big stuff."

Perhaps the best way for me to end this chapter is with a personal prayer regarding my own struggle with facing what hasn't happened yet:

> Lord, as I face an empty nest, I am afraid. I'm afraid for Jason's safety. I'm afraid he doesn't really understand what's involved in his choices. I'm afraid he'll be introduced to habits and language that are foreign to his protected life. I fear an unworthy woman may steal his affection.
>
> God, I'm afraid the house will be so empty without the noise of a teenager's laughter and the reverberation of his karate practice. I'm afraid to pass his unslept-in bed and fearful of facing the next stage of my own life. I'm not used to less laundry, greater freedom. I may feel worthless with no lunch bags to fill or car pooling to provide. God, I worry that he may not need me anymore, and my anxious heart feels unable to put this in Your hands.
>
> Father, teach me that "letting go" involves a total surrender of my will and a faith-filled decision to practice what Mary said: "Be it unto me according to Thy will." Help me to affirm my son's manhood and trust his choices. Teach me to "be anxious for nothing" and to quit worrying about tomorrow.
>
> Lord, with Your help, I will quit making my son feel guilty for growing up. Help me to stop depending on him to make me happy and to realize that only You can fill the empty places in my heart. I dedicated him to you when he was in my womb, and I affirm today that he belongs to You and is only "on loan" to me. Help me to look around and use my gifts to help others now that my "hands on" parenting is almost over. Amen.

REVIEWING FIVE SIMPLE TRUTHS

As we work together through our fears, let's take a moment to reflect on the five truths discussed in this chapter:

1. Life is full of negative things that might happen.
   - Have I faced the reality of living in a fallen, sinful world, or am I still expecting life to be easy and free of pain?
2. As long as I choose a path of personal growth, I will face fearful situations.
   - Have I accepted the fact that saying yes to new opportunities and challenges brings numerous fearful situations that I must deal with?
3. Acknowledging my anxieties is a positive first step.
   - Am I so fiercely independent that I refuse to admit I need help, or am I willing to admit my fears to God and key people in my life?
4. An attitude of optimism will make today more enjoyable.
   - Have I added one humorous thought to my life during the last twenty-four hours? (To help you get started, ponder this: "The people who tell you never to let little things worry you have never tried sleeping in the same room with a mosquito."[19])
5. Choosing a faith-filled decision is much less frightening than living with the underlying fear that comes from feeling helpless.
   - If I have assimilated a pattern of "learned helplessness," will I choose to face my problem and take progressive steps toward learning how to practice making faith-filled decisions in my daily life?

MOVING FORWARD

In the next chapter I will confess my greatest fear—losing control. I know you already guessed I have that problem. It deals with my fear of vulnerability—and I'm encouraged to know I'm not alone.

PART THREE

OVERCOMING THE FEAR OF BEING VULNERABLE

"Why Does Everything I Do Have to Be Perfect?"
FEAR 3: LOSING CONTROL

*Control is an outgrowth of fear, insecurity and lack of self-esteem.
The more anxious a woman is the more she wants to control and, conversely,
the more secure a woman is the less likely she will need to control.*

BARBARA SULLIVAN
The Control Trap

I've always been impressed by competent women. Intelligence, confidence, and a strong commitment to the work ethic is an attractive combination. As a young married woman, I selected a few "worthy" mentors and decided to become one of the super-achievers.

Average was a word I loathed. When I committed myself to a task, it was done well. I enjoyed tight schedules, impossible agendas, a full calendar, and demanding opportunities. After all, I believed God was worthy of excellence—and I always felt more spiritual when I was buried in work. I wasn't sure excellence, by God's standards, was defined by an insurmountable schedule and unrealistic workload, but godly people applauded my efforts and that only increased my desire to please them. Their affirmations and enthusiastic approval assured me I was selecting the right path.

LEARNED BEHAVIOR?

As the firstborn of six children, being "in charge" came naturally. I was the built-in baby-sitter, which made me the frequent disciplinarian of my four younger sisters and one brother. Dad always said, "The oldest person in the house gets to be the boss." Mother taught me to cook and clean at an early age, and I was convinced that "Cleanliness is next to godliness" was a verse in the Bible. I was also a charter member of the "Clean Up Your Plate" club; we were reminded that many people in the world were starving, so we should eat *everything* in front of us—and we did!

Dad was the adult child of an alcoholic and had learned to take charge at a very young age. He valued strength, leadership, authority, personal discipline, obedience, self-control, and commitment to God. Dad taught me the following slogan: "Be a leader, not a follower; the whole world is made up of followers, but it takes a real individual to be a leader."

My early years were filled with strict Christian training, overflowing love from my precious Dutch mama, more than a little self-imposed fear of not pleasing Dad with high enough grades or noteworthy accomplishments, and a lot of work as I helped care for all of those babies who kept coming. I rather enjoyed being "Mom's right arm" and the big sister in charge of the little kids. Also, earning Dad's approval helped to mask my insecurities.

THE MAKING OF A PERFECTIONIST

My father accepted the call to pastor his first church when I was in junior high. After running from God's will for many years, Dad left a comfortable position in business, went back to Bible school, and finally moved our family to a little railroad town in Michigan. There were forty-two people in the first congregation—so *everybody* had a job. During my teenage years I was the church pianist, and later on, I functioned as the "acting" senior high youth director.

I started to love being in control. Leadership was natural for me. Mother and Dad were very busy with the young, growing congregation, so I was often in charge of my five siblings, meal preparation, "media" control (phone, front door, and disgruntled church members). In my spare time I functioned as the program director and publicist for every event sponsored by my youth group.

Life was fast paced. Men and women were coming to Christ through the outreach of my parents—and I *loved* being part of the ministry. The more I accomplished, the more people in and outside of the family expected from me. I savored the comments I overheard as people spoke to my parents, "Your daughter Carol is such a good girl, and she's such a hard worker."

As long as saying "yes" felt like a spiritual decision for a worthy cause, I accepted every opportunity, challenge, and invitation. I wanted to please God with my whole heart, and I secretly liked pleasing the people who told me how wonderful I was. I was also convinced that being "on fire for God" meant working harder and doing things more perfectly.

DEFINING THE FEAR

One of the most difficult fears to recognize is the fear of losing control. Why? In its early stages it looks so appealing. Women caught in "the control trap" appear to be dynamic, sharp, aggressive leaders — the "movers and shakers." They get things done. Their résumés are impressive and their list of accomplishments is unending. Christian women who fit into this category are publicly honored for their commitment to worthy causes.

So how does something that looks so good become so wrong? Barbara Sullivan, in her book *The Control Trap*, asserts that few women set out to control and dominate their friends, coworkers, husbands, or children. But it's happening all the time. She says,

> One of the most widespread factors in a woman taking control is *fear*. Even though there may be legitimate reasons for the seeds of fear in us — a sensitive nature, past hurtful experiences, present unfavorable circumstances — what we *do* with fear as adults is our responsibility. We must see fear for what it is — a trap we fall into, causing us to subtly or overtly take wrongful control of the lives of those around us.[1]

Many of us who get entangled in this snare fail to see our problem until we are hopelessly addicted to the adrenaline of prestige and power. Even then, we tend to overlook the danger signs because of our obvious accomplishments and our internal belief that *no one can do the job as well as we can*. We don't see our mind-set as egotism. It's just a fact. We have deluded ourselves into believing that we are using our God-given giftedness to manage people, circumstances, and events in the best possible way, for the good of all concerned.

If you're thinking you don't fit this description, so you must not have this problem, read on. Dr. Les Carter, in a book titled *Imperative People: Those Who Must Be in Control*, gives helpful insights. He defines "imperative people" as "those whose need for control disrupts their closest relationships."[2] Many of us expect all people with the fear of losing control to be firstborn, Type A, workaholics, but that's not so. He states,

> The Type A personality is driven by an incessant need to per-
> form endless tasks for personal fulfillment. This is done at the
> expense of loving, accepting relationships with other people.
> Certainly Type A personalities are imperative people . . . [but]
> people with all sorts of temperaments are susceptible. . . . Con-
> trolling behavior is quite common to Type B personalities, those
> quiet, easy-going individuals; they just express their imperative
> thinking differently. Often these people use "the silent treat-
> ment" to control their loved ones.[3]

I winced as I read Dr. Carter's explanation, because I'm a Type A person who sometimes uses "the silent treatment" in order to feel more spiritual when I'm controlling family members who I think need my direction. Sometimes I "switch personalities" so I don't have to admit the truth about my problem. When we face reality, we must admit— *silence can be just as powerful as screaming* when we are trying to "manage" (manipulate) people!

THE MANY FACES OF CONTROL

Since the fear of losing control is evidenced in many different ways with a wide variety of disguises, take a few minutes to read through the following list and ask yourself if you have ever assumed any of these ten controlling identities.

1. The *manager*—This person always leads every group she participates in. She is quick to volunteer and slow to delegate—because someone else might not do the job as efficiently or effectively as she does.

2. The *manipulator*—This woman's technique is so perfected that

she gets people to do what she wants and they actually believe it was their own idea. Frequently the manipulator comes from a home where one or both of her parents were dysfunctional, so she learned to manipulate difficult people and situations at an early age—just to keep the peace and have the semblance of a normal life.

3. The *martyr*—The woman who controls situations and people "because no one else in the family will help" often becomes a martyr. Frequently, she "sacrificially" gives up her own rights and financial resources to meet the needs of others. Then, after all she's done for them, she controls them with guilt and obligation.

4. The *meanie*—The woman who finds herself in this category knows she is a nag capable of intimidating the people around her. Known for her negative attitude about everything, she wears her family down by constant criticism. She controls by her forcefulness, browbeating, and policing of activities.

5. The *most spiritual*—Women who are married to nonChristians or "less spiritual" spouses sometimes fall into the trap of flaunting their organization of the religious training of the children. They do this in such a way that they subtly make their husbands feel like worthless, uncaring creeps for their lack of interest or involvement in church-related activities. On occasion I have met women who withhold sex if their husbands don't attend services with them. Married and single women use their "spiritual prowess" to gain control in church and family situations.

6. The *mother of the extended family*—Women with very honorable motives often control their children far into adulthood by "protecting them from serious mistakes" or "helping them to make right choices." Sometimes a firstborn woman (or one raised in a dysfunctional home) assumes the decision making related to family reunions, care of elder parents, and the coordination of birthday parties and special events. She thinks she's doing it because no one else cares as much as she does. Later, she resents being left with all the work and responsibility. This woman sometimes tries to "mother" her husband and robs him of masculinity and self-esteem.

7. The *most perfect person*—The most subtle disguise of all is perfectionism. Christian women try to achieve "excellence," which brings a pat on the back and a word of affirmation. The perfectionist has trouble delegating—no one can do things as well as she can! The perfectionist

has trouble with fatigue—there are never enough hours in a day to get everything done properly. She has few (if any) close friends—people are intimidated by her workaholism, time constraints, and "superior" image. And she doesn't *allow* anyone to get close enough to discover her insecurity beneath the carefully constructed image.

8. The *mime*—This woman is not a "screamer," but she has powerful control over others by a certain look in her eye, the raising of an eyebrow, a grimace, or a body-language signal, all of which are understood only by another family member. The woman in this category could be reading this description right now and be shocked as she realizes (for the first time) she is exerting forceful control over her family members with this highly perfected technique.

9. The *morbid weakling*—Some women have learned to control by exhibiting physical or emotional problems. When a woman is ill, she becomes the center of attention. Family members change their plans in order to be close to her in her "hour of need." Often, she feebly tells them they don't need to worry about her, but she seeks to control their decisions by making them feel guilty if they don't focus on her needs before their own.

10. The *main attraction*—An insecure woman often learns how to control men by her feminine charm. As a child, batting her "baby blues" at Daddy always resulted in a "yes" to her requests. As she grew older, dating became a game, and when flirtatious behavior won the heart of a man, she moved on to the next challenge. Afraid of intimacy, this woman controls men by enticing them with her looks and childlike flirtation. She may appear outgoing and confident, but fear keeps her from developing a meaningful relationship with anyone. Since women are not attracted to a woman exhibiting these behaviors and she rarely can control them using the same methods, loneliness becomes her companion.

WHAT DOES THE FEAR OF BEING VULNERABLE HAVE TO DO WITH CONTROL?

Looking at the list of disguises we sometimes put on to hide our fear of losing control, I admit I have worn several of these masks at different times in my life. Underneath my facade I was terrified of becoming vulnerable. Webster says the vulnerable person is "open to attack, hurt or injury; (to have the capability) of being . . . wounded (either because of being insufficiently protected or because of being sensitive and tender); liable to greater penalties than the opponents."[4] That's me!

At the deepest level, I know opening myself up to other people, instead of controlling them, means I am vulnerable to letting them hurt me deeply. Instead of admitting that I have sensitive and tender feelings, I'd rather choose a path of control, so I never have to give myself an opportunity to experience the potential pain in an honest, open relationship with coworkers or family members. In my youth, I observed a vulnerable relative experience emotional abuse in the name of biblical submission. That wasn't going to happen to me! I was too smart to fall into that degrading and helpless trap!

When I was newly married, my problem with insecurity and low self-esteem was hidden behind a carefully constructed, aesthetically pleasing wall of perfectionism. Controlling my own behavior and that of others with my ability to manage everything well was the only way I knew how to protect myself from disclosure. And no one guessed what I was doing. After all, I was only carrying on with what I had done in my early years. Big sister Carol could organize anything. If my to-do list wasn't full, I questioned my worth. I was always focused on the next big project.

One day I was reading Paula Rinehart's book *Perfect Every Time* and realized she was a fellow struggler.

> When you live in the future you are always internally in motion, moving toward the next achievement, the next need to be met. You can be months, even years, ahead of yourself. It's a "when I finish . . . then" approach to life where real living is put on hold. Yet I found, ironically, that when I did reach the next juncture—when I finished the degree or delivered the baby or wrote the article—I couldn't really enjoy that either. It slid off me like water on a duck's back. I was mentally way down the road.
>
> . . . As long as I was immersed in a project or moving toward a goal, life had meaning and purpose. But as soon as a blank space appeared or my schedule eased up, I was more anxious than relieved. And the only way to address the anxiety, it seemed, was to get busy again. The illusion was that some inner blessing awaited me just around the corner. Another degree,

another book written, always the next accomplishment promised to put me over the top. Then I could relax.[5]

Paula's description of her cycle of anxiety was just like mine. Because of my inner insecurities, I wound up controlling people and situations in very subtle, but powerful ways, while demanding perfection of myself. When I saw flaws in my pattern, I would get off the "gerbil wheel," but I felt so worthless when I wasn't achieving, leading, and organizing that I soon resumed my former ways. Total exhaustion and a feeling of personal and spiritual failure eventually revealed my deception.

PLAYING GOD?

Dr. Chris Thurman refers to perfectionism as "the crushing weight of playing God." Most of us who fit the pattern of the controlling perfectionist would be appalled to be accused of trying to take God's place—but that's exactly what we work to do.

> One of the primary causes of most psychological and spiritual problems is perfectionism, the belief that one can be just like God—all knowing, . . . all powerful . . . , and all places. What happens when most people run into situations they can't control? They respond with, "I'm going to do something about this!" They try to control the uncontrollable. What are they implying? Somehow, they should be so powerful that nothing should be beyond their control. Only God is that powerful.[6]

Once again our problem is rooted back in the Garden of Eden. Satan tempted Adam and Eve with the fruit of the forbidden tree by saying, "God knows that when you eat of it your eyes will be opened, and *you will be like God,* knowing good and evil."[7] It's tempting to "bite the apple" and take the control of our lives right out of God's hands. We don't think of it as "usurping His authority," but that's exactly what we do!

For years my fear of vulnerability was hidden in a mask of false confidence. If I did God's work for Him, "helping Him out," maybe the pain of low self-esteem would go away. I didn't think I was "playing

God," but my "I'll do it myself" actions were demonstrating a lack of sorrow for my sinful self-reliance and certainly were not leading me toward repentance.

WARNING SIGNS

If you're wondering if you've entered the danger zone, check out how many "yes" responses you have to the following questions:

- When situations arise that need leadership, direction, and a "voice of authority," do I find myself mentally solving the problem and then jumping in to help, even if my advice or assistance has not been requested?
- Do I organize family events or take charge of family crises and later resent my siblings for not "doing their fair share"?
- Do I often feel like nothing will get done unless I take care of the situation or problem?
- Is it hard for me to enjoy a day off or a week's vacation? Is my mind preoccupied with the work I've left at home or at the office? Do I feel less valuable if I'm not doing something "constructive"?
- Do I have trouble letting people get close to me emotionally? Is it easier and less threatening to have many acquaintances but few, if any, real friends?
- Do I focus more on the goal, product, or end result (the future) than on enjoying the process of getting there?
- Do I often set impossible goals and then mentally put myself down for low achievement?
- Do I feel uncomfortable dislosing my weaknesses and needs to other people?
- Would I rather not take on a project if my work couldn't be as good as or better than the last person who attempted the task? Am I uncomfortable with being "average"?
- Do I get tired of controlling situations and people, but feel terrified of giving up the "status quo" and releasing my grip?

If you answered "yes" to more than half of these questions, you and I have a lot in common! In my interviews with women prior to beginning this book, I became convinced that we have an epidemic of Christian women who have a fear of being vulnerable, which has catapulted us into a "tyranny of terror": If I give up my control, I will be weak, powerless, average, open to attack, exposed, and unprotected.

ELIZABETH'S STORY

Liz was one of the most capable women I had ever met. She was the Christian education director of a fast-growing church, wife of a busy doctor, and mother of three energetic, intelligent children. She and her husband had purchased a charming three-story Victorian home, which they had systematically remodeled and redecorated. With her talent, this woman could have done anything. She could manage, direct, teach, inspire, persuade, and create like no woman before her! Every time we were together I felt motivated to achieve new goals and serve God with greater fervor.

To my surprise, one day I received word that Liz had been hospitalized for depression. Could we be talking about the same person? Elizabeth, the achiever, church staff member, encourager, organizer, and super-mom of three future leaders? There must be some mistake. But it was true.

After Liz went through treatment, we had dinner together, and she shared her story. Later, she put more of her thoughts on paper.

> For me, clinical depression was waking up one morning in the fortieth year of my productive, Christian life feeling as if I had entered a foreign country. Something was happening to me I had never experienced before, and I didn't like it. One day I tried three times to measure and count four cups of flour for Christmas baking. My mind couldn't hold a thought. I could no longer concentrate.
>
> I couldn't feel emotion. Even when my family took me to our favorite vacation spot, where we had spent our most precious family times, where I had always been drawn closer to God in the quiet and splendor of His creation, I could feel nothing. I was dying inside.
>
> My job on the pastoral team at our church required compassion and sincerity, but I remember walking down the church

corridor secretly wishing I could punch someone in the nose. On my days off I wanted to hide from people. Once, while shopping, panic struck—and I had to get out!

My confidence was lost, and I no longer had that valuable "passport to joy."

I was going through the motions with a smile on my face while I traveled further down into a place of sadness and despair. I couldn't tell anyone what was happening because I didn't know—and besides, I was a Christian leader. What would they think of me? I just kept trying harder and harder to do all the right things. After all, I was a highly educated firstborn, so I could handle this myself, thank you very much!

Besides, I had always given the help; I had never learned how to ask for it.

There wasn't enough time to do all the "right" things in the day, so I began to rise in the middle of the night—every morning at three or four o'clock—so I could work. In the beginning, panic attacks woke me as my past fears surfaced in my sleep. In my slumbering state I was not in control enough to push the fears down again. As the panic attacks increased, it was easier to get up and work than to wrestle with my fears in the dark. But the fears grew.

As I continued reading Liz's words, I wept for my friend. She went on to describe how her coping strategies quit working. She had tried to serve God with her whole heart, and He didn't seem to be helping her. Maybe He didn't love her. Perhaps she was going crazy. She continued,

Since my conversion experience twenty years before I had never questioned God's grace. I had lived it, loved it, taught it, and shared it with undaunted childlike faith. Now, battle weary, lost and helpless, my mind could arrive at only two conclusions:
1. This "God thing" and faith didn't work.
2. There was something basically not good about me. God couldn't love me. I was hopeless and I knew God couldn't use me. I was broken. God didn't want me. I had no value. God had forsaken me. I was not worthy.

This was the most terrifying moment of my life!

In a pool of tears, one night she expressed to her husband what was happening. With tenderness and deep concern, he made arrangements for professional help at a reputable Christian clinic. Liz said feelings of failure engulfed her as the former "super-mom" waved goodbye to her three children as she left home for treatment.

CAN CONTROLLING WOMEN EVER BREAK THE PATTERN?

As we consider the development and defeat of fear, it helps to see ourselves in process.

Triggering event/situation/person: For both Liz and me, being firstborn children with high goals, expectations, and obligations, it seemed quite natural to cover our own low self-esteem and insecurities by "control."

Reactive emotion: Panic set in for me when I realized I could never work hard enough to make everybody happy. No matter how much I did, there was still more to do. I was afraid. After all I had done, I still wasn't feeling fulfilled and happy. I was afraid God would be displeased with me if I slowed down, but I knew I couldn't keep up the pace forever.

Sense of powerlessness: My fear soon led to an overwhelming sense of powerlessness. Paula Rinehart describes the feeling perfectly:

> All of us who recognize ourselves as a woman "who does too much" hold this characteristic in common: We rarely realize how close to the edge we live until we have almost stepped over the line. We don't start to read the messages on the wall until we have painted ourselves into a corner. We are too busy—doing too much.
>
> No matter how high your energy level, you can give for only so long without adequate replenishment. The well eventually goes dry. It is God's way of puncturing the myth that you can make it on your own as a strong, independent woman who has no needs herself.[8]

Rage: Both Liz and I experienced an unconscious, growing, inner rage when we realized other people were using us because we were hard workers who always got the job done. When God didn't give us a continuing abundance of fresh energy as we continued to abuse our bodies and minds with work, it felt like He betrayed us too.

Internal negotiating: Controlling women are very good at internal negotiating. We convince ourselves that people who are as competent as we are shouldn't be struggling like this. After all, we don't really have a *problem*, we have a *challenge*. If we could just find a "how-to" book on more effective organization, or if we could find a better system for getting things done more efficiently, or if we could get by on fewer hours of sleep, we could resolve our fear of losing control. When we refuse to see that our total self-reliance is a sinful state, we are catapulted into a destructive resolution.

Destructive choices: I chose a destructive resolution of *denial*. Even though I saw danger signs, I was convinced I did not have a "big" problem. Dr. Les Carter pointed out, "Imperative people just refuse to admit the truth—to others and sometimes even to themselves. They so strongly believe the lie that humanness is debilitating that they cannot bring themselves to admit even simple deficiencies."[9]

Liz, after a while, chose the destructive resolution of *defeat*. The God she trusted appeared to have let her down. Apparently, He didn't love her or want to use her in ministry any more.

Some women who are afraid of losing control choose a resolution of bitterness. They become resentful of the heavy workload that *always* ends up on their desk or the family responsibilities that continue to fall on their shoulders.

Liz and I both chose *escape into perfectionism* as our resolution for dealing with our fear of losing control. I continued in a pattern of workaholism for years (and still struggle at times). Liz wound up facing clinical depression. Other women choose a destructive resolution for their fear by escaping into eating disorders or addiction to alcohol, tobacco, or other drugs.

If Liz and I had allowed our internal negotiating to lead us to a constructive resolution, we would have honestly faced our fear of losing control and admitted it was a stubborn form of sinful self-reliance. We would have experienced genuine *sorrow* for our sin and for the misery of our lives. We had expected life to be easier, and we had anticipated rewards from God for working so hard. But the endless demands we placed on ourselves brought only emptiness. That was sad. Our growing perfectionism brought more anxiety into our relationships. That was sad. We both experienced a deep loneliness (even in the middle of crowds of people). That was sad. We felt alienated from God. That brought the most sadness.

This deep level of sorrow brings us to *brokenness* before God. Job knew what brokenness felt like and, in spite of all his losses, felt okay about voicing his emotions to God: "Though I cry, 'I've been wronged!' I get no response; though I call for help, there is no justice. . . . Those I love have turned against me."[10]

Here lies that great challenge for the woman who is afraid of losing control: Our *internal negotiating* can allow us to convince ourselves we have no problem—which sends us right back to our escape into denial, defeat, bitterness, or compulsive behaviors. Or, it can lead us to genuine *sorrow* for the sin of relying on ourselves, instead of on God. David said it so well:[11] "Have mercy on me, O God, according to your unfailing love; according to your great compassion blot out my transgressions."

His sorrow led to *brokenness*, and then to *surrender*: "For I know my transgressions, and my sin is always before me." He experienced guilt, but he knew what to do about it: "Against you, you only, have I sinned and done what is evil in your sight. . . . Cleanse me . . . and I will be clean; wash me, and I will be whiter than snow."

True repentance always leads to *surrender*. It has been true for Liz. It was true for David—"Create in me a pure heart, O God, and renew a steadfast spirit within me."

The final step for all of us is a *faith-filled decision*. Liz chose to resign from her prestigious position in Christian education, to accept wise counsel from her husband, and to submit to treatment for her perfectionism, which had led to depression. She has fully recovered and now paces her life in a whole new way. She has time for her children's activities. She recently accompanied her husband on a short-term mission trip to Nigeria. She has time to entertain friends in her home. I believe Elizabeth's ministry is more powerful than it was when she was in bondage to perfectionism. She is relaxed, happy, and at peace.

I had to come to the painful decision of realizing that people will always ask me to do more than God asks me to do. I began saying "no" to worthy opportunities to speak when my calendar was getting full. In the beginning it was hard to force the words out of my mouth. When I was home for a day with nothing "important" to do, I would fall into old patterns of feeling worthless and vulnerable.

But I discovered something significant. Every time I made the *faith-filled decision* to release the old control reflex, I took a step forward. I began developing a "real" friendship, for the first time, with someone who held me accountable for following through with my decision. I learned how precious an intimate friendship is—no strings attached. By allowing myself to be vulnerable with another human being, I sometimes experienced misunderstanding or hurt, but the love I received so greatly outweighed the risk, I would never choose to go back to my old ways. I finally believe God loves me just because I exist, not because of what I do for Him.

The next chapter begins where we leave off here. I'm living proof there's hope for those of us who have denied our problem and covered our anguish with perfectionism and excessive work. Being vulnerable isn't easy. But it's a start. Old habits *can* be changed. Honest relationships can replace superficial ones. As we make progress, I think God smiles. He knows we'll be so much happier when we quit equating *doing* with *being*.

"If I Let You Get Close to Me, Will You Still Like Me?"

FEAR 4: REVEALING WHO I REALLY AM

No one can develop freely in this world and find a full life
without feeling understood by at least one person. . . .
[She] who would see [herself] clearly must open up to a confidant
freely chosen and worthy of such trust.

DR. PAUL TOURNIER
Quoted by John Powell in *Why Am I Afraid to Tell You Who I Am?*

Abby was hard to love. In fact, Abby was even hard to *like*. Every time I tried to get close to her, she pulled away. And she never looked at me with steady eye contact. What was this girl trying to hide, anyway? Her body language begged for human compassion, but when I reached out to her, I was shut out.

My husband and I had accepted the invitation to become the youth directors at our local church. We were young university graduates with lots of enthusiasm and big ideas for redefining "effective youth programming." We accepted the challenge.

In the beginning, the job was fulfilling and rewarding. The group was growing. Eager volunteers were there to help out. Kids were coming to Christ. We felt successful and happy. But then frustration set in.

In addition to the normal exhaustion of a busy ministry schedule, we had a new problem that put us in a quandary. Our phone started to ring regularly at late hours. At first we thought the calls were a prank. When we picked up the receiver and said, "Hello," no one would speak on the other end of the line. After a moment, the caller would hang up. I finally figured out that the mysterious caller always rang our number after a youth event or church service—and I had a sneaking suspicion it was Abby—just checking to see if we were at home yet. The girl irritated me!

One day Abby confessed to me that she thought she was pregnant. I tried to mask my disappointment in this girl. After all of my attempts to help her, Abby always seemed to turn her back. She rejected every attempt I made to have an intimate conversation with her—and I felt like giving up!

WHY AM I AFRAID TO TELL YOU WHO I AM?

Years ago John Powell wrote a book by that title, and the answer to the question reveals the total vulnerability of every one of us: "BUT IF I TELL YOU WHO I AM, YOU MAY NOT LIKE WHO I AM, AND IT IS ALL THAT I HAVE."[1]

That's a powerful statement. If I open myself up to another human being and they laugh at me, ridicule me, or make my ideas seem unimportant and stupid, I will feel overwhelming embarrassment and shame. If I reveal something painfully personal and you handle the information carelessly or act like you don't really care, the emotional anguish will be more than I can bear. "Who I am" is all I have to offer another person. If you make me feel awkward and unworthy of your friendship, I may die of humiliation.

ABBY'S FEAR

My awkward relationship with Abby continued throughout her high school years. At times I felt totally ineffective as a youth specialist because she rejected my attempts to get close to her.

She mysteriously "lost" the baby she was carrying. I couldn't decide if she'd had an abortion or if she'd made up the whole pregnancy story to get attention. Either way, Abby was not on my "favorites" list.

Years later a letter came from Abby, and she finally revealed her secret:

> Several years ago . . . I came to you with the fear that I was pregnant. Do you remember? I need to explain to you the circumstances surrounding that situation.
>
> During that time in my life I was being violently and repeatedly sexually abused. Because of the nature of the abuse and the

threats that were ever present, I didn't dare tell you what was happening.

I hoped you would ask and prayed that you wouldn't. I was very scared. I could tell by your reaction that you were disappointed in me. I felt so ashamed because I knew what you must have thought. (Sometimes I still feel ashamed and dirty, but I'm working on that!)

I want you to know that I wasn't in that situation because I willingly slept around. I wasn't like that. If I had any control over what was happening, I wasn't aware of it. I thank God for pulling me out of that horrible situation. I was so afraid.

Her letter went on to explain that she had received counseling, was in a Twelve Step program, and was busy working through the past so she could get on with the present and future. Tears brimmed in my eyes as I realized how wrong I had been about Abby. I had been totally blind to the nonverbal signals that were screaming at me.

BEING VULNERABLE—A RISK WORTH TAKING?

In the last chapter, we looked at the meaning of the word *vulnerable*. It seems to indicate the person who is "unprotected" emotionally or is vulnerable physically. When we feel like victims (due to past experience or current situations) we are particularly open to attack, hurt, or injury.

For those of us who have been victimized in the past, it's easy to fall into a habit or pattern of withdrawal in order to avoid the potential of being wounded again. After a while, we become convinced that we are susceptible to greater penalties in life than other people. This defeatist attitude is quickly detected by "users"—those who make themselves more powerful by selecting weak victims to control or hurt.

However, if we're honest, we must admit that sometimes *we are our own worst enemy*! Our minds have a tremendous capacity for exaggeration and distortion of truth. Sometimes we convince ourselves we have an aggressive enemy who doesn't exist. We can even persuade ourselves and others that being vulnerable is always a negative experience.

But there is a flip side to all of this. Being vulnerable with the right people has the potential of bringing deep joy, emotional connection, and personal growth. To be vulnerable in the positive sense is to be accessible, innocent, and exposed. When we peel back the protective layers of our carefully crafted image and reveal ourselves to another human being who is worthy of that trust, true vulnerability brings an intimacy that breeds affection, transparency, tenderness, and understanding.

SO WHERE DOES THE PROBLEM COME FROM?

If you have ever had a friend you tried to be open and honest with who clammed up and shut down every time the conversation turned to her personal life, thoughts, or feelings, you've asked the question: *What causes women to become emotional misers who are afraid to reveal themselves to someone else?*

After talking with hundreds of women about this topic, I've determined the fear of being vulnerable has many causes. Some of them are listed below. As you read through the descriptions, look for any similarities in yourself.

TRIGGER POINTS
THAT TURN A WOMAN TOWARD A CYCLE OF FEAR

LACK OF TRUST

Dr. Carla Perez, a San Francisco psychiatrist, says, "A lack of trust in others—usually dating from childhood—is the basis of the guarded woman's problems."[2] In an article in *Cosmopolitan* she goes on:

> Very early in life . . . this person was given good reason to conclude that she would be hurt if she let people know too much about her. . . . [This can happen when she] is condemned instead of comforted by her parents when she shows fear, ridiculed instead of praised for her dreams, or raised in a way that fosters intense mistrust of anyone outside her family.[3]

Lack of trust turns a fearful little girl into a grown woman who has great difficulty allowing herself to enjoy the luxury of intimacy with a spouse, friends, or other family members.

SHYNESS

Researchers have said that as many as 93 percent of all people have experienced shyness. We usually think being "shy" means we are quiet, timid, or fearful of interacting with other people. Psychologists sometimes refer to shyness as "social anxiety," and that can mean mild nervousness when you are around people all the way to the other extreme of having a social phobia.

Psychotherapist Jonathan Berent described this more intense shyness disorder as an "interaction-related anxiety [which] is so extreme that a person actually avoids the specific situations that cause it."[4] If you've ever been so afraid of people that you avoided certain individuals, places, or events, you understand that statement very well. Extreme shyness can hurt us in our job situations, love relationships, ministry opportunities, and in other aspects of our general social lives. It's very painful!

LOW SELF-ESTEEM

Years ago Dr. James Dobson wrote a book called *What Wives Wish Their Husbands Knew About Women,* and he documented a survey concluding that low self-esteem was the number-one problem of women. Sometimes early rejection by peers or family members is the cause. Another trigger point is repeated failure in everything from athletics to academics to career choices to relationships. Low self-esteem is an epidemic and is a major cause of our fear of revealing ourselves to others.

Max Lucado told a story of needing time to be alone during a busy workday. He found some "space" in a local cemetery during his lunch break (creative idea!), and he began wandering around, reading the engravings on tombstones. He came to one that said:

Grace Luellen Smith
Sleeps, but rests not
Loved, but was not loved
Tried to please, but pleased not,
Died as she lived — alone.[5]

Some of us will have more positive statements on our gravestones — or maybe just our names. But I wonder how many of us can identify with the unknown Grace Smith—the woman who tried to earn love and failed, tried to please people and didn't, and died emotionally lonely. Low self-esteem has nothing to do with economic status or level of education. It kills relationships, stifles creativity, and holds people in bondage to hidden fear.

SHAME

This category involves embarrassment, humiliation, abuse, and dishonor. Whatever happened in the past that brings a loss of reputation, painful memories, and repeated bouts of depression seems to keep us "locked up" in our emotions so we are unable to relate to other people in a healthy way. Dr. David Seamands wrote, "Memories involving times when we were deeply humiliated produce the most painful emotions we experience, and are some of the chief causes of . . . depression."[6]

MISSED OPPORTUNITIES

This category almost writes itself. How many times have you and I joined the millions of women who contemplate:

- If only I had selected a different career. . . .
- If only I had married a different man. . . .
- If only I had chosen to have children. . . .
- If only I had more perfect children. . . .
- If only I had a chance for a university education. . . .
- If only I had not come from such a dysfunctional family. . . .
- If only I had a supportive friend/spouse. . . .
- If only I had a church/denomination that allowed women to use all their God-given gifts. . . .
- If only I were not trapped by financial problems. . . .
- If only I had better health. . . .

Lost opportunity can lead us on a destructive mental course. We begin to see that all of these causes of fear overlap and interweave. Lost opportunity can lead to low self-esteem. Constantly looking in the "rear-view mirror" sometimes breeds humiliation or shame. The negative effects of missed opportunity multiply over time as we internalize and mentally magnify the fear connected with our regrets and second thoughts. Our frayed emotions lead us to poor interaction with people as we try to cover our hurts with an image of "I'm okay . . . and how are you?" Surface talk keeps us from appearing as unhappy, hurting, and fearful as we really are.

POOR COMMUNICATION SKILLS

I've spent part of the past ten years training Christians in communication skills through the "Speak Up With Confidence" seminars. I have met many women who are thinking, creative, educated, and attractive, but they are enveloped in fear when it comes to expressing what they know to other people. According to the *Book of Lists*, public speaking is the number-one fear of people in the United States. Depending on the year, the fear of death fluctuates between number two and six on that list. I have always been surprised by that. People are more afraid of speaking in public than of dying!

But far greater than the fear of public speaking is the fear some people have of private, interpersonal speaking. Many women are convinced that every time they open their mouths, they can't formulate what they want to say in a meaningful sentence. Some struggle with getting their thoughts organized. Or they experience extreme nervousness in front of people they perceive as powerful. Others have been teased by siblings (or parents) about their strange gestures, word pronunciations, or oral mistakes. The majority simply believe they do not have the ability to share their thoughts in an articulate, clear, and concise manner. Rather than risk being laughed at or because they fear looking mentally "slow," they prefer withdrawal to the potential of public ridicule.

LEARNED INTERPERSONAL COMMUNICATION LEVELS

John Powell once stated, "To refuse the invitation to interpersonal encounter is to be an isolated dot in the center of a great circle . . . a small island in a vast ocean."[7] He began to study the way we reach out to each other and determined that most of us function at one of five different levels in our interpersonal communication.[8]

Level 5: Cliché Conversation

This is the "weather talk" level where we reach out to people on the surface, but say nothing meaningful or personal. "How are you?" "New glasses?" "Great outfit!" We appear interested in people, but never get past the superficial level.

Level 4: Reporting the Facts About Others

Career women and mothers are very good at this kind of communication. They say things like, "Have you heard about what happened to Sally?" or "My daughter is going to wilderness camp next week." At this level we offer nothing personal or self-revealing, but we do report the facts about other people, share gossip items, or we engage in office chit-chat. It's still a very lonely level of communication.

Level 3: My Ideas and Judgments

This level of communication represents the first step out of the prison of "I'll talk to you, but I'm not telling you anything about myself." Women who risk communicating at the level of ideas and judgments begin to share a few personal thoughts, even some decisions they've made, but they are watching the "receiver" very carefully. Is there a raised eyebrow or grimace that would indicate disapproval? If so, it might feel safer to retreat to a less personal level of communication.

Level 2: My Feelings and Emotions

John Powell refers to this as "gut level" communication. At the previous level, as long as we are only discussing ideas we have, judgments we've made, or decisions that are forthcoming, we still have not revealed our hidden passions. At this level we divulge what makes us feel strongly about our political persuasion, our child-rearing techniques, our commitment to issues or causes, and our approach to our faith.

For instance, I might make a judgment about you: "I think you are a very beautiful woman." There are many possible emotional reactions I might have regarding that observation. I may choose to share them with you—or choose to stay "safe." My potential "gut level" feelings are numerous. Keep in mind that my judgment is simply: "I think you are a very beautiful woman." But my *feelings* could have a wide range:

- . . . and I hope my daughter is like you on the inside and out when she grows up.
- . . . and I'm very jealous of you.

- . . . and I feel good about myself when I'm with you.
- . . . and I'd like to have your advice the next time I go shopping for clothes.
- . . . and I feel threatened whenever you are around my husband.
- . . . and I find myself putting you down so I can mentally elevate myself.
- . . . and I'm usually intimidated by attractive women, but you make me feel comfortable and at ease.

Powell stated,

> Most of us feel that others will not tolerate such emotional honesty. We would rather defend our dishonesty on the grounds that it might hurt others, and, having rationalized our phoniness into nobility, we settle for superficial relationships. . . . Any relationship, which is to have the nature of true personal encounter, must be based on this honest, open, gut-level communication. The alternative is to remain in my prison, to endure inch-by inch death as a person.[9]

Level 1: Peak Communication

All of us who have ever experienced an honest, truthful, authentic friendship have had moments of peak communication. Notice, I say, "moments," because with our human imperfections, we don't communicate at this pinnacle level every day. But when we share our heart and mind with someone who empathizes completely with our elation or grief, there are times of unexplainable oneness of spirit. It is the experience of knowing someone has "heard" us, accepted us, and felt our sadness or joy. We know a complete emotional and personal communion with another human being.

FACING THE CONSEQUENCES OF "THE FEAR TRAP"

As I talk to women who have chosen to retreat into the "safety" of not revealing themselves to someone else, I wonder if the consequences of that choice are far worse than the risk of facing the fear, feeling the panic, but making personal progress. Some of the negative results women have shared with me are listed here.

EMOTIONAL ISOLATION

Intimate conversation is the way most of us get to know each other, and it's an essential part of deepening a friendship or a marriage. When we deprive ourselves of gut-level communication with someone else, we become withdrawn and lonely. We are robbed of intimacy.

THE IMPOSTER PHENOMENON

Psychologists use the term "the imposter syndrome" to describe "a deep sense of fraudulence or unworthiness that bears no relation to reality."[10] When our sense of self-esteem is very low, though we may actually be educated, talented, and dynamic, we are convinced that we've gotten where we are only by fooling the rest of the world. We are fearful of letting anyone get too close to us—because they might find out what a "nobody" we really are and tell someone else.

COMPULSIVE BEHAVIORS AND ADDICTIONS

When we internalize our feelings and emotions, we often give in to the destructive path fear takes. We don't have meaningful communication with anyone else, which leads to *a sense of powerlessness*, which fuels our *fearful emotion*. We react with a feeling of *betrayal*, leading to reactive emotions of *defeat* or *denial*. The final step always seems to lead to the refrigerator, or perfectionism, or workaholism, or substance abuse, or to twisted perceptions of people and reality. The control issues discussed in the last chapter overlap here. We hate this destructive cycle, but we always seem to choose it.

A FANTASY WORLD

The imagination is a wonderful thing when we dream the right dreams or engage in playful activities that come to life as our creativity helps us mentally to paint the picture of "what might be." However, when we constantly live "inside ourselves" with no opportunity to unload emotional baggage with a caring person, our mental pictures can breed untrue perceptions. We imagine that people aren't reaching out to us because we have a strange personality, or odd looks, or because we always make a fool of ourselves in public. This distortion of reality is magnified if we are struggling with a lack of trust in people due to the shameful events of our past.

INTERNAL RAGE

Emotions boil when some women who are afraid to reveal themselves to others observe happy, well-adjusted people interacting well with each other. Every time the fearful woman is around these "examples of perfection" a fuse inside of her is lit. She doesn't know if it's extreme jealousy or resentment because they haven't reached out to her.

Regardless of what the trigger point is, an inferno of anger begins to build as she realizes how unhappy, unfrequented, and unknown she is. Internal rage finally exhibits itself in the form of ulcers, strained work and family relationships, severe depression, or inappropriate comments or outbursts.

SPIRITUAL DEFEAT

Most Christian women have been challenged by sermons on the Great Commission, the passage at the end of Matthew where Jesus challenges His leadership team: "Go and make disciples . . . teaching them to obey everything I have commanded you. And surely I will be with you always, to the very end of the age" (Matthew 28:19-20). We don't need to be reminded that spiritually active Christians are in the process of telling other people about their faith. And not only are we supposed to speak of our own personal commitment to Christ, we *should* be coming alongside young Christians and teaching them what we know about the Word of God and the faith-walk.

To feel like a social failure because of our inability to reveal our emotions and feelings to others is one level of defeat. But compounding that guilt is our knowledge that we aren't fulfilling Christ's command. We seem to be afflicted with mental and verbal paralysis when it comes to expressing our faith out loud. Often, because of our guilt we feel unworthy of God's love.

THE SECRET POWER WITH PEOPLE

People were always bringing hurting friends and relatives to Jesus. What was there about Him that made Him so approachable? The Bible seems to indicate that He wasn't drop-dead gorgeous—so it wasn't looks that made Him so appealing. What was the secret of His ability to relate to people so well? Close observation gives us the answer. Even before He opened His mouth to speak to individuals who came for help, He was already revealing who He really was in a nonverbal way.

The account of Jesus' life in the four gospels gives us the answer to His amazing power with people. (I'm not talking about the obvious deeper theological meaning behind His deity. I'm talking about the human traits we can learn from how He related to men and women.) Repeatedly the text reads, "*He looked at him [her] with eyes of compassion.*" Within a verse or two, something else becomes apparent. "*He touched them.*" Everywhere Jesus went He did those two things.

1. *He looked at people, showing He really cared about them.* Compassion always makes me feel like people are concerned about my feelings, emotional responses, and hurts. Instead of feeling threatened, I feel valued and loved. I know someone desires to make it easy for me to share my feelings or voice my fears. Usually that feeling comes nonverbally from someone before he or she speaks a word.

2. *He touched people.* Appropriate touch through a handshake, a hug, a squeeze on the arm, or a pat on the shoulder conveys a volume of meaning. It's a way of letting people know we are genuinely glad to be with them. It's a nonverbal way of making them feel comfortable and desirable. The woman who touches others with a warm greeting or affirming pat appears much more approachable and is perceived as a person of warmth. Intimidation is not present. Fears begin to melt away.

WHAT DOES THIS HAVE TO DO WITH OUR FEARS?

Most of us suffer from varying degrees of the fear of vulnerability. It's a risky, frightening thing to offer our feelings and emotional responses to someone who might not hold what we reveal of ourselves with tender loving care. We long for intimacy, but we are afraid to be the first one to offer it.

When we finally conquer this fear, we often find ourselves on the receiving end of a relationship with someone who is just learning how to trust. The person may have experienced years of low self-esteem or feelings of shame. It might be someone who still struggles with communicating what she means, or perhaps she feels victimized by lost opportunity.

The type of fear we've been discussing often progresses to a paralyzing "inner state of the mind." We can choose to remain a victim of our fear, or we can decide to admit the fear and do something about it.

A great way to start is by following the example of Jesus, the Master Teacher. When we begin looking at other people with eyes of compassion, we see a whole myriad of other women just as frightened as we are. It's been a long time since they saw another woman look at them as if she wanted to reach out and communicate in a meaningful way. If we take the second step of communicating through meaningful touch, we are often surprised by the warmth of the response.

LOOKING BACK AT ABBY

Remember the teenager in my youth group? In her situation the *triggering situation* that initiated her fear was sexual abuse. Her *reactive emotion* was panic, followed by betrayal. Was she pregnant? Would people think she was promiscuous? People she trusted abused her. Her own youth director didn't pick up on her nonverbal cries for help. These emotions soon turned into a sense of *powerlessness*. As a teen with no place to go and no one to ask for help, she felt totally unable to change her situation.

It didn't take long for Abby's emotions to turn to *rage*. Why would a God of love have allowed her to become so deeply damaged at such a young age? Why didn't the youth leaders she tried to communicate with understand her desperate cry for help? Why did family members allow the sexual abuse to continue when they probably knew what was going on? Nothing about the entire situation was fair!

Her *internal negotiating* could have led her to a lifetime of compulsive addictions. Instead, as the years went by, she had the maturity to realize that we live in an imperfect and unfair world. Instead of giving in to the destructive resolutions of denial, defeat, bitterness, or escape, she sought counseling and gave herself permission to feel deep *sorrow* for the loss of her virginity by a violent act. She grieved over her loss of innocence and trust.

In time, this grieving led to **brokenness**. The brokenness she experienced was not caused by false guilt for what had been done to her.

Here's where a lot of us have problems. Because of the emotional response of shame and embarrassment that often accompanies sexual abuse, sometimes victims feel as if they have to confess sin. They're not sure why, but they feel dirty and guilty. Satan powerfully deceives them into believing they caused the problem.

We often spend a lot of time asking God for forgiveness for the wrong things. It's the willful dependence on ourselves (trying to "play God") that gets us into trouble. Abby discovered that when we repent of the legitimate sin of self-reliance (not shame inflicted by other people), it leads us to **surrender** to God's authority in our lives. And finally, we are able to come to the place Abby arrived at—a **faith-filled decision** to change the future with God's help.

I saw Abby a few weeks ago. What a difference there was! She looked at me with confidence and didn't pull away when I gave her a hug. There was a sparkle in her eye as she told me of her immediate plans for this year and of her hopes for the future. She briefly shared her feelings about the benefits of her counseling and the positive changes in her life.

As I said goodbye, I realized Abby had become a well-adjusted, happy, and outgoing person and was fun to be with. I didn't recognize the teenage girl I met fifteen years before. This "new" woman was open, honest, vulnerable, and accessible. She shared emotions and feelings. She was the kind of person I would want for a close friend. Before I left, *she* looked at *me* with eyes of compassion and asked how *I* was doing in my personal life and ministry. Abby's gentle touch assured me she really cared and my heart responded to her genuine warmth.

A FINAL CHALLENGE

If you have been "locked up" and unable to reveal your feelings and emotions to someone else, will you face your fear and risk rejection in order to make progress? Practice my husband's instruction to me when I was first learning how to ski. When you face your fear, say "So what?" Ask yourself, "What's the worst thing that could happen to me?" Well, let's say that if I share at the "feeling" level, someone might laugh at my idea or remind me of my past. So what? Move on to someone else.

I also have a little hint. Be a person with eyes of compassion and a warm and friendly handshake. The rewards of intimacy are many. But prepare yourself. Your phone will ring more often, and there will be knocks at your door—occasionally at inconvenient times. The costs of intimacy can be great, but do you really want fear to rule such a potentially fulfilling area of your life?

PART FOUR

OVERCOMING THE FEAR OF ABANDONMENT

CHAPTER SEVEN

"If I Don't Meet the Expectations of Others, What Will Happen to Them and Me?"

FEAR 5: DISAPPOINTING PEOPLE

When we face how deeply disappointed we are with our relationships, it then becomes possible to recognize the ugliness of what before seemed reasonable. When I realize how badly I want someone to come through for me in a way no one has, then (and not until then) can I see how hard I work either to get what I want or to protect myself from the anguish of more disappointment.

DR. LARRY CRABB
Inside Out

The headline was not unusual: "San Diego Man Put On House Arrest To Await Trial." But my heart was racing. Breath was short. Eyes brimmed with tears. Terror gripped my heart. The article continued:

> A judge Wednesday ordered that a San Diego man charged with attempted murder of a police officer be jailed and then held under house arrest until trial.
>
> Michael Jensen, 37, will wear an electronic monitoring bracelet in his home. . . . The bracelet will allow law enforcement officials to keep track of Jensen, who allegedly shot at his wife and two sheriff's deputies during a domestic dispute at the home on Wednesday, March 4.
>
> . . . Judge Anthony J. Markham said that according to a report, Jensen "shot up everything in the house that reminded him of his wife." . . . One bullet apparently went right over a sheriff's head and hit a squad car. . . .
>
> The Jensens had been seeing a counselor, and their marital problems "came to a head." . . . On the night of the domestic dispute, Megan Jensen left the home and called the sheriff. . . .

A standoff began at 7:45 p.m., when Jensen allegedly fired shots from a scope-equipped rifle at his wife and sheriff's deputies. . . .

Jensen held sheriff's deputies at bay and kept his neighbors away from their homes almost three hours . . . [before he] surrendered to about 30 Special Operations Officers [and] was taken to a mental health center.[1]

As I viewed the videotape on the local news that night, it was my sister's face that appeared on the screen of my television set. The paralyzing fear that accompanied a phone call on the fateful night of March 4 returned to imprison me. My own sister a victim of domestic violence? How could she have stayed married to an abusive man for nineteen years? What about her ten-year-old son—my nephew!

My thoughts came like water over a dam, filled with anger and rage and guilt for not being more involved in her life—guilt for not being there to "save" her from this situation. From that man. From the humiliation and public embarrassment. Then in the middle of my "Messiah complex" came the reality of the oppressive fear that consumed me—fear for her life!

This article was not just one more case of spousal abuse. This was my sister, my family member, my flesh and blood—and all the prayer in the world could not quiet my heart.

WHY DO WOMEN PUT UP WITH SO MUCH?

All of us have an indescribable desire for love. We spend much of our lives trying to make relationships work so we can fill the vacuum inside our souls. For most of us, no punishment could be worse than being abandoned by someone to whom we have given our love, loyalty, and commitment.

But this problem goes far beyond the personal feeling of rejection we might experience. Our gripping fear is that significant other people in our lives will know we failed at the one thing Christian women are supposed to be good at—making relationships work. Especially marriage and family relationships!

Most of us would prefer to live with personal pain, emotional deprivation, and spiritual paralysis rather than risk the possibility of disappointing people who we think expect us to be models of Christian womanhood. Sometimes we choose sick marriages, plastic family reunions, and phony church fellowship instead of admitting we have a problem and asking somebody for help. Some of us have functioned at this level for so long, we think it's normal.

KEY QUESTIONS THAT DEMAND PERSONAL INTROSPECTION

Answer the following questions as honestly as you can:

- In one or more of your closest relationships, do you always give more than you receive?
- Are you fearful of arousing someone's anger or rage if you don't perform certain tasks to their liking?
- Do you "cover the tracks" for someone you are close to by making excuses, justifying what they haven't done, doing work for them, or even lying to make them look better?
- Do you have trouble communicating in an open, honest, and appropriately confrontational manner with a certain person in your life?
- Do you find yourself "giving in" or "giving up" in order to keep peace in a relationship?
- Do the emotional mood swings of another person drastically affect your personal planning and emotional well-being?
- Do you find yourself constantly "fixing things" so someone else is in a good mood or behaves in a civil manner?

If you answered "yes" to more than half of these questions, this chapter is for you. The fear of disappointing people is rooted in the fear of abandonment and most of us struggle with this problem at some level throughout our lifetime.

UNDERSTANDING THE BUZZ WORDS

A few years ago some new words started cropping up in informal conversations everywhere. People with any "awareness" or education, basic savvy, or experience in counseling were using terms like *dysfunc-*

tional, codependency, and *enabler.*

There were also special initials that the "in" crowd referred to. I remember feeling totally ignorant in a gathering of my peers when someone referred to an ACA group; I had no idea she was talking about "Adult Children of Alcoholics." I was more than a little irritated that this whole new vocabulary had evolved—and no one had written a lay person's glossary for these new terms.

Since then, my basic understanding has extended to include at least an elementary knowledge of these terms, and the more I learn, the more interesting the words have become. The three specific buzz words mentioned above play vital roles in the lives of all of us who are afraid of disappointing people.

DYSFUNCTIONAL

How dysfunctional is *your* family? The names in the following scenarios may be different, but are the people the same?

- Have you ever participated in a family reunion and looked over at weird Uncle Harry and negative Cousin Ethel and wondered if *all* of the strange people are in *your* family?
- Have you ever attended a family dinner and heard your father/mother argue with your aunt/uncle/grandmother/ grandfather for two hours of the three hours they were together? Do you wonder why they choose to get together, because this *always* happens?
- After a perfectly miserable time with relatives, has your mother tried to convince you that all families have a few people who don't get along, but overall it was "a warm and wonderful time at the reunion"?
- Do you or the people in your home blame others for the family tensions with words like: "If only he hadn't said that . . ." or "I wouldn't yell at her if she . . ." or "I can't be responsible for the way I am . . ."?
- Do you prefer being alone to spending time with a family like the one you're in?
- In desperation have you ever given in to an angry out- burst directed toward the stupidity of the family members around you?

So what does it mean to be in a "dysfunctional" family? Curt Grayson and Jan Johnson, in a book titled *Creating a Safe Place*, tell us that some people look at the destructive tendencies of dysfunctionality and think it's a fancy name for sin. But that's not true! "Dysfunctionality is not sin; it's a by-product of sin. It's the handicap of an inability to relate to God and others because we were nurtured improperly as children."[2]

During his early years of ministry my father pastored a little country church. This church had some members who were vibrant, effective, growing Christian men and women. It also had some very odd, obstreperous people in attendance. At times I looked forward to leaving for college and getting on with my life so I could go to a church with more "normal" people than we seemed to have in our town.

The day finally came. I grew up and visited several other churches. My husband and I became active in the "perfect" local church. Then one day we faced a milestone in our maturity: *All churches have a few strange people.* As we looked at our families and talked to our friends, we realized: *All families have a few unconventional relatives.* It was somewhat comforting to know: *All of us struggle with dysfunctional people!* Not all of the strange people are in my family or in my church! Some of the dysfunctional people are in *your* family and in *your* church! And the final revelation? *Sometimes I'm the dysfunctional person other people are dealing with!*

When the dysfunctional people we struggle with are in our church or work places, we can sometimes hold them at arms length and make them someone else's problem, but when they're relatives or close friends, it's often a far different story. Because we long so desperately to "help" those we love and because our own successful image is strongly tied to those we are close to, codependency is often triggered.

CODEPENDENCY

Nancy Groom, in her book *From Bondage to Bonding*, defines this word as follows:

> Codependency is a self-focused way of life in which a person
> blind to his or her true self continually reacts to others — being
> controlled by and seeking to control their behavior, attitudes,
> and/or opinions, resulting in spiritual sterility, loss of authentic-
> ity, and absence of intimacy.[3]

Experts in the addiction-recovery field find this word very difficult to define because at one time or another *all* of us have dealt with some level of codependency. Codependents feel controlled by someone else much of the time, regularly adjusting their behavior to keep the status quo in relationships—even those that are abusive and demeaning.

Groom wrote,

> Think of a relationship continuum with healthy mutual interdependence at one end and debilitating codependency at the other. We all fall somewhere in between . . . [but] the longer a person pursues codependent strategies for dealing with life, the more codependent he or she becomes. Eventually those strategies become an addictive way of life—a person's primary and compulsive method for relating to self and others.[4]

ENABLER

This role is often played by the spouse, parent, or loyal friend of a dysfunctional person and it overlaps with codependency. The enabler becomes the "shield" for the alcoholic, workaholic, drug abuser, rageaholic, or depressed person. (After all, we still want this person to "look good" in front of our friends, coworkers, and relatives!) Authors Katherine Ketcham and Ginny Gustafson describe the enabler:

> The chief protector, hiding the Dependent's mistakes, covering up, lying, and making excuses for his behavior. The Enabler acts out of a sincere sense of love and loyalty, is motivated by fear of the consequences of the Dependent's behavior ("If I don't lie for him, he'll lose his job," "If I don't take care of him, he'll die,") . . . and believes that there is no choice but to continue covering up and taking responsibility. As the Enabler tries harder and harder to make things right and as things get worse and worse, she suffers from growing self-doubt, self-hatred, guilt, anger, and fear.[5]

MEGAN'S STORY

Megan was raised in the same home I grew up in. Because we loved our parents and wanted to make them proud of us we were very careful not to do anything that would put a question mark over the validity of their ministry. Since Mom and Dad were visible Christian leaders in our town, the thought of disappointing them by doing something publicly embarrassing was unthinkable!

When Megan met Michael, sparks flew. He was a flamboyant, flashy Italian who enjoyed living on the wild side. Mom and Dad were concerned about his religious upbringing, which was very different from our conservative evangelical training, but when Michael realized an important step in his relationship with Megan's father was to "pray the prayer" and invite Christ into his life, he quickly obliged. Within a few months the wedding date was set.

Michael and Megan tied the knot in lavish celebration of what appeared to represent the portrait of an ideal marriage. Soon after the wedding, they moved to San Diego—far from the watchful eyes of Mom and Dad, and far from the potential of casting a negative shadow over the ministry.

In the beginning they were happy. Michael was possessive in his love and Megan was young enough to enjoy being his "private obsession." But after a while, his heavy domination and control became a burden to her. Megan had to answer twenty questions after she returned from short shopping trips. She had no freedom to pursue personal friendships apart from Michael's total involvement in the relationships.

Megan gave birth to a baby boy and began staying at home to run Michael's construction business from an in-house office. She became the bookkeeper, the office and personnel manager, and the charming voice that booked future business over the phone. Michael's outrageous emotional ups and downs and his lack of interest in the details and paperwork of self-employment left Megan in charge of "making Michael look good"—to the clients, the IRS, the relatives, the neighbors, and even to his young son.

When Michael was in a good mood, no one could be more fun. But when he was raging mad or feeling threatened or overwhelmed with financial problems, he was in a frenzy. He had developed a library of pornographic material and began insisting that Megan live up to the models of perfection on his favorite videos. She would be summoned to the bedroom on a moment's notice—even when guests were in the house. At one point Michael stated, "I only feel safe when I'm inside of you." Megan was always quick to make "appropriate" excuses for his demanding and bizarre behavior.

His sessions of rage started to come more frequently. When he was upset, he destroyed property—expensive personal property. The next day he would apologize and try to "fix" his mistakes by buying new things.

As the financial crunch hit, Megan acquired her credentials for selling real estate and joined a prestigious firm in the city. Soon she had a large automobile, a car phone, important appointments, and her own growing income. Megan no longer had the time and energy she once possessed to cover all of Michael's tracks. But she tried.

When her parents or sisters phoned, she hid the truth from them, indicating life with Michael was blissfully happy. She even began using her own income to cover debt incurred by Michael's wild spending sprees. Megan's codependency had brought her to a place of enabling Michael to continue in his self-destructive mode. And she was almost killed in the process.

WHAT CAUSES CODEPENDENCY?

How do we wind up with this problem of codependence? Most of us long to be loving women who reach out to the needs of family members and friends in healthy, authentic, and appropriately intimate ways. How does something that sounds so correct become distorted and destructive?

Why does the fear of disappointing people play such a major role in our lives? Why do we wind up feeling emotionally bankrupt and spiritually empty? There are many potential trigger points, but some vital causes that women have shared with me are listed below:

FEAR OF DISAPPOINTING GOD

This fear is a natural for Christian women. Most of us have been raised with a strong work ethic and we believe in the concept of "serving people in love." We believe that giving of ourselves to help others is basic to what Scripture teaches. We know that Christians are supposed to go the second mile and give the second chance. With our deep desire to have a strong Christian home, we wind up enabling our "less spiritual" spouses or family members to look more "godly" by controlling their behavior, attitudes, and opinions.

This cycle of failure often continues for years without the codependent person realizing she has taken Scripture out of context. When we wind up adding our own flawed interpretations to what the Word of God says, we come up with a distorted view of a biblical concept.

MISUNDERSTANDING SUBMISSION

Christian women know the Bible teaches that the husband is the head of the home, as Christ is the head of the church. The guidelines for a successful and happy marriage are definitely found in Scripture. However, some verses have been lifted from their context to authenticate an erroneous teaching about Christian marriage.

In *Love Is a Choice* Doctors Hemfelt, Minirth, and Meier explain this false understanding of Scripture:

> In 1 Corinthians 7:4 [we] accept Paul's teaching that the husband rules over the wife's body—ignoring the rest of that verse . . . that says the wife rules over the husband's body. In that same chapter, verse 10, Paul declares that a wife should not separate from her husband. Yet, how few women are counseled in the rest of that same verse—*"but if she does"* . . . Paul left the door open for extreme cases.
>
> The wife is called upon to be subject to her man (Ephesians 5:22), but hardly anyone notices that in 5:21 Paul has used exactly the same word to call every Christian into similar submission to every other. . . . The abusive husband quotes Hebrews 12:7, which extols God's disciplining of His faithful, and twists it to suggest that the man ought to keep his mature adult wife in line in the same way one might discipline a small child, or God might discipline an errant saint.[6]

Often, the woman who has been taught that her chief duty is to "stand by her man" believes that since divorce is unthinkable for the Christian woman, she should just put up with mental, physical, and sexual abuse. She fails to fully understand that the same Scripture (1 Corinthians 7:32-37) just as firmly states that the husband should please his wife.

The doctors quoted earlier state:

Especially in Christian marriage, denominational interpretation and tradition bind the woman to an unholy union of fear and pain. Because of her erroneous concept of submission and her strong abhorrence of divorce or separation, the Christian wife may have little recourse but to take refuge in terrible denial . . . [which] is compounded by false guilt.[7]

This woman often hears her husband say, "If you would just submit to me the way the Bible teaches, I wouldn't have to yell at you (or discipline you)." The codependent woman believes that *she* is responsible for his negative actions and attitude. Her self-esteem is so fragile, she quickly accepts the blame for almost anything!

FILLING THE DONUT HOLE

As a child I was fed Lifesavers during church services. I always wondered where those delicious "holes" had gone. Later, I mused over donuts in the same way. Once, as I twirled a sumptuous, glazed Krispy Kreme on my finger before attacking it with the first crushing bite, I realized my "real self" was a lot like the hole in the middle. Empty. Lost. Abandoned. But never declared missing, because it was never noticed.

When we come to this point, most of us begin to experience a dull ache in our soul. On the surface we appear to be functional women, but we have at last realized on a cognitive level that the donut hole inside does indeed exist. It's the realization that no matter how hard we've tried to please other people and God by doing more for Him or them, it hasn't brought contentment. So we move into "managing" another person who needs our help. We think that will make people happy with us. We're convinced our actions will please God. But the hole in our soul is still there.

LOST CHILDHOOD

Women who were abused as children easily fall into a codependent relationship in their adulthood. They often experience an undercurrent of guilt, which leads them to believe they could have stopped the perpetrator of the abuse if they were smart enough or strong enough. This leads to low self-esteem, which reinforces a cycle of trying to be helpful or good enough to please the powerful people around them. They feel the most self-worth when they are "fixing things" for the alcoholic, workaholic, rageaholic, or drug-addicted person.

The firstborn woman frequently fits into this category as well. If there were several siblings, she may have taken on adult responsibilities at an early age and learned how to "make peace" between arguing family members and "rescue" brothers and sisters from the wrath of a dysfunctional parent. The habits of a lifetime often lead the firstborn woman into becoming an adult enabler, who is so absorbed and enmeshed in the life and conflicts of someone else that she loses her own sense of self in the process.

THE DESTRUCTIVE PATH OF FEAR

Life is very complicated. I am one of five sisters. All of us were raised under the same roof with the same parents. We had the same theologically sound upbringing, with similar opportunities and challenges, but our lives have taken very different turns.

When the call came on that March evening, announcing that my sister had run from her home as shots were fired in her direction, I was numb. Why would my brother-in-law get a gun from his collection and begin shooting up the house? Why did he randomly place bullet holes in family pictures, furniture, and sentimental items? Why did he "go over the edge" in such a violent way?

Other thoughts consumed my mind. Why did my sister keep her mental and sexual abuse such a secret? Why did she enable him to continue in his destructive path by making calls to appease his creditors? Why did she always make excuses for him when family members visited? Why did she justify his childish behavior to her ten-year-old son? When he became raging mad and destroyed expensive personal property, why did she welcome him back into her good graces the next day when he offered his predictable "I'm sorry"?

It's much easier to evaluate codependency from a gallery seat as a spectator than when we are living through it in a dysfunctional family situation. The subject is very complex. The fear of disappointing people has deep foundations in our past. For a time, the outward characteristics of codependency have the appearance of everything we admire in a caring Christian woman: helping, meeting needs, making peace in the middle of chaos, creating a "good testimony" for the family, keeping people with addictions from making fools of themselves, and protecting children from a dysfunctional parent. The list could go on and on. How could something that looks so "spiritual" become so destructive?

Megan's story has been repeated, with a few variations, in every city in North America. What happened?

Triggering situation: Prior to Megan's whirlwind romance with Michael, she had been in love with a man her father had disapproved of. With a deep desire to meet the expectations of her family and to protect her father's ministry from potential controversy, she broke off the relationship, even though the decision brought her deep personal pain.

She married Michael within a year after saying goodbye to her first love. Michael was the fifth child born to an economically deprived family, and he was the only child in the family released for adoption. Although he was raised by parents who adored him and gave him every benefit money and love could provide, Michael still knew he was the only child abandoned by his birth parents. Thus, his "love tank" was always on empty and the only way he knew how to compensate was to control Megan with an unhealthy, obsessive love.

In the beginning, Michael and Megan had many happy times together. They both enjoyed outdoor sports in sunny California, but a dark cloud came over the marriage as Michael's control began stifling Megan's personhood.

Reactive emotion: Megan began to experience fear on many levels. Michael began destroying property when he was angry. At times, she feared for her own safety and that of her son. On another level, she was deeply afraid of hurting the testimony of her mother and father if word of Michael's violence and their marriage problems became widely known. She had recurring fears that *she* might be the person causing Michael's problems. Perhaps if she was a more submissive wife, he wouldn't become so violent.

Had marrying Michael been the worst mistake of her life? Was it *her* fault he went into an angry rage and threw the telephone on floor, demolishing it in the process? And what about the time he destroyed the television in a spurt of anger? If only she met his needs more completely, he wouldn't buy pornographic magazines and videos. Maybe if she was a better wife, he might be a better man.

Powerlessness: It didn't take long for Megan to feel powerless and betrayed. Earlier, her conservative Christian father had kept her from marrying the man she cared for so deeply. Later, Michael eroded her confidence and made her feel incapable of changing her downward spiral. Finally, she felt betrayed by God.

Rage: After a while, anger began to fester. It didn't take long for Megan's sense of betrayal to turn to rage. She had tried her best to be an obedient daughter and a submissive wife. Did God see what was happening and how miserable she was? Apparently not!

Internal negotiating: At times like this, most of us struggle deeply. During the powerless stage, we tend to get our focus off Christ and on our own crisis and our intense need. After rage sets in, we decide *to do something ourselves*—since the people we may have trusted haven't come through for us. Thus, self-reliance becomes our crutch. Our internal negotiation leads us to take action.

Destructive resolution: When internal negotiating brings on a rigid "I'll do it myself" decision for dealing with fear, we often choose denial, defeat, bitterness, or escape into obsessive/compulsive behaviors. In the beginning, Megan chose *denial*. She had married this man and she was going to make it work. She began convincing herself his emotional fits of rage were the same as any man venting his disapproval. His sexual obsession and outlandish physical demands were sometimes unbearable, but God said she was supposed to give herself to her husband and she did.

In the end Megan chose a "survival mode" through the *escape* called codependency. She wasn't happy, but at least she could "manage" this difficult situation. She became skilled at hiding Michael's mistakes, covering up the aftermath of his violent rage, and making excuses for his behavior. For years, it seemed like the right decision. It made her feel like a "biblically correct" wife; it kept her from embarrassing her parents with a divorced daughter; it kept a raging husband under control much of the time. But her life was spiritually sterile. She had a loss of self-respect, and a total absence of intimacy.

RISKING CHANGE

Redesigning our lives with the benefits of time, maturity, wise counsel, and hindsight is time consuming and costly. People may question our judgment. We may feel unspiritual for changing codependent habits. Family members may feel temporarily displaced.

Our long-term struggle with low self-esteem asserts itself with determination, begging us to accept the blame for making the lives of those around us uncomfortable—and perhaps deplorable, during the transition to wholeness. Their words reverberate: "*You're abandoning us and all of your 'Christian' duties. You are responsible for this chaos!*"

The journey to self-respect is full of challenges, questions, second thoughts, and hope for a better future. As you begin to release the fear of disappointing people, remember:

- The controlling person in your life did not take a look in your direction, judge you "unworthy" and decide to make you miserable. He or she is responding out of dysfunction: an inability to relate to God and others, perhaps because of improper nurturing as a child. *Can you forgive him or her for that?*
- We are all flawed human beings. If you have identified yourself as an enabler, you hurt the person you want to help by allowing this codependency to continue. *Are you willing to pick up a phone and find out where you can get Christian counseling?*
- God's plan for marriage is not a dictatorship. The reference to the husband being the head of the home as Christ is the head of the church is often misinterpreted. The day-to-day outworking of that level of love means serving each other sacrificially, with *mutual respect and honor.* The husband who treats his wife like a wayward child or a disobedient servant in the name of "biblical submission" is misunderstanding or misinterpreting Scripture. *Are you willing to appropriately confront your husband if you are being treated like a doormat?* (A similar scenario could be present in any relationship where there is an imbalance of power.)
- God's ideal is for unbroken, intimate fellowship in our significant relationships. But we live in a fallen world where people make sinful choices. When problems arise, every effort should be made to bring about biblical reconciliation; however, if we allow our fear of disappointing people to keep us from confronting serious codependency issues, we are making a mistake. When these serious concerns are dealt with, there is the potential of a relationship that exceeds our

expectations. But sometimes, if both parties are not willing to face their responsiblity for discord, ending the relationship becomes necessary. There are no easy answers. *Has your fear of disappointing people kept you from taking a biblical step toward confronting an unhealthy relationship in your life?*

If this chapter has "hit a nerve," make a faith-filled decision to do something specific. You might want to begin by reading one of these books:

- *Love Is a Choice, Recovery for Codependent Relationships* by Drs. Robert Hemfelt, Frank Minirth, and Paul Meier (Thomas Nelson)
- *From Bondage to Bonding* by Nancy Groom (NavPress)
- *One-Way Relationships: When You Love Them More Than They Love You* by Alfred Ells (Thomas Nelson)
- *Married Without Masks* by Nancy Groom (NavPress)

POSTSCRIPT

Megan practiced "tough love" when Michael refused to continue with counseling over their marriage problems and codependency issues. She made arrangements for a separation, which triggered Michael's violent response. Megan is now living in another state, pending a final divorce settlement.

Megan's story does not have a fairy-tale ending. Most of us don't have storybook lives. But she has made some important faith-filled decisions and she no longer lives in fear for her life.

Megan knows that confronting her husband about past abuses was a godly decision. She has realized she is not responsible for the wrong choices of her husband. She knows Mom and Dad will still be dynamic Christian leaders even though they will have a divorced daughter.

Many years have passed since Megan's father rejected her first love. All of us mature in our spiritual understanding and application of biblical principles over time, and my dad had the wisdom to write a beautiful letter of apology to Megan recently. He told her he had come to realize he was very wrong and should not have interfered in her relationship with this man so many years ago. There has been some precious healing in our family.

The "donut hole" inside of Megan is in the process of being filled. She has grieved for her losses, which are many. She no longer needs to hide behind self-protective pretense. She is learning the meaning of God's empowering grace and is finding help beyond herself. Her life is honest and authentic—and she is learning how to develop intimate relationships based on mutual trust and nonpossessive love. Megan is a courageous woman. You can be, too.

CHAPTER EIGHT

"What If the People I've Given My Love to Leave Me Or Betray Me?"

FEAR 6: BEING REJECTED

Few things make us more aware of our need for the Lord than rejection.
The only final cure for the frowning face of rejection
is His smiling face of love and acceptance. And the more we wait for Him,
the less we'll wait in fear of future rejection.

DR. LLOYD OGILVIE
12 Steps to Living Without Fear

The letter had an out-of-state address. I opened the handwritten note and began to read:

> My husband left me three years ago to live as a homosexual. . . .
> He admitted he came back to me for the kids. . . . Can you give
> me any advice on how to live with a totally self-centered man?
> I'm expected to be perfect — right down to keeping a flawlessly
> tidy laundry room (is there such a thing?), yet he denies me
> sexually and will not try to see our relationship in a positive
> light. . . . I have two children who love their dad, but my hus-
> band doesn't love me. I am going through a dark emotional
> time. I don't want to be his maid or prostitute . . . he said he
> loved me before he married me, but he betrayed me on our first
> anniversary.

As I continued reading the lengthy account of Nancy's rejection, I realized how many other women face the same emotion, even when the triggering situation is different.

• A flight attendant wrote: "I have been going through a 'gray period' for quite a long time, which has become even blacker lately. I keep making decisions and choices in my life that I think are 'right,' but they continuously leave me alone and unhappy. . . . I appear superficially happy, but I'm sad inside most of the time."

● An executive woman recounted her story: "I dated a man for two years who led me to believe he cared deeply for me. I was a virgin who always planned to 'save myself' for the one man I would marry. This man convinced me he had several business problems during our two year relationship and kept putting off setting a wedding date. I finally 'gave myself' to him physically, thinking it would be a short time before we were married anyway. He made promise after promise but never followed through. I finally realized he *never* planned to marry me. He was enjoying the single life too much. I feel angry, hurt, betrayed, and robbed!"

● A young mother voiced her fear: "When I married Mark, I trusted him completely. We had dedicated our lives to the Lord and fully expected to go into full-time Christian ministry. Over a period of months following our marriage, I began to realize that my husband was hopelessly addicted to marijuana. He knew I wouldn't approve, so he hid his habit, used money needed for our bills to support his addiction, and then began lying to me.

"After he 'came clean' two years ago, I caught him again. You can imagine how I felt when the truth came out—for the second time! We have two small children who need their father to be a positive role model. I am angry—even bitter, wondering how on earth I am ever going to respect this person I'm supposed to be submissive to. . . . I'm having a hard time dealing with my feelings toward him. I feel like he has betrayed my love and our future in ministry for his habit."

● A single female missionary in Europe voiced her anguish: "Carol, I work among people who have a spirit of self-sufficiency. On my mission field people seem to feel that they have everything they need, so they don't require a God. No matter how hard I work there are very few visible results to report to my supporting churches when I'm home on furlough.

"I have just been devastated by a letter from my mission requesting that I submit my resignation. I was told that my home church had questions about the degree of effectiveness of my last term of ministry. I have given the best years of my life to the Lord through this mission, and I am being totally rejected by the ministry I love the most.

I feel betrayed and angry!"

● A woman in her sixties wrote: "Last spring my husband of forty-one years left me when I discovered he had been involved in a long-term affair with a woman in our church. He also left his position of leadership in our denomination. He says he plans to divorce me, marry this woman, and start a church for 'hurting people.'

"I am bitter and confused. I cry all the time. I used to be so happy and carefree, but I can barely function anymore. I don't see how God can get any glory through the things that have happened to me. I have been rejected by my husband—and now I feel rejected by my church and my denomination. I have never needed help more, but instead of reaching out to me, the people in my church seem to want me to go away—along with the embarrassment this whole incident has caused in our community."

WHAT IS THE FEAR OF ABANDONMENT?

Lonely. Abandoned. Misunderstood. Rejected. Betrayed. How many times have you and I needed more than one of those words to describe what we're feeling?

When we have poured our energy, passion, and time into the lives of people, we instinctively expect something in return. Are those expectations wrong? Why do friends consistently let us down? Why are we lonely in the middle of a crowd? How can someone we trust completely betray us? Why would anyone reject a genuine offer of love?

When we are abandoned, someone deserts us. Whether the experience is an emotional or a physical desertion, the experience of being "cast off" is the same. We are unwanted. Unfrequented. Undesired. The fear of abandonment is closely linked to the fear of rejection. When we believe we might be "thrown away as worthless" by someone we desired to have a relationship with, the fear can be paralyzing.

One woman described her fear of abandonment in this way:

It is the dread of not being wanted. I am never sure the people who are displaying love toward me are doing it because they really want to. Maybe they feel obligated. It's the fear of being an imposition upon someone. Rooted deeply in false guilt, it shows up in a sense of insecurity when I'm with others.

The fear of abandonment often binds women to the compulsive behavior of clutching at people so closely they feel strangled. When we believe that letting go of someone means we will be left behind, we are in bondage to fear. This fear inhibits intimacy and causes deep pain. One pastor states, "The fear of rejection not only keeps us from deep relationships, it often robs us of courage. We become solicitous and compliant. Eventually like a chameleon we try to blend into the background of other people's values and attitudes."[1]

Abandonment issues can be hidden deeply and covered up in many subtle disguises. Think about the people you care about the most or the people you would like to develop a closer relationship with. Do you ever entertain the following thoughts?

- I'm afraid you will leave me.
- If I tell you the truth about my past, you will push me away.
- If I'm vulnerable with you, I could become embarrassed and humiliated.
- I have been betrayed by someone in the past, and it won't happen to me again.
- If I don't change my appearance, you will think I'm fat and unattractive, and you might reject me.
- I feel threatened when you develop a close friendship with someone else.
- I feel unworthy of your love.
- I know you have many important things to do and many influential people in your life, so you probably don't really want to develop a friendship with someone like me.
- The people I've trusted the most in the past have let me down. I wonder when you will abandon me.
- I will work hard to avoid disappointing you, because if you reject me, I will have nobody.

WHAT CAUSES WOMEN TO FEAR REJECTION?

LONELINESS

The fear of rejection is often precipitated by loneliness. In an article titled "All Alone: The New Loneliness of American Women," Margery Rosen points out that researchers know loneliness is triggered when our need for an intimate, caring relationship goes unmet. She quotes psychologist Anne Peplau who said, "At any given time, at least ten percent of the population feels lonely."[2]

According to Robert S. Weiss, Ph.D., who's a research professor at the University of Massachusetts in Boston and a pioneer in loneliness research, there are actually two types of loneliness: emotional and social.

> We *feel* emotionally lonely when we aren't sharing our life with . . . an attachment figure. . . . People who suffer this form of loneliness often display real physical symptoms—an intense restlessness that makes it difficult to concentrate, a heaviness in the chest.
>
> But while some women—especially those who live alone— have always felt emotionally lonely, now they are increasingly susceptible to what Weiss calls social loneliness. "People who are socially lonely feel marginal." They tend to blame themselves for their isolation. "They may harbor a feeling that people don't like them—a sense that everyone was invited to the party but them."[3]

The woman who has built a wall of isolation around herself often feels abandoned. Even if she is alone by her own choice and can't name an individual who has rejected her, she still feels rejected.

Past Issues

Women who were victims of abuse often feel abandoned by the adult who overlooked obvious evidence of their exploitation and did nothing to help. One woman wrote, "My mother would have had to be blind to be unaware of my father's sexual relationship with me. *Why didn't she do something to protect me from that sickening animal?* I was only eight years old when it started."

Those who felt abandoned as children often carry those feelings into adulthood. Rejection can be real or imagined, but this genuine emotion often leads to a sense of abandonment. Sherrie writes:

> As an adopted child, I was never sure that I was wanted, even though I was told I was. My parents had never worked through their own grief about having been childless, and I translated their

subtle sadness to mean they were disappointed in me. So I worked hard to make them proud of me, because if I disappointed them, they might reject me, and then I would have no one in this world. No one. So I never felt the freedom just to be me. Out of a fear of abandonment, I had to pretend to be somebody "special." This produced a drivenness in my lifestyle from childhood.

BETRAYAL

Looking back at the excerpts from letters that were printed at the beginning of this chapter, it's easy to see why betrayal is a triggering cause of the fear of rejection:

- The homosexual husband who kept his secret until the first anniversary
- The flight attendant who felt betrayed by a fallen world that promised fulfillment
- The executive woman who was betrayed by the man she believed would marry her
- The young mother who was betrayed by the addiction of her husband
- The missionary betrayed by her Christian financial and prayer supporters
- The older woman betrayed by her husband, his lover, and the church congregation

Max Lucado reminds us of the sting of betrayal:

Betray. The word is an eighth of an inch above *betroth* in the dictionary, but a world from "betroth" in life. It's a weapon found only in the hands of one you love. Your enemy has no such tool, for only a friend can betray. Betrayal is mutiny. It's a violation of trust, an inside job. . . . A sandpaper kiss is placed on your cheek. A promise is made with fingers crossed. You look to your friends and your friends don't look back. You look to the system for justice—the system looks to you as a scapegoat.

You are betrayed. Bitten with a snake's kiss.[4]

Betrayal's worst insult is the pilfering of innocence. Once we have felt the barb, endured the mockery, and experienced the insult, our relationships are never the same again. Betrayal bleeds the heart of its ability to trust. Insecurity replaces confidence. Hesitancy displaces certainty. Skepticism uproots faith. The fear of rejection erases acceptance.

SPIRITUAL VOID

An intriguing story is recorded in 1 Kings 17. It had been fifty years since Israel was at the pinnacle of spiritual success under David and Solomon. Now Ahab was king. Jezebel was his wife. This was more than a marriage—it was an evil alliance. Under this diabolical leadership, Israel was plunged into the appalling rituals and sexual orgies of Baal and Ashteroth, pagan deities dedicated to violence and sexual perversion.

At this crucial time in Israel's history Elijah was selected to be God's public speaker for his generation. God's change agent. But when the script for his first talk came from God, it was one line long and it was the last time Elijah was allowed to speak publicly for about three and a half years! "As the LORD, the God of Israel, lives, whom I serve, there will be neither dew nor rain in the next few years except at my word."[5]

Immediately after God opened such a major door of ministry for Elijah, he got new instructions: "The word of the LORD came to Elijah saying, 'Go away from here and hide yourself by the brook.' So he went and did according to the word of the LORD *and it happened after a while, that the brook dried up.*"[6]

Did you get that? After what appeared to be a big-time opportunity for powerful and visible ministry, God sent Elijah to the brook—but it dried up. It shut down. It quit meeting his needs. It left him thirsty and dehydrated.

Those words jump off the page as I think about my own relationship with God. When was the last time in my life "the brook dried up"? Dry brooks take many forms:

- The opportunity for ministry or work that was going to bring me fulfillment didn't.
- The promised job never came through.
- The baby I asked God for has not been conceived.
- The friend who had cancer was not healed, in spite of my fervent prayers.
- The child I nurtured is on drugs.

- The friend who led me to Jesus contracted the HIV virus from her husband.
- The teenage daughter I love is pregnant.
- The pastor I trusted left his wife.
- The intimacy I long for with God is elusive.

When the brook dries up, dreams are shattered. Hopes are dashed. God seems far away. We feel abandoned by people we were hoping would satisfy our needs. But more than that, we feel rejected by God. Rejected by a God who should have intervened in our situation. The One who is Living Water and says He loves us and wants to meet our needs has allowed the brook to dry up.

SHERRIE'S GREATEST FEAR

Sherrie was released for adoption at ten days of age. As an adopted child, she wanted to please her parents. She had perceived their sadness regarding infertility. So Sherrie tried hard to be "good enough" to please them and take away their pain.

She was convinced her mother and father's grief over not being able to conceive a child meant they were very disappointed in the little girl they adopted. Sherrie's fear of rejection followed her. When she became pregnant out of wedlock, she took the fear of abandonment into marriage. The question always haunted her: "Did Bob marry me because he really wanted to, or because he was stuck with me?" Her life became consumed with the need to be "special" enough to keep him from being disappointed in her—and abandoning her. She became a driven wife and mother.

During twenty-seven years of homemaking and motherhood she tried to be the perfect hostess, laundress, gourmet cook, maid, and interior decorator. As she contemplated returning to college, she wondered, "Would my husband abandon me if I no longer did these tasks so well? Would he find another woman who is more like I used to be?" It was hard for Sherrie to accept Bob's total acceptance and unconditional love.

Sherrie's adoptive parents both passed away and she had a growing desire to find the answers to the abandonment issues that left her feeling powerless and hurt. After a long search, Sherrie's birth mother was located. An emotional phone call was made and within ten days, Sherrie and her husband were on a 727 headed for Seattle, Washington.

Initially, the reunion was a fairy-tale experience. Sherrie's birth mother greeted her with open arms and every imaginable sign of acceptance: a bouquet of her favorite flowers in the hotel suite, a diamond-studded pin from Tiffany's, and a sign over the front door of the family home that said, "WELCOME TO YOUR FAMILY."

Within ten days, Sherrie went from being an only child, with both parents dead, to being a sister and a daughter. During the visit her birth mother's words were tender as she looked at Sherrie and spoke softly, "When I look at your sweet face, I know you're mine." With sensitivity she continued, "You are my angel. I love you."

As the next few days progressed, Sherrie felt the Master-Healer doing a deep work within her soul, healing wounds of the past. It was so much fun discovering all the similarities: same voice, same facial features, same tastes and talents. Every discovery was a gift, a piece of the puzzle that had been missing all of Sherrie's life.

But as the week progressed, Sherrie's birth mother began to get in touch with her pain—pain from the past that had never been resolved. Her pain threw her totally out of control. Her choices were clear: she could face the pain of the past and get help, or put Sherrie out of her life and regain the control that provided a false sense of security. And without warning, she closed the door on any future relationship with her daughter. As Sherrie boarded the plane to return home, she knew her mother was saying "goodbye."

HOW DID THE CHAIN REACTION WORK?

Triggering event: Sherrie's cycle of fear was triggered by the knowledge that her birth mother had "given her up" for adoption at ten days of age. She knew nothing of her nationality, her family's medical history, and very little about why she had been released for adoption by her family of origin.

Reactive emotion: Sherrie's fear of rejection started in childhood when she sensed her parents' longing to conceive a child. She was convinced that meant they were displeased with her. She knew she'd been abandoned by her birth mother. Now Sherrie feared rejection by her adoptive parents.

Powerlessness: As a child with no place to go and no one to talk to about her fear, Sherrie was totally powerless to change her circumstances or deal with her fear of rejection in a constructive manner.

Rage: Sometimes we think of rage as a violent show of emotion—and it can be. But for Sherrie, the anger was inside. Why had she been given away? Why was she placed with a family that wanted a biological child? Why did she feel so alone? Why did God allow this to happen to her? On the surface Sherrie was a model child. But her internal rage boiled with unanswered questions.

Internal negotiating: Sherrie needed to find a way to "fix" her problem. There had to be a way out of her emotional pain and fear. It's at this point when each of us has a choice. We can choose the path of self-reliance and say, "I'll take care of the problem myself." Or we can choose the path of God-reliance and focus on a constructive course of action.

Escape: It didn't take Sherrie long at all to escape into a lifelong pattern of perfectionism, first as an adopted daughter who tried to be "good enough" to please her parents. As a young, pregnant newlywed, she tried to be "perfect enough" to please her husband. For twenty-seven years the pattern continued—with a lot of happiness mingled in with the compulsive perfectionism. During the first years of marriage, two beautiful daughters were born, and Sherrie tried to make a warm, open, and loving home for Bob and the girls.

THE TURNING POINT

A major turning point for Sherrie came with the gut-wrenching rejection from the birth mother she had longed to know. When we face our fears and allow our pain, insecurities, and anger to bring us to our knees, we can reach a God-honoring resolution.

Sorrow: Sherrie had spent years in a self-destructive escape pattern of perfectionism as she sought to cover up her feelings of betrayal, powerlessness, hurt, and rejection. Her mother's cold goodbye at the airport brought Sherrie deep pain. Then the report came to Sherrie via her half-sister. She simply stated that her mother "didn't feel much like mothering." When Sherrie realized her birth mother wanted to put her out of her life, the grief was overwhelming.

Sometimes we forget that it's okay with God if we feel the sadness profoundly. We live in a world of imperfection, broken relationships, and unresolved conflict.

Brokenness: We take a major step when we come to the place of admitting how needy we really are.

Sherrie describes the sorrow that lead her to brokenness in this way:

> I was in intense pain. I felt the anguish of being rejected. I felt so in touch with the little girl inside of me who was never sure she was wanted. I felt used. I felt disposable and discarded. I called my friend and when she arrived, I began sobbing and shaking uncontrollably.

The Sherrie of former days would have buried her pain by escaping into perfectionism. She would have figured out a way to be "good enough" so her mother would accept her once again. Instead, she let go of self-reliance and, with a humble heart, asked for help.

Surrender: People who control their lives by perfectionism often find letting go very difficult. Sherrie surrendered her desires to God. She asked Him to remove the false guilt she had carried for years. She quit blaming her adoptive parents and her birth mother for her problems. As Sherrie focused on Him, Christ made His presence very real to her through Isaiah 49:15—"Can a mother forget the baby at her breast and have no compassion on the child she has borne? Though she may forget, I will not forget you!"

Faith-filled decision: Surrender always leads to a supernatural strength that enables us to make God-honoring faith-filled decisions. I have known Sherrie for fifteen years, and I have observed a powerful change in her life. Instead of constantly longing for her family of origin, she is finding deep fulfillment with her brothers and sisters in the Body of Christ. She is leaning on them during times of need, instead of trying to be good enough to earn acceptance. She made the decision to go back to school and will earn her bachelor's degree in journalism. Taking a risk, she recently submitted an article to a well-known Christian periodical, and it was accepted!

Sherrie is still a gourmet cook and entertains her guests with a touch of class, but she is no longer a slave to her home. Life with her husband is happier and more balanced. Bob and Sherrie support each other in being whole, complete individuals. God is doing a powerful, healing work in Sherrie's life. I am proud to call her my friend.

LESSONS FROM ELIJAH

If Elijah were living today, I'm sure he'd be under contract with a major Christian publisher. The possible titles for his book would be tossed around by creative minds in a publisher's boardroom, but the final decision would probably be *Trusting God When the Brook Dries Up*.

Elijah must have felt abandoned. First, by God as he waited patiently for new instructions. Then came total rejection by Jezebel. Four hundred and fifty prophets of Baal had been destroyed. She was not a happy camper! Remember the note she sent him after the big scene on Mount Carmel?

> Dear Elijah,
> You are dead meat.
> Love, Jezebel
> (*Loose paraphrase of 1 Kings 19:2; to get the whole story read 1 Kings 17–19.*)

When Elijah faced his worst fear, he chose a destructive resolution for his problem—defeat!

> Elijah was afraid and ran for his life. . . . [He] went a day's jour-
> ney into the desert. He came to a broom tree, sat down under
> it and prayed that he might die. "I have had enough, LORD," he
> said. "Take my life; I am no better than my ancestors."[7]

But the end of the story reminds us that we never have to remain in the dead end of defeat. It is never too late to resolve our fear in a God-honoring way. God sent an angel to minister to Elijah. Then the word of the Lord came—but not in an expected way. One would think He would come dramatically—in the wind, the earthquake, or the fire. But not so. He came in a gentle whisper.

Today, because we have the completed Word of God readily available to us any time of the day or night, we have an advantage. So—the next time you fear rejection and you feel abandoned, remember:

We do not have to wait for the Lord to come to us, for He has never left us. What we are to wait for is the complete fullness of His healing. The only way that this can be speeded up is to trust Him with our hurts sooner.[8]

As we experience the deep *sorrow* of rejection and abandonment, our *brokenness* before God leads to a *surrender* of our stubborn, self-reliant will and paves the road for future *faith-filled decisions* that bring healing, acceptance, and nonpossessive love.

A GLANCE AT GETHSEMANE

Those of us who fear rejection and have experienced abandonment need only a look back at the garden where Jesus spent His final pre-crucifixion hours to forever stamp the truth in our hearts: *He knows what abandonment feels like. He knew the ultimate rejection.*

Calvin Miller reminds us of that night:

The life in question was His own. He needed friends to watch with Him and support Him as He faced death. He reached. Oh, how He reached! But His stretching, hungering touch went unfulfilled. There was but one gift He desired—to see His friends stand by Him as He carried out His faithful purpose.

In Gethsemane, Christ found Himself abandoned—not because His friends were gone, but because they took His giant needs too casually. . . . They never wanted Him to be alone, but His need escaped them as they focused on themselves.

Here and there we stumble blind in grief through our Gethsemanes and find the ground already stained with His blood. In our Gethsemanes there's an unseen plaque on every twisted tree, "Jesus was here." He is still here, and we can bear with our Good Fridays if we let our Thursdays call to mind the glorious solitude of Him who conquered loneliness.[9]

We are not alone!
   . . . when our brook dries up,
   . . . when our friends and family abandon us,
   . . . when today's cross blinds us to tomorrow's opportunities.

This is my prayer: "God, in the middle of my Gethsemanes help me to remember that You conquered loneliness. You know what my agonizing pain feels like. The total rejection. The 'Judas kiss.' The abandonment. Change my focus from lonely Gesthemane to Easter Sunday morning."

PART FIVE

OVERCOMING THE FEAR OF TRUTH

"If I Remember and Reveal What Happened to Me, Will the Pain Be Insurmountable?"

FEAR 7: FACING MY PAST

You have been damaged. But you have great hope.
The mercy of God does not eradicate the damage, at least not in this life,
but it soothes the soul and draws it forward to a hope that purifies
and sets free. Allow the pain of the past and the travail
of the change process to create fresh new life in you and to serve
as a bridge over which another victim may walk from death to life.

DR. DAN ALLENDER
The Wounded Heart

As a young child, I had a strictly enforced bedtime. But I was so deeply terrified by the darkness that my mother installed a night light. That minuscule stream of light provided just enough illumination for me to use my hands to form all kinds of amusing shadows on the wall. I remember my excitement when I first learned how to form the image of Mickey Mouse. Then I went on to create a variety of unique animal shapes.

However, when my experimental shadows produced monster images instead of familiar facsimiles of delightful creatures, my fears resurfaced. Knowing my father would be angry if I was a "fraidy cat," I developed a series of reassuring phrases I could call out. Each response demanded an answer from a parent—and when I heard the return call, I knew I was safe from the shadow monsters.

Some of my favorite nighttime proclamations were:

- "See you in the morning!"
- "Hugs and kisses . . . sweet dreams too!"
- "I love you."
- "Sleep tight . . . don't let the bedbugs bite."

SHADOW MONSTERS FROM THE PAST

Each of us has a set of our own "shadow monsters." This time, however, we're not playing a child's game. We are remembering a vivid image from our personal history.

Our fears related to past events loom over us at unexpected times. They crowd out present happiness and cast a dark cloud over future success. As time erodes the exact memory of key events and people that produced our pain, hurt, or disillusionment, the shadow gets larger and the potential for shame, guilt, anger, and hatred is enhanced.

Some of the shadow monsters faced by women I have talked to include the following:

● "I despise my father for leaving my mother, my two sisters, and me to marry his secretary. I can never forgive him for deserting us."

● "I was abused by a church that took advantage of my eagerness to serve the Lord by giving me so many responsibilities and obligations that I nearly had a nervous breakdown."

● "When I was twelve years old my father began sexually molesting me. The need for my father's love and affection was so great that I could not stop him or tell anyone about the problem. My mother knew, but she was a victim of the fear of abandonment, so she looked the other way. We were members of an evangelical church, and I attended a Christian school. I used to wonder what my father thought about when he drove our family to church every Sunday. After several years the incest ended, but the shame and guilt continued.

"When I married, I never told my husband. I didn't want him to hate my father. I knew it would destroy the image he had of our 'perfect family.' The problem did not go away. I built a wall around myself, giving the outward appearance of a vibrant and confident Christian, while frustration and anger grew within me. My rage was vented on my children—and I hated myself for it!"

● "My parents paid for my brother's university education because he would be the 'breadwinner' in his future home. Even though my academic record was much better than my brother's, I wasn't encouraged to go to college. I resent my parents to this day for treating me like an inferior human being because I am a female."

● "I aborted my first baby when I was eighteen years old. I was not in love with the father of the child. I was too young and immature for single parenting, and an abortion counselor convinced me that I was getting rid of excess 'tissue' and an unnecessary responsibility by making the best decision for my future. I now struggle with severe guilt over the life I took."

● "I had an affair with my best friend's husband several years ago. Even though the physical intimacy with this man ended quickly, my 'emotional affair' with him continued for two years. I'm afraid of getting found out—but I'm even more afraid of facing my own image in the mirror every morning. What kind of a woman am I, anyway?"

● "I stole money from my boss when funds were tight at home a couple of years ago. He's a very successful, highly motivated employer who has done everything to make my job mentally stimulating and personally challenging. I feel tremendous guilt for having taken advantage of someone who has treated me with such respect."

● "The man I dated for five years just married someone else— after knowing her for only six months. How could God allow this to happen after I invested so much time and energy in the relationship? I feel bitter and angry."

● "Someone else received the promotion that should have been given to me. I have invested my loyalty and the best years of my life in this company and have gotten *nothing* in return! I am hurt, angry, and resentful."

● "My parents *drove* me to achieve. I went to an accelerated preschool, a private elementary, middle school, and secondary school. I was forced to take years of lessons in music, art, gymnastics, ballet, and swimming. I feel like I totally lost my childhood. I had no opportunity to learn how to develop intimate friendships, and I am ignorant when it comes to developing an appropriate male/female relationship. I am angry at my parents for ruining my life by being so controlling."

THE FEAR OF TRUTH

Whether through victimization or our own behavior, many of us have been held in the grip of our fearful "shadow monsters" for too many years. Some of us spend a lifetime trying to work hard enough and smile long enough to convince ourselves and other people that we're okay. But we're always looking over our shoulder, remembering an event from yesterday or recounting the details of a failed relationship or reliving the horror of abuse—and we are running from the truth.

We seem to believe that if we gave ourselves permission and time to face our past, we would be overwhelmed by shame and guilt—and more anger. Rather than exploring the feelings those memories reveal, it's easier to bury our fears in denial, defeat, bitterness, or a wide variety of socially acceptable and not-so-socially-acceptable escapes. And the cycle of fear continues.

AN UNWANTED CHILD

My mother-in-law is an amazing woman. She is hard-working, committed to her children, generous with her grandchildren, firm in her convictions, and energetic in her determination to make a positive difference in the lives of individuals who are physically or mentally challenged. Watching her get behind a cause and implement a plan is like watching a one-person army move a whole platoon into formation for the desired aim. She gets things done!

At the age of seventeen she found herself pregnant and unmarried. On the day of that baby's birth, her own mother walked into the room, looked at the infant in her daughter's arms and said, "For the last nine months I prayed that this child would be born dead."

When I heard this story, I felt weak in the knees and faint in my heart. You see, the baby my mother-in-law was holding in her arms that day is my husband today. If Grandma had gotten her wish then, I would have missed out on marrying an incredible man. I'm able to tell the story now since Grandma has passed on. She was filled with the fear of facing her friends and family with the news of a child conceived out of wedlock. Mom married the father of her child and as time passed, Grandma did grow to love the grandchild she had rejected earlier.

Thinking about my mother-in-law's situation, I wondered how she was ever able to face her past and get on with her future in such a successful way. In spite of the initial disapproval and condemnation from her own mother, she became confident, energized, focused, and determined to look on the positive side of a negative life situation.

I wondered about the fears she had faced in the past. What gave her the courage to get beyond the shame, rage, bitterness, and pain? How does *anyone* find "life" beyond the damaging events and hurtful memories of the past?

Triggering event: There must have been a growing fear when Mom began to suspect she was an unwed, pregnant teenager. I'm sure the fear was deepened on the day the suspicion became a known fact.

Reactive emotion: Grandpa was a tall, gruff, authoritarian, controlling man. Mom must have been filled with terror at the thought of telling her parents about the pregnancy. What would the family think? What would her angry parents do? Her fears went far beyond the initial panic. If she married the father of the baby, it would calm her parents down a bit. But would it be the *right* decision for her and for the child in her womb? How could she support herself and this baby?

Powerlessness: One of the most debilitating aspects of fear is its ability to sap our strength, drain our energy, confuse our ability to make wise choices, and rob us of confidence. To be powerless is to experience a void at several levels. Suddenly, we have no control over our own situation, no inner strength for hard times, no physical stamina to carry on with routine activities, and no hope that our dark cloud will lift. We feel robbed of the basic rights *the Constitution* promises to all citizens—life, liberty, and the pursuit of happiness. Instead of focusing on God and a spiritual resolution to our fear, we seem incapable of focusing on anything but our own loss of control.

Rage: When we get tired of being victimized by our own bad choices or by the pain inflicted upon us by people we trusted, anger replaces the sense of powerlessness. Sometimes the anger seethes within us and is not clearly identifiable to the people who are in close proximity. But at other times, the fury of our rage surprises us with its outward intensity. One woman expressed it this way: "I was so shocked to hear my mother's angry voice coming out of *my* mouth!"

When it comes to the fear of facing our past, our anger seems to be highly selective in *who* it targets. At times, we are extremely angry with *ourselves*—reasoning that if we had been smarter or stronger, we could have stopped the person or event triggering our fear. At other times, we get angry at *the people who caused our pain*. If they had cared more about us and less about themselves, we would not have been in bondage to all of this fear. Finally, we direct our anger at *God*. Where was He when questionable situations emerged and when these people exhibited wrongful power over us? Where was He when we were tempted to make bad choices? Why didn't the sovereign God of the universe do something?

When we get angry because fear has stripped us of our power, we have a deep desire to become self-reliant, since relying on other people or on God hasn't seemed to help at all.

Internal negotiating: In our anger and sense of betrayal, we begin our "fix-it" program with internal negotiations. Feeling let down by other people and by God sends us into an internal battle. We are sick and tired of being controlled by fear and *something* has to change or we will break down emotionally.

This a crucial point—because each of us has to face our own past. Will we rigidly choose a destructive resolution for our fear, or will we be willing to explore the depth of painful feelings our fear has produced and discover the path to wholeness?

Mom's choice: I have never wanted to pry into the details of all that transpired between my mother-in-law and Grandma during the days following the birth of the baby Grandma disapproved of, but I can quickly assume that Mom chose a constructive resolution for dealing with her early fears. How do I know? Because I've observed her making faith-filled decisions on a regular basis for many years—and that takes practice!

THE DESTRUCTIVE CHOICES OF UNRESOLVED FEAR

Often, as we think about our fears, we rationalize about *why* certain things happened. Sometimes we come up with questions that have no answers:

- Why did I take that position in the first place?
- Why didn't I set an earlier curfew for my daughter?
- Why did I always give in to peer pressure?
- Why did I allow myself to get involved with a married man?
- Why did I take the first drink?
- Couldn't I have stopped the incest earlier?
- Why did I steal from my employer?
- Why did I listen to the abortion counselor instead of following my own convictions?
- Why did I destroy her reputation?
- Why did I sacrifice my virginity in order to be accepted?

- Why did I become a slave to my church instead of looking to God for my self-worth?
- Why did I allow my mother to tell me who to marry?
- Why did I stay in a job I hated for twenty years?

When we get no answers to those questions, we often seek a destructive course of action for dealing with the fears that resurface. We can sometimes convince ourselves to *deny* there was ever a fear in the first place. More often, we feel *defeated* by the fears from the past that haunt us today. We give up. In time, we successfully convince ourselves that the future will only be another version of a terrible past.

Sometimes we begin to blame all the negatives in our lives on the events, people, and situations that caused us to fear in the first place. At this point *bitterness* takes over. Larry Crabb says, "Bitterness develops when people don't respond to our demands."[1] Sometimes our bitterness drives us to seek revenge on the institutions or individuals who caused our pain. At other times, we have a negative attitude toward life itself: "I've been dealt a bad hand—and I will *never* be able to overcome the pain in my past."

The end result for many of us is escape into obsessive/addictive patterns. We run from the past by jumping into too much work, exercise, or perfectionism. Each of these addictions wins us the applause of the crowd and momentarily our inner void is forgotten. But when the negative escapes turn us toward alcohol, codependency, and eating disorders, we discover we're stuck in a bottomless pit.

LOOKING BACK AT YESTERDAY

Sometimes I wonder if I can ever get beyond the damage of the past. Is there any way to let go of the shame, rage, bitterness, pain, and anger? Is there any way to let the past become part of my life in a positive way—to use yesterday's mistakes and wrong choices to become part of the hope I have to offer others?

One of my major fears from the past deals with losing my second child in the early stages of pregnancy. The complete story of the miscarriage is told in my book *Secret Longings of the Heart*. After I experienced the loss of this much-wanted child, fear enveloped me. I had been warned to slow down, rest more often, reduce my schedule, and take care of my body. But in my drive to carry on with ministry responsibilities and do "important work for God," it did not seem prudent to slow my pace. There were so many urgent needs. The phone kept ringing. Slowing down felt like a sign of weakness. I wanted to prove to myself and everybody else that I was *not* going to use pregnancy as an excuse for taking it easy.

And I lost the baby in the middle of a hectic schedule. Instead of seeking help when the cramps began, I continued to drive to the location of my speaking engagement. Instead of calling for assistance, I walked to the ladies' room alone—and in the middle of a run-down community center restroom, I sat in a stall surrounded by graffiti and filth, while my baby, just in the embryo stages of life, spontaneously left my womb.

I have lived with the guilt of wondering if I could have saved that little life if I had followed the doctor's instructions more carefully. Often, our lives are made up of afterthoughts.

- If I could just live that one day over. . . .
- If only I hadn't married the first man who showed an interest in me. . . .
- If only I had taken the other route home. . . .
- If I could just take back those words of criticism. . . .
- If I could erase that one night from existence. . . .
- If I had left this miserable job earlier. . . .
- If only I had resisted the flirtations of that man. . . .
- If only I had spent more time with my children. . . .
- If only I had the courage to confront my father about his abuse. . . .
- If only I had understood that *I* was the victim. . . .
- If only I hadn't waited so long to have children. . . .

When we allow ourselves to look back at the past and meditate on all of those "if onlys," we wind up being victimized by guilt and shame for much of our adult lives. The enemy boldly articulates his message of fear, despair, and hopelessness. He wants to convince us there is no God of love and that we are damaged beyond repair. This is the worst fear of all! It's not just the past events that are so scary, but it's the fact that the memories of past events and mistakes we've made bring up our feelings of worthlessness.

UNDERSTANDING GUILT AND SHAME

If competitions were held for "Guilt Queen of the Year," many of us would be in the running. Sometimes it makes us feel better to take the full responsibility for *why* our lives are so miserable. Most of us have never wanted to be negative women who grovel in our mistakes, but when life isn't turning out right, we eagerly take the blame.

Someone once told me the definition of "mounting apprehension." It's the feeling experienced by a pet who is owned by a taxidermist! I think guilt is a lot like that. God certainly isn't a taxidermist who is going to take our lives when we are no longer useful to Him, but He does have power over us. We know a "day of reckoning" is coming. We feel mounting apprehension about the mistakes of the past. What gets confusing is figuring out if we've brought the problem on ourselves, or if we have been victimized by someone else. Our anxiety continues to grow until we've convinced ourselves we could have done *something* to stop whatever happened. In time, shame often replaces guilt.

In his book *Restoring Innocence*, Alfred Ells says,

> The single most hurtful legacy many families leave their children is shame. . . . Where guilt says, "I made a mistake," shame says, "I *am* the mistake." Shame is often an excruciating and punishing awareness of one's own insufficiency and inadequacy, and it is probably the most painful emotion one can experience.[2]

The shame felt so deeply by women who were sexually abused is a false shame, but they don't know it. It feels real. It follows them everywhere. And if they experienced any sexual pleasure during the process of being victimized, they often cling to shame. But it's illegitimate shame—a trick of our enemy to place them in confusion and bewilderment.

Though we may not be dealing with the heavy burden of sexual abuse, we *are* dealing with the mistakes of our former days. We know our bad choices caused someone else pain. We know we made errors in judgment that hurt our Christian testimony. We know there is no way to take back words that have already been spoken or to undo a wrongful deed. We know there is no way to bring life back to an aborted child. There's no way to relive a day of life that is already history.

As we get the courage to face the past in order to get on with the future, we need to understand the difference between *illegitimate shame* and *legitimate shame*. Simply stated, false shame accepts the blame for inappropriate things. Illegitimate shame causes thinking like this: "If I could have controlled someone's drinking, he wouldn't have had the accident," or "If I had been more obedient, this evil thing would not have happened."

Conversely, legitimate shame is facing our failure to trust God with the healing of our souls. That level of humility is the basis of our return to the Father.[3] We experience deep sorrow over the evil that has been done to us during victimization, which brings us to a brokenness before God. For example, legitimate shame does not lead to confession for our role in childhood abuse. The child was the victim. Legitimate shame leads to humility before God as we acknowledge our sinful self-reliance—our efforts to run from the pain or to protect ourselves from the God who seems to have let us down.

Whether our pain is caused by victimization or by our own mistakes and wrong choices, we have a natural tendency to rely on ourselves to get out of a distressing situation. Our immediate reaction is to escape our pain and look for an antidote—which usually leads us down the destructive path of denial, defeat, bitterness, or compulsive behavior. The best course of action, even though we often don't see it at first glance, is to allow our pain to lead us back to God.

THE BENEFITS OF PAIN

I'm not very good at allowing myself to *experience* the depth of past pain. I would much rather read a book on how to manage my problem or read a success story about someone else who overcame obstacles. But looking into the face of my own shame, guilt, unforgiveness, or personal sorrow is too frightening!

C. S. Lewis once said, "Pain insists on being attended to. God whispers to us in our pleasures, speaks to us in our conscience, but shouts in our pains. It is His megaphone to rouse a deaf world."[4] Exploring our feelings is always frightening. Old wounds fester. Relationships that are now tolerable are once again threatened. Plastic smiles fade. Honesty replaces the game of "let's pretend." Long hidden fears are resurfaced. Our past "shadow monsters" make images on the wall of our minds and bring flickers of dreaded emotion.

When we choose a constructive resolution for our fears, *sorrow* is the first major step. It's important to grieve over the injustices of the past, the mistakes we've made, and the consequences we've brought on ourselves. The first step to a faith-filled decision is to acknowledge the deep pain we have experienced.

David Biebel describes the greatest benefit of pain: "The old center has collapsed, and I am helpless."[5] In other words, instead of following our former, rigid path of handling our emotions and taking care of our problems, we begin to yield. We acknowledge that our system for dealing with fear failed and we cannot "fix" things ourselves.

Biebel wrote,

> Pain gives you new eyes, eyes to look beyond these temporary things we normally label "life" and see into eternity. And now you have new ears, too, to hear His voice. Your mind is sensitized to understand, and your will is ready to respond. But most of all, by coming to the end of yourself, you have learned this most difficult of lessons, the folly of integrating life around anything other than God.
>
> . . . Perhaps your center was material things, and now they're gone. Or it was good health, and that is threatened. Or maybe it was another person—your son or daughter, wife or husband, or someone else you loved very dearly—and now that person is gone. Or maybe it was friendship, and you have been betrayed. Or fame, and you have been defamed. Perhaps it was career or intellectual pursuits, or maybe it was even theology or ministry. Whatever it was, if it took the place of God as the central focus of your life, the house had to fall . . . because nothing other than God can ever be enough.[6]

I think we need to add that many of us are in that kind of bondage to the memories of our mistakes or to the reminders of the violations by others. When we allow ourselves to grieve over injustices and bad memories, our sorrow brings us to the place of *brokenness* that has just been described. Our old center (everything we could do to fix our problems) has collapsed—and we are helpless.

One day while reading the Sermon on the Mount I came to the verse where Jesus says, "Blessed are the poor in spirit, for theirs is the kingdom of heaven."[7] I had always assumed that the phrase "poor in spirit" had something to do with being needy, but after further study, I saw the verse in a whole new light.

Jesus was saying, "You are right on target if you have quit relying on your own dynamic personality, your personal wealth, or your grand accomplishments to get you into Heaven. You are truly blessed if you have come to the end of your resources—and you can admit you are needy." In other words, a spirit of humility is the first step toward spiritual wholeness—and that level of humility often comes after we grieve over injustices and wrong choices and when we experience true brokenness before God.

Brokenness turns to surrender when we say, "Lord, I can no longer pick myself up by my own bootstraps. I *need* You and I surrender myself to You—my pain, my bad memories, my mistakes, my disappointments, and my expectations. I yield myself to You and will choose to stop living with the fearful shadow monsters of the past. I willfully hang my weakness on Your almighty strength."

A FAITH-FILLED DECISION TO FORGIVE

Much of our ability to face the past in order to get on with the future is wrapped up in the power of forgiveness. Surrender to God brings us to the point of being able to make the faith-filled decision to forgive.

When we choose unforgiveness for the injustices of the past, we hurt ourselves most of all. Booker T. Washington once made the statement, "I will not permit any man to narrow and degrade my soul by making me hate him."[8] I think Washington knew that the opposite of forgiveness was to put himself in bondage to those who had wronged him—to be powerless and fearful of injustice. To forgive is to be set free!

Author Judith Sills wrote,

Forgive, and you can heal, move on, reduce your health risks, lighten your spirit. . . .

Forgive, and you free all the energy you are currently using in reviewing old injuries, fantasizing revenge, craving justice. Forgive, and the piece of you that was tied up with rage is free to be much, much more. . . .

. . . Forgiveness is not approval. It is not your way of saying, "Oh, never mind. It doesn't really matter." Forgiveness does not mean that what the other person did was acceptable or even tolerable. Quite the contrary. Forgiveness says, "What you did hurt me deeply and you were wrong to do it. I have hated you for what you did long enough. Now I want to let go of my hatred. I forgive you."[9]

The concept of forgiveness is so powerful that we can understand it only by experiencing it. Most of us have no idea how much control we give to people who have hurt us or wronged us by allowing them rob us of weeks, months, even years of happy, productive lives. When our days are consumed with thoughts of revenge, or a recounting of the abuses of the past, or a rehearsed itemization of why we hate ourselves for the wrong choices we have made, we are chaining ourselves in a prison of our own making.

For a lesson in forgiveness, look at Jesus. Nail-pierced hands. A crown of thorns. No complaint coming from His lips. No blaming accusations hurled at His abusers. That day Innocence hung on a cross. Injustice prevailed. Pushing up on nails in His feet to get the breath to speak, He uttered the most empowering words in Scripture, "Father, forgive them, for they know not what they do."

I think of my mother-in-law. Grandma's words to her after the birth of her infant son reverberate in my mind: "For the last nine months I prayed that this child would be born dead."

What gave Mom the grace to make a faith-filled decision to choose a constructive resolution for the fears that plagued her? I believe she grieved over the injustice of the situation—and probably over her own questionable choices. But I believe that sorrow led to brokenness, which brought a humility before God that led to *surrender* of her will. This surrender gave Mom the power to make the *faith-filled decision* to forgive her mother and forgiveness freed her from the bondage of the past.

TAMING OUR "SHADOW MONSTERS"

Facing the truth involves seeing our fears as they really are.

- Have we exaggerated our fears of the past?
- Have we run from past fears, hoping they will disappear?
- Do we carry any false guilt or illegitimate shame?
- Have we grieved over the injustice in our lives and experienced the sorrow of painful memories?
- Have we chosen the empowering freedom of forgiveness?
- Have we looked back at Calvary lately? Hear Jesus once again, "Father, forgive them, for they know not what they do."

Occasionally, I try to "take back" fearful memories. As my shadow monsters resurface on the videotapes of the past, I hear His reassuring voice in the middle of the darkness. "Let go, Carol. I'll see you in the morning."

CHAPTER TEN

"How Can I Have These Doubts About God and Call Myself a Christian?"

FEAR 8: LOSING MY FAITH

*For every confirmed skeptic I encounter,
I meet at least a dozen sincere believers who struggle with doubt.
At times their apprehension is casual, but at other times it is grave.
These people want to believe God, but for whatever reason,
wrestle with thoughts and feelings to the contrary. And, unfortunately,
when doubt enters the believer's experience,
it threatens to paralyze him.*

JOSH MCDOWELL
Quoted by Jackie Hudson in the foreword of *Doubt, A Road to Growth*

Jackie Hudson had spent years of her life in full-time Christian service with a well-known international ministry. She was vitally involved in helping with the preparations for EXPLO, a conference that was designed to train over 80,000 Christians in principles of evangelism and discipleship.

When the first day of the event finally arrived, she watched the crowd spilling onto the playing field of the Cotton Bowl in Dallas. Without warning, a frightening and foreign thought flashed through her mind: "How do all these people really know there is a God?"[1] Jackie describes the avalanche of thoughts that immediately engulfed her mind:

> I was stunned. Did I think that? After all, I'm one of the 250 staff members working on this evangelism training conference. We've planned and prayed and worked for months for this. I'm in full-time Christian work! How can I think a thought like that?[1]

During the next few weeks Jackie tried to push the haunting thoughts out of her mind. But to no avail. She was drowning in a sea of doubt.

Questions engulfed my mind. How do I know God exists? Is the Bible really His inspired Word? What about the 2.5 billion people who have never heard about Christ? Are they going to hell? That seems so unfair![2]

Jackie had great difficulty eating and sleeping. Fear, anxiety, and panic became her constant companions. Small doubts became giant boulders. Skepticism and uncertainty replaced faith and assurance. In desperation Jackie confessed her doubt to God, memorized lengthy passages of Scripture, and asked for help from Christian friends. But the doubts stubbornly persisted.

Maybe I'm not really a Christian, I thought. Maybe I can't believe because I'm not one of the "chosen ones." If I'm not predestined for salvation, I must be going to hell—and I can't do anything about it.[3]

Jackie had heard someone say that if you're not *sure* you're a Christian, you should pray one final time and write the date in your Bible. That way, when the doubts come, you can look the date up and be reminded of the time when the commitment was made. As she scanned the front of her Bible, Jackie found *five* different dates when she had prayed "the prayer"—just to be certain! But the doubts returned.

WHY DO WE KEEP OUR DOUBTS A SECRET?

Christians who are struggling with doubts about their faith almost never talk about it. They are too ashamed. They could be estranged from relatives and friends who think they are heretics. And if they are Christian leaders—especially if they receive financial support from other believers—to admit their intense fear is to risk being fired from a ministry position, followed by malicious gossip, and bankruptcy. Who would want to give money to support a missionary or worker who had doubts about Christian theology?

So with no one to turn to, the doubts increase and the fear is magnified. For most of us, it becomes easier to live a lie and to fake confidence than to say, "I'm struggling. In fact, I'm having major questions about things I've believed for years. My doubts are plaguing me, and I don't know what to do."

Gary Parker, in his book titled *The Gift of Doubt*, makes this statement:

> To admit to doubt is just like taking the little finger out of the dike for many Christian believers. I suppose our natural inclination to be afraid of uncertainty is basically the fear of opening up a Pandora's box of questions. We resist all uncertainty because we fear that the first question will lead to an avalanche of questions. Most of us believe that even a little doubt will push us down a slippery slope into disbelief. So we fall into the trap of closing our minds to honest inquiry because we think an open mind will let us slip into deep waters over our heads.[4]

Are we are afraid that if we admit doubts about God—or about heaven or hell or the supernatural—we will become infidels and traitors? If we have no one to talk to, we stay locked up, hurting, uncertain, fearful, and in some cases, paralyzed. This mental and spiritual imprisonment is based on the fear of facing the naked truth of all that is raging in our minds and hearts.

WHAT KINDS OF DOUBTS DO WE HAVE?

I've heard women ask riveting questions related to the fear of losing their faith. The first entry on this list came from one of my former junior high students who as a grown woman came to visit me, ten years after she sat in my classroom.

● "Carol, you led me to Jesus when I was in the eighth grade. All these years I've kept a secret from you. My mother was extremely abusive and my father was an alcoholic who was very uninvolved in my life. In my teen years, mostly in order to escape from my unhappy home, I became very close to another woman and developed a lesbian relationship with her. I became hopelessly involved in homosexuality, and it has a grip on my life. I know the Bible teaches against this lifestyle, and I've tried to quit a hundred times—but I always go back. I have *begged* God to take this curse from me, but He doesn't. Is the God I trusted in the eighth grade still alive?"

- "I used to believe in a loving God, but when I see the extreme injustice and horrific violations of human rights in the world, I just can't continue to trust in a God who allows things like that to happen."

- "I made a childhood decision to accept Christ, but now I wonder if I'm really a Christian."

- "I used to give financial support to a well-known TV evangelist and later found out his life was filled with sexual addictions and immorality. If Christianity is real, why would God have allowed that man to preach against the evil he practiced on a regular basis? I feel confused and disillusioned."

- "I have prayed for my children since they were in my womb. They were raised in a loving home and given every opportunity for spiritual growth and encouragement. In spite of all the positive, Christian input, my son has dropped out of school and is addicted to cocaine. My teenage daughter is an unwed mother. My husband feels too embarrassed to go to church and face our friends. And I'm beginning to wonder if there really is a God out there who hears and answers prayers. Many of my nonChristian friends who *never* prayed for their children have had no apparent problems."

- "I went to a university of higher learning for a specific purpose—to enjoy the parties, the wide variety of gorgeous men, and to experience the freedom from parental control. My weekends were filled with alcohol, drugs, and promiscuity. Then I met Jesus through a campus ministry—and He totally changed my desires. My lifestyle took an abrupt turn, and for the first time I had a purpose for living beyond the thrill of the moment. Two years later I was engaged to a vibrant Christian man when I discovered I not only had two different kinds of venereal diseases—I was also infected with the HIV virus. The grief my fiancé and I are experiencing cannot be expressed in words. *Why* would God allow this to happen? I'm trying to believe He still cares about me, but I'm afraid my faith is weakening."

- "My earliest memory dates back to when I was five years old. I was being violently raped by a male relative and I was terrorized. In our family incest was an everyday occurrence. By the time I was old enough to leave home, I had been sexually abused by my grandfather, father, brothers, and a few male cousins. I can name twelve men who victimized me. Today I find it impossible to receive love properly from my husband. The thought of physical intimacy makes me sick. I once believed in God—but if He exists, why would He let a child be damaged so badly?"

• "I was raised in a Christian home, but after doing some of my university studies overseas and since being exposed to several large and diverse world religions, I'm having real doubts that there is only *one* way to get to heaven. The God I believe in would not let all of those sincere, religious people go to hell—just because they don't believe in Jesus Christ."

• "My husband has been unemployed for two years and I was just pink-slipped. We have used our entire savings account, and if this goes six more months every dime saved for our retirement will be spent on household necessities. My daughter will have to drop out of college, because there's no way to pay her tuition. We have always tithed our income, giving God the 'first fruits,' but now I'm beginning to doubt Him. We've given to Him all these years, but our whole world is falling apart—and it appears He is unconcerned."

• "My only child was killed in an automobile accident by a drunk driver. She was just becoming an adult—her whole life before her! I have been robbed of her love and companionship. Any future grandchildren I might have enjoyed will never exist, never bring happiness and spontaneity to our holiday reunions. I have been given loneliness, pain, and grief. If God is all powerful and all knowing, He could have stopped this accident. My faith is faltering and I'm afraid."

DISAPPOINTMENT WITH GOD

Perhaps the most haunting thought a Christian woman can ever have is this: What if the beliefs I have always held about God, the faith I have affirmed to others, and the beliefs I have taught my children are inaccurate? If the Bible has errors, if God is not real, if my convictions are faulty, or if there is no heaven or hell—I am left with absolutely nothing to give lasting purpose to my life. The thought of having a meaningless life, void of supernatural strength, biblical counsel and encouragement, and hope for an eternal life is so devastating that we often prefer to live with our unspoken doubts, pushing them down into our subconscious, rather than risk voicing them and wrestling with them.

What expectations did you have when you "signed on" to become a disciple? I'm sure many of us thought we could anticipate health, wealth, joy, love, peace, adventure, contentment, and happiness. We may not have understood a lot about the Bible at that point, but we knew Christianity was supposed to offer a new, satisfying, more fulfilling life.

One of the benefits was supposed to include an improved social life—hundreds of other believers who loved God and wanted to be friends with us. But perhaps the biggest expectation was having a direct line to God. We knew He would be available on the tough days and during the major decisions. We expected a personal protector to shield us from doubt, discouragement, and despair. But our expectations sometimes become bitter disappointments.

Ken Abraham, in a soul-searching book called *The Disillusioned Christian*, says:

> Nobody ever warned you that there would be times when God seemed a million miles away. Or you might pray for somebody to be healed and they would die. Where were those financial blessings when you needed them, like when it came time to pay the rent? And what about all those great Christian superstars who have let you down?[5]

As we look back at some of the fears voiced earlier, we see a whole list of disappointed disciples:

- The Christian leader who now has doubts about the faith she taught others.
- The lesbian who confessed her sin a hundred times and feared God might not exist, since He didn't deliver her from her desires.
- The woman who doubted her faith after viewing the extreme suffering and injustice in the world.
- The woman who prayed as a child to receive Christ and now has fears about how "real" her decision was.
- The Christian who doubts her beliefs after seeing a TV preacher's moral demise.
- The mother who tried to "train up" her children according to

biblical principles, but watched them fall into sin—in spite of her faithful prayers.

- The university graduate who came to Christ following a wild life of parties and promiscuity, only to discover she had sexually transmitted diseases.
- The woman raped repeatedly throughout her childhood who can't believe in a God who would allow a child to be so damaged.
- The intellectual who studied world religions and concluded that Christianity couldn't be the only viable path to eternal life.
- The believer who questions God's love because of the severe financial reversals she suffered after faithfully giving to His work.
- The mother, robbed of her daughter and the possibility for grandchildren because of a drunk driving accident, who now wrestles with the reality of an all-powerful God.

THE GIFT OF DOUBT

Philip Yancey once said, "Fear, not doubt, is faith's opposite." In other words, if we are willing to look into the face of doubt, seeking truth (not fearing it), we will find a renewed faith. When we shrink back, unwilling to face legitimate doubt about the truth of God's Word, the justice of God's plan, and the disappointments in our lives—we live in a fearful cage of growing disillusionment.

Many of us have believed the only answer to the fear of doubt is to confess it as sin and to decide, once and for all, never to doubt again. But on a closer look, it's easy to see a hidden destructive pattern in this decision.

Sometimes when we follow this course, it looks like this: Our *triggering event* could be the loss of an unborn child, a severe financial reversal, or huge doubts about the goodness of God. We respond with an overwhelming *reactive emotion*: terror that we'll lose our faith in the God we have always trusted. Our sense of *powerlessness* is foreign. We have always counted on God for guidance and comfort. But we certainly sense no supernatural help in our situation. He seems to be out of the picture. It appears He doesn't care. As we focus on our desperate condition, we turn to *rage*. How could the God we looked to for protection, love, and guidance all these years let us down? If He is real, why doesn't He make Himself more obvious? Our focus has now moved from God to ourselves and our self-reliance leads to *internal negotiating*.

THE RIGID RESOLUTION

If that internal battle leads to a destructive course of action, it follows a rigid, uncompromising path. For the woman who makes this negative choice, there are four different potential end results.

1. *Denial*—When we follow the path of confessing our doubt as sin and telling ourselves we will never talk about our doubt again and we will never allow ourselves to question the goodness of God, we often live in a state of denial. It's almost like saying, "God, if I really investigated my doubts, I might find out something that would destroy my faith completely, and I just can't risk that!"

2. *Defeat*—Defeat leads us to a total lack of faith. It closes the door to hope and makes our world smaller and smaller. We feel let down by God, Christian friends, and biblical principles. We allow our disappointment with God to lead to a final decision of, "Lord, I'm giving up on You, the Bible, the church, and Christian friends. I quit!"

3. *Bitterness*—A sense of betrayal leads to bitterness. When we have given our lives to God and have worked for Him and taught His principles as truth—and He allows injustice, misery, poor health, infertility, and deep disappointment to enter our lives, we sometimes choose bitterness.

Gordon Aeschliman, in a book addressed to disillusioned and disappointed Christians called *Cages of Pain*, says: "Resentment and bitterness are cousins, but it is bitterness that works for the destruction of our souls. Resentment recognizes an (apparent) injustice for what it is. It is, in a sense, a true measure of the degree of pain inflicted on us."[6]

When bitterness takes root, we begin to believe a lie: God has dealt me a bad hand. He picked me out of all the other Christians and betrayed me by allowing deep hurts and injustices to rob me of my faith.

4. *Escape*—In an attempt to ease the pain caused by a huge void that

now exists where faith used to be, we sometimes cling to a diversion that provides momentary relief from our fear of being rejected by God and left without hope. Depending on our personality and background, we choose from a wide range of obsessive/compulsive behaviors. From perfectionism to alcohol to workaholism to prescription drugs to *anything* that can cover up the festering wound of a broken spirit and a disillusioned heart. Our unspoken response is, "God has deserted me and I will fill up the vacuum in my soul. I can fix this need myself. I don't need Him anymore!"

THE DAY THE ACCELERATOR STUCK

I had been married about six months. My husband and I had moved to Grand Rapids, Michigan. My husband, Gene, was taking some graduate classes, and I was working as an executive secretary for the Steelcase Corporation.

One morning on my way to work in rush-hour traffic, my accelerator stuck as I was approaching a red light. No matter how hard I pressed my foot to the brake, my car picked up speed. As I swerved into an open lane, I had difficulty guiding my fast-moving vehicle to make the turn and I hit the car waiting to make a left-hand turn—and that car hit the car behind it.

As my car continued on I glanced at the gas gauge. It was half full. Thinking quickly, I knew I could not run the car out of gas before causing a horrible accident in the next intersection. After trying the emergency brake to no avail, in a desperate attempt to stop the car, I steered the automobile toward a telephone pole before evacuating. The car hit the curb, missing the pole, and went right into the next intersection and hit another car, which hit the car behind it. (That's a five car collision so far!) It did a circle in the intersection and then pulled out a fire hydrant, did another circle in the intersection and destroyed a park bench, and did one more circle before crashing into the plate-glass window of the prestigious IBM building.

Police sirens descended and after listening to my explanation of what happened, an officer said, "Why didn't you turn the ignition off?" I never thought of it. The day after this horrible experience we discovered we had no insurance. When we left the Christian organization my husband and I worked for previously, they "gifted us" with six additional months of insurance, but due to a clerical mistake, we were uninsured for this disastrous accident.

Two women sustained minor injuries, and we were grateful there was no loss of life—but the property damage was extensive! We were dirt poor, still paying off education loans, and the day after we made the second large payment to our attorney (with borrowed money), the newspaper ran an article on *our* attorney. It read, in part: "This man has been disbarred from practicing law in the State of Michigan because of indecent exposure in his office."

We were financially ruined, emotionally exhausted, and spiritually devastated! We were in a brand-new marriage and suddenly all of the hopes, aspirations, plans, and dreams we had for the future were crushed by the fear of what the next phone call would tell us.

THE QUESTIONS WE ARE AFRAID TO ASK

Looking back, it's easy for me to see the *triggering event* that caused my initial fear. In a fast-moving car that was out of control I feared for my life. But my fears quickly accelerated. My *reactive emotions* brought the fear of financial ruin, the fear of abandonment by God, and the hidden fear of losing my confidence in the God I had always trusted to meet my needs. My sense of *powerlessness* became overwhelming when we discovered our insurance had been mistakenly transferred to another vehicle by the Christian organization we had served so faithfully.

When my focus gets off God and on my problems—watch out! I turned to *rage*. As a "slow boiler," I didn't express my anger on the surface immediately, but I was mad! How could the organization we had served with such loyalty let something like this happen? They never even called to tell us the insurance had been dropped! But the anger intensified when I thought about my all-knowing God who should have been overseeing this situation more carefully!

I remained in the "rage stage" for a long time. I was mad at the Christians who made the mistake on my insurance. I was mad at the "Statute of Limitations" in Michigan that allowed cases revolving around this accident to be brought to court for up to seven years! My husband and I had wanted to teach missionary children at an academy in Brazil—and because of this I could not get a visa to leave the country. I was mad at God. This disappointment led to *internal negotiating*.

- Why would a God of love allow this to happen? Gene and I had dedicated our lives to Him, looked forward to short-term missionary service—and we faced more red lights than green lights.
- Why did God allow a young Christian couple in the middle of their first year of marriage to have such an avalanche of financial problems—through no fault of their own?
- Why didn't the God of the universe "fix" the stuck accelerator? Surely it would have been a small item on His daily agenda. Where was He when the car was out of control and I was yelling for help?
- If God couldn't be trusted to protect the people most eager to serve Him, why should we rely on Him in the future?

RESOLVING TO BELIEVE

For the first time in my Christian life, I began to doubt the goodness of God. With that came an erosion of what had been strong faith. I felt betrayed by the God I had served with pure motives and energetic service. I never got to the fear of losing all faith in God, but I faced unanswerable questions that left me uncomfortable and immobile as a Christian. It's at this point many women choose the destructive resolution. The rigid choice brings on denial, defeat, bitterness, or escape.

But I had another alternative. I remember talking at length with my husband and voicing my doubts about God out loud for the first time. It was freeing to admit that I felt God had been unfair to us and that He didn't seem to be answering prayer or intervening in our situation at all.

After a long time, I knelt beside a kitchen chair with my husband at my side and my internal negotiating finally moved to genuine *sorrow*. I told God how disappointed I was. I voiced my doubts about His love. I spoke of my anger for what appeared to be unjust treatment. I told Him how unfair it felt to be in financial limbo for seven years—knowing *everything* we owned could be taken away from us with one lawsuit. I allowed myself to grieve over the financial devastation of the accident. For the lawyer who had taken our money unethically. My sorrow soon turned to *brokenness*. We were in a mess, and it was too big for me to solve. In spite of my pain and doubt, I knew I needed God's help through all of this. I humbled myself before Him, giving up the deep desire I had to control the situation myself.

This led to a *surrender* I had never known before. I stopped telling God how to change my situation. My heart began to believe the words as I prayed, "Lord, I submit myself to Your authority. I choose to trust You—even if in this lifetime I am never allowed to understand why You have allowed this terrible accident to happen. I believe You still love me." I was surprised by my own words. I was even more amazed that I *believed* them.

This constructive resolution to fear brings us to an ability to make *faith-filled decisions*. Paula Rinehart describes the faith that emerges out of broken dreams:

> "How is faith that comes on the far side of disappointment better than (the) faith that preceded it?" . . . There is room for mystery—for *not* knowing all the answers. The passage of faith that follows disillusionment begins when there is no experiential reason to believe. It is born in the fearlessness that comes when you've already lost a good portion of what you were so afraid of losing in the first place.[7]

This process defies being understood until it is experienced. It's part of the mystery—and part of the inexplicable freedom from the fear of losing my confidence in God. In the middle of the journey, I stumble over the answer to one of my lifelong questions: *Where is God when I'm in pain?*

> Somehow, you know God is there in the midst of this passage—in ways you didn't expect. He makes His presence known by the pain of His seeming absence. He doesn't necessarily change the circumstances; He gives you the courage to face and move through them.[8]

In time, I was able to see some of the many beneficial effects of the accident. I made some faith-filled, though at time times humbling, decisions:

- I gave up my "I'll do it myself" attitude and allowed some of

God's people to help meet severe financial needs. (That was a *huge* step for me!)

● I better identified with the many people I had ministered to who had experienced doubts about God and their faith. (It made my outreach much more genuine than when I always had textbook answers but no major personal experience with the fear of losing my own faith.)

● I let myself feel the pangs of living in a fallen world, filled to the brim with disappointments and unfulfilled expectations. (It caused me to realize *every* day brings an opportunity to make decisions to move forward by faith—not by sight!)

● I learned to be thankful for the grace of God in the middle of the disaster. Each time a lawsuit reached the courthouse, I was declared innocent of any wrongdoing. The report read: "The accelerator was stuck and the driver did everything in her power to stop the vehicle." So in spite of years of attorneys' fees, we were spared huge financial liability for multiple lawsuits.

● I learned the importance of talking out loud about my doubts, fears, and discouragements. One of the greatest benefits of the accident has been the lesson learned on my knees at the kitchen chair: Doubts about God need not lead to denial, defeat, bitterness, or escape. Instead they can lead to a "truth-search." Asking questions related to our doubts will lead to a strengthened faith as we discover truth in the process.

I long to reach a plateau in my spiritual experience that ensures I will never doubt again—a faith that promises I will never question God's truth or love or goodness. But in this world, that would be idyllic.

Gary Parker mirrors my thoughts:

Although my "fear and doubt" may not have ended, they have at least been transcended by a faith that lives vibrantly, in spite of the storms of life that create uncertainty. . . . When our faith in God transcends our doubts about God, we will not find, in the same moment, the key that unlocks the door to all of life's mysteries. We will not find ready-made answers to all of life's questions. And we will not find solutions to all of life's problems or acquire protection against all of life's tragedies. We will, however, find a framework for life that brings purpose to our days, meaning to our hearts, and solace to our hurts. We will find a spiritual Father in whom we can place our trust.[9]

This level of trust involves risk and uncertainty that can be transcended by a faith that gives us an eternal perspective.

PETER LEARNED THE SECRET

Peter is often described as the "open mouth, insert foot" disciple. He spoke before he thought. He sometimes acted without thinking through the consequences. He was quick to speak, slow to listen. But, at times, this spontaneous personality had to be refreshing to Jesus. He never had to guess what Peter was thinking.

The account in John 6 says that people were following Jesus. Anywhere this man went, exciting action followed! Think of it. He fed the five thousand with one little boy's lunch—no small feat! The crowd must have been mesmerized. Some of these "new disciples" were following because of the incredible miracles. Others joined the group for free food. Jesus rebukes them and says, "I tell you the truth, you are looking for me, not because you saw miraculous signs but because you ate the loaves and had your fill."[10]

Then Jesus begins teaching in word pictures. He talks about the Bread of life. And then He speaks in a puzzling way, saying *He is the living bread* and if anyone eats of this bread, that person will live forever. That is too much for some of the "fringe followers." After Jesus explains the meaning of this statement, many of these disciples grumble and some say, "This is a hard teaching. Who can accept it?"[11]

It reminds me of an elementary teacher who assigned book reports on an animal story. She got back one report that was only one line long. It said, "This book tells more about penguins than I want to know!"

I think some of those disciples were a lot like that student. They *loved* hanging around Jesus while there was drama and excitement—but when tough teaching came, they were through! Imagine how they might have voiced their thoughts: "This man gives me more confusing information than I'm interested in hearing. I wish He'd stick to miracles and quit talking in riddles. I'd rather leave than have to figure out what these hidden messages are all about!"

The contrasts in that crowd tell the whole story. They were seeking a circus. Jesus was offering truth. They demanded outward drama. Jesus sought inward change. They looked for a hero. Jesus came to be a servant. When they did not get what they wanted, many of those brand-new disciples packed up their marbles and went home.

At that moment Jesus turned to the Twelve and said, "You do not want to leave too, do you?" And Peter, in typical, fast-responding and enthusiastic form, said, "Lord, to whom should we go? You have the words of eternal life. We believe and know that you are the Holy One of God."[12]

Peter went on to deny Jesus three times—but over time his early conviction took root. Read the story in the epistles Peter wrote later on. He wrote to Christians who were hurting. They were scattered in the five provinces of the Roman Empire. The heat had been turned up on these believers. In the 105 verses of 1 Peter, the word *suffering* appears sixteen times. They knew what persecution felt like.

If we look closely, Peter gives us the secret of an eternal perspective. He reminds us of two important faith-builders:

- Our hope rests in the power of Christ's resurrection.
- Our hope is fixed on the promise of our reward.

No matter what life dishes out along the way, there is nowhere to go but to Christ! Peter's entire challenge to people in pain involved reminding them they were pilgrims—people who were just passing through this fallen world. Then he helped them focus on "goin' home."

Think of it. One day doubts and fears will all be in the past. We will be in a Kingdom that cannot be shaken. No more unanswerable questions. No more unexplainable suffering. No more riveting doubts. No more paralyzing fear. We will see Him as He is. As we look at the nail prints, we will finally understand.

PART SIX

OVERCOMING THE FEAR OF MAKING WRONG CHOICES

"What If I Never Live Up to My Potential?"
FEAR 9: GETTING TRAPPED

In the middle of our lives, from about ages thirty-five to forty-five,
our marriages and careers have generally settled into a routine.
This is a time when many women question their life choices and ask,
Is that all there is?

JEAN LUSH
Emotional Phases of a Woman's Life

As early as I can remember, I always wanted to make a difference in the lives of other people. I desired to be a woman of vision, passion, and commitment. As a teenager I had made a covenant with my best friend, Janet. We were both idealistic, empowered with youthful enthusiasm—but we were serious. We decided that if Jesus Christ was who He claimed to be, He was worth *everything* we had to give Him. We made a commitment to hold each other accountable for becoming Christian women who would change our corner of the world in a positive way for the sake of God's Kingdom.

In my quest for meaning, I began collecting quotations that inspired me to pursue God's highest and best calling. Some of my favorites follow:

- Choose a goal for which you are willing to exchange a piece of your life.
- All of us have 168 hours each week. We sleep about 56 hours, and use approximately 12 hours for personal hygiene. That leaves 100 hours a week for you to plan. How are you choosing to use those hours? Do not give your life's energy to something that does not ultimately count.

- When I come to the end of my life, will it have mattered that I was here?
- What makes life worthwhile is having a big enough objective, something which catches our imagination and lays hold of our allegiance; and this the Christian has, in a way that no other man has.[1]

SEARCHING FOR THE "DOT"

With energy and idealism, I continued my quest to find the "dot" in the center of God's will for my life. After coming to Christ at my mother's knee at the age of five, I had often been instructed to seek God's "perfect plan" for my life. Being totally convinced there was an ideal blueprint was comforting. It meant if I could just find the right niche, difficult decisions and hard choices would no longer plague me. I would not have to be afraid of getting trapped in a losing situation or vocation. I wouldn't need to grieve over lost opportunity. I would be right on target for total happiness and contentment in my life—and I wanted that!

Finding God's "dot" was important to me. It would abolish the headaches brought on by heavy decisions. It would make me feel secure. It would get rid of haunting questions and second thoughts. It would eliminate the gripping fear of choosing a path of "second best." That was my worst fear—making choices because I felt indefinite about the "perfect" will of God and finding out years later that I should have followed a different path in order to please Him more fully.

I spent many hours meditating on Scripture, trying to make sure I didn't miss the right signals. I began to devour Bible passages that reinforced my belief in the "dot." Psalm 32:8 (KJV) was my favorite, and I immediately claimed it as my "life verse": "I will instruct thee and teach thee in the way which thou shalt go; I will guide thee with mine eye." Surely that verse meant that God was going to give me specific instructions. But where were they hidden?

Another passage I clung to was in Proverbs 3:5-6—"Trust in the LORD with all your heart and lean not on your own understanding; in all your ways acknowledge him, and he will make your paths straight." I delivered devotionals to my church youth group using these verses and challenging my friends to find the center of God's will. I earnestly warned against settling for His second best. And I waited for God to tell me what His "straight path" for my life was.

THE FEAR OF A DEAD-END LIFE

As a visual thinker I am endowed with a powerful imagination! As a young woman about ready to leave home and make her mark on the world, I had nagging apprehensions about being sure I was making choices that would result in the use of my full potential. I was obsessed with the fear of getting trapped in a situation that would mean I had lost out on an "A" choice because "B+" looked good at the time.

I worried about what university to attend. A few years later I was anxious about whether or not I should get married. The day finally arrived—my wedding day. I had dated the man I was about to marry for four years. He appeared to be the ideal choice for a lifetime of fulfillment and joy. But as I sat in the home of my best friend before leaving for the church, panic struck.

With profound sincerity I articulated my fears: "Janet, it's not too late for me to back out of this marriage. Could I be ruining the rest of my life? It would be embarrassing to call everything off at this point. Guests are en route to the church; the food for the reception is ordered. But I am so afraid of making the wrong decision. I wonder if God would use my gifts more fully if I remained single."

Some of the fears that came out of my "dot theology" went like this:

- If I attend the wrong college or university, I could meet people who will negatively influence my life.
- If I don't major in the right field, I could wind up in a job that is unfulfilling, beneath my potential, and out of God's will.
- If I don't marry God's ideal man for my life, I will totally ruin my life—and the lives of the man I was supposed to marry, the man I did marry, and the woman my husband was supposed to marry. (This thought got even more complicated as I pondered the birth of children and wondered

if they too were "messed up for life" because of my wrong choice.)
- If I don't buy a home in God's choice of neighborhoods, I may lose out on meeting a neighbor God wanted me to win to the Lord. (At this point, I realized there was a flaw in my thinking—but I still didn't know what it was.)

One day I picked up a book that put me into shock. It asked questions I was afraid to think about. It attacked some beliefs about God's will I held close to my heart. It made me feel uncomfortable but intrigued. It was addressing fears that I had hidden deeply—fears I didn't want to admit. Even the title of the book sounded controversial: *Decision Making and the Will of God: A Biblical Alternative to the Traditional View.*

Garry Friesen, a Bible professor who had grappled with this major dilemma, voiced the same questions that had been flickering in my mind:

1. Does God have a perfect will for each Christian? Does it matter?
2. Does the Christian have the right to choose and still be in the will of God?
3. Can you be 100 percent sure of God's individual will for your life?[2]

Each of these questions revolved around my great fear—getting trapped outside of God's ideal plan for the potential He placed within me.

If we ask, "How can I know the will of God?" we may be asking the wrong question. The Scriptures do not command us to find God's will for most of life's choices nor do we have any passage instructing us on how it can be determined . . . the Christian community has never agreed on how God provides us with such special revelation. Yet we persist in searching for God's will because decisions require thought and sap energy. We seek relief from the responsibility of decision making and we feel less threatened by being passive rather than active when making important choices.[3]

All of this made so much sense. I knew I was created in the image of God and that He had given me the ability to reason and think out the answers to perplexing problems. I held in my hands the completed Word of God. But I was still in quest of an easy way to find complete joy and fulfillment in life. I wanted "divine roadmarks"! Other people talked so confidently about receiving insight from God and about "signs" in the Bible that gave them specific direction. Was I wrong to expect the same thing?

FACING THE FEAR OF MAKING WRONG CHOICES

Many Christian women grapple with varying degrees of the identical problem. Most are not as obsessed as I was about the fear of falling out of God's perfect plan, but other questions stalk in the background of our minds. Here are some of the fears women have voiced regarding making wrong choices:

- If I can't get away from the ugliness of my past, I will be destined for failure.
- If I take *this* job now because of economic necessity, I may close the door on a better opportunity for career advancement in a position more suited to my background and education.
- If I don't work harder and outdo the competition in my office, I may not get a promotion.
- If I'm promoted I may feel pressured to "succeed" at a level that will compromise balance in other important areas of my life.
- If I say "no" to personal or professional opportunities in order to stay physically and emotionally healthy now, I may never have other opportunities when I'm ready for them.
- If I choose to marry, I may get a man as dysfunctional as my father, and I will never let that happen!
- If I don't marry *this* man, someone I'm more compatible with might not come along, and I'd be sorry I turned him down.

- If I *do* marry this man—even though we seem perfectly suited for one another—I may discover later I have shut myself out from reaching my highest potential in my work or ministry because of the "encumbrances" of marriage and family responsibilities.
- If I leave a relationship that is destroying me, I will never have a better relationship.
- If I have a baby now, I may interrupt my career and never recapture the momentum and job success I've worked so hard to obtain.
- If I wait to have a child until I'm older and more established in my marriage and in my career, I may increase my risk of having a baby with mental or physical disabilities.
- If I don't pursue infertility treatment, I will never know complete fulfillment as a mother and eventually, as a grandmother.

As I have listened to the heartfelt fears of so many women who struggle with the whole concept of "lost opportunity," one thought becomes predominant: All of us have an earnest desire to make choices that will result in personal fulfillment and spiritual satisfaction.

LOOKING BACKWARD

How many times a week do we start a sentence with, "If only"?

- If only I could live this week over again. . . .
- If only I had known what I know now. . . .
- If only my dad (or mom) had not been an alcoholic. . . .
- If only I had become a Christian earlier. . . .
- If only I could have gotten a better education. . . .
- If only I were as gifted as my sister (or brother). . . .
- If only I were married. . . .
- If only I had married a different man. . . .
- If only I had remained single. . . .
- If only I could make that choice over again. . . .

And often we believe in our hearts that it's much too late to change anything now.

Does this sound familiar? Of course it does. Who among us can claim to have never made a mistake or missed a goal, never regretted a choice we made—or suffered because of someone else's action? Did you marry the wrong person? Take the wrong job? Fail to tell your mom how much you loved her before she died? Recognized opportunity only after you'd let it slide by? Did you goof not once but often? Do you get the feeling that it's become your way of life?[4]

Most of us have struggled with the fear of making wrong choices at some point in our lives. On certain days all of us feel trapped. And when we are changing dirty diapers, doing laundry, working in a job beneath our potential, or pouring so much of ourselves into work that we miss the rest of our lives, it's easy to envision ourselves as one of the few women in the world who is experiencing lost opportunity, because of the options we've selected.

JANET'S MISSION

Janet changed my life. My best friend lived in a modest house on the other side of the railroad tracks. Her father was an alcoholic who was totally absent from her life—except for the handful of times he showed up on the doorstep looking for a handout. He offered Janet, her mother, and two sisters no financial or emotional support. They were on their own! Janet's mom worked in a local factory to put food on the table.

Both of Janet's sisters dropped out of high school and married at a young age. But not Janet. There was a spontaneity, enthusiasm, and energy about her that could turn the lights on in a dark room. Wherever she went there was laughter—combined with deep discussions about life and God and the future. When I was with Janet, I felt full of hope.

Janet became the first person in her family to graduate from high school. She was the first to get a university degree and the only one to get a master's degree. Janet majored in elementary education because she wanted to give hope to kids who came from single-parent backgrounds like hers. She would look a struggling child in the eyes and say, "I didn't have a dad either. It sure is hard. But you can make it. I know you can."

Every year Janet selected the neediest student in her classroom and made an appointment to take him or her out for dinner at one of the finest restaurants in town. Before going to dinner, Janet took the child shopping for a new outfit. Janet has a God-given gift for building self-esteem in children like no one I have met before or since.

By human standards, Janet should have been a dropout. Fear of facing an unknown future and anxiety over making wrong choices could have immobilized her. Talk about lost opportunity: She had no father, no hope for getting her education funded, and most of us would have said, "I quit," if we had been in a similar situation.

Had I been in Janet's position, my story might have been very different than hers. If my *triggering event* had been an alcoholic, absentee father, my *reactive emotion* would have been fear, first of all for my daily needs. Later, the fear of getting trapped in a situation similar to my mother's would have been all-consuming. I'm sure my sense of *powerlessness* would have been overwhelming—no money, no dad, no visible opportunities for a positive change in my circumstances. With my focus on how little I could do to change my situation, it would not have taken me long to move to *rage* and begin venting my anger, probably in subliminal ways first. I would have been furious with God for allowing my life to be so difficult before I even had a chance to become "somebody."

One author speaks of *frozen rage*:

> We become extremely angry that our parents weren't emotionally (or physically) available to us. The anger seethes within us, and there seems to be no resolution to it. Sometimes we turn this anger inward, and we become deeply depressed.[5]

With my self-reliant tendencies, my *internal negotiating* would probably have led to a destructive, rigid resolution of denial, defeat, bitterness, or escape.

But Janet selected a different course of action. I never observed her in the process, but because I saw the end result of a life based on faith-filled decisions, I wonder if she went through a process much like this.

Sorrow: I'm sure there was a day when Janet grieved over her losses. Other girls had fathers who loved them and applauded their successes. She did not. Others had bigger, fancier houses and no fear of financial hardship or limitations on future education. Not Janet. Others had fathers with a deep faith in God who provided strong spiritual leadership. Her friends would have a loving father walk them down the aisle on their wedding day and a dad to respond to the question: "Who giveth this woman to be married to this man?" But Janet had none of those basics.

When the deep sadness of lost opportunity hits us, there is an ache in our soul. And when we are surrounded by people who appear to have everything we desire, the sting of sadness can be very deep. It is a pain that defies description.

As we experience the sorrow of lost opportunity, the pain can lead to brokenness before God.

> "Pain" is the fundamental human predicament. No one escapes life without experiencing pain, although many become pre-occupied with attempts to alleviate it. Pain is the overriding, inexplicable condition of life . . . the touchstone of our lives. In this "trysting place" heaven and earth meet. Here we meet each other in humanity, and more important, God meets us.[6]

Brokenness: The constructive resolution of fear always brings us to a place of brokenness. Our emotional pain is deep and we long for an escape. But in time, our pain becomes a friend that brings a humility before God. Instead of telling Him how to "fix" our hurts, we say, "God, You are in charge. I'm tired. I'm hurt. I will quit trying to alleviate the problem myself. I need You."

Surrender: It's difficult to determine the exact point where brokenness turns into surrender, because a broken heart before God moves to surrender very naturally. For Janet, surrender meant giving up fantasies about "the easy life" that could not be hers. It meant experiencing the all-encompassing love of her heavenly Father and releasing resentment. Surrender meant trusting God without knowing the answers to all of her questions, beginning with "Why me?"

Faith-filled decision: I wish I could invite everyone reading this book to a lunch with Janet, because you would be filled with hope. You'd leave encouraged. You would feel valued and loved. You would know you have a personal mission in this world that is different than any other woman alive. You would soon understand that you don't have to be afraid of getting trapped in a dead-end situation, no matter what your lost opportunities have been. You would know it's possible to grieve deeply over your losses and experience brokenness before God without shame. You would be convinced that God can change the future generations because Jesus lives.

You would learn how to make faith-filled decisions in the process of listening to her talk about daily life. You would have to remind yourself that the gracious, attractive, dynamic, magnetic educator before you was the product of a broken home and an alcoholic absentee father — a woman who paid her way through her university years by working in a factory.

Her love for children and belief in God's future potential in each of them would convince you that past fears do not have to place dark shadows over the days to come. Your faith would increase. You would know it is possible to overcome huge personal obstacles and your own personal fear monster.

JANET'S LEGACY

Janet made many faith-filled decisions. I've listed some of them below:

- Instead of getting bitter over life without a dad, she encouraged her hard-working mother in unique, creative ways.
- Rather than being defeated in her spiritual life, she surrounded herself with Christian friends and families who provided encouragement and wise counsel.
- Instead of expecting all men to be like her father, she chose to marry and defeat the negative statistical odds about her potential marital success.
- Unlike her peers with similar backgrounds, she worked hard to pay for a university education so she could positively impact the lives of kids with difficult home situations.
- After teaching for several years, Janet became a school principal — but not for long. She soon realized it was possible to have a much greater influence on children in the classroom than through the lofty doors of the administrative office — and she left a higher salary behind to go back to her precious students.
- Through the years, Janet made *me* — her old best friend from

high school—a prayer project. Janet phoned and wrote regularly, letting me know that she believed God had a major mission for me to do—and she was committed to being an encouraging supporter in my life.

That *is* Janet's story. But it's far more than the story of a girl from the wrong side of the tracks who had an alcoholic father and many seemingly impossible challenges in her life. It's the story of one woman who said, "I will not let the fear of getting trapped in life paralyze me. I will not live with the ghost of lost opportunity leering over my shoulder. I will believe there is a constructive resolution to fear. I believe my focus can be on God and my future with Him in a better place, rather than on myself and my personal misery. I know God can change the future generations in my family."

Instead of choosing self-reliance as a way of coping—which might have driven Janet to a life of compulsive/addictive behaviors—she chose to grieve over the sadness in her life, which led to brokenness, surrender, and a lifetime of faith-filled decisions. Her consistent example has inspired me to be a woman with a passion for God.

CURING THE "IF ONLY" SYNDROME

It's possible to spend most of our lives looking back at the mistakes we might have made or at the opportunities that never appeared or the will of God that we think we missed. We can spend our days filling the pauses between sentences with "If only. . . ." The choice is ours.

Barbara Johnson says it well:

Saying "IF ONLY I had done this," "IF ONLY I had gone there," or "IF ONLY I had done that," can lead to all kinds of situations, most of them bad.

IF ONLY can fill your stomach with ulcers.

IF ONLY can give you high blood pressure.

IF ONLY can deprive you of fun in your profession.

IF ONLY can take the zing out of your marriage.

IF ONLY can depress you to the point of suicide.

You see, yesterday is gone forever and tomorrow may never come. TODAY IS IT! So give it your best shot, and at the end of the road you will be at the place of your choice instead of being haunted by IF ONLY, IF ONLY, IF ONLY.[7]

The fear of making wrong choices has a thousand different faces. For some, it's a lifetime of looking in the rear-view mirror — the "If Only Syndrome." For others, it's bondage to a past that convinces us there is no way to escape unhappy and unproductive choices. It can be the fear of not being able to undo past mistakes. If can involve regrets based on low self-esteem that keep us from believing God has a meaningful future for our lives.

Dee Brestin writes,

> The fascinating Book of Ecclesiastes is a portrait of a person who is drifting, attempting to find fulfillment outside God because he does not fathom that God has a purpose for his life. Often, he's wearing blinders, and then his vision is limited to life "under the sun." During these times the author of Ecclesiastes tries to find meaning in life with earthly pursuits: worldly wisdom, parties, the building of a fantastic house and garden, promiscuous sex with concubines. . . . Yet, after each pursuit, he crawls back broken, crying, "Meaningless, meaningless, my life is utterly meaningless!"[8]

It all boils down to the fact that we want to make choices that affirm a meaningful life. We are obsessed with the fear of getting trapped in the "no outlet" alleys of life, and we certainly don't want to miss out on opportunities that were designed to bring fulfillment to our lives.

My big obstacle was the fear of missing out on God's perfect will and having to settle for the dreaded "second best." As I matured and sought wise counsel, I began to find the hidden dangers in my "dot in the center of God's will" theology. My study revealed some important information that was in the Bible, but I had never discovered it for myself.

I soon ascertained that New Testament examples pointed out that direct, supernatural guidance for specific decisions was the *exception* to the general rule in Scripture. Further study helped me to see that direct guidance was given to people who played a strategic role in the drama of world evangelization and that direct guidance was provided only at critical points during the formative years of the church. My investigation further led me to understand that this direct guidance was always communicated by means of supernatural revelation.[9]

For a while it was hard to give up convictions I had clung to and taught to others. But I soon discovered a far better alternative. I went back to the same verses I had memorized in my youth: "I will instruct thee and teach thee in the way which thou shalt go; I will guide thee with mine eye."[10] I turned to another passage and my eyes fell on these now familiar words: "Trust in the LORD with all your heart and lean not on your own understanding; in all your ways acknowledge him, and he will make your paths straight."[11]

For the first time, instead of seeing a rigid, unyielding "only-perfect-plan-for-my-life" kind of option, I understood a truth discovered by someone else:

> God took humankind very seriously when He gave us the gift of choice; perhaps more seriously than we take ourselves. We frequently and almost carelessly . . . abdicate our autonomy and let the community, the government, or the church decide for us.[12]

I finally realized that every day, for the rest of my life, I will be making choices. Some of them will determine major courses of action; others will involve shorter blocks of time. God has given me His Word as a guide, and as I apply my heart to obeying biblical principles and as I pray for wisdom, the "straight path" He has for me will become obvious.

I had been making myself miserable with the fear of making wrong choices. Gordon Graham describes my internal conflict: "Decision is a sharp knife that cuts clean and straight; indecision is a dull one that hacks and tears and leaves ragged edges behind it."[13] My second thoughts about God's will constantly left me with confusion, indecision, and a "hacked-off" edge on my attitude.

I began to realize that God was not playing a cruel game up in Heaven, making Christians guess which path they should be on. He gave us very specific direction about being people of integrity, honesty, and commitment. For the first time, I read Scripture with a sense of release, instead of seeing my life choices based on inflexible rules and regulations. I read, "The fear of the LORD is the beginning of wisdom, and knowledge of the Holy One is understanding."[14] and "Commit to the LORD whatever you do, and your plans will succeed."[15] Another principle seized my attention: "Wisdom is found in those who take advice."[16]

It was freeing to base my choices on my knowledge of God's character and His Word. As I prayed for guidance related to major decisions, I looked for individuals who were capable of offering wise counsel. I asked God to put a "check" in my spirit if I was headed in a direction that was inappropriate.

This new liberty was an exciting adventure. Instead of being filled with anxiety over the past "if onlys" or my present trap of circumstances or my lost opportunities of the future, I was experiencing a desire to dedicate my potential to Him. I realized that in former days my paralyzing fear had often led to a destructive resolution of escaping into a fog of indecision and then expecting God to come through for me with a lightning bolt of insight or a neon sign in the sky. As I learned to yield to Him with a heart attitude of humility and surrender, faith-filled decisions—even on the tough issues of life—became a natural outgrowth of a dynamic and growing relationship with Him.

The process felt risky at first. I kept looking for those well-marked road signs and God's voice through a megaphone. But I made progress. My faith grew. Instead of fearing the journey, I was learning to fear God with an awesome respect I had not known. Courage replaced hesitation. Insecurities were exchanged for confidence. I knew I could never go back to my old fears. The future was filled with opportunities. The prospects for serving Him were limitless. Godly wisdom would allow me to make the hard choices. This new lifestyle brought a peace I had not known before. And one day I knew something was missing—my lifelong fear of making wrong choices.

Elizabeth Dole summarizes what it took me so long to learn:

It is not what I do that matters, but what a sovereign God chooses to do through me. God doesn't want worldly successes. He wants me. He wants my heart in submission to Him. Life is not just a few years to spend on self-indulgence and career advancement. It's a privilege, a responsibility, a stewardship to be lived according to a much higher calling—God's calling. This alone gives true meaning to life.[17]

Janet learned the secret. No blaming the past. No paralyzing anxieties about the future. Walk through open doors and do what your hand finds to do with all your might! Touch some lives along the way. Forgive as you've been forgiven. Hold your head high. Laugh hard. Show compassion. Love passionately. Let go of fear. Life on earth doesn't get better than that!

"What If Reaching My Goals Isn't Enough?"
FEAR 10: ACHIEVING SUCCESS/ADMITTING FAILURE
❖

Biographies of bold disciples begin with chapters of honest terror.
Fear of death. Fear of failure. Fear of loneliness.
Fear of a wasted life. . . . Faith begins when you see God on the mountain
and you are in the valley and you know that you're too weak
to make the climb. You see what you need . . . you see what you have . . .
and it isn't enough . . . but He is! . . .
Faith that begins with fear will end up nearer the Father.

MAX LUCADO
In the Eye of the Storm

M y stormy emotions are in sharp contrast to the sunshine outside.
I've been trying to swallow the lump in my throat since early this morning. Why am I fighting back tears when I should be celebrating? My
mind is playing back the recording of almost two decades of time—and
I've been pausing to remember significant events, places, milestones,
challenges, and laughs—a lot of laughs. The playback simultaneously
brings exhilarating joy and unbearable pain. I feel fearful and weak. An
important era of my life is ending in a few days.

The call came from the congressman's office: "Congratulations!
Jason Paul Kent has been awarded an appointment to the U.S. Naval
Academy. If he accepts the appointment, he'll be heading for Annapolis
soon. Mrs. Kent, you have an extraordinary son. You must be very
proud of him."

I was proud, all right. The competition had been fierce. The interviews were long. And the paperwork was endless. I made appropriate
remarks to the district liaison, put the phone down, and faced reality as my tears flowed shamelessly. My son was headed for a military
career. My baby was leaving home very shortly. The child of my womb
was saying yes to an unknown future and would never return home in
quite the same way that he had in the previous eighteen years. My nest

would be empty. My "fear of something that hadn't happened yet" was becoming a reality!

RUNNING THE TAPE

Mental flashbacks took me to his first day of school and on to the first time he was allowed to ride his two-wheeler on the street. I thought about our hot, week-long car trip to visit the Grand Canyon and of our mission trip to Mexico. I remembered the day he came home from school with tears in his eyes because he was shunned by fellow students for being the only one on his row who refused to participate in a cheating scam during math class.

Then I recalled the day shortly before his fifth birthday when I was helping him memorize Romans 6:23. He looked up quizzically and said, "Mom, what are the wages of sin?" That was the day he asked Jesus to be his personal Savior.

In addition to the high points, which were many, there were challenges. Dirty laundry. Lots of dirty laundry. A messy room. Questionable posters. Testing limits. Confrontations. A few tears. Setting guidelines. Learning to let go. Taking back authority. Overreacting. Apologizing. Forgiving. Laughing. Loving. How could eighteen years have ended so abruptly?

EVALUATING SUCCESS

Each of us comes to specific crossroads in life when we stop and ask ourselves if we are achieving the success we so desperately want. I'm at one of those junctions of introspection right now. And for most of my lifetime I've had a tough time judging whether or not I'm succeeding or failing. And I'm so afraid of failing!

Some people would say I've had a lot of successes. A growing ministry. A few books published. A couple of appearances on national television. A few articles in Christian periodicals. But sometimes I have this haunting feeling that I might have picked the wrong definition of success.

My mind went back to an incident I first shared in *Speak Up With Confidence*:

I had jumped out of bed early, showered, dressed hurriedly, and sat reading the paper at the kitchen table while enjoying a freshly brewed cup of coffee.

J.P. (Jason Paul) came downstairs a few minutes later. I made him some breakfast and returned to my coffee. Minutes later while peering at me over his cereal bowl, he said, "Mama, you look so pretty today."

I couldn't believe it. On most days I'm quite dressed up—always a bit more comfortable in a suit and heels than in a pair of blue jeans and sneakers. On the day in question, I had dressed for leisure—nothing special, just slacks and a sweater.

We made eye contact, and I questioned him: "Honey, why do you think I look pretty today? These are old clothes, and usually Mother's wearing something nicer."

He flashed his gorgeous blue eyes and smiled at me. "It's because," he said thoughtfully, "when you're all dressed up, I know you're going out some place, but when you look like this, I know you're all mine!"

His answer was like an arrow, piercing my heart and pinning me to the back of the chair. It had never dawned on me that this little boy could tell if I had *time* for him by what I was wearing on any given day.[1]

It was at that time in my life when I faced the fear of becoming a failure at the one thing I most wanted to succeed at—motherhood. I was allowing my success in ministry to drive me into the potential of failing at one of my main tasks on this earth—being a great mom to Jason Kent. New choices were necessary, but in the middle of my fear of failure, I did not know how to begin making faith-filled decisions that would redirect my priorities. I bottomed out!

THE GREAT PARADOX: FEARING SUCCESS AND FAILURE

As we grapple with the fear of making wrong choices, we make a surprising discovery. If we achieve the success we think we desire, we may have difficult decisions and time constraints that require sacrifices. Fear builds as we give months and years to organizations, companies, and even churches—but we're not sure we've spent our energy on the most important goals. Erwin Lutzer once said, "Many who are climbing the ladder of success have their ladders leaning against the wrong walls."[2]

But then, if we *don't* live out our dreams and if we have no driving goals, we may flounder in a sea of failure, doomed to a life of boredom, inactivity, and unrealized potential. One author summed up the problem this way: "Undefined priorities are at the root of much of our success-or-failure frustration."[3]

Triggering situation: Most of us experience a sense of elation when we finally find our niche in life. I've always believed that success is finding out what God wants us to do with our uniqueness and then doing it with all our might. The problem comes when we enjoy our work/ministry so much that it begins to take over every area of our lives. In my case, a growing ministry was demanding more days away from home and more preoccupation at home while I answered mail and returned phone calls from faraway places.

The situation that triggered my fear went right back to undefined priorities. I had never taken the time to decide what was most important to me, so I let phone calls, aggressive meeting planners, urgent mail, and ministry preparation keep me so busy I never thought about saying "no" and choosing a more relaxed schedule. In the beginning I was having fun. I was in demand. I enjoyed having the acclaim of "doing it all." And I felt spiritual. After all, I was doing God's work—at least I'd convinced myself that this move into overcommitment was for Him.

Reactive emotion: It didn't take long for me to begin fearing success and failure at the same time. The more successful I became in ministry, the more time demands were placed on my schedule. And the more I began writing books and accepting speaking engagements, the less time I had to be an at-home mother. I was afraid of success because I didn't know how to set limits. I was also afraid of failure, because in my mind, if I hurt my child by being too busy, no other form of success could make up for that type of failure. This monster fear began preoccupying my mind and produced tremendous guilt.

Rage: I experienced an inner boiling cauldron of rage, and it was often directed at different people. During the times I lived through an impossible schedule, I was furious with myself. I would return home in the middle of the night from Detroit Metro Airport, tiptoe into my son's bedroom, pray over his sleeping figure—and realize I had just missed three days of his life. I hated myself!

At other times I would walk into a room and see my husband reading a good book or playing a game with Jason and a surge of anger would envelop me. I was filled with rage as I saw Gene with extra hours to enjoy reading and being a father. I wanted the same freedom and privilege—but my schedule was so full I rarely had time for those personal luxuries.

Occasionally my rage was vented toward other people. Several years ago I was in Minneapolis speaking at a weekend conference. After finishing the opening keynote address, a woman I had never met walked toward me, stared with furrowed brow over her half-glasses, and spoke with a critical tone, "Who watches your little boy when you're off speaking like this?"

This woman irritated me. Anger was mounting, and it was fast turning into rage. What right did this person have to suggest that I was a bad mother? What business was it of hers *who* watched my child in my absence? It's a good thing I didn't speak my thoughts aloud, because I was more than tempted to respond, "Oh, no one does. We just let him play in the streets."

Internal negotiating: Living every day in the middle of rage is so uncomfortable that we usually move to internal negotiating. I had to ask myself why my husband's legitimate and wise use of his leisure time made me so angry. It was hard for me to admit I resented him because he had chosen what I wanted—time for Jason and time to breathe. I realized that the woman from Minneapolis made me so full of rage because she was asking a question that hit too close to home. She made me face my fear of failing as a mother—and I continued to seethe inside when I thought of her remark.

Destructive solutions: I had great coping skills, so my internal negotiations immediately turned to finding a resolution for my fear of failure. Many individuals select only one of the negative techniques for dealing with fear. But at different times, I tried each of the following resolutions.

1. *Denial*—This was one of my favorite techniques. I convinced myself that I always spent "quality time" with my son, and that's what mattered—not the quantity of time. He was doing well in school and had a very involved father. I was only making myself guilty and

fearful because of a silly self-imposed standard of excellence that no parent could ever live up to. I did not have a problem!

2. *Defeat*—Exhaustion is the constant companion of women who don't set limits and when I was tired, I threw personal pity parties. I was smiling on the outside, but inside I was convinced that my worst fear had come true—I was a rotten mother. In fact, I was a screaming mother, an irritated wife, and an agitated human being. Phone calls and interruptions overwhelmed me. I started to prove to myself and my family that I was a failure! I was too busy to attend family reunions with them. I was too tired to entertain company at home. I certainly could not work as hard as I did and be an energized bed partner with my husband. I could not cook well-rounded nutritious meals while simultaneously keeping the house in impeccable condition. My mother *always* had a clean house and cooked big dinners. I was a failure, and I was defeated!

3. *Bitterness*—I never experienced an extended period of bitterness, but I remember "seasons of embitterment." The year I missed all but two Little League games was the time bitterness hit me in the face. We had experienced some financial challenges that year, and I was realizing that my income had become a necessary part of meeting our monthly obligations. In the beginning I had worked hard because I enjoyed it. Now I was working even harder and I couldn't slow down because we needed the money to meet our financial commitments.

Bitterness always looks for someone or something to blame and my mind was great at creating a list to fault others:

- If my husband would work harder and make more money, I wouldn't have to be on the road so much.
- If the Little League committee had an ounce of compassion, they'd schedule the games when I could come. They *always* scheduled Jason's games for when I was out of town.
- If we hadn't bought this big house, I wouldn't have to work so hard and I could spend more time with my son.
- If God really cared about me, He would give me back the joy I lost.

Bitterness is a debilitating choice. It always poisons *us* more than it contaminates those we blame.

4. *Escape*—My fear of failing as a mother was closely tied to my fear of losing control. For a while, I found myself sinking deeply in the compulsive addictions of work and perfectionism. Both of these forms of escape gave me enough affirmation to continue down my destructive path. I was miserably unhappy, and my fear of failure loomed in the background, reminding me that success had a price tag.

WIDENING THE SCOPE OF A SECRET FEAR

I have never met a woman who has not struggled at some level with the fear of success or the fear of failure. Most of us struggle with both! One woman wrote, "I have desperately wanted everyone, anyone, or someone to think I was wonderful, talented, exciting, and spiritual. But I have been so afraid of failure that I have turned off my ability to accept success as well." This woman's self-esteem was so fragile due to past issues that she was in bondage to the fear of failure.

On the other hand, some of us are overwhelmed by the secret fear that to be successful, we must do something so spectacular that the whole world will validate our worth. When we get caught up in this philosophy, we often *do* accomplish something worthy of applause, but often the fear of failure looms in the background because of the personal sacrifices that have allowed the success.

Helen Keller once said, "I long to accomplish a great and noble task; but it is my chief duty and joy to accomplish humble tasks as though they were great and noble. The world is moved along, not only by the mighty shoves of its heroes, but also by the aggregate of the tiny pushes of each honest worker."[4] I've struggled with exactly what Helen Keller talked about. Why did I always feel more successful when I was writing a book or speaking to a large crowd than when I was doing laundry for my family or making peanut butter sandwiches for Jason and his friends? Sometimes I think one of life's most important challenges is to understand the value of humble tasks. We are so afraid that being "ordinary" and taking time to relax means we are not successful.

This last fear is a giant force in most of our lives. As women who desire to achieve greatness and accomplish worthy deeds for God, we face many fearful challenges. A few of the fears women have shared with me follow:

- I'm afraid I'll be looked at as less competent if I don't work through my lunch hour. I have to work harder all the time to outdo the competition, but I'm also afraid even more will be expected of me if I keep working at this pace.
- I'm afraid to get more education even though I'm unhappy in my job. What if I'm not smart enough to get decent grades? Then I'd really feel like a failure.
- I'm afraid to look too competent in my job because the men I work for won't think I'm feminine.
- I'm afraid to have a child because I might not be a good enough mother.
- I'm very unhappy in my current position, but I'm afraid to try something new because I might not be successful. If I fail, how could I face my friends and how could I pay my bills?
- I'm afraid to approach my boss about a raise, because I might be turned down and I'd feel like a total failure.
- I'm afraid to accept the chairmanship of the organization because I've never led a group before and I might not have the skills to be successful.
- I'm afraid to get married to this man because he might be disappointed in me and I couldn't risk that.
- I'm afraid of accomplishing my goals because then what would there be for me to live for after that?
- What if I work hard for my entire life and discover I'm still empty inside?

Much of our fear centers on being unable to identify what will bring a sense of purpose, joy, and fulfillment to our lives. Fear of making the wrong choice in our life's work. Fear of getting trapped in dead-end marriages and/or vocations. Fear of *not* having children. Fear of *having* children and being bad parents. Fear of not knowing how to handle success. Fear of not feeling fulfilled when everyone says we are successful. Fear of trying something new because we've never succeeded in the past.

David Frähm wrote,

If you don't dream your own dreams, others will project their dreams onto you. Then your direction will be by default, not by choice. The only real direction you'll be headed in is around in circles. . . . The Christian who lacks a sense of personal vision for her work, who has yet to clarify the mental picture of what she'd like to do in her world, lacks passion and purpose. Her work life will feel more like purgatory than a privileged cooperation with the One who made her.[5]

As we try to break out of bondage and tame the fear monster, we will always experience some failures along the way. To dream our own dreams means to risk failing more than once. It means developing a constructive resolution for the way we process fear. As we develop the ability to arrive at faith-filled decisions instead of being paralyzed by our fears of success and failure, we discover that every successful person we know has gotten where they are by learning how to process their failure feelings in a constructive way.

REMEMBERING FEARS OF THE PAST

We've looked at five major areas of fear in this book. I've come through many of them—but I'm still in the process of facing others. Dealing with lifelong fear is a dynamic process of choosing to face the fear, acknowledging the pain, and implementing a constructive resolution. Here's a quick reminder of those five major fears.

THE FEAR OF THINGS THAT HAVEN'T HAPPENED . . . YET!

Engraved on my mind is a list of the paralyzing phobias that have at times kept me frozen in a state of inactivity. At times I documented a huge list of the potential disasters I was sure would happen. Reading this list makes me laugh and cry simultaneously. I chuckle when I realize that more than half of the dreaded possibilities never took place, but I feel sad when I'm reminded of all my wasted mental and spiritual energy—energy that could have been invested in something productive!

THE FEAR OF BEING VULNERABLE

This fear haunts me the most, because at times, I still feel more secure when I'm "in control" of people and events, instead of letting people get close enough to share my personal hurts and failings. As I daily choose to reveal myself without debilitating anxiety about what people will think of me, I take a step in the right direction.

THE FEAR OF ABANDONMENT

Some of us are plagued by the fear of disappointing people. Even though old patterns tempt us, it's encouraging to see ourselves leaving codependency behind and allowing the people around us to be responsible for their own actions. The fear of abandonment may occasionally tempt us with thoughts of insecurity. But every time we face rejection, we can choose to allow the pain to draw us closer to God. Instead of feeling trapped in our pain, we can choose a constructive resolution to this fear.

THE FEAR OF TRUTH

Lloyd Douglas once said, "If a man harbors any kind of fear, it makes him landlord to a ghost." Looking back is often painful, and if there has been severe emotional, physical, or spiritual abuse, we've faced two ghosts—shame and guilt. The shame of victimization can be brutal, but sometimes the guilt for the wrong choices we've made is even worse—until we understand the power of forgiveness. When life brings disappointments that jolt our confidence in God, we have a decision to make. We can wind up defeated and bitter, or our brokenness can lead to surrender and a future based on a faith-filled decision to forgive ourselves and others.

THE FEAR OF MAKING WRONG CHOICES

A few years ago a friend sent me a cartoon of a woman who came to a fork in the road and wound up crashing into a pole in between the two choices. As she stumbled out of her car with blurred vision, broken bones, and open wounds, she said, "I just couldn't decide which way to go."

This book is all about choices. Will we be consumed with the fear of getting trapped in the "dead ends" of life? Will we be afraid of success because of the hard decisions we'll have to make and the personal limitations we'll have to face? Will we allow the fear of failure to keep us from trying to achieve? Or will we use the events and situations that trigger our fears to move us toward faith-filled decisions? It inspires me to know that I have a choice—every day. It's the daily choices that produce lifetime results.

THE VALUE OF FAILURE

When we allow our internal negotiation to lead us to a constructive resolution for our fears, we get a new perspective on the value of failure.

Christian psychologist and author H. Norman Wright says,

> You have failed in the past. You are failing now in some way. You will fail in the future. You weren't perfect in the past. You won't be perfect in the future. Your children will not be perfect, either. When you fail, allow yourself to feel disappointment, but not disapproval. . . . You can fail and not be a failure![6]

In other words, failure's positive contribution to my life is that it leads me to explore the depth of my disappointment, which has the potential of bringing me to a place of personal and spiritual growth. Instead of covering up my fear with denial, beating myself up with defeat, picking victims for my bitterness, or selecting an escape into a compulsive/addictive pattern, I can allow failure to launch me in a different direction.

I think the Apostle Paul understood this concept.

> But one thing I do: Forgetting what is behind and straining toward what is ahead, I press on toward the goal to win the prize for which God has called me heavenward in Christ Jesus. (Philippians 3:13-14)

LESSONS LEARNED THE HARD WAY

Thinking back on my life brings a realization of the tension in my heart as I have battled the fear of success and failure throughout Jason's growing-up years. It would be absolutely wrong for me to suggest that on a certain day I learned how to practice a constructive resolution for that fear and I never had a problem with it again. Many times I fell back into old patterns and had to make new choices. You're probably a fellow struggler or you wouldn't be reading this book. But, in time,

I have learned how to come to a constructive resolution faster. And I've also learned how miserable I am when I go back into my "I'll take care of the problem myself" mode. It just doesn't work! So what *does* work?

Sorrow: When I allow my fears to bring me to a place of grieving, I've already begun to "give up my rights," and I've started to release my tenacious grip on the situation. As a young mother, I grieved for the time I had lost with my child because of overcommitment. I felt deep sadness for the times I had yelled at him because of my own fatigue level, not because he was doing something wrong. I wept for the false guilt I had placed on my husband for not being as committed to his work as I was. I lamented over my own total inability to know how to relax.

Brokenness: This sorrow led to a brokenness I had never experienced before. For me, it was a total role reversal. Instead of figuring out how God could fix a situation and giving Him all of the multiple choice options I had constructed, I quit telling Him what to do. With a heart of humility, I said, "Lord, I'm hurting. I'm broken. I'm a failure as a wife and a mother. I'm a phony Christian leader, and I'm at the end of my resources. None of the successes I've had mean anything to me, because they have not brought happiness. I cannot go on like this."

Surrender: For me, surrender meant getting on my knees with my precious date book in my hand and offering it to God. That book represented important ego-gratifying speaking engagements, a book deadline with a major Christian publisher, and a week of appearances on a national television program. It also represented the birthdays of important people in my life, an anniversary with one of the best husbands in the world, family vacations, and lunch dates with friends who were wondering if I cared about them anymore. I confessed my self-reliance to God, admitting that I had allowed urgencies and personal pride to crowd out the important things in my life. I no longer wanted to fear success because of the fear of failing at home. I wanted to learn how to be successful by God's standards.

Faith-filled decision: Out of the yielding pattern of sorrow, brokenness, and surrender comes an empowerment that sets us free from fear. Instead of being in bondage to indecision, we have a supernatural strength to make wise choices. Timothy said it best: "For God did not give us a spirit of timidity, but a spirit of power, of love and of self-discipline."[7]

As I surrendered my calendar, my plans, my ego, and my insecurities to God, I experienced a new understanding of success. I was able to make the hard choices more easily and form the words, "Thanks for asking, but I'm not available," with greater authority and joy. I moved to a new plan for defining my priorities. I saved days on the calendar ahead of time—just for our family—before making them available to the first person who called. I began to suggest other speakers to retreat directors instead of accepting every opportunity that came along.

I was freed to make the choice of taking a whole month off every summer to be with my family—with no ministry interruptions or obligations. I had time to read God's Word and let it say something fresh to my exhausted, hungry soul. I had time to go for jeep rides with Jason and let my hair blow in the breeze on a sunny day.

This month I had time to listen to my son voice his fears regarding the temptations and loneliness that he might face at the Academy. I had time to grieve the "passage of life" I'm in the middle of. Instead of running to catch the next plane, I had time to make strawberry Jell-O and chocolate chip cookies. I had time to *enjoy* folding laundry, knowing that what was once a burden is now a privilege—almost gone. I had time to read the high school graduation cards and remember with love the precious faraway friends and family who still bless our lives at unexpected moments.

When my focus was on God, instead of me, self-reliance was relinquished and I was infused with a joy and personal relaxation I forgot was possible. I was no longer afraid of success, because I had a new definition of it. I was no longer afraid of failing as a mother. I had *time* to *be* a mother.

I rediscovered the truth of Isaiah 41:9-10,13—

"You are my servant";
>   I have chosen you and have not rejected you.
So do not fear, for I am with you;
>   do not be dismayed, for I am your God.
I will strengthen you and help you;
>   I will uphold you with my righteous right hand. . . .
For I am the LORD, your God,
>   who takes hold of your right hand and says to you,
Do not fear; I will help you.

Fear is energy draining. The surrender that leads to faith-filled decision making is energizing and freeing.

FAITH OR FEAR?

The opposite of fear is faith. Fear makes us withdraw and hide behind our escape mechanisms. Fear exposes our disappointments and makes us choose a rigid or a yielding resolution for those fears. Faith or fear? The choice is ours.

Bruce Larson says, "Fear is a handle for laying hold on God. When you stop running and face your fear head on with faith, you find God. It is His presence and power that move us beyond our fears—past, present, and future."[8]

Sometimes faith feels risky and fear seems like a comfortable burden. What will we choose? Reva Nelson, the author of a book on risk taking, describes the kind of risk that leads to faith: "To decide to take action, beyond your usual limitations, for a vision, when the results are not guaranteed, but look positive." Every day I have a choice. Will I allow fear to overcome me, or will I take action, even though the results are not guaranteed, and look with faith into the face of my Savior?

HEADING FOR ANNAPOLIS

Tomorrow I will get into a car with my family and head for the Naval Academy for my son's induction into the future he believes God has called him to. I'm facing another day of choices. Fear or faith? Will I give in to the bondage of past fears—or will I be set free to make new goals, dream new dreams, and use my new freedom from the laundry room to make a major difference in God's Kingdom?

Lord, as I enter a whole new experience in my life, give me the grace to realize life on this earth will never be completely free from anxiety. I know the enemy will harass me with memories of failure from the past and I will be tempted to fall back into old patterns of handling my fears.

Protect me from the bondage of denial and defeat. Guard my heart from the cancer of bitterness. Keep me from my favorite escapes into perfectionism and workaholism.

Lord, when fear surfaces, help me to grieve over the pain without shame and let my broken heart turn me to humble surrender and forgiveness. Enable me to practice making faith-filled decisions as I submit to Your authority in my life. Keep me from demanding instant answers and help me to understand the simple truth: *Faith that begins with fear will end up closer to You.* . . .

Notes

✥

CHAPTER ONE—
"IF I'M SUCH A GREAT CHRISTIAN, WHY DO I HAVE THIS PROBLEM?"

1. *Webster's New World Dictionary of the American Language*, David B. Guralnik ed. (Nashville, TN: The Southwestern Company, 1966), page 274.
2. *Webster's New World Dictionary*, page 274.
3. Excerpted from the book *The Trauma of Transparency* by J. Grant Howard (Portland, OR: Questar Publishers, Multnomah Books, © 1979), page 32. Used by permission.
4. Peter McWilliams, "Happiness . . . Understanding Happiness," *Bottom Line*, vol. 14, no. 1, 15 January 1993, page 1.
5. Henri J. M. Nouwen, "Prayer and the Jealous God," *New Oxford Review*, vol. LII, June 1985, pages 9-10. Used by permission.
6. Paraphrased from 1 John 4:18.

CHAPTER TWO—
"WHAT HAPPENS INSIDE MY HEAD WHEN I'M AFRAID?"

1. Paul Moede, "Facing Down the Giants in Your Land," *Discipleship Journal*, issue 52 (1989), page 24.
2. Paraphrased from Matthew 14:22-33.
3. Paraphrased from many books and dictionaries.

CHAPTER THREE—
"WHY DO I LET IRRATIONAL PANIC IMMOBILIZE ME?"

1. Marcia J. Pear, "How to Turn Off the Anxiety Alarm," quoted from *Nation's Business*, August 1992, page 60. Copyright 1992, U.S. Chamber of Commerce.

2. Pear, page 60.
3. Jacqueline Wasser, "Phobias, Panic, and Fear—Oh My!" *Mademoiselle*, vol. 96, April 1990, page 162.
4. Carl Bard, quoted by Barbara Johnson, *Pack Up Your Gloomees in a Great Big Box* (Dallas, TX: Word Publishing, 1993), page 26.
5. Lawrence Richards, *Lawrence Richards' 365 Day Devotional Commentary* (Wheaton, IL: Victor Books, 1990), page 342.
6. Richards, page 342.
7. *Webster's New World Dictionary of the American Language*, page 755.
8. Amanda Warren, "Scare Tactics—Living With Your Secret Fears," *Mademoiselle*, October 1991, page 98.
9. Nicky Marone, *Women and Risk: How to Master Your Fears and Do What You Never Thought You Could Do* (New York: St. Martin's Press, 1992), page xi (Preface).
10. Marone, page xi (Preface).
11. This account is found in Exodus 3:11-12, 4:1-13.
12. Susan Jeffers, *Feel the Fear and Do It Anyway* (New York: Ballantine Books, 1987), pages 218-219.

CHAPTER FOUR—
"WHY DOES THE FEAR OF THINGS THAT MIGHT HAPPEN CONSUME MY MENTAL AND SPIRITUAL ENERGY?"

1. Karen Randau, *Conquering Fear* (Houston and Dallas, TX: Rapha Publishing/Word, 1991), page 5.
2. Randau, page 5.
3. Jane and Robert Handly with Pauline Neff, "Why Can't I Stop Worrying?" *Ladies' Home Journal*, January 1991, page 88.
4. Sharlene King, "How to Feel Better About the Future," *Ladies' Home Journal*, May 1992, page 94.
5. King, page 94.
6. Larry Burkett, *The Coming Economic Earthquake* (Chicago, IL: Moody Press, 1991), page 40.
7. Burkett, page 112.
8. Romans 8:22.
9. 1 Peter 5:7.
10. Quoted in King, page 94.
11. Barbara Johnson, *Stick a Geranium in Your Hat and Be Happy* (Dallas, TX: Word Publishing, 1990), pages 72-73.
12. Marone, page 17.
13. Marone, page 17.

14. Handly and Neff, page 88.
15. Matthew 6:34.
16. This incident is found in Luke 1:28-38.
17. Luke 2:49.
18. Sue Monk Kidd, *When the Heart Waits* (San Francisco, CA: Harper & Row, 1990), page 114.
19. Barbara Johnson, *Splashes of Joy in the Cesspools of Life* (Dallas, TX: Word Publishing, 1992), page 101.

CHAPTER FIVE—
"WHY DOES EVERYTHING I DO HAVE TO BE PERFECT?"

1. Barbara Sullivan, *The Control Trap* (Minneapolis, MN: Bethany House, 1991), page 73.
2. Les Carter, *Imperative People* (Nashville, TN: Thomas Nelson, 1991), pages 14-15.
3. Carter, page 15.
4. *New Webster's Dictionary and Thesaurus of the English Language*, Bernard S. Cayne ed. (Danbury, CT: Lexicon Publications, 1992), page 1104.
5. Paula Rinehart, *Perfect Every Time* (Colorado Springs, CO: NavPress, 1992), pages 18-19.
6. Chris Thurman, "Perfectionism," *Today's Better Life*, Spring 1993, page 48.
7. Genesis 3:5, emphasis added.
8. Rinehart, page 25.
9. Carter, page 47.
10. Job 19:7,19.
11. See Psalm 51:1-10.

CHAPTER SIX—
"IF I LET YOU GET CLOSE TO ME, WILL YOU STILL LIKE ME?"

1. Dr. Paul Tournier, as quoted in John Powell, S.J., *Why Am I Afraid to Tell You Who I Am?* (Allen, TX: Tabor Publishing, © 1969), page 20.
2. Susan Jacoby, "The Guarded Girl: What Is She Hiding?" *Cosmopolitan*, October 1992, page 231.
3. Jacoby, page 231.
4. Jonathan Berent, *Beyond Shyness: How to Conquer Social Anxieties* (New York: Simon & Schuster, 1993), page 9.
5. Max Lucado, *Six Hours One Friday* (Portland, OR: Multnomah Press, Part of the Questar Publishing Family, 1989), page 36.

6. David Seamands, *Healing of Memories* (Wheaton, IL: Victor Books, 1985), page 84.
7. Powell, page 52.
8. Powell, pages 54-61. (The five levels of communication were first introduced in this way by John Powell.)
9. Powell, page 61.
10. Jacoby, page 232.

CHAPTER SEVEN —
"IF I DON'T MEET THE EXPECTATIONS OF OTHERS, WHAT WILL HAPPEN TO THEM AND ME?"

1. Although this is an accurate portrayal of my sister's story, names and identifying details have been changed to protect the privacy of people involved.
2. Curt Grayson and Jan Johnson, *Creating a Safe Place* (New York: HarperCollins, 1991), page 23.
3. Nancy Groom, *From Bondage to Bonding* (Colorado Springs, CO: NavPress, 1991), page 21.
4. Groom, page 21.
5. Katherine Ketcham and Ginny Lyford Gustafson, *Living on the Edge* (New York: Bantam Books, 1989), page 77.
6. Robert Hemfelt, Frank Minirth, and Paul Meier, *Love Is a Choice* (Nashville, TN: Thomas Nelson, 1989), pages 98-99.
7. Hemfelt, Minirth, and Meier, page 99.

CHAPTER EIGHT —
"WHAT IF THE PEOPLE I'VE GIVEN MY LOVE TO LEAVE ME OR BETRAY ME?"

1. Lloyd Ogilvie, *12 Steps to Living Without Fear* (Waco, TX: Word Books, 1987), page 111.
2. Margery D. Rosen, "All Alone: The New Loneliness of American Women," *Ladies Home Journal*, April 1991, page 218.
3. Rosen, page 218.
4. Max Lucado, *And the Angels Were Silent* (Portland, OR: Multnomah, Part of the Questar Publishing Family, 1992), page 159.
5. 1 Kings 17:1.
6. Paraphrase and summary of 1 Kings 17:2-7.
7. 1 Kings 19:3-4.
8. Ogilvie, page 128.
9. Calvin Miller, "Alone," *Moody*, March 1991, pages 22-23.

CHAPTER NINE—
"IF I REMEMBER AND REVEAL WHAT HAPPENED TO ME,
WILL THE PAIN BE INSURMOUNTABLE?"

1. Larry Crabb, *Inside Out* (Colorado Springs, CO: NavPress, 1988), page 120.
2. Alfred Ells, *Restoring Innocence* (Nashville, TN: Thomas Nelson, 1990), page 51.
3. Paraphrase from Dan B. Allender, *The Wounded Heart* (Colorado Springs, CO: NavPress, 1992), page 57.
4. C. S. Lewis, *The Problem of Pain* (New York: Macmillan, 1978), page 93.
5. David B. Biebel, *If God Is So Good, Why Do I Hurt So Bad?* (Colorado Springs, CO: NavPress, 1989), page 128.
6. Biebel, pages 128-129.
7. Matthew 5:3.
8. Compiled by George Sweeting, *Great Quotes & Illustrations* (Waco, TX: Word Books, 1985), page 119.
9. Judith Sills, Ph.D., *Excess Baggage* (New York: Viking Penguin, 1993), pages 229-230.

CHAPTER TEN—
"HOW CAN I HAVE THESE DOUBTS ABOUT GOD
AND CALL MYSELF A CHRISTIAN?"

1. Jackie Hudson, *Doubt, A Road to Growth* (San Bernardino, CA: Here's Life, 1987), page 13.
2. Hudson, page 14.
3. Hudson, page 14.
4. Gary E. Parker, *The Gift of Doubt: From Crisis to Authentic Faith* (San Francisco, CA: Harper & Row, 1990), page 18.
5. Ken Abraham, *The Disillusioned Christian* (San Bernardino, CA: Here's Life, 1991), page 11.
6. Gordon Aeschliman, *Cages of Pain* (Dallas, TX: Word Publishing, 1991), page 88.
7. Paula Rinehart, "Passages of Faith," *Discipleship Journal*, May/June 1993, page 19.
8. Rinehart, page 19.
9. Parker, pages 142-143.
10. John 6:26.
11. John 6:60.
12. Paraphrase of John 6:67-69

CHAPTER ELEVEN —
"WHAT IF I NEVER LIVE UP TO MY POTENTIAL?"

1. J. I. Packer, *Knowing God* (Downers Grove, IL: InterVarsity, 1973), page 30.
2. Garry Friesen, *Decision Making and the Will of God* (Portland, OR: Multnomah, 1980), book jacket.
3. Haddon W. Robinson, quoted in the foreword of Friesen, page 13.
4. Dr. Arthur Freeman and Rose DeWolf, *Woulda, Coulda, Shoulda* (New York: HarperPerennial, 1990), page 23.
5. Curt Grayson and Jan Johnson, *Creating a Safe Place* (New York: Harper SanFrancisco, 1991), page 118.
6. Edward Kuhlman, *An Overwhelming Interference* (Old Tappan, NJ: Revell, 1986), page 18.
7. Barbara Johnson, *Pack Up Your Gloomees in a Great Big Box* (Dallas, TX: Word Publishing, 1993), page 66.
8. Dee Brestin, *The Lifestyles of Christian Women* (Wheaton, IL: Victor Books, 1991), pages 15-16.
9. Paraphrased from Friesen, page 92.
10. Psalm 32:8 (KJV).
11. Proverbs 3:5-6.
12. Mary Lou Cummings, quoted in *Inspiring Quotations*, compiled by Albert M. Wells, Jr. (Nashville, TN: Thomas Nelson, 1988), page 56.
13. Gordon Graham, quoted in *Quotable Quotations*, compiled by Lloyd Cory (Wheaton, IL: Victor Books, 1985), page 96.
14. Proverbs 9:10.
15. Proverbs 16:3.
16. Proverbs 13:10.
17. Elizabeth Dole, quoted from a speech given at the National Prayer Breakfast, 5 February 1987.

CHAPTER TWELVE —
"WHAT IF REACHING MY GOALS ISN'T ENOUGH?"

1. Carol Kent, *Speak Up With Confidence* (Nashville, TN: Thomas Nelson, 1987), page 172.
2. Erwin Lutzer, *Quotable Quotes*, complied by Lloyd Cory (Wheaton, IL: Victor Books, 1985), page 371.
3. Max Lucado, "The Applause of Heaven and Earth," *Leadership*, vol. 13, no. 3, Summer 1992, page 20.
4. Helen Keller, quoted in *Leadership*, vol. 13, no. 3, Summer 1992, page 30.
5. David Frahm, *The Great Niche Hunt* (Colorado Springs, CO: NavPress,

1991), pages 144-145.

6. H. Norman Wright, quoted by Judy Anderson, "Learning Unconditional Love," *Moody*, February 1993, page 53.

7. 2 Timothy 1:7.

8. Bruce Larson, *Living Beyond Our Fears* (New York: HarperSanFrancisco, 1990) page 150.

Author

❖

Carol Kent is the founder and director of "Speak Up With Confidence" seminars, a ministry committed to helping Christians develop their communication skills.

A member of the National Speakers Association, Carol speaks at conferences and retreats throughout the United States and Canada. She is also a frequent guest on a wide variety of radio and television broadcasts.

Carol has a B.S. degree in speech education and an M.A. in communication arts from Western Michigan University. She is listed in *Who's Who Among Students in American Universities and Colleges* and was twice selected to appear in *Outstanding Young Women of America*.

Her background includes four years as a drama, speech, and English teacher and two years as director of an Alternative Education Program for Pregnant Teenagers. After a brief time of working as a director of women's ministries at a midwestern church, she went into full-time speaking.

Tame Your Fears is Carol's third book. A companion study guide will be available in 1994. *Secret Longings of the Heart* was published by NavPress in 1990 and her first book, *Speak Up With Confidence,* was released in a new paperback version in 1993 by Thomas Nelson Publishers.

Carol and her husband, Gene, live in Port Huron, Michigan. They have a teenage son, Jason, who at this writing is a midshipman at the United States Naval Academy. They also have a Himalayan cat named Bahgi who has a very low I.Q.

Carol Kent Ministries
In addition to conference and retreat speaking, Carol Kent presents "Speak Up With Confidence" seminars in many cities each year. The seminars are designed to train Christians to communicate more effectively. Presented in a three-day format, participants learn how to find and use illustrations, how to gain the attention of an audience, how to organize and file speaking material, and how to overcome stage fright

For more information on Carol's cassette tapes and "Speak Up" seminars, or for details related to scheduling her to speak in your area, contact:

Carol Kent Ministries
P. O. Box 610941
Port Huron, MI 48061-0941
Phone: (810)982-0898
Fax: (810)987-4163

began, Pileggi (already a certified fitness fanatic) went for a refresher course to the famous Goosen Gym in Los Angeles.

"It makes me happy that some people will assume there was a stunt double in the ring," he says. "There wasn't! As a matter of fact, before I took my little dive, I hit that guy I was boxing with a couple of good ones. We both had a great time."

Pileggi has an altogether different set of recollections about waking up in the middle of the night, driving into the studio, and sitting motionless long past sunrise while wide-awake *X-Files* makeup artists glued monstrous black veins onto his face, arms, and torso.

"They did a beautiful job and it looked awesome, but man, I hated it! I really don't know how those guys on *Star Trek* or *Babylon 5* can stand having that done to them every day. I just wouldn't work if that's what it took.

"There was one positive aspect, though. I was so wiped out by the process that it really helped me play dead and dying. Remember that shot where the camera pulls back from my open eye? The truth is, I was having a hard time keeping even one eye open."

For the record, Pileggi's chief tormentor on "S.R. 819" was special effects makeup supervisor John Vulich, who constructed Skinner's ravaged features from a latex mask of the actor's face shot through with hollow rubber veins—many of them hooked up to hand-operated air bulbs to make them pulse and quiver on command. "He was covered with a lot more rubber than you would probably think," says Vulich, proudly. "The only part of his actual face that you really see are his nose and upper lip."

To show Skinner (and the unfortunate scientist Kenneth Orgel) progressing from extreme illness to near death, Vulich constructed two entirely different sets of makeup. For the scene in which Krycek tortures and kills Orgel by remote control, visual effects producer Bill Millar morphed the two levels of makeup together electronically in postproduction. Millar also designed the bloodstream-borne nanobots ("It took a few tries. One of our attempts looked too much like the CBS eye," he says); inserted them in actual through-the-microscope footage of blood and plasma; and "cloned" them with a handy computer animation program.

Krycek's lethal palm computer was actually a small working television set, modified and embellished by prop master Tom Day's minions. Its screen displayed graphic images broadcast from a computer—programmed and operated by consultant John Markham, who was located just out of camera range. "It was amazing," recalls Day, with relish. "John could enter his commands, change the display on the little TV, and get instant feedback by watching what the TV camera attached to our film camera was showing."

Location manager Ilt Jones, in contrast, remembers 6X10 as "the damn parking lot episode." He says

grumpily, "There were three or four of the damn things in the script. Above ground. Below ground. Big. Small.

"You wouldn't believe how many we scouted for each one we finally chose! I'm now the world's greatest expert on the parking lots of Los Angeles. I started to wake up screaming about barriers and parking tickets and entrances and exit ramps."

As for set decorator Tim Stepeck, the teeth-gritting tension of "S.R. 819" centered around the real-life electronic blood analyzer, borrowed from a friendly medical device manufacturer, used in the scene with Scully and Dr. Plant. The $12,000 device worked perfectly during filming, then vanished into thin air.

"We looked frantically for it everywhere, for weeks," says Stepeck. "All around our office. All our storage facilities. We even went over to *Chicago Hope*, which shoots on the Fox lot also, to see if somebody had taken it by mistake.

"We didn't find it until we were wrapping the whole season. By mistake, somebody had taken it away and dressed it into the Lone Gunman set. I guess they felt it fit just right with all that junk and weird equipment on their shelves."

Ⓧ

Special makeup effects supervisor John Vulich is the founder and owner of Optic Nerve Studios, a Sun Valley, California—based firm that provides makeup, prosthetics, and other related nondigital special effects for movies and TV series. He and his company have won Emmys for their work on *Buffy the Vampire Slayer* and *Babylon 5*.

Ⓧ

"S.R. 819" is the third "Skinner episode" in *X-Files* history. The first two were "Avatar" (3X21) and "Zero Sum" (4X21).

Ⓧ

Composer Mark Snow says that his complex score for "S.R. 819," filled with tension and foreboding, was inspired by Daniel Sackheim's subtle direction and "a lot of big-time feature-like action." It was nominated for an Emmy for Outstanding Music Composition for a Series (Dramatic Underscore).

Ⓧ

Dr. Katrina Cabrera, one of the physicians who treats Skinner, was named after a current researcher on *The X-Files* staff.

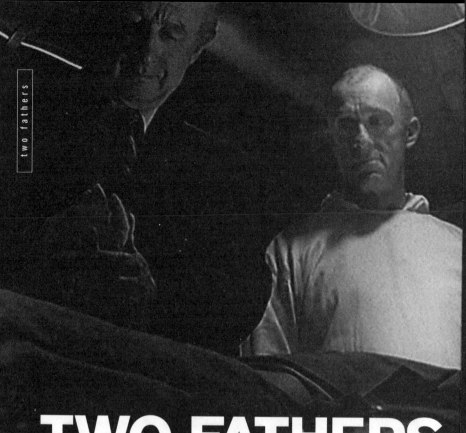

TWO FATHERS

As a prelude to the colonization of Earth, Syndicate scientists successfully create a human-alien hybrid. The slave-race prototype is abductee Cassandra Spender, who returns, reveals many secret conspiracies and connections—and plunges Mulder and Scully into a climactic battle for global domination.

EPISODE: 6X11
FIRST AIRED: February 7, 1999
EDITOR: Lynne Willingham
WRITTEN BY: Chris Carter & Frank Spot
DIRECTED BY: Kim Manners

GUEST STARS:
Mitch Pileggi (AD Skinner)
William B. Davis (The Cigarette-Sm
Chris Owens (Agent Jeffrey Spende
Nicholas Lea (Alex Krycek)
Veronica Cartright (Cassandra Spen
Mimi Rogers (Agent Diana Fowley
George Murdoch (The Elder)
Don S. Williams (Second Elder)
Nick Tate (Dr. Openshaw)
Al Ruscio (Third Elder)
Frank Ertl (Fourth Elder)
James Newman (Lead Surgeon)
Damon P. Saleem (Pick-Up Player)

PRINCIPAL SETTINGS:
Arlington, Virginia; Washington, D.C.;
Silver Springs, Maryland

6⊗11

"MOM, IT'S ME, JEFFREY. MOM, WHAT HAPPENED TO YOU? YOU'VE BEEN GONE SO LONG I THOUGHT I'D NEVER SEE YOU AGAIN."
—Jeffrey Spender

Cassandra is silent for a long moment.

"I need to talk to someone," she says, finally.

"You can tell me," says her son, urgently.

Cassandra shakes her head.

"I need to speak to Agent Mulder," she says.

At this, Skinner turns and walks toward his car. Spender pursues him and shouts that he doesn't want Mulder talking to his mother.

"Why?" says Skinner, curtly.

"He's forbidden from the X-Files. He's to stay out of this."

"She's asking for him," says Skinner. "What are you afraid of, Agent Spender?"

"Of Agent Mulder filling her head with alien abduction nonsense."

"Are you afraid of the truth?"

"I want to know who did this to her—and why. That's all I want."

"Then why not use every resource available to you?" says Skinner.

"I'll send you a progress report," says Spender, moving off.

At the same time and place as before, the Cigarette-Smoking Man continues his narrative:

"My son refused to believe that his mother had been abducted, though it had been going on for years. Even after I schemed to put him in charge of the X-Files, where Fox Mulder had amassed so much evidence of our secret plans, he still could not bring himself to accept the possibility of alien life. When he did come to believe—when the facts became so glaring—he turned. Not to me, his father, but the man I drew him to."

At a Washington, D.C., gymnasium a sweaty Fox Mulder—in shorts and a New York Knicks T-shirt—plays in a pickup basketball game. He dribbles, drives to the hoop, and scores. Mulder takes the ball out beyond the key for the next play—and sees Scully entering the building. He stares at her curiously.

"Hey, Milk! Let's play ball," yells one of the guys on the opposing team. "Yo, homestyle! Cough up the rock!"

Mulder flips the ball to his opponent, who bounces it back. Mulder fakes left, pulls up, and sinks a jump shot from the top of the key.

"Game!" declares Mulder, who turns his back and walks toward Scully.

"Hey, homegirl! Word up!" he says.

"Mulder, it's my distinct impression that you just cheated. And that you're not coming in again."

"Oh, Scully!" he replies, grinning. "I got game!"

"Yeah, you got so much game that I'm worried if you've got any work left in you."

"I'm ready to j-o-b," protests Mulder. "Just not on some jag-off shoe-shine tip. No background checkin' jag-off shoe-shine tip."

Scully grins wryly.

"Well, about your j-o-b, Mulder, somebody's been trying very hard to reach you by phone. Somebody who wants you back at the FBI, ASAP."

"About what?" asks Mulder.

"About an X-File," says his partner.

At FBI headquarters later that day Spender is sitting at Mulder's desk in the bullpen, absorbed in writing.

"You looking for work, Agent Spender? Because if you are, I've got a whole pile in that middle drawer that I'd love to shove down someone's throat."

Spender looks up at Mulder.

"I was just writing you a note," he says tersely. "I think you know why I'm here. She wants to talk to you."

"I didn't hear the magic word."

"Look, Agent Mulder," says Spender. "I'm not going to get down on my knees here."

"Are you asking me, Agent Spender?"

Spender struggles to control himself.

"My mother has been gone for almost a year," he says. "She turns up in a train car, where she's been operated on by a group of doctors who were burned alive. I just want the truth."

Mulder smiles thinly.

"The truth is out there, Agent Spender. Maybe you should find it for yourself."

At St. Mark's Medical Center in Arlington that evening, Dr. Openshaw—critically burned—lies in a hyperbaric chamber. The Cigarette-Smoking Man enters the hospital room and approaches him. Openshaw opens his eyes.

"I expected you sooner," he says, in a weak voice.

The Cigarette-Smoking Man is in some distress.

"I've been at the train yard," he says. "Trying to tidy things up."

"Yes," says Openshaw. "The overkill will be hard to divert attention from. But not as hard as from Cassandra."

The Cigarette-Smoking Man stares down at him blankly. Openshaw explains that the experiments on Cassandra were a success and that he was preparing to kill her when he was interrupted by the alien rebels.

"They saved her to expose us," says the Cigarette-Smoking Man, shocked. "I won't let her out of our hands."

Openshaw looks the Cigarette-Smoking Man in the eye.

"They'll run medical tests on her. It's only a matter of time. Cassandra must be terminated."

The Cigarette-Smoking Man turns away, troubled.

"They will come and question me," says Openshaw.

"I know," says the Cigarette-Smoking Man, softly. "I'm sorry."

He reaches down and turns off the oxygen to Openshaw's chamber. A beeping alarm begins to sound.

"A man," says Openshaw, "should never live long enough to see his children—or his work—destroyed."

Inside an expensive home in Silver Springs later that evening a phone rings. The First Elder picks it up; as he does so he notices a car pull up to the front of his house.

His caller is the Cigarette-Smoking Man. The Cigarette-Smoking Man fills him in on the events in the rail car, including Dr. Openshaw's death. He tells the shocked leader that he's called an emergency meeting of the Syndicate.

"Only the future rides on our response," says the Cigarette-Smoking Man.

"I'll be on a plane," says the Elder.

The Elder hangs up. There is a knock on his door. Standing on his front porch is Dr. Openshaw—apparently uninjured.

"I've come to see you," says the scientist.

The Elder attacks, reaching out and grabbing Openshaw's face and ripping downward. The outer skin peels away revealing a faceless rebel underneath. The alien grabs him by the throat, forcing him to the floor. There is a sudden explosion of flame, then a muffled scream.

At FBI headquarters later that night, Mulder sits at his desk, staring at photos of the rail car carnage on his computer monitor. Scully enters, and says she's surprised to find her partner still there.

"Where'd you expect to find me?" replies Mulder.

"I thought Agent Spender offered you an X-Files assignment," says Scully.

"It wasn't exactly an offer," says Mulder. "It's an opportunity. Made to order for the powers that be."

"You think it's a setup?" asks Scully.

"This is exactly the kind of mistake they've been waiting for to come down on me full force."

"But Agent Spender asked you."

"Like I said," says Mulder. "Not exactly."

Scully walks to Mulder's side of the desk, looks at the images on the monitor, and recoils.

"We've seen this before," she says. "Bodies set aflame with no conclusive cause of combustion. Mulder—"

"I know," says her partner.

"I was with Cassandra Spender when she disappeared," says Scully. "You sat with me when I was under hypnosis, when I spoke of just these sort of details."

Mulder nods.

"I have no doubt what Cassandra could tell us

might expose more than just what happened to her," he says.

"I was taken to one of those train cars," says Scully. "I was tested just like Cassandra. What if what she tells us could expose who did this to me?"

She considers this question for a moment.

"Mulder, Agent Spender doesn't have to know."

At a nearby hospital the next morning, Cassandra Spender is ensconced in a room guarded by FBI agents. She is pleasantly surprised to see Scully at her door, and greets the agent warmly.

"If we can get ahold of a wheelchair, do you want to go out for some fresh air?" asks Scully, smiling brightly.

Cassandra's smile is even brighter.

"I don't need a wheelchair," she says.

She throws back her covers, pulls herself to her feet, and looks the astonished Scully in the eye.

"But I am dying for a cigarette!" she says.

The two women walk into the corridor. Cassandra tells Scully that her doctors are baffled by her recovery, and that they would never believe what had happened to her. So she hasn't told them.

"I'm only going to tell somebody I can trust and who can do something about it," she says. "I was hoping when I saw you that Agent Mulder was going to be coming in the door behind you."

"I've got a surprise for you, Cassandra," says Scully.

They enter a hospital storage room where Mulder has been waiting for them.

"Oh, my God!" says Cassandra. "I think I'm going to pee on the floor!"

She and Mulder hug.

"I told you about their power," she says. "You said you didn't believe it."

"Well, I had reasons for doubt when I met you, Cassandra," says Mulder.

"You just doubted yourself. You were just doubting you'd ever see her again, weren't you? Your sister."

Cassandra tells Mulder that the woman who looked like his sister, whom he saw the previous year (in "Redux II," 5X03) was not Samantha Mulder. The real Samantha, she adds, is still being imprisoned by the aliens.

Scully asks Cassandra whether the doctors in the rail car had cured her.

"No, the aliens cured me," says Cassandra. "The doctors were working with the aliens. That's what I wanted to tell you. I told you that the aliens were here to do good. And that I was being used as an oracle to spread the word. Only now I know what the aliens are here for and it isn't good."

"What are they here for?" asks Mulder.

"To wipe us off the planet. They're taking over the universe. They're infecting all other life forms with a

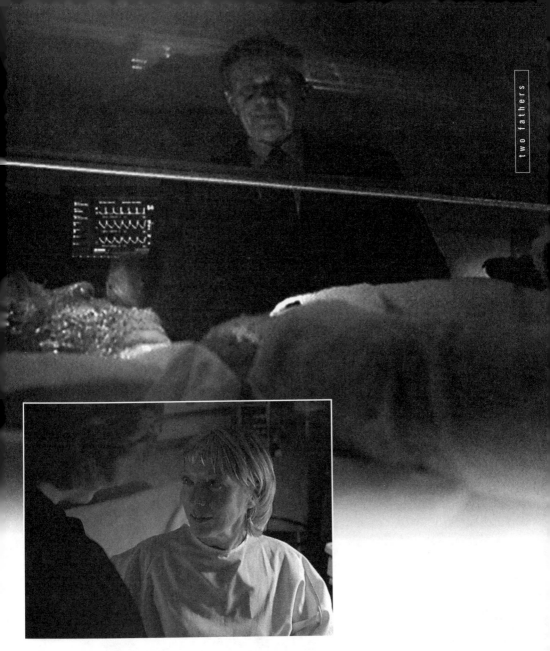

"I TOLD YOU THAT THE ALIENS WERE HERE TO DO GOOD. AND THAT I WAS BEING USED AS AN ORACLE TO SPREAD THE WORD. ONLY NOW I KNOW WHAT THE ALIENS ARE HERE FOR—AND IT ISN'T GOOD."

—Cassandra Spender

"WHAT DO THEY WANT?"–The Second Elder

"TO EXPOSE OUR ENTERPRISE. EVERYTHING WE'VE WORKED FOR."–The Cigarette-Smoking Man

black substance called Purity. It's their life force. It's what they're made of."

Mulder nods, grimly.

"It's the virus. The black oil."

"But those doctors weren't infected—they were burned," says Scully, puzzled.

"By another race of aliens," says Cassandra. "A rebel force that are mutilating their faces so that they won't be infected. This was what I couldn't tell my son Jeffrey, because he doesn't believe me, even though his life is in danger by these same rebel aliens. He's in with the men that have been working with the alien colonists for fifty years."

"Working to do what?" asks Scully.

"Whatever it is they did to me. And to you, Dana."

"And you know who these men are?" asks Mulder.

"Oh, sure," says Cassandra, bitterly. "One of them is my ex-husband—Jeffrey's father."

The Cigarette-Smoking Man's narrative continues:

"Cassandra was beginning to realize her role in the greatest science project that man had ever known. She was the center of fifty years of work—key to all our plans. Something that even my colleagues didn't realize yet.

"I killed to keep them unknowing. I killed Dr. Openshaw so they wouldn't discover him. It was Cassandra I should have killed, Cassandra who needed to die. I couldn't do it. With all the blood on my hands, I couldn't kill the mother of my own son. The woman I never even loved.

"My colleagues never knew, focused as they were on the new threat, the faceless alien rebels who'd burned our doctors alive. But my colleagues had become old men. Blind to the fact that the faceless rebels already held the upper hand. That they'd used their powers of disguise to infiltrate our group."

At Syndicate headquarters the next day, Alex Krycek delivers a report to his masters. He tells them that the alien rebels have destroyed project facilities all over New Mexico and the Southwest and killed staff at the Arizona research facility; that the death of Openshaw and his colleagues has severely disrupted work on creating an alien-human hybrid.

"What do they want?" asks the Second Elder.

"To expose our enterprise," says the Cigarette-Smoking Man. "Everything we've worked for."

The Fourth Elder complains that that's precisely what is going to happen. The Cigarette-Smoking Man counters that he's in control of the situation, especially so with his new man in place inside the FBI.

The First Elder—or someone who looks exactly like the man killed the night before—speaks up.

"Why not side with the rebels?" he says. "Join their alien resistance?"

Silence.

"It's . . . an option," says the Third Elder, tentatively.

Krycek is incensed by the proposal.

"It's an option you declined long ago!" he protests. "Resistance was futile then, why would it be any less so now? That's why you voted against it, against men like Bill Mulder. Collaboration has allowed you to prepare, to stall colonization. How close are you to developing a human-alien hybrid? That alone ensures your survival—"

"As slave labor for the aliens," says the First Elder.

Krycek glowers at him.

"What about your vaccine? By collaborating you buy yourself some time to secretly develop a way to combat the aliens. To fight the future."

"Alex! Enough!" shouts the Cigarette-Smoking Man.

He takes a long drag on his Morley, then turns to the First Elder.

"For fifty years, we've worked on this project. Fifty years, since Roswell. We can't sacrifice ourselves for every new threat, can we now?"

That night Mulder and Scully push past the door of their old X-Files office. Mulder switches on Spender's computer.

"Why risk getting caught here?" asks Scully.

Replies Mulder, "They'll be monitoring any work on our machines, in or out. We need access to files. A name that'll raise flags."

Mulder types in several commands; full-face photos of Jeffrey and Cassandra Spender appear. Several more keystrokes: a beep; then a photo of the Cigarette-Smoking Man appears. It is labeled: SPENDER, C.G.B.

Mulder turns to Scully, astonished and pleased.

"Smokey's got a name," he says, triumphant.

He types several more commands. The words NO INFORMATION AVAILABLE appear.

"Get up from the desk," says a male voice.

The agents look up, startled. Skinner is standing in the doorway.

"Get up and turn the computer off, grab whatever you took or printed out and give it to me!" says the AD. "Let's go, Agents! They're coming."

Mulder and Scully stand and quickly follow Skinner into the corridor. They round a corner—and come face-to-face with Jeffrey Spender, backed by a posse of agents.

Spender eyes Skinner with a faint smirk.

"Assistant Director," he says. "I'll assume you came down to apprehend these agents for unauthorized entry into my office. I'll make sure it's duly noted in the report of their dismissal."

At Syndicate headquarters sometime afterward a depressed-looking Spender enters, sits in front of an ornate-looking desk, and talks to its occupant through a cloud of blue-gray cigarette smoke.

"I've done as you've asked," says Spender. "Mulder's been brought up to his superiors. He and his partner will be processed out of the FBI. I've done as you asked. Now I would like you to do for me."

The Cigarette-Smoking Man takes a slow drag.

"Do for you?" he says.

"I think I'm entitled," says Spender.

"To?"

"The truth. The truth about my mother. She won't tell me."

"Because you won't believe her," says the Cigarette-Smoking Man, evenly. "Maybe you won't

believe me. Maybe it's better not to know."

"I need to know!" insists Spender.

This irritates the Cigarette-Smoking Man.

"You need to show me," he says, cuttingly, "that you're capable of handling the responsibility that comes with this knowledge."

"Don't try me, old man!" shouts Spender.

The Cigarette-Smoking Man rises, shaking with anger, and slaps Spender across the face. Spender recoils, and gasps.

"I gave you responsibility!" says the Cigarette-Smoking Man, furious. "I gave you a position. I gave you the things that you couldn't get yourself! And you can't do the job!"

"Keeping Fox Mulder down is not a job!" replies Spender. "It's your dirty work!"

The Cigarette-Smoking Man slaps Spender across the face once more.

"You pale to Fox Mulder," he says, contemptuously.

At the D.C. gym that day Mulder shoots baskets, alone. Scully enters, carrying a cardboard file box. Mulder greets her unenthusiastically.

"Aren't you curious about 'C.G.B.'?" says his partner.

"What's that?" says Mulder.

"C.G.B. Spender. His name—the Cigarette-Smoking Man."

"What's it stand for?"

"An alias, as far as I can figure. One of hundreds." Mulder turns to face her.

"Scully, you wanna go one on one? We've got nothing but time now that we're on administrative leave."

"Aren't you curious what I've got in the box?" says Scully. "Everything I could find on him."

Mulder stares at the floor.

"Nothing you could ever find would be accurate or credible."

"Maybe," says Scully. "But there's a picture here you'll want to see."

She hands him a black-and-white photo showing two men, apparently arguing. They are the Cigarette-Smoking Man and Bill Mulder, Mulder's father.

"It was taken in 1973," says Scully. "I traced the connection to something they worked on together for twenty-five years at the State Department. A highly classified project. There's more, if you're ready."

Mulder nods. Scully confirms that Cassandra is indeed Jeffrey Spender's mother and the Cigarette-Smoking Man's ex-wife. She says she's also discovered that Cassandra was first abducted on November 27, 1973—the same night as Mulder's sister.

Mulder is rocked by this news. Scully adds that C.G.B. Spender is connected to several noted medical researchers, including Eugene Openshaw, a Nobel Prize winner for early work in genetics. She shows him a picture of Openshaw and tells her partner that he was the man who died in his hospital room before being questioned.

Mulder considers the implications of all this.

"The project is still going on," he says.

In his office, the Cigarette-Smoking Man continues:

"If Mulder hadn't known of his father's history with me," he says, "he was fueled now with names, dates, and certainties. I couldn't stop him any longer. Stop him from learning our sins. His father's, and my own.

"The truth was out there, patently exposed. I had one last hope. One chance to preserve my legacy."

That night Jeffrey Spender stands alone on a D.C. street corner. A black limousine pulls up, and the Cigarette-Smoking Man emerges.

"I waited, like you asked," says Spender, nervously.

"Good. I'm pleased," says the Cigarette-Smoking Man. "I was doubtful after our last meeting."

Spender looks around nervously.

"You have a new job for me?" he asks.

"Yes. I may have been unduly harsh. You deserve a fighting chance. To prove your father wrong."

He pulls an alien stiletto from his pocket.

His son asks what it is.

"A weapon," says the Cigarette-Smoking Man. "A man has infiltrated the group I work with. That's to kill him."

"I don't understand," says Spender, confused.

"He's pretending to be a member of our group, disguising himself as a man he's already killed. You will greet him as that man, engage him in conversation, and put that in the back of his neck. You can do it, Jeffrey."

He opens the limo door for Spender. Spender slides in, studying his weapon with curiosity and horror. At the wheel of the limo is Krycek.

"Watch where you point that," he says.

Shortly afterward Krycek drives the limo to the First Elder's house. Spender gets out, knocks on the door, and faces a man who appears to be the First Elder.

"Sir, my name is Jeffrey Spender," he says. "My father sent me to see you. I have a message from the group."

"They changed their minds?" says the man.

"That's what I'm here about," says Spender.

They enter the living room and sit facing each other.

"What have you to tell me?" asks the man.

"Something I've been entrusted with. It's a name, actually," says Spender. "One that will mean something to you."

He pulls a slip of paper out of his pocket and lets it "accidentally" slip to the floor. The man bends down toward it. Spender pulls out the stiletto and moves to stab the man in the back of the neck—and hesitates. The man reaches up and grabs Spender's throat in a death grip. Frantically, Spender rips the false face off his adversary. At that moment Krycek appears and kills the alien with the stiletto, unhesitatingly.

That night Skinner knocks on the door of Mulder's apartment. Mulder lets him in. Scully is also present. Mulder thanks him for coming to meeting with them against FBI orders.

"You said Cassandra Spender's life is in danger?" says Skinner.

"Her life's been in danger going on thirty years. Just not the way I think it is now," says Mulder,

"In danger from whom?"

"Men who've conducted medical experiments," says Mulder. "On what began as a secret government project, but what is now the most private government enterprise—to develop human-alien hybrids who can survive the viral apocalypse when aliens colonize the Earth."

Skinner asks Mulder if he has proof. Mulder tells him about the documents Scully has found and of the connections between Cassandra, Jeffrey Spender, and the Cigarette-Smoking Man. Skinner asks Scully if she believes Mulder's conclusions. Mulder answers him.

"I know that Agent Scully has her doubts about the purposes of these experiments," he says, "but I also know that she herself knew that she was a test subject when she was abducted four years ago."

"Then why is Cassandra Spender's life in danger and not Scully's?" asks Skinner.

Mulder explains that Cassandra may well be the first human-alien hybrid.

"What I don't understand," says Skinner, "is if she's a success, then why is her life threatened?"

"Because," says Mulder, "the men who created her would rather kill her than let her expose the enterprise."

"She's on twenty-four-hour guard," says Skinner.

"Assigned by Agent Spender?" replies Mulder.

At the First Elder's house, the creature whom Krycek killed is dissolving into a pile of green ooze.

"You've never seen one, have you?" says Krycek. "It's shocking at first—the acceptance of the ideas. Something you thought only children and fools believed in. It undermines your beliefs in yourself and in the world. But then you come to understand."

"Understand what?" says Spender.

"The responsibility this knowledge demands by the men who have it. The great sacrifice. By great men like your father."

"What sacrifice?"

"The sacrifice of your mother."

Krycek explains that the Cigarette-Smoking Man is in charge of the experiments, and that he, not the aliens, was the direct cause of Spender's mother's abductions. The revelation makes Spender furious.

"So I'm protecting her now?" says Spender. "So that the experiments can continue?"

"It's why your father sent you here tonight," says Krycek. "You're protecting the project, Jeff. Making sacrifices. So that you can be a great man, too."

Spender heads for the door. "I'll be my own great man," he scowls.

Says the Cigarette-Smoking Man:

"I've trusted no one. Treachery is the ultimate result of all affairs. Every man believes he has his own good reason. I have little doubt of my son's disloyalty. Certainly he led Mulder and Scully to us. His mother must know by now her central role in the grand plan—that she's as much alien as human. Do you wonder why I've chosen you? You've never betrayed me. And now I need someone to trust."

Diana Fowley has been sitting across from the Cigarette-Smoking Man, listening, all this time. She stands.

"I'll help you," she says. "It's not too late."

AD Skinner enters Cassandra Spender's hospital room and calls her name. She is not there. Jeffrey Spender enters.

"Where's my mother?" he demands.

"You tell me, Agent Spender," says Skinner.

143

"He took her," says Spender, realizing.

"Who?"

Spender walks quickly to the phone and begins to dial.

At Mulder's apartment that night someone is knocking frantically on the front door. Mulder opens it, his partner close behind him. It is Cassandra Spender, nearly hysterical with fear.

"I can't believe I found you!" gasps Cassandra.

"How did you find us?" says Scully. "Cassandra?"

"How'd you get out of your room?" says Mulder.

Says Scully, "How'd you get your clothes?"

Someone begins knocking on the front door. This makes Cassandra even more frantic.

"Oh, Agent Mulder! Agent Scully! You cannot let them find me!"

Cassandra reaches for Mulder's holstered gun. Mulder stops her, but she keeps fighting for it.

"You cannot let them have me! You've got to kill me now!"

She pulls away.

"If you don't kill me, it all starts! There won't be any stopping it! I am the one! You have to shoot me! Please!"

The knocking grows louder, more insistent. Mulder draws his gun—and points it at Cassandra.

"Mulder, what are you doing?" asks Scully.

"Stand away, Scully," says Mulder.

"Mulder! Mulder! We have to protect her!"

Mulder ignores her. He grimaces, aims, and fingers the trigger.

To be continued . . .

BACK STORY/6X11

She has worked with the best: Alfred Hitchcock, William Wyler, Rod Serling. She has done it all: movies, television, theater. She has been a child actor, a leading lady, and an award-winning supporting actress. She has starred in comedies, dramas, horror films.

She cannot get over the public's reaction to her four-episode arc on The X-Files.

"People stop me on the street!" says Veronica Cartwright, over a small salad at a cozy Italian restaurant near her Burbank-area home. "They ask me: 'Are you dead?' 'Are you alive?' 'Were you abducted?' 'Are you crazy?' 'Could you really have been married to that creep who smokes those cigarettes?'"

In all of these outdoor encounters Cartwright responds that she believes Cassandra Spender is telling the truth: that the multiple abductee is indeed a selfless representative of homo sapiens, willing to sacrifice her life to derail a very real alien conspiracy.

She'll also add, with little prompting, the fact that working with the X-Files company ranks with her most interesting career experiences in or out of Hollywood.

"Remember last year?" she says. "The time I was abducted from that bridge? Well, they had me in this wire harness dangling over the special bridge set they built for six hours."

She adds, "But that's not the whole story. Originally, they were going to put me in a special seat for that shot, so I had to go to the special effects place where they could make a—well, anyway, I had to be on all fours on this table while they put Vaseline all over me, wrapped me with bandages, and then covered everything with goop.

"Then I had to wait until it all dried, and they pulled everything off me. In the end, they didn't wind up making the seat. But who cares? Somewhere in Vancouver, there's an exact mold of my ass!"

Cartwright laughs delightedly at her only-in-the-movie-biz story. For their part, many members of the X-Files cast and crew say they've enjoyed working with such an experienced and well-grounded performer.

Indeed, Veronica Cartwright has been a working actress for more than forty years. Born in Bristol, England, the daughter of a soon-to-emigrate engineer and his wife, a nurse, she was brought to Canada as a toddler along with her older sister Angela, who would herself go on to star in Make Room for Daddy and Lost in Space, among many other things.

After two years north of the border the Cartwrights moved to an apartment building in El Segundo, a suburb just south of Los Angeles. "Our building manager used to take calls for a little girl named Whitney Robinson who also lived there," recalls Cartwright. "I can't remember what Whitney's mother's name was, but one day the manager said to my mother: 'Why don't you ask Mrs. Robinson how to go about getting your own daughters into modeling? You can meet a lot of interesting people that way.'

"Whatever possessed my mother to actually do this I have no idea," smiles Cartwright. "But that was the beginning of everything."

At the age of seven Cartwright became a kind of junior spokesmodel for Kellogg's, doing commercials for Corn Flakes, Sugar Smacks, and Rice Krispies. Millions of graying Baby Boomers remember her well as Violet Rutherford, Jerry Mathers's first girlfriend on Leave It To Beaver. Connoisseurs of early TV science fiction know her as the girl with a robot grandmother in "I Sing the Body Electric," a classic 1962 episode of The Twilight Zone written by Ray Bradbury.

In 1961 she started her film career near the top, with a supporting role in The Children's Hour, the second screen adaptation of Lillian Hellman's famous stage play. It was in 1963, however, that Cartwright truly ensured that her image would never vanish from film schools or movie rental shelves: she played Cathy Brenner, the girl presented with a pair of caged lovebirds by Melanie Daniels (Tippi Hedren) to get the horrific ball rolling in Hitchcock's much-analyzed

maniac you'd get wiped out like a bowling pin. Everybody was a mutilated wreck by the time we finished with that.

"But he had a wonderful side, too. I turned thirteen while we were filming; they threw me a big surprise party right on the set. One of my presents was a pair of love birds, and Hitchcock sent me an enormous bouquet of lilacs and tulips. And then he took a piece of white poster board, and drew that famous caricature of his face, and he wrote: 'To The Woman I Love, Veronica—Alfred Hitchcock.' I had it framed. It's hanging in the front hall of our house right now."

Like almost all child stars, Cartwright had difficulty finding work when she grew into her teens. Unlike the great majority, however, she worked through her difficulties, moving back to England in her early twenties to study acting and work in live theater.

Her movie career picked up again in the mid-1970s, with significant roles in films like *Alien, Goin' South, The Right Stuff*, and *Witches of Eastwick*. On television she's played such diverse roles as Ethel Kennedy in the miniseries *Robert Kennedy & His Times* and Marceline Jones, the wife of the mad cult leader, in *Guyana Tragedy: The Story of Jim Jones*. She's gotten considerable notice for guest roles on such contemporary series as *L.A. Law, American Gothic*, and *E.R.*

As for *The X-Files*, she admits to being a relatively late convert to the cult. When she first won the part of Cassandra Spender, she had seen the show only a few times.

"I'd watched it in the beginning, and maybe drifted off a little because I missed an episode or two. But when I got Cassandra they sent me the episodes with Steve Railsback ["Duane Barry" and "Ascension"; 2X05 and 2X06], because there was a connection to my character.

"Then, one of the first days on the set [of "Patient X"; 5X13] Chris took me aside and told me the difference between all the different kinds of aliens. After that, I was hooked. And you know what? So is my sister Angela, and lots of the other people I talk to."

Ⓧ

paean to the cruelty of nature, *The Birds*.

Her memories of the film are vivid, if perhaps slightly different than those of the rest of us. "Hitchcock and I had a special relationship," says Cartwright. "When he learned that I was from Bristol, he told me that the most fabulous wine cellars in the world were in that city and that's where he got all his wine from.

"On the set he'd go around telling dirty jokes all the time. I had no idea what he was talking about, but I'd laugh anyway. I would take him his tea every afternoon at 4:30. Everything would stop while he would sip away.

"He had his wicked side, of course. When we were all on a sort of treadmill device, shooting the scenes where we were running away from the birds, he'd get that thing going faster and faster so that if you didn't run like a

Veronica Cartwright's first appearance as Cassandra Spender was in "Patient X" (5X13).

Ⓧ

For her role in "Two Fathers" and "One Son," Cartwright received an Emmy nomination for Outstanding Guest Actress in a Drama Series. She was nominated in 1998 for the same award for "Patient X" (5X13) and "The Red and the Black" (5X14).

Ⓧ

Cartwright is married to TV director Richard Compton (*Charmed, Babylon 5, Home Improvement*). They have an eight-year-old son.

ONE SON

EPISODE: 6X12
FIRST AIRED: February 14, 1999
EDITOR: Louise A. Innes
WRITTEN BY: Chris Carter & Frank Spotnitz
DIRECTED BY: Rob Bowman

GUEST STARS:
Mitch Pileggi (AD Skinner)
Chris Owens (Special Agent Jeffrey Spender)
Veronica Cartwright (Cassandra Spender)
Mimi Rogers (Agent Diana Fowley)
William B. Davis (The Cigarette-Smoking Man)
Nicholas Lea (Alex Krycek)
Laurie Holden (Marita Covarrubias)
Tom Braidwood (Frohike)
Dean Haglund (Langly)
Bruce Harwood (Byers)
James Pickens, Jr. (AD Kersh)
Don S. Williams (Second Elder)
Al Ruscio (Third Elder)
Frank Ertl (Fourth Elder)
Peter Donat (Young Bill Mulder)
Scott Williamson (CDC Team Leader)
Robert Lipton (Head Surgeon)
Mark Bramhall (Surgical Team Member)
Jo Black-David (Nurse)

PRINCIPAL SETTINGS:
Washington, D.C.; New York City; Arlington, Virginia;
El Rico Air Force Base, West Virginia

Cassandra Spender outlines the real connections between the Syndicate, the warring alien factions, a half century of sinister experiments, and the abductions of Scully and Samantha Mulder. Using her information, the agents reach the end of their long quest—and confront a worldwide apocalypse.

The black-and-white 1973 photograph of C.G.B. Spender and Bill Mulder, seen in the previous episode, reappears. The voice of Fox Mulder is heard. He says:

"Two men: young, idealistic, the fine products of a generation hardened by world war. Two fathers whose paths would converge in a new battle; an invisible war between a silent enemy and a sleeping giant on a scale to dwarf all historical conflicts. A fifty-year war; its killing fields lying in wait for the inevitable global holocaust."

Tongues of flame lick the edges of the photograph; it blackens and burns.

"Theirs was the dawn of Armageddon. And while the world was unaware—unwitting spectators to the hurly-burly of the decades-long struggle between heaven and earth—there were those who prepared for the end. Who measured the size and power of the enemy and faced the choices: to stand and fight, or bow to the will of a fearsome enemy. Or to surrender, to yield and collaborate. To save themselves and stay the enemy's hand. Men who believed that victory was the absence of defeat; and survival the ultimate ideology—no matter what the sacrifice."

It is October 13, 1973. Inside a massive empty hangar stands a small group of men in their forties recognizable as the leaders of the Syndicate. At exactly 10:56 P.M. a blinding light pierces the translucent doors of the structure. They turn and squint into the brightness. The doors open slowly.

The Cigarette-Smoking Man steps forward. He is holding an American flag folded into the traditional triangle shape. He kneels and places it on the ground in front of him. As he does so, twenty or more small gray aliens emerge from the midst of the white light. They array themselves in formation, then pause.

The action from 6X11 resumes: Mulder is a split-second away from shooting Cassandra Spender. As he is about to pull the trigger the front door of his apartment explodes inward. A moon-suited attack team enters, shouting at Mulder, Scully, and Cassandra to lie down on the ground. The intruders blast the area with anticontaminant, then seal it with heavy strips of translucent plastic.

"Who are you?" shouts Mulder.

"We're with the Centers for Disease Control," says the squad leader, his voice muffled by his plastic-windowed helmet. "Remain calm and where you are—for your own good. You're going to be transported to a quarantine facility as soon as we can secure the environment."

"Quarantine for what?" shouts Scully.

"A contagion," says a female squad member. "A contagion of unknown origin."

The woman's voice is badly muffled, but the agents recognize her. She is Diana Fowley.

Later that night Mulder and Scully stand silently under decontamination showers. Afterward, dressed in hospital scrubs, they are scanned for radiation.

"There must be some kind of mistake," says Mulder, deadpan. "I signed up for the aromatherapy treatment."

Unamused, Scully asks the men examining her if anyone will explain what's been happening to them. There is no response. Mulder asks his partner where she thinks they are. Scully guesses that they're at Fort Marlene, a government facility designed for high-risk decontamination and quarantine. Diana Fowley—wearing business clothes now—enters the room.

"I'm going to beg for your forgiveness and understanding and offer my humblest apologies for the way this went down," she says quickly. "I didn't have a lot of choices.

"I owe your neighbors apologies as well. It's going to be some time before they get back in the building. We're still acting on a CDC Level Four quarantine protocol."

"Based on what information?" asks Scully.

"That Cassandra Spender had contracted a highly contagious vectoring organism which produces spontaneous cellular breakdown and combustion.

"She was and remains the only surviving victim of an unspecified medical experiment that killed seven doctors with violent and unexplained burning."

"Who called you?" asks Mulder.

"Agent Spender."

"Where's Cassandra?" asks Scully, alarmed.

"She's isolated. Pending full and satisfactory medical examination."

Scully protests that Cassandra is not contagious and that Fowley's actions are unjustified and suspicious. Brushing aside Mulder's attempts to stop her, she demands to see Cassandra.

"I told you," says Fowley, curtly. "She's isolated."

"Yes. And I am a medical doctor—"

"Who's been suspended indefinitely," says Fowley, "from her position at the FBI."

Scully stands and storms out. A few moments later Scully stands in a locker room, grimly contemplating the shapeless gray garment she's been given to wear. Mulder enters.

"They burned our clothes," says Scully.

"I heard gray is the new black," offers Mulder, helpfully.

Scully turns to her partner, disgusted.

"Mulder, this stinks. And not just because I think that this woman is a . . . well, I think you know what I think that woman is. Agent Spender calling the Centers for Disease Control? Mulder, this is just somebody using their position to stage a high-tech government kidnapping."

"Apparently not," says Mulder. "I just spoke to AD Skinner. He was at the hospital when Cassandra went missing. He heard Spender make the phone call to the CDC."

Scully protests that Cassandra was not sick—in fact, the opposite.

"Then why did she come to my apartment and ask to be killed?" says Mulder.

"Because of everything that had been done to her!" replies Scully, angrily. "Because of the tests, because of the medical experiments, and the implant put in her neck. The same thing that was done to me. She just wants it to stop. I am telling you, they have taken her so it can continue!"

Mulder shakes his head.

"No, it won't continue," he says. "It doesn't have to anymore. She knows what she is, Scully. That's why it's so dangerous for her to be alive—that's why she came to my apartment asking to be killed."

"What is she?" asks Scully.

"I think she's the one, Scully," says Mulder, quietly.

That night at Syndicate headquarters Alex Krycek briefs the remaining leaders on Cassandra's escape. Their doctors had discovered, he says, that she might be the first successful human-alien hybrid.

"That's why the rebels struck," says the Fourth Elder. "They wanted to kill her."

"They killed everyone *but* her," says Krycek, scornfully. "They struck to keep her alive. To keep us from killing her."

"What do the rebels want?" asks the Second Elder.

"To destroy us," says the Fourth Elder. "They know that when the aliens learn of Cassandra, colonization will begin."

"We must destroy Cassandra," says the Third Elder.

The Cigarette-Smoking Man steps forward.

"No," he says. "Let colonization begin. We must turn over Cassandra. Save ourselves."

"Bill Mulder was against this!" says the Third Elder. "He said this would be our tragic mistake."

"Bill Mulder sacrificed his only daughter because he knew this day would arrive," says the Cigarette-Smoking Man. "What choice have we, if we want to see our families survive? If we want to see those who we sacrificed return to us?"

At Fort Marlene that evening Mulder—wearing clothing definitely not his own—explores a deserted corridor. A middle-aged female nurse appears.

"Oh, ma'am!" says Mulder. "These shoes, they're two sizes too small. I was wondering if I could get a—"

The nurse looks at Mulder. Then she turns and disappears through a doorway.

"—pair that fit."

Mulder hobbles down the corridor. He spots a woman, dressed in a hospital gown, at the far end. She turns and walks quickly down another corridor. Mulder follows. He hears the sound of a door closing, retraces his steps, and enters a storage room. The woman cowers at the far end. It is Marita Covarrubias, the UN official last seen in "The Red and the Black" (5X14). She is emaciated, agitated, and obviously very ill.

"NO, IT WON'T CONTINUE. IT DOESN'T HAVE TO ANYMORE. SHE KNOWS WHAT SHE IS, SCULLY. THAT'S WHY IT'S SO DANGEROUS FOR HER TO BE ALIVE—THAT'S WHY SHE CAME TO MY APARTMENT ASKING TO BE KILLED."—Mulder

"I can't be seen here," she whispers. "If they catch me with you, they'll kill me this time."

Mulder approaches the terrified woman. He examines several scars on her arms, wrists, and neck.

"Who?" he says.

"The Smoking Man. And his group"

"What have they done to you?"

"Tests. Terrible, terrible tests."

"Like the tests on Cassandra Spender?"

"No."

Marita tells Mulder that unlike Cassandra, she was infected with the alien virus—the black oil—as part of a project to develop a vaccine against it.

"Secret from the alien colonists," says Mulder, to Marita's anguished nod. "The hybrid program was in cooperation with the aliens, but the conspirators never intended to succeed. To finish the work."

"They were buying time," whispers Marita.

"To make a vaccine. To build a weapon," says Mulder.

"But Cassandra Spender happened," says Marita.

"She's the first, isn't she?" says Mulder. "She's the first successful alien-human hybrid."

"If she is, and the aliens learn a hybrid exists, colonization of the planet will begin. There's no stopping it."

In another part of the Fort Marlene facility Cassandra Spender lies on a hospital bed in the center of a high-tech operating room. Jeffrey Spender enters, with Diana Fowley close behind. He moves quickly to his mother's bedside. Cassandra greets him worriedly.

"I feel fine," she says. "Why are they keeping me here?"

"*I'm* keeping you here," says Spender. "Because you're safe here."

"Safe from who?"

"You know. From my father."

Cassandra frowns and turns away.

"You can't keep me safe from him," she says.

"I can, Mom. And I'm going to. There won't be any more tests on you."

"You don't understand," says Cassandra. "You don't understand about me. You don't understand what will happen, what will happen to you if they find me out. *You've got to let me go.*"

"They'll just hurt you, Mom."

She clasps his arm tightly.

"Yes! You must let them!" she says. "Or everyone dies. *Everyone.*"

Without another word Spender turns to leave. Crying out in fear and frustration, Cassandra calls after him.

"Please, Jeffrey! Please!" she begs.

Her son does not respond.

The next day at the Lone Gunmen's office Frohike responds to an insistent buzzing noise by unlocking the

"I CAME HERE LOOKING. EVIDENCE THAT YOU'D LIED TO ME THAT YOU HAD LOYALTIES OTHER THAN TO ME OR THE X-FILES."
—Mulder

"NOTHING COULD BE FURTHER FROM THE TRUTH, FOX. NOTHING."
—Agent Diana Fowley

dozen or so locks that secure the front door. It is Mulder; he tells Frohike that he's responding to an urgent call from Scully. She is waiting for him inside, along with Langly and Byers.

"I'll ask you to hear me out before you launch any objection," Scully tells her partner. "Mulder, I asked them to pull up everything they could on Diana Fowley."

"I don't have time for this," he replies, frowning.

"Mulder, she's playing you for a fool."

"I know her, Scully. You don't."

"You knew her," says Scully. "You don't anymore. I think we can prove it to you."

With the help of the three Gunmen, Scully briefs Mulder on Fowley's recent history: Having joined the FBI's Foreign Counterterrorism Unit in 1991, she spent seven years in Europe—without leaving any trace of her activities in FBI files. Travel records pulled from airline manifests purged from her FBI records show extensive movement through Western Europe, including almost weekly travel back and forth to Tunisia.

Logs of the Mutual UFO Network—MUFON— indicate that the agent had paid visits to every European chapter, collecting data on female abductees.

"So she's collecting data. Big deal," scoffs Mulder.

"Or hiding it," says Scully.

"Scully, you're reaching."

"Mulder, when I was abducted a chip was put in my neck. When I happened on a MUFON group filled with women who'd had the same experience—"

"So you're suggesting that Diana is monitoring these abductees? Monitoring these tests?"

Scully frowns, pauses, and tries again.

"You tell me that Cassandra Spender is the critical test subject," she says, carefully. "The one who can prove everything and, yet, who is watching over her? Mulder, I can prove what you're saying or I can disprove it. But not when Diana Fowley is keeping us from even seeing her.

"Mulder, ask yourself why there is no information whatsoever on Special Agent Diana Fowley! Why she would suddenly happen into your life when you are closer than ever to the truth. I mean, you ask me to trust no one, and yet you trust her on simple faith."

"Because you've given me no reason here to do otherwise," says Mulder, brusquely.

Scully turns away.

"Well, then, I can't help you anymore," she says, heading for the exit.

Mulder turns to face her.

"Scully, you're making this personal," he says.

"Because it *is* personal, Mulder," says Scully, forcefully. "Because without the FBI, personal interest is all that I have. And if you take that away, there is no reason to continue."

At the Watergate Apartments at 7:04 that evening, Mulder knocks on an apartment door.

"Diana?" he says.

No answer. He pulls a lock pick from his pocket and lets himself in. He pulls out his flashlight, scans the living room, then searches the drawers of Fowley's desk and bedroom bureau. He hears a noise behind him— somebody else opening the front door—and conceals himself in the bedroom, gun drawn. A tall figure—the Cigarette-Smoking Man—enters the bedroom and finds himself staring into the barrel of Mulder's automatic.

"Sorry. Nobody home," says Mulder. "What are you doing here?"

The Cigarette-Smoking Man eyes Mulder with a hint of a smirk.

"The door was open. I came in," he says, coolly.

"Interesting company you keep," says Mulder.

"No more interesting than your apparent lingerie fetish," says the Cigarette-Smoking Man.

Mulder smiles thinly and shakes his head—then grabs the Cigarette-Smoking Man by the collar and pushes him backward into a chair.

"You feeling smug, C.G.B.?" he says. "Yeah, I know your name. I know your game and I got nothing to lose."

"I remember looking at you over a gun barrel once before, Agent Mulder," says the Cigarette-Smoking Man. "You couldn't pull the trigger then. What makes you think you can do it now?"

Mulder cocks his gun. The Cigarette-Smoking Man cringes slightly.

"I came here looking for my son," he says quickly. "Because he's betrayed me. He's chosen the wrong side. He's chosen to believe in your cause."

"That presumes my cause is wrong," says Mulder.

"Oh, it is, Agent Mulder. It is!"

Mulder tells the Cigarette-Smoking Man angrily that it wasn't he who's been using innocent women as lab rats—or creating a race of human slaves so that the collaborators with alien invaders will survive. The Cigarette-Smoking Man smiles.

"You find that funny?" demands Mulder, furious.

"Your father was against it, too. Back in '73. The lone dissenter. But he came to his senses. And gave up your sister, Samantha—"

"He didn't give up my sister! He was forced to! You made him do it!"

"You're wrong, Agent Mulder," says the Cigarette-Smoking Man, mockingly. "I can't tell you how wrong you are. How wrong you've always been."

Mulder slowly lowers the pistol to his side. The Cigarette-Smoking Man continues.

"We had agreed to cooperate with the alien colonists," says the Cigarette-Smoking Man, "by a majority vote taken by the group your father and I worked for. A group that came together at the State Department on a project dating back to 1947. To

151

Roswell. The vote changed that, though. It changed everything. We no longer cleaved to any government agency. We now operated privately, on our own project. That was your father's objection—that we would align ourselves with the alien colonists."

"Toward your own selfish end," says Mulder.

"We forestalled an alien invasion!" says the Cigarette-Smoking Man, vehemently.

"No, no, no. You only managed to postpone it."

"We saved billions of lives!"

"You put those lives on hold so that you alone could survive!"

"No, Agent Mulder," says the Cigarette-Smoking Man. "So *you* could. It's exactly what your father failed to realize. He railed at us and our plans even as the process had begun. While the group had agreed to the most painful sacrifices, sacrifices

remove an alien fetus—first seen in "The Erlenmeyer Flask," 1X23—from a cryogenic transport container into a vat of liquid nitrogen.

"You see," says the Cigarette-Smoking Man, forcefully, "the alien fetus gave us the alien genome: the DNA with which we could make a human hybrid. A new race, Agent Mulder! An alien-human hybrid who could survive the holocaust! So *you* could survive and live to see your sister!"

Overwhelmed, Mulder turns away. He slumps into a chair at the other end of the room.

"And now you've succeeded?" he asks.

"Quite in spite of ourselves," says the Cigarette-Smoking Man. "The plan was to stall, and resist."

"To work secretly on a vaccine," says Mulder.

"That was your father's idea. To use the alien DNA to make a vaccine. To save everyone. The world. It's the

"I KNOW WHERE THEY'RE TAKING HER. I KNOW HOW THEY'RE TAKING HER. YOU'VE GOT TO TRUST ME, JEFFREY."
—Marita Covarrubias

that no one else would be asked to make."

"You gave them your children!" says Mulder, enraged. "You gave them your wife! You sent them away like they were things! You sent them to be tested on!"

"We sent them away so they would come back to us!" says the Cigarette-Smoking Man. "Don't you see?"

"You're a liar," says Mulder, quietly. "My sister wasn't taken from any hangar. She was abducted from our home, right in front of me."

"Because your father was late to understand the necessity! That he, too, must give up one of his children to the alien colonists! The aliens insisted on it. It was the only way they would give us the one thing that we needed. The one thing without which we could not proceed."

In 1973 moon-suited scientists at Fort Marlene

reason he went along. But it's too late now. Colonization is going to begin.

"There will be a sequence of events. A state of emergency will be declared, because of a massive outbreak of the alien virus, delivered by bees. Then the takeover will begin. I have only to hand over Cassandra."

"You can't do that," says Mulder.

"Our hand's been forced," says the Cigarette-Smoking Man. "The Faceless Rebels leave us no choice."

Mulder stands, his rage renewed.

"Stop it now or I will stop it," he says.

"No, Agent Mulder. You won't stop it. Not if you want to see your sister again."

Mulder points the gun at his adversary's face.

"You stop it or everyone dies."

"No. I live. You live—to see your sister return."

The Cigarette-Smoking Man stands and lights a cigarette.

"It's what your father realized. It's what you'll realize as your father's son. Or die in vain, with the rest of the world."

Mulder says nothing. The Cigarette-Smoking Man hands him a slip of paper.

"Save her," he whispers. "Save yourself."

At the abandoned Syndicate headquarters that night, Krycek tells a shocked Jeffrey Spender that the leaders of the conspiracy have fled.

"Where did they go?" asks Spender.

"To West Virginia," says Krycek. "They'll be transported by the colonists and begin medical preparations to receive the hybrid genes. Except for your father. He's gone to get your mother."

"Nothing could be further from the truth, Fox," says Fowley. "Nothing."

"I didn't find anything, Diana," he replies. "But something found me."

"What?"

"Fate. Destiny. Whatever it's called when the choices you thought you had in life are already made."

Fowley walks over to Mulder, kneels in front of him, and takes his hands.

"Fox, what happened here?" she asks.

"You were being paid a visit by Young Jeffrey Spender's father. The Cigarette-Smoking Man came looking for his son, who has now taken up the futile cause that used to be mine. Against his father."

"Why futile?"

"Because there's nothing to be done. And at some point you just have to accept that the only way those

Spender protests that Cassandra is under his protection. Krycek scoffs at this.

"She's probably being prepared as we speak, Jeffrey," he says.

At Fort Marlene Cassandra Spender is still in her bed. A surgical team enters and—over her cries of anger and defiance—holds her down and tranquilizes her into semi-consciousness. The Cigarette-Smoking Man enters the room. Cassandra sees him.

"The biggest bastard of all," she murmurs.

In Washington that night Diana Fowley enters her Watergate apartment—to find Mulder seated in the living room, waiting for her.

"Fox? What are you doing?" she asks.

"Nothing. Not a damn thing," says Mulder. "I came here looking. Evidence that you'd lied to me. That you had loyalties other than to me or the X-Files."

you love are going to survive is if you give up."

Diana's hand finds the piece of paper that Mulder took from the Cigarette-Smoking Man. It reads:

EL RICO AIR FORCE BASE.

"That's where it all begins," says Mulder. "That's where we need to be if we want to survive it."

Diana shakes her head and kisses Mulder tenderly. They embrace. A tear runs down Fowley's cheek.

At Fort Marlene at 10:13 that evening, Spender bursts into his mother's room to find her gone. He is stunned and furious.

"Please help me," says a female voice behind him. "They're going to leave me here!"

It is Marita, even more distressed and ill than before. She tells Spender that the facility is being deserted and pleads with him to take her with him.

"I know you! I can help you!" she begs.

153

"You can't help me," says Spender, backing away in disgust.

"I know where they're taking her," says Covarrubias. "I know how they're taking her."

Spender turns and faces her, horrified.

"You've got to trust me, Jeffrey," she whispers.

In an isolation room nearby the head surgeon dons a protective hood and carefully removes an alien fetus from its cryogenic container. A woman—the middle-aged nurse whom Mulder had encountered earlier—opens the door to the room. The surgeon frantically shouts at her to leave. She doesn't. He turns back to the container.

The nurse comes up behind him, rips off his headgear, and begins to strangle him. The surgeon rips at the nurse's face, revealing a faceless alien underneath. A few moments later the head surgeon calmly exits the room.

Mulder dials Scully's cell phone from Fowley's

move forward. At that moment Scully drives her sedan—with Mulder sitting alongside her—onto the dirt road paralleling the track. They see the train approaching. Mulder tells her to turn around. She skids into the opposite direction and races alongside, then ahead of, the train. She swerves her car onto the tracks and stops. The agents get out, draw their weapons, and fire again and again at the locomotive. The bullets bounce off.

Inside the train a surgical team is tending to Cassandra, who is unconscious.

"What the hell is that?" asks the surgeon, alarmed.

The locomotive plows into Scully's car—and with an awful grinding of metal pushes it ahead and off the tracks. Mulder and Scully leap for their lives. The train rolls on.

Inside the medical car the lights flicker off and on. The Cigarette-Smoking Man regards all this calmly. At the other end of the car stands the head surgeon—or

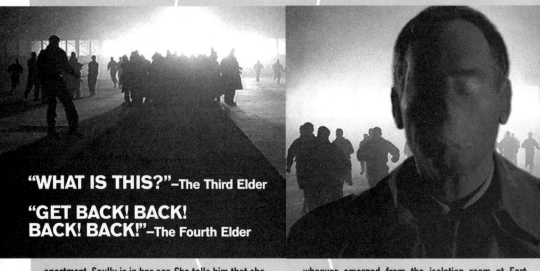

"WHAT IS THIS?"–The Third Elder

"GET BACK! BACK! BACK! BACK!"–The Fourth Elder

apartment. Scully is in her car. She tells him that she knows where Cassandra's being taken, and will pick him up and take him there.

"Cassandra's gone, Scully," says Mulder. "It's no use."

"Mulder, I'm going there whether you're coming or not."

"Going where?"

"To the Potomac Yards. They're transporting her by train car."

"Who gave you this information?"

"Agent Spender called me."

Mulder abruptly clicks off. He turns to Fowley.

"I'm going to send you on ahead," he says. "This may be our last chance to stop them."

At the Potomac Yards later that night, the Syndicate rail car is hooked to a locomotive. The train begins to

whoever emerged from the isolation room at Fort Marlene.

At El Rico Air Force Base at 11:21 P.M., the members of the Syndicate, with their families, file into the huge hangar. Carrying suitcases, they walk steadily toward the giant doors.

At the Potomac Yards Mulder and Scully stand beside their wrecked car. Another sedan pulls up. Inside is AD Skinner.

"You going to tell me what the hell's going on?" Skinner asks.

"Our lives are in danger," says Mulder. "We don't have much time."

"Why couldn't you tell me that over the phone?"

"If somebody overheard us, it might create mass panic."

"Mass panic? Over what?"

"El Rico Air Base," says Mulder, getting into the car. Scully also gets in. They speed off.

Inside the hangar a military ambulance drives toward the assembled Syndicate members, and stops. Cassandra Spender, strapped to a gurney, is unloaded carefully. Supervising this is the Cigarette-Smoking Man. The Elders approach him. He tells them that shots were fired at the train.

"By whom?" asks the Fourth Elder, nervously.

"I don't know," says the Cigarette-Smoking Man, scanning the crowd. "We have people missing. Where's Alex Krycek?"

Krycek is at Fort Marlene, walking quickly through the nearly deserted facility. Dressed in protective garb, he enters the isolation room and sees the head surgeon, dead, his face flash-frozen into a grotesque mask. He rushes past him to the cryogenic container. It is empty; the alien fetus gone. Krycek rips off his headgear and screams in frustration and rage.

A short time later Krycek moves quickly toward the exit and is flagged down by Jeffrey Spender.

"I'm trying to get out of here," says the agent, urgently.

"What are you talking about?" asks Krycek.

"We're trying to get past security. They won't recognize my authority to remove a patient."

Krycek looks past Spender. Behind him cowers Marita—his former lover in "Patient X" (5X13).

"My father did this to her," says Spender. "She wants to tell her story."

Krycek eyes him with contempt.

"You sorry sonuvabitch," he says. "You don't get it, do you? It's all going to hell. The rebels are going to win. They took it."

"They took what?" demands Spender, uncomprehending.

Inside the giant hangar a sedan pulls to a stop and Diana Fowley gets out. She sees the Cigarette-Smoking Man. He sees her. They walk slowly toward each other.

As they reach each other a brilliant white light penetrates the hangar doors. The Syndicate leaders and their families stare into the brightness.

"Who sent the communication?" asks the Third Elder.

"No one," says the Fourth Elder.

The Cigarette-Smoking Man and Diana edge away from the main group, then run for their car. Alien figures emerge from the light and walk toward the humans. They are not gray aliens.

"What is this?" asks the Third Elder.

"Get back! Back! Back! Back!" shouts the Fourth elder, terrified.

Panicked, the humans try to run away. Dozens of faceless aliens, brandishing their fire weapons, pour through the open hangar door. The head surgeon turns, faces the fleeing men, women, and children, and

morphs into a faceless alien. The aliens surround their victims.

The humans begin to scream.

Sometime later AD Kersh sits at his desk, paging through color photos of horribly charred corpses.

"The way these people died," he says, swallowing hard. "The loss of life here—it is beyond words. I can't imagine how it must be for you, losing your mother."

"Yes, sir," says Jeffrey Spender, softly. "But that's not why I asked for this meeting."

Spender is sitting across from Kersh. Also present are Skinner, Mulder, and Scully.

"Why did you ask for it?" asks Kersh.

"Because I'm responsible for the deaths of those people at the air base hangar in no small way," says Spender. "I certainly didn't prevent them."

"I can assume, then," says Kersh, "that you can explain how they died, because I've yet to hear any explanation."

"Agent Mulder can explain it," says Spender. "I think Agent Scully to an extent. They might have even prevented what you see in those photos."

"Agents Scully and Mulder have been suspended from the FBI—" says Kersh, harshly.

"Also my doing," says Spender. "And my mistake."

"I would ask—"

"I'd ask, sir, before you tell me that it's not my business, you do everything you can to get them back on the X-Files. Far worse can happen. And it will."

Spender stands and prepares to leave.

"Where are you going?" asks Kersh.

"To pack up my office," says Spender.

Spender exits. Kersh leans forward and eyes Mulder and Scully angrily.

"You have answers *now?*" he says. "Why didn't I hear about those answers before?"

"I've had answers for years," says Mulder, calmly.

"Then why didn't we hear about them?"

"No one would ever listen."

"Who burned those people?"

"They burned themselves," says Mulder. "With a choice made long ago, by a conspiracy of men who thought they could sleep with the enemy. Only to awaken another enemy."

"What the hell does that mean?"

"It means that the future is here. And all bets are off."

Kersh turns to Mulder's partner.

"Agent Scully, make some sense," he orders.

"Sir, I wouldn't bet against him," she says.

In the X-Files office the Cigarette-Smoking Man sits at Mulder's old desk, gazing at the photograph of himself with Bill Mulder. Spender enters.

"Get out of here," says Spender.

The Cigarette-Smoking Man does not move.

"This picture you have," says the older man. "I

haven't seen it since you were born. You probably don't even know who the other man is."

"I don't care. Get out."

"It's Bill Mulder," says the Cigarette-Smoking Man. "Fox Mulder's father. Isn't that something?

"He was a good man. A friend of mine, who betrayed me in the end."

Spender stares at his father.

"I know more than enough about your past," he says. "Enough to hate you."

The Cigarette-Smoking Man turns away. He puts the photo down and takes Spender's pistol from the desk drawer.

"Your mother was right," he says. "I'd come here hoping otherwise. Hoping my son would honor me. Like Bill Mulder's son."

The Cigarette-Smoking Man aims the gun at the young man standing across from him. A shot rings out. A few seconds later the Cigarette-Smoking Man emerges from the office, puts the photo carefully into his coat pocket, and walks away.

BACK STORY /6X12

An excellent case can be made that "Two Fathers" and "One Son" are the most important, revelatory, and shockingly unexpected episodes in X-Files history.

In the relatively short term, they bring to a definitive close Mulder and Scully's estrangement from the FBI's X-Files and Walter Skinner; reveal Cassandra Spender's relationship with the Cigarette-Smoking Man and the alien colonization project; and draw the final curtain—at least as final a curtain as is ever drawn on The X-Files—on the fatally conflicted FBI agent Jeffrey Spender.

In the very long term, 6X11 and 6X12 bring to an end the Shadowy Syndicate and the conspiracies that formed the basis of its existence, as well as much of the complex mythology that has helped to drive the hit series since Season One.

As a bonus, the two-parter also has an important relationship to the X-Files movie and the quibbles of some hard-core fans who rushed to see it in June 1998.

"I think if there was any trouble with the movie," explains Chris Carter, "it was that we promised so much that we didn't deliver all of it. I think we wanted to deliver a lot, and all at once, in these two episodes."

"I think we ran into a problem," says executive producer Frank Spotnitz, cowriter with Carter on the movie as well as on 6X11 and 6X12, "when they advertised the movie with the tagline 'The Truth Is Revealed.' I didn't object, but it crossed my mind then what a dangerous idea that was to say, because everybody's idea of the truth is a different thing. To my mind, the movie delivered the truth about what was going on in the conspiracy. But

it wasn't the truth that a lot of other people were thinking the movie was going to reveal."

Carter and Spotnitz reveal now that the plan to eliminate the Syndicate—and relaunch the series in a fresh mythological direction, beginning with the two-parter and culminating in the season-ending "Biogenesis" (6X22)—was hatched in late September 1998.

Originally, they add, much of the story was to be told in flashback: with several important scenes (only a fraction of which survive in the final cut) set in the early 1970s and peopled with younger versions of Bill Mulder, the Cigarette-Smoking Man, Dr. Openshaw, the Elders, and others.

"It didn't work on several levels," says Spotnitz. So the writers decided to give the Cigarette-Smoking Man a narrative monologue instead, which was filmed and edited under classic X-Files levels of extreme last-minute pressure. "I think things got a little dense from time," comments 6X12 director Rob Bowman, "but all in all I think Chris and Frank did a wonderful job getting it all to tie together."

Most insiders rank the scenes shot at "El Rico Air Force Base" as among the most powerful and awe-inspiring of the season. They were filmed inside a real gargantuan hangar: the largest freestanding wooden-framed structure in the world. Located at a decommissioned Marine Corps helicopter base in Tustin, south of Los Angeles, the hangar is more than a thousand feet long and 240 feet from floor to ceiling. Built in the 1920s to shelter nine or more tethered U.S. Navy blimps, it nearly swallowed up whole the seventy-five-plus members of the X-Files crew, who managed to fill only a small corner.

Occupying even less space were the dozen or so young girls, dressed in form-fitting costumes and alien masks, who played the small gray aliens in the 1973 flashbacks. "They were great," recalls Rob Bowman, smiling. "It was freezing cold outside, where they all had to start. The hangar doors didn't open very quickly, so they waited in their coats and sweaters with their mommies and daddies. When we yelled 'action' they peeled off all their outer layers, handed them to their parents, and ran inside."

At another point unchaperoned adult actors, playing the faceless alien rebels in 1999, retraced their steps. They were made faceless by special effects makeup supervisor John Vulich after consultations with Vancouver-based makeup wizard Toby Lindala, who created the unique effect during Season Five. The Close Encounter-ish light display that marked both sets of aliens' entrances was created in situ, then enhanced by special effects producer Bill Millar in postproduction.

Second place on the Most Memorable Location list goes to the open-air rail yard where scenes for both 6X11 and 6X12 were filmed. Located in Wilmington, a stark industrial district—especially ominous after dark—near Los Angeles Harbor, its sidings were filled for the occasion with railroad cars completely re-sided and repainted (under the supervision of production designer Corey Kaplan) to appear identical to the cars first established in "Nisei" (3X09). The unfortunate sedan hastily abandoned by Mulder and Scully, then crunched by an onrushing locomotive, was a water-damaged Ford LTD donated by the car company and prepared by transportation department mechanic Kelly Padovic—who removed the engine and drivetrain—for crunching. The bullets that Mulder and Scully fire ineffectually at the engineer's cab were computer-generated by Bill Millar and his helpers.

More than any other X-Files episodes this season, "Two Fathers"/"One Son" made extreme demands on department makeup head Cheri Montesanto-Medcalf and her crew. In addition to "de-aging" the numerous flashbacked Syndicate members with strategically applied highlights and shading, wrinkle-erasing bits of adhesive tape, even a prosthetic device or two, she also had to "burn" Dr. Openshaw in 6X11 and "freeze" the Head Surgeon in 6X12.

Says Montesanto-Medcalf: "For the burns we used a combination of gelatin, coloring, and latex 'tissue.' I remember thinking as I did it: 'Is this too much?' Because it looked gross. I'd never gone so far on any other TV show. But they loved it. They got in so close to it when they framed the shots. I'm proud of that."

To create the frozen Head Surgeon, Montesanto-Medcalf initially gave the actor's face a blue makeup tinge, then carefully glued on "icicles" carved out of blocks of silicon.

"The funny thing about that one," she recalls, "was that when we were doing it the guy kept leaving my chair to 'blow his nose' or 'get a Tylenol.' But I knew he was actually going out to smoke. I could smell the cigarettes on him. So one time, after he'd been gone a long while, I told him: 'Oh, by the way, don't smoke with that stuff on your face. It's flammable.'"

Other notable inspirations, improvisations, and frustrations:

To equip the operating theaters in the rail car and inside "Fort Marlene," set decorator Tim Stepeck made a pilgrimage to a local high-tech medical equipment firm—and was pleasantly stunned when its owners and employers immediately stopped virtually their entire design and production activities to help their favorite TV series. For the scenes in which supposed Syndicate members are revealed to be alien rebels, John Vulich applied two complete masks—one on top of the other, separated by a layer of gelatin—to each appropriate actor.

To get the 1973 photo of the Cigarette-Smoking Man and Bill Mulder to burn just right—slowly and from the edges inward—producer Paul Rabwin and his "insert" camera crew went through fifteen takes, fifteen color photographs, and uncounted applications of kerosene and/or fire retardant.

In the final analysis, of course, the two-parter will not be primarily remembered for the feats of X-Files crew members—or even its actors and writers—but for the epochal way it moved the mythology and series forward, revealing solid truths that many loyal viewers had despaired of ever discovering.

Concludes Frank Spotnitz: "There was an awful lot we wanted to accomplish—a lot of questions we wanted to answer—at the same time we were creating two entertaining episodes. The truth is, unfortunately, that there have been so many questions raised in the course of the series that not all of them will be answered to everyone's satisfaction. But by and large, I think we delivered what we promised."

Although the train carrying the Cigarette-Smoking Man and Cassandra Spender near the conclusion of "One Son" appears to be traveling at high speed, in reality it never got above eight miles per hour—the speed limit in the rail yard used for filming. The illusion was created with sound effects; music; clever camera angles and quick cutting.

The mammoth blimp hangar used in 6X11 and 6X12 should be familiar to West Coast X-philes and others: It was the venue for the Los Angeles X-Files Expo, held in March 1998.

Second-unit production manager Harry Bring is a TV industry veteran whose resume includes stints on Northern Exposure, Models, Inc., and Melrose Place.

Actress Jo Black-David, who played the murderous nurse in "One Son," was casting director Rick Millikan's high school drama teacher.

"One Son" marks Agent Jeffrey Spender's—and actor Chris Owens's—last appearance on The X-Files for the foreseeable future. Owens recalls fondly how William B. Davis, playing the Cigarette-Smoking Man, became upset when it came time to film Spender's final scene. "Bill said, 'I don't want to shoot you! I enjoy working with you!'" says Owens. Then he adds, "Of course, he didn't have any trouble slapping me."

The Emmy Award for Outstanding Makeup for a Series went to Cheri Montesanto-Medcalf, Laverne Basham, John Vulich, Kevin Westmore, Greg Funk, John Wheaton, Mark Shostrom, Rick Stratton, Jake Garber, Craig Reardon, Fionah Cush, Steve LaPorte, Kevin Haney, Jane Aull, Peri Sorel, Jeanne Van Phue, and Julie Socash for their work on "Two Fathers"/"One Son."

6⊗13

ARCADIA

Residents of an upscale,
uptight suburb are disappearing
without a trace. Mulder and Scully go undercover—as a "typical" married couple—to
investigate.

EPISODE: 6X13
FIRST AIRED: March 7, 1999
EDITOR: Heather MacDougall
WRITTEN BY: Daniel Arkin
DIRECTED BY: Michael Watkins

GUEST STARS:
Peter White (Gene Gogolak)
Abraham Benrubi (Big Mike)
Tom Gallop (Win Shroeder)
Marni McPhail (Cami Shroeder)
Debra Christofferson (Pat Verlander)
Tim Bagly (Gordy)
Tom Virtue (Dave Kline)
Juliana Donald (Nancy Kline)
Mark Matthias (Mover)

PRINCIPAL SETTING:
Northern San Diego County, California

At "The Falls at Arcadia," an immaculate gated community, a fortyish man named Dave Kline pulls his SUV up to the front entrance, stops, and punches in his access code. The gates swing open.

"Welcome home, Mr. Kline," says a computerized female voice.

Kline drives past a series of good-sized, immaculately kept, nearly identical split-levels. He parks in his driveway, gets out, and opens his pristine white mailbox. To his surprise, it is covered with fresh wet paint.

"Oops! Did you get some on you, Dave?" says a thirty-fiveish man—whose name is Win Shroeder—standing nearby, holding a paint can and brush.

"Didn't want you to get fined! Just trying to be neighborly. Gotta be up to code!"

Kline stalks inside his house. The smugly smiling Shroeder ambles over to touch up his neighbor's fingerprints.

A few moments later Kline angrily flings his mail—including a largish manila envelope—onto the kitchen counter. His wife, Nancy, is already in the kitchen, calmly tending to her flower arrangement.

"Shroeder's out there painting our mailbox!" shouts Kline. "You know what I'm gonna do? I'm gonna paint the whole damn house pink—forget about the mailbox, huh? I'm gonna make the whole damn place look like you won it selling cosmetics. How about that, huh! That'll show these Nazis!"

Nancy Kline smiles indulgently.

"Honey, would you just calm down?" she says. "Rules are rules."

"They're repainting our mailbox because it's desert sienna instead of desert sage! I mean, this guy is a freakin' weirdo."

"Honey, what about that package?" asks Nancy.

Dave opens the envelope, which has no return address. Inside is a whirligig: a painted plywood yard sculpture. When the wind spins the propeller on one end, a little man chops wood with an ax on the other. It's more tasteful than a pink plastic flamingo, but not by much.

"Boy," says Nancy, laughing. "The neighbors would really hate that."

Her husband's eyes light up immediately.

That night the whirligig—attached to a post on the Klines' front porch—is chopping noisily away in a steady breeze. In the upstairs bedroom, Dave and Nancy sleep soundly. The chopping noise stops. Dave awakes, reacting to the sudden silence. So does Nancy. They both hear a faint creak of floorboards.

"Stay here," says Dave to his wife, getting out of bed.

He snatches a bowling trophy off a dresser, holding it like a club, and creeps cautiously downstairs. There are large bloody footprints, leading to the kitchen, on the white pile carpet. He enters the breakfast nook, hears something behind him, and turns to see a hulking black mass. He screams in horror. There is a crash, then another. Then another.

"Dave? Honey?" says Nancy, terrified.

She cowers in her bed. The entire house shakes with the impact of something massive crashing clumsily up the stairs. The water in a glass on her bedstand ripples with each step. Her gruesome screams rend the night air.

Seven months later, a pudgy, sweet-faced woman holding a huge gift basket waits anxiously in front of the Klines' house. A small moving van, followed by a spanking-new minivan, pulls up and stops.

Mulder and Scully get out of the minivan: he wearing a pink alligator shirt and Dockers and she clad in the height of high-end mail-order fashion. Mulder gazes at the house, hands on hips, and smiles.

"Wow! Take a look at this!" says Mulder. "Honey? What do you think? Is this place us or what?"

Scully smiles gamely. The woman thrusts the gift basket into her arms.

"You must be the Petries! Hi!" she bubbles. "Welcome to the Falls!"

"I'm Rob," says Mulder. "And this is my lovely wife, Laura."

"Rob and Laura Petrie," says the woman.

"We pronounce it 'Pee-tree,' actually," says Scully.

"Like the dish," says Mulder.

"Oh," says the woman, confused. "Well. It's so nice to meet you. I'm Pat Verlander. I live six doors down. I'm the neighborhood Welcome Wagon!"

Smiles and handshakes all around. A hint of a frown crosses Pat's face.

"I really must say," she says, worriedly, "it's already ten after five. I don't think you're going to make it."

"I'm sorry?" says Scully.

"The six o'clock cutoff? All move-ins are required to be completed by six P.M."

Mulder and Scully stare at her blankly.

"It's in the CC and Rs," she says, her smile fading. "It's one of our rules."

A few moments later Mulder and Scully cross the threshold of their new home. Pat trails after them, urging the moving men to move faster. She approaches Mulder and asks him what he does for a living.

"I work mostly at home," says Mulder.

He gives Scully an affectionate hug.

"Which is great for Laura," he adds, "because she gets me all to herself."

Mulder beams at Scully. Scully manages to avoid his eyes.

"This place really is immaculate, Pat," Scully says. "I wouldn't mind sending a thank-you note to the previous owners."

"Oh, that's sweet. Um, good," says Pat, nervously.

She dashes out of the house and joins a growing crowd of smiling, Stepfordian neighbors—all eagerly pitching in to move the contents of the moving van into the house. Their leader joins the flabbergasted Mulder and Scully in the driveway.

"Rob and Laura Petrie?" he chirps.

"Pee-tree," says Scully.

"Win Shroeder—next-door neighbor. Welcome! Welcome! Don't you folks worry. We'll have you moved in before six. TIME?"

A male neighbor—Gordy—checks his wristwatch.

"Five-nineteen!" he shouts, hustling a packing carton into the house.

Scully smiles weakly and sees something that alarms her: a large man is unloading a large cardboard box marked china from the moving van. Before she can stop him, the man hoists it onto his shoulder—from which it slips, falls backward, and hits the ground with an ominous crash.

He apologizes profusely before being interrupted by a pretty, thirtyish woman who soothingly directs him to another task. She helps Scully pick up the fallen box, then introduces herself as Cami Shroeder, Win's wife.

"Nice to meet you," says Scully. "I'm Laura."

At the back of the moving van Mulder supervises a moving man unloading a large portable basketball backboard. He tells the mover to put it in the driveway. Win Shroeder rushes over.

"Whoa, whoa. Hold on! Hold on! Let's talk," he says to Mulder. "Um, b-ball fan. Shooting hoops. That's, um, that's not good. That would definitely stand out in your front yard over there."

"Stand out, Win?" says Mulder.

"Well, as in 'not be aesthetically pleasing.' To the eye."

Mulder says nothing. Shroeder smiles encouragingly.

"But, hey! Maybe you can get special dispensation from Mr. Gogolak, the president of the Homeowner's Association. I'd take it up with him. But, in the meantime, let's keep that in the garage."

Mulder shrugs, smiles crookedly, and agrees—delighting Shroeder to no end. By 5:59:55 P.M. all the contents of the moving van are out of sight inside the house, the van is on its way, and all the helpful neighbors are waving good-bye. Mulder and Scully wave back, then enter the house.

"Oh, *yeah*," says Mulder. "Nothing weird going on around here! Oh, hey! Wait a minute. You didn't let me carry you over the threshold."

Scully ignores this. She pulls on a pair of latex gloves, opens the "china" box, and pulls out a piece of obviously broken scientific equipment.

"Thanks to our friendly neighbors," she says, "there will be no fluorescein bloodstain enhancement."

"Might not make much difference," says Mulder. "This place is so clean you can build computer chips."

Scully pulls out a camcorder, turns it on, and as she

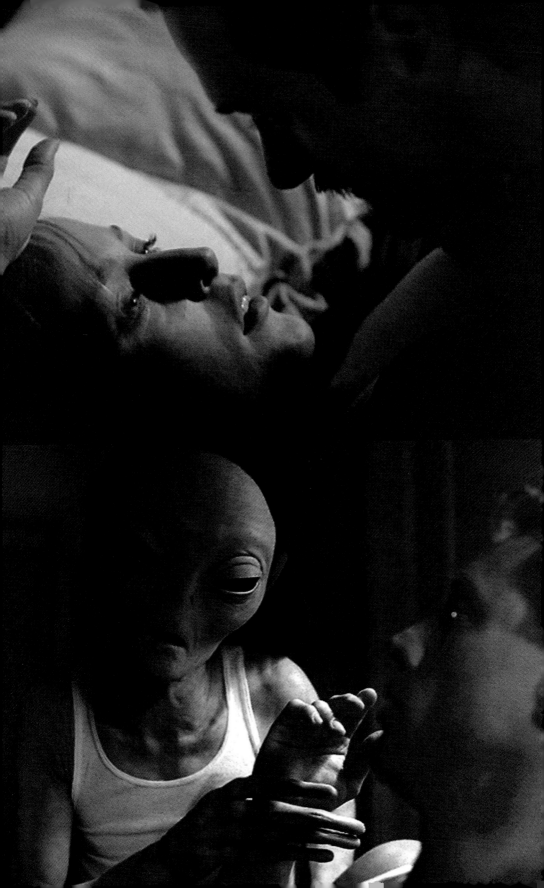

"BOY, THE NEIGHBORS WOULD REALLY HATE THAT." –Nancy Kline

pans slowly around the interior of the house she narrates her case notes. She says:

"6:01 P.M., February 24. Agents Scully and Mulder in the former home of David and Nancy Kline, who disappeared without a trace last July. The Klines were the third such couple to disappear since this neighborhood was built in 1991. All were apparently stable professional people with no history of violence, domestic discord, or mental illness. And it took a family member or employee to realize that they were gone, including their cars and few personal items.

"What local police found in each case was nothing. Just impeccably manicured homes and a community of neighbors who professed total ignorance that anyone had disappeared."

Mulder comes up behind her.

"Pretty surprising," he says. "considering how nutty this bunch is about being neighborly."

Scully continues:

"The local police were at a dead end, so they turned to the FBI. AD Skinner, in assigning us this case, thought a fruitful approach to the investigation would be if we went undercover, posing as prospective home buyers, as this planned community would seem to hide a dark, possibly murderous conspiracy of silence."

Mulder steps in front of Scully's lens.

"Wanna make that honeymoon video now?" he says.

Scully grimaces and asks Mulder why he picked the names Rob and Laura Petrie—and whether that means he's not taking the assignment seriously.

"Pee-tree," corrects Mulder. "And no, I am taking

it seriously. I just don't understand why we're on it. It's our first catch back on the X-Files. This isn't an X-File."

"Sure it is," says Scully. "It's unexplained. What do you want? Aliens? Tractor beams?"

A lightbulb goes off over Mulder's head.

"Wow!" he says. "Admit it. You just want to play house!"

The doorbell rings.

"Woman!" says Mulder. "Git back here an' make me a samwitch!"

Scully turns, strips the gloves from her hands, and tosses them into Mulder's face.

"Did I not make myself clear?" he deadpans.

Scully answers the door. On the front step stands the man who'd ruined her scientific equipment. He's carrying a cardboard box filled with dishes and cups. Scully tells him his offer is appreciated, but unnecessary.

"Oh, please," says the man. "I have more dishes than I need. I just usually use one, then wash it. I'm Mike Raskub, by the way. 'Big Mike,' for obvious reasons. I just live the next street over."

Big Mike wears a gold winged ornament on a chain around his neck. Scully notices.

"That's a caduceus. Are you a doctor, Mike?" she asks.

"No. Uh, veterinarian," says Big Mike, blushing. "If you folks are planning on getting a dog or any pet, I'd be happy to check it out for you, no charge. Just, uh, you're not allowed to have more than sixteen pounds of pet. That's one of the CC and Rs."

"Mighty nice of you, Mike," says Scully, beaming. "Gosh, with all this hospitality, I can't believe the Klines ever left!"

At the mention of the Klines' name, Big Mike becomes visibly uncomfortable. He quickly hands Scully the box of dishware and departs.

"Mulder—" says Scully.

"The name is Rob," he replies.

Mulder is standing atop an end table, carefully examining the blades of a designer ceiling fan. He scrapes off a small patch of black goo and places it carefully in an evidence Baggie.

"Looks like whoever cleaned this place maybe missed a spot," he says. "Look like blood to you?"

"Uh-huh," says Scully. "How'd it get way up there?"

That night at 7:49 P.M., a small dinner party is assembled in the home of Gene Gogolak, the Homeowner's Association president.

"I, uh, didn't really learn much about them," says Pat Verlander, nervously. "He just said he works at home, which tells me she has money."

"They seemed nice," says Cami Shroeder. "Cute couple."

"Very cute," says Big Mike. "I mean, uh—"

"What do you think, Gene?" asks Win Shroeder, turning to Gogolak: a lean, tanned, sixtyish man with too-white teeth.

"Ladies," says Gogolak, smiling evenly from his seat at the head of the table, "my compliments to the chef."

The women take the hint, clear the table, and remove themselves to another room. Gogolak's smile fades.

"These Petries," he asks. "Are they going to play ball?"

"Pee-trees," says Shroeder. "So far, so good. I'm keeping my eye on them."

Shroeder nods. Big Mike, who is visibly agitated, works up the courage to speak.

"Mr. Gogolak?" he says, voice quavering. "Don't you think that, uh, maybe this time it would be better if we told them? It's just that there are so many—so many—rules. I think that maybe they would be able to keep up with them better if they knew what happened if they don't.

"It's the neighborly thing to do. I really think we should do this."

Gogolak looks Big Mike straight in the eye.

"Son," he says. "Godspeed."

Pleased to hear this, Big Mike stands and asks directions to the bathroom.

"Second door on the left," says Gogolak. "Glade's under the sink."

After he leaves, Win tells Gogolak that he thinks he can keep Big Mike in line. Gogolak is unmoved.

"Win, the boy's a weak link," he says. "And a strong chain can't survive with a weak link."

Later that evening Big Mike is slumped on his living room couch watching TV—a documentary about rules and conformity in primitive tribes. He glances through his window and is shocked to see that the lamppost in his front yard is unlit. In a panic, he rushes outside to fix it. He burns his hand trying to unscrew the burnt-out bulb. Something dark begins rising from a patch of lawn behind him.

He screws in the new bulb, heads back toward his front door, and hears something behind him. He turns.

"No. No! I fixed it! I fixed it!" he yells.

Something dark and wet envelops him. He screams—and blood splashes over the welcome mat by his door.

The next morning Win Shroeder, looking stressed, washes the blood from Big Mike's porch with a garden hose. Mulder and Scully amble up; Mulder is carrying the box of Big Mike's dishes. Startled, Shroeder sprays them with the hose, then asks them about their first night in their new home.

"It was wonderful," says Mulder. "We just spooned up and fell asleep like little baby cats. Isn't that right, Honeybunch?"

"That's right, Poopyhead!" says Scully, with a pained smile. "Win, aren't we at the right place? Isn't this Big Mike's house?"

Win nods and tells them that Big Mike has left town on business.

"What kind of business?" asks Scully. "He's a veterinarian."

"Veterinarian business, I guess," says Shroeder, quickly. "All I know is that he's gone for weeks at a time."

Mulder moves to leave the box on Big Mike's front porch. Win steps in front of him.

"Let me take those!" he says. "Just tidier-looking than leaving them on the front porch."

"It would be more aesthetically pleasing," says Mulder.

"Exactly. Say, would you two like to join Cami and me for dinner this evening? About six? We eat early."

Later that morning Mulder and Scully sit in Gene Gogolak's den, which is decorated with all manner of exotic Far Eastern statues, masks, and totems. Gogolak thumbs through a hefty three-ring binder containing The Falls' all-important Contracts, Covenants and Restrictions.

"Nope. I'm sorry. It's not allowed," says Gogolak, emphatically.

"You're kidding!" protests Mulder.

"I'm afraid not. Rules are rules. It may not sound like anything—a simple basketball hoop—but from there, it's just a few short steps to spinning daisy reflectors and a bass boat in the driveway."

"In other words," says Mulder, "anarchy."

"THIS PLACE IS SO CLEAN YOU CAN BUILD COMPUTER CHIPS."—Mulder

Gogolak nods self-importantly.

"It may sound tough, but ours is a system that works. That's why The Falls is one of the top-ranked planned communities in all of California. Most of our homeowners have been here since Day One."

Mulder smiles and compliments Gogolak on his decor. The older man tells him that it's mostly Nepalese and Tibetan.

"I go twice a year on business," he says. "I run Pier Nine Imports. I can get you a great deal on rattan furniture, if you're interested. Indoor only—outdoor use is prohibited by our CC and Rs."

At 6:37 P.M. Mulder and Scully dine with Cami and Win Shroeder at their home.

"You know, Win," says Mulder, "when you told us this morning Big Mike was out of town on business, I don't think that's true. Because we called his office, didn't we, honey?"

"We did!" says Scully, perkily.

"We're thinking about getting a dog," says Mulder. "So we wanted to call him and ask him his advice, whatever, and we asked his office if they had a forwarding number. But guess what?"

"They didn't know where he was," says Scully. "Do you know where he is, Win?"

Win looks uncomfortable, his wife even more so.

"I really couldn't tell you," he says.

Mulder's eyes sparkle.

"It's gotta be something freaky-deaky, huh?" he says. "I mean, for him to lie about it like that. Maybe he's got some wild, secret life going on. But every community has its dark underbelly, don't you think?"

Win frowns.

"We don't have any underbelly," he says, coldly. "As far as I'm concerned, this community is the American Dream."

Cami rises from her chair, doing her best to sound casual.

"I, uh, I'm sorry, but I realize it's past time I walked Scruffy."

"Would you mind some company?" asks Scully, brightly.

A few moments later they're walking Scruffy—an impatient white Chihuahua—down a deserted, pristine street. Scully asks Cami if she thinks The Falls is really the American Dream.

"Oh," replies Cami, nervously. "It's a nice neighborhood. Lot of people who want the best for their families."

"So it's just not your dream?" says Scully.

Cami says nothing.

"You know, Cami," says Scully, "I've noticed that you've walked us past Mike's house. Twice. Are you worried about him?"

Cami averts her eyes and mumbles that she isn't. At that moment Scruffy barks, pulls the leash out of Cami's hand, and scampers into a curbside storm drain entrance. Cami calls frantically after him, then kneels down and peers into the drain. Nothing.

Scully kneels down herself, pulls out her flashlight, and shines the beam into the drain entrance. Her beam falls on Big Mike's caduceus. She reaches down for it.

At that moment Scruffy blasts out of the storm drain as if shot from a cannon. Cami grabs the hysterically whimpering dog, whose muzzle is covered with a familiar black goo. Scully wipes it off on her handkerchief, and the women walk home. Behind them, on the sidewalk, a manhole cover lifts open slightly.

Later that night, in the Klines' house, Scully—in pajamas and robe—talks on the phone with a local policeman. Mulder enters, strips off his hooded sweatshirt, and tosses it carelessly onto a valet stand. Pausing to shoot her partner a dirty look, Scully passes on the latest info: There have been no

"THE KLINES? WHAT IF THEY'RE STILL HERE?"
—Mulder

"YOU MEAN, BURIED IN THE YARD? WELL, ONCE WE
START A FORENSIC EXCAVATION OUR COVER IS BLOWN."
—Scully

sightings of Mike Raskub or his '97 Mercury Villager and nothing charged to his credit cards.

"There's no sign of him in his house, and I didn't see him in the storm drain, either," says Mulder. "I take it he's dead, Scully."

"Laura," says Scully from the bathroom, her mouth filled with toothpaste. "Win Shroeder?"

"Maybe Win cleaning up," says Mulder.

"Cleaning up for whom?" says Scully. "Mulder, speaking of cleaning up, whoever taught you how to squeeze a tube of toothpaste?"

Mulder asks what his partner knows about the black goo. Scully tells him she's driving to San Diego in the morning to have it analyzed.

"Third warning: toilet seat," she adds.

There is a clang as the aforementioned is flipped down.

Playfully, Mulder assumes a seductive position and is shocked severely by the sight of Scully emerging from the bathroom—a lime-green beauty mask smeared on her face.

"Why kill Big Mike?" she asks. "What's missing is intent. What would be the motive?"

Scully picks up Mulder's discarded sweatshirt and flings it at his head.

"Compulsive neatness," says Mulder. "Or lack there-of. These people are obsessed with the neighborhood rules and the CC and Rs. You know, you fit in really well here."

"And you don't."

"Anyway," says Mulder, "tomorrow I've got a sure-fire way of testing my theory."

He pats the space on the bed next to him.

"C'mon, Laura," he says, tenderly, "we're married now."

"*Scully*, Mulder," she says, not very tenderly. "Good night."

Mulder pulls himself wearily to his feet and leaves the bedroom.

"The thrill is gone," he says.

The next morning Mulder strides out his front door and plants a large pink plastic flamingo on his front lawn.

"Bring it on," he says, defiantly.

He strides back inside and swigs from a carton of orange juice from the fridge. He walks to the front window and peers out—the flamingo is gone. He goes outside, kicks the mailbox's white wooden support to a cockeyed angle; opens the box and leaves its door dangling; and pours orange juice over it. He walks back inside and keeps watch through the window. Nothing.

He sits, watching intently, until 5 P.M. Still nothing. He makes a much-needed pit stop, then walks outside to the mailbox. It is now perfectly perpendicular, clean, and closed. Inside the box is a note.

It reads: BE LIKE THE OTHERS . . . BEFORE IT GETS DARK.

At 10:37 that evening Win Shroeder exits his house quickly, an anxious Cami right behind him. Mulder has set up the basketball backboard in the driveway and is shooting hoops. Win hustles over, furious.

"Hey, Win!" says Mulder. "Wanna play 'Horse'?"

"What the hell are you doing?" demands Shroeder.

Shroeder begins dragging the heavy backboard toward the garage.

"What am I doing?" says Mulder. "What are you doing?"

"Help me get this thing inside!" says Shroeder.

"Why?" says Mulder. "What's going to happen if we don't?"

From the lawn next door Cami Shroeder watches all this tearfully. Something big emerges from the earth behind her. She screams. Mulder races next door just in time to see a large black figure running around the corner of the house and out of sight. Mulder turns, runs back to Cami, and follows her frightened gaze. The glass on their lamppost is broken, as is the now-dark bulb.

Later that night someone drags the basketball hoop into the "Petries'" garage. Scully pulls up in the minivan, parks in the driveway, enters the house, and calls for Mulder. No reply. She hears a creaking noise upstairs. She takes a poker from the fireplace and heads toward the stairway.

In front of the Shroeders' house Mulder investigates, his flashlight beam stabbing the darkness. He stumbles, nearly falling, and realizes that he's stepped into a depression on the lawn. He pulls away the thin cover of grass and turf. Underneath is sort of a huge gopher hole, lined with loose dirt.

Inside her house Scully rounds a corner into an upstairs bedroom. She hears another noise, this time from the ground floor. She creeps cautiously down the stairs, spots someone, and swings the poker—at Mulder, who manages to deflect it at the last second. Scully pauses to get her breath back.

"Somebody was in the house," she says.

"Tidying up," says Mulder. "Whoever it was that put away my basketball hoop. Somebody's looking out for us, Scully, which may not be a bad thing."

"What do you mean?"

"I got a look at that thing that's been scaring everybody. And I take it back—this is an X-File."

Later that night Gene Gogolak, in his house, con-templates the Shroeders' broken lightbulb. Win Shroeder—angry and frightened—comes up behind him.

"What did we do wrong, Gene?" says Shroeder. "Was our welcome mat not to your liking? Did I coil my garden hose clockwise instead of counterclock-wise?"

Gogolak turns around slowly to face him.

"Son, you'll want to take a deep breath and rethink that theory," he says. "It's your next-door neighbor. He's a rabble-rouser, Win. He's trouble with a capital *T*. And you and I both know it only takes one rotten apple to spoil the entire bunch."

In front of his house Mulder rolls back the grass and uncovers a hole just like the one in front of the Shroeders'.

"Here we go," he says. "I'm guessing there's one of these in every yard. I think this is how this thing travels. How it lives."

"Look, Mulder," sighs Scully, standing nearby. "Huge creatures aside, do you care to hear what I think?"

"Always," says Mulder.

They walk inside. Scully tells her partner that the lab reports are in; that the goo they found on the fan blade is predominantly ketchup and brake fluid. The sample they took from Scruffy's muzzle is similar: It consists of egg shells, coffee grounds, and motor oil.

"In other words, Mulder," she says, "it's garbage. Which makes perfect sense, because this entire neighborhood has been built on an old landfill. We found this stuff everywhere because it is everywhere; it's just beneath the topsoil.

"And that protrusion in the front yard may occur from the venting of methane gas. But, Mulder, I don't see how any of this has to do with the disappearances."

"It does," says her partner. "Somehow, it's one and the same. The Klines? What if they're still here?"

"You mean buried in the yard? Well, once we start a forensic excavation our cover is blown."

Mulder smiles faintly.

The next morning a horrified crowd of neighbors watches as a noise- and fume-emitting backhoe gouges out a huge hole in Mulder and Scully's front yard. Standing nearby, supervising, is Mulder. Pat Verlander rushes over and—fighting a serious fit of apoplexy—quotes the CC&Rs' prohibition against swimming pools.

"Not a swimming pool," says Mulder, genially. "It's a reflecting pool. I checked the rules. There's no rule against putting in a reflecting pool. Very tranquil. You'll like it."

Standing nearby, Gogolak and Shroeder take this all in. Mulder waves to them.

"Let him dig his own grave," says Gogolak.

That evening the backhoe is silent, but there is a large, deep trench in the front yard. Scully peers down into the hole. Mulder's head pops into view. He's filthy, and he groans with exhaustion.

"Mulder, the Klines aren't down there," Scully says, softly. "And I think it's time you called it a night."

Mulder grimaces, stretches, and turns. He looks up at the backhoe's bucket and sees a big chunk of the Klines' whirligig. On it is a small label reading: PIER 9

IMPORTS MALAYSIA. Mulder turns to his partner.

"Can we get an excavation team out here?" he asks. "We need to dig deeper."

Mulder climbs out of the hole.

"Where are you going?" asks Scully.

"To price some rattan furniture," he says.

Scully enters the house. At the bottom of the hole, a pool of water bubbles weirdly. A gnarled black hand reaches into view.

A few moments later Scully is alone in the bedroom. She dials her cell phone and orders a forensic team dispatched—to 450 Autumn Terrace—immediately. She hears a noise below her and grabs for her holster, placed above a pile of folded clothes. It's empty. Something big and black comes up from behind and grabs her, clapping its huge hand over her mouth.

"It's come for you, Laura," says a male voice. "You can't make any noise."

The creature releases Scully—who turns to face Big Mike, still alive but filthy and viciously mauled. He is holding Scully's pistol.

"Mike? What happened to you?" whispers Scully, frantically.

"You have to get out of here," says Big Mike.

"Why? Who's downstairs, Mike? Who did this to you?"

Mike puts his fingers to his lips, then barricades the door with several heavy boxes and pieces of furniture. He turns to Scully.

"The *Ubermenscher!*" he says. "It's our fault! The original homeowners—we asked for it. Now we can't stop it."

"Stop what, Mike?"

"I tried to give it Shroeder," says Mike, terrified. "You know, tit for tat. Just like Shroeder did for me!"

"Mike, please settle down!" says Scully. "Just give me my gun. I'm a federal agent."

"The *Ubermenscher* wants you, Laura!" says Mike. "Your husband's broken way too many rules. I've been hiding in the sewer. I tried to warn him!"

There are heavy footsteps right outside the bedroom door. Big Mike grabs Scully, shoves her into a clothes closet, and barricades it with a dresser. The bedroom door bursts open and Big Mike empties the pistol into the charging monster. Something starts clawing its way through the closet door. Scully recoils toward the back wall.

Inside a house nearby Mulder slaps a pair of handcuffs on Gene Gogolak.

"FBI? What did I do?" he says.

"Let's start with the Klines," says Mulder. "You're responsible for them being in little pieces in my front yard. You gave them that lawn ornament, the guy with the ax. It's tacky enough to break your rules, your CC and Rs. Tacky enough to mark the Klines for death."

Gogolak smirks.

"Won't that sound good in a court of law?" he says. "When the judge asks you who killed the Klines, what exactly will you tell him?"

Mulder turns. His eyes fall on a nearby primitive carving.

"A *tulpa*," he says. "It's a Tibetan thought form. It's a living, breathing creature willed into existence by someone who possesses that ability. An ability I think you picked up on your whirligig-buying excursions to the Far East."

"Son," says Gogolak, condescendingly, "my lawyers are going to make you sound so stupid that not only will I never see the inside of a jail cell, but you'll be signing all your paychecks straight to me."

spattered. Scully calls out to him from inside the closet. He yanks several louvers off the closet door, trying to free her.

Out front Gogolak struggles to free himself from the mailbox post. He asks Win for help. Cami rushes up the driveway and begs him not to.

"He deserves what he gets," she tells her husband.

Upstairs, Mulder pulls at the closet door with all his strength.

"Mulder, it was here," says Scully, voice quavering.

There is a loud scream from outside. Mulder races out the front door to see the *Ubermenscher* attacking Gogolak. Gogolak falls, dying, and the monster turns toward Mulder. It takes several heavy steps toward the

"LET HIM DIG HIS OWN GRAVE."
–Gene Gogolak

Mulder shakes his head, then hauls Gogolak to his feet and out of the room. He marches him to his front yard, where he sees his front door gaping open. He quickly cuffs Gogolak to the mailbox post and sprints inside.

Standing on his lawn next door, Win Shroeder peers at Gogolak, appalled.

"Win!" says Gogolak, smiling cruelly. "You've got two FBI agents living next door to you. Cheer up! It won't be for long."

Inside the house Mulder sees bloody tracks leading upstairs. He calls for his partner. No answer. He follows them into the bedroom, which is wrecked and blood-

agent. Gogolak draws his last breath and the creature collapses into itself, disintegrating into a pile of earth at Mulder's feet.

The next morning the trench is ringed with crime scene tape. Movers carry furniture out of the house to a waiting moving van. Mulder and Scully exit; Mulder locking the front door behind him. They enter the mini-van and drive away.

Sometime afterward, Scully dictates her case report. She says:

"Several residents of The Falls have now come forward to blame the deaths in the neighborhood on Homeowners Association President Gene Gogolak.

These same residents deny Agent Mulder's allegation that they were in some sense all responsible for the demise of Gogolak, claiming ignorance as to what actually killed him.

"It would seem that the code of silence that hid the sins of this community has not only survived, but in its creator, claimed a final victim. Meanwhile, The Falls at Arcadia has been named one of the top planned communities in California for the sixth year running."

BACK STORY/6X13

"Gumby on steroids."

"Mr. Butterworth."

"Fecal Fred."

"The S*** Monster."

All of the above are some of the nicknames X-Files staffers gave to the creature that emerges from the sewer in "Arcadia." Creating the creature, however, was a challenge.

"The problem," says assistant director Bruce Carter, "was that although the basic concept was good, no one could really envision what that this strange beast—a psychologically manifested compilation of garbage—should look like. Should it be a conventional monster, a creature that has somehow grown muscle and sinew through the force of Gene Gogolak's personality? Or should it really be made of garbage, covered with banana peels and coffee grounds and old bedsprings?"

Working under tremendous time pressure, special effects makeup supervisor John Vulich came up with a costume t was basically a foam rubber suit," says Vulich. " poured urethane foam on it to give it a sort of bubbly appearance, then glued on some shredded rubber and coated it with gunk." During filming the costume was worn by Roger Morrissey, a very tall actor with whom Vulich had worked on numerous previous occasions.

During successive waves of cutting, reediting, darkening, and visual effects jiggering, less and less of the monster became visible so that it became more of an unseen menace than an actual monstrous presence.

As a mid-year standalone episode, "Arcadia" more than held its own as the seventh highest-rated episode of the year. Hardcore fans reacted especially warmly to Mulder and Scully's make-believe "marriage," which good-naturedly consummated some of their most heartfelt fantasies about the two characters without violating the bedrock tenets of their platonic relationship.

The idea for this semi-comedic story—the first X-Files written by first-year staff writer Daniel Arkin—came partly fr a 1991 incident in which Arkin, then an instructo t New York University, moved into a co-op apartment in Manhattan's Greenwich Village.

"Our movers were late," says Arkin, "and we didn't start moving in until 4 P.M. Little did we know—not having read all three hundred pages of our CC and Rs—that we were going to be fined for moving in after 5 P.M. It cost us a thousand dollars."

Over the following years, adds Arkin, several of his more successful friends moved out of their apartments and older houses and into uptight planned communities—a development that he frankly found "kind of frightening." In other words, good raw material for an X-File.

"The story definitely went through many incarnations," says Arkin, describing the typical collaborative marathon experienced by first-time X-Files writers.

"My first idea actually dealt with some notorious person—an infamous character or an accused criminal—who moves into the planned community, to the horror of the residents, creating a sort of 'bogeyman,' a manifestation of all their worst fears. I think it was Chris who suggested we turn the bogeyman into a monster.

"The theme of the 'Tibetan thought forms' was something I'd arrived at early on, so it was relatively easy to make this Gogolak's ability, give him some travel experience through the Far East where he could pick it up, and place the community over a landfill to give him some sinister material to work with.

Arkin adds, "The idea of 'marrying' Mulder and Scully seemed to arise spontaneously at one of our many meetings. Someone said: 'We've never put them undercover together. If we're ever going to do it, why don't we do it in this episode?'"

Many drafts, staff rewrites, and polishes later, Arkin's idyllic community was ready for immediate occupancy. Shortly before the Christmas hiatus, platoons of X-Files artists and technicians headed up the 101 Freeway toward "North Shore at Sherwood": an uncannily Arcadia-like gated community just north of the border between Los Angeles and Ventura Counties.

Inside this suburban Shangri-La—in real life almost exactly as Daniel Arkin imagined it—strictly color-coordinated mini-mansions march in gently curved lines toward the security perimeter.

To amplify the feeling of numbing community harmony, set decorator Tim Stepeck purchased and installed thirty identical lampposts and thirty identical mailboxes. Production designer Corey Kaplan replicated the interior of the houses on the X-Files sound stage.

For the most part, the non-monster portion of the filming schedule went smoothly. "I enjoyed this episode," says Gillian Anderson. "I got a big kick out of sitting next to David and doing all the little things to pretend we were married. I also liked calling him 'Poopyhead.'"

Others had their triumphant moments, also. To fill the vital role of Big Mike, casting director Rick Millikan worked hard to pry Abraham Benrubi loose from his recurring role of orderly Jerry Markovic on NBC's ER. "They were filming the final George Clooney episode at the time and they didn't want to let up on his schedule at all," says Millikan. "But there was a small window—he had a few days off—and we were able to squeeze him in here."

Once on the set, Benrubi came under the aegis of make-up department head Cheri Montesanto-Medcalf, whose job it was to turn him into the mauled and bedraggled apparition who emerges from the sewer to confront Scully.

"It took four hours," says Montesanto-Medcalf, who used several prosthetic appliances and a head-to-toe application of dirt, red clay, glycerin, and a thickening agent called Cabosil to give him a "cracked and crusty" appearance. "But we had to watch out for his palms," she says, "because he had to grab Gillian later on and they didn't want any of this stuff on her face.

"He was a real trouper. He had the stuff on him for maybe twelve hours without complaining," says Montesanto-Medcalf, who adds that Benrubi initially wanted to keep his makeup on to surprise his fellow attendees at a dinner party that night.

"But about halfway through he realized he was looking *really* terrible," she says. "He told me, 'There's no way I can go to a party looking like this.'"

Makeovers of a slightly different sort were carried out by costume designer Christine Peters, who modified Mulder's and Scully's usual wardrobe to help them blend into their undercover assignment as Yuppie clones.

"For David: Lacoste Izod alligator shirts, Dockers, Bass Weeguns," says Peters.

She adds, "Gillian was a little tougher, because she has a 'look' that she doesn't want to give up. She's very savvy that way. So we weren't going to see Gillian in jeans and a sweatshirt or Gillian in khakis and sneakers. So basically she wore the same kind of clothes she always wears, just in lighter colors. It was khaki and tan Tahari; it was mint green Calvin Klein. Obviously, it worked for her. She fit into the scenes without looking ridiculous."

Special effects supervisor Bill Millar remembers "Arcadia" particularly well for the fact that he was asked to completely modify Scully's "evidence video"—adding the framing lines and the digital counter to the shot—at noon on the Friday before the show aired. "They wanted to show Scully's point of view rather than the Handicam's point of view," says Millar. "Luckily, the video playback guy had Scully's camera in the trunk of his car, and he was about five blocks from my editing facility because he was getting fitted for a tuxedo for the Director's Guild awards that night. He dropped it off within a half hour and we were finished only six hours later."

Property master Tom Day, however, has the last word in hard work—and hard luck—in the making of this episode. "When I read the script," he says, "I realized that the most important prop in the show would be that wood-chopping whirligig, and the last thing I thought I would have a problem finding. Well, I simply couldn't lay my hands on one.

"I went around to all the thirty different places in town where you might buy a whirligig, and all of them were totally filled with Christmas stuff. No whirligigs.

A nightmare! Finally, I got hold of someone—a friend of a friend of a person who works on the show—who had the exact thing in his yard. I borrowed it and had duplicates made."

Long pause.

"Then, over the Christmas vacation," he says, "I get on an airplane with my family and fly to Mystic, Connecticut, to visit my mother-in-law. The first day there, we all go shopping in a little place called Mystic Village. There's a store that sells *nothing* but whirligigs. The little man chopping wood? They had a dozen of them."

The name "Polizzi" painted on one of the neighborhood mailboxes is in honor of Lauren Polizzi, one of the art directors on design director Corey Kaplan's staff.

To depict Cami Shroeder's dog Scruffy being ejected from the storm drain, the special effects department rigged up a small device to propel a rubber dog model through the air. No Chihuahuas were harmed in the making of this episode.

In ancient Greece, Arcadia was the name of a district famous for its rustic peace and simplicity. There are towns and cities by that name in twenty states of the Union.

As part of his work on this episode, researcher Lee Smith investigated the explosive properties of landfill; learned how to determine what garbage comes from a sewer (you look for a certain level of bacteria found in human feces); and obtained diagrams of sewer systems from cities and towns across the country. He hit a snag when he asked for one from New York City. "They laughed, they howled, they thought it was the funniest thing they ever heard," said Smith. "They said there was one guy—he was eighty-two years old—and he was the only person who even vaguely knew what was under the streets of New York. They were trying to get him to write it all down and draw diagrams before he died, because when he died, the knowledge died with him."

6X14

AGUA MALA

EPISODE: 6X14
FIRST AIRED: February 21, 1999
EDITORS: Lynne Willingham & Heather MacDougall
WRITTEN BY: David Amann
DIRECTED BY: Rob Bowman

GUEST STARS:
Darren McGavin (Arthur Dales)
Joel McKinnon Miller (Deputy Greer)
Valente Rodriquez (Walter Suarez)
Diana Maria Riva (Angela Villareal)
Jeremy Roberts (George Vincent)
Silas Weir Mitchell (Dougie)
Nichole Pelerine (Sara Shipley)
Max Kasch (Evan Shipley)

PRINCIPAL SETTING:
Goodland, Florida

A deadly creature is slithering through the water system of a seaside town. Mulder and Scully are called down to investigate—and arrive in the midst of a killer hurricane.

On a violently stormy night, angry surf pounds the Gulf Coast community of Goodland, Florida. Inside a beachfront bungalow, Sara Shipley—an attractive woman in her late thirties—works frantically by the light of emergency flashlights and lanterns. She wields a hammer, nailing up her front door against the gale, and calls out for her twelve-year-old son, Evan, who is in the laundry room.

Evan spins the faucets on the utility sink. Nothing. He yells to his mother that the water has been cut off.

Sara runs to the laundry room, passing a portable radio announcing that Tropical Storm Leroy has just been upgraded to hurricane status.

"Mom! Is Dad going to be all right?" cries Evan. "What about Dad? Mom? What about Dad?"

His mother does not answer. A floor drain in the middle of the room is spewing foaming water. Sarah stares at it with dread and fascination and comes to an awful realization.

"We need water. Right now!" she says.

She runs over to the washing machine and lifts the lid. It is filled to the brim with wet clothes and soapy water.

"*Mom!*"

"Just do as I say, Evan! Help me pull the washer out!"

Evan squeezes into the space between the washing machine and the wall. He spots the family's pet cat, as wet and frightened as they are.

Sara tells him to unplug the washer, pull out the drain hose, and help her to tip the machine over. He pushes while she pulls, but despite her frantic cries the washer is too heavy to topple. Again, water surges through the floor drain. Evan stops pushing. Something is pulling him down behind the washer. His mother scrambles forward—to see him being strangled by clear, shiny tentacles.

"*Evan!*" she screams.

Panicked, she pulls at the octopus-like limbs, but the creature only grips the boy tighter. Another limb thrusts up from the floor drain. Sara is pulled backward, screaming.

The next day in Arlington, Virginia, Mulder's answering machine picks up in his empty apartment. After the beep, a grouchy-sounding male voice kicks in. The message is:

"Agent Mulder, this is Arthur Dales calling from Florida. I don't know if you're watching the news, but we're in for a hell of a blow in the next twelve to twenty-four. I've been through hurricanes, Mulder—been through the alphabet—but I just got a distress call from my neighbor down the road that set my teeth on edge. You don't have much time to get to the airport, but if you're the X-Files man you say you are, you better get your butt in gear."

That evening, inside a rainswept—and messy—dwelling in the Tierra Nueva Trailer Park in Goodland, someone tops off a glass of liquor with water from the kitchen faucet, then walks over to a bank of radios and listens to a female voice announcing that Hurricane Leroy is now twenty miles off the coast.

He switches over to a police-band scanner. On it, a cop with a deep Southern accent is reporting that he is in the Shipley house. The entire family seems to have vanished without a trace, even though the house is boarded up from the inside and their only vehicle is still in the carport.

"Well," drawls another cop on the frequency, "that sounds like a real mystery, don't it?"

"It sure does, you dumb fathead!" growls the grouchy-looking old man sitting in front of the scanner radio.

The eavesdropper takes a healthy swig of his drink. He is retired FBI agent Arthur Dales—last seen in "Travelers" (5X15).

Headlights shine through the trailer window. Dales—who is dressed in a ratty bathrobe, old slacks, and a dingy undershirt—heaves himself to his feet, grabs a cane, and hobbles to his front door. He flings it open. Standing outside in a godawful downpour are Scully and Mulder, wearing long black slickers.

"Well!" says Dales, recoiling from the rain and wind. "It couldn't be that all the planes out were fully loaded, huh?"

"Mr. Dales!" says Mulder, nearly drowned. "There's a reason that people don't head out into hurricanes! Mr. Dales, can we come in?"

Dales grumpily steps aside. Mulder introduces him to Scully, who is also thoroughly drenched. Dales grunts skeptically at the news that she is Mulder's partner.

"Well, don't get too comfortable," he says. "You're going to want to get right back out there."

"Out where?" says Scully.

Dales turns to Mulder.

"Did you tell her what I told you?" he snarls.

"SEA MONSTERS CAN ONLY BE READ ABOUT, MULDER. BECAUSE THEY DON'T EXIST."
—Scully

"Yes!" says Mulder. "But she's not the type who's easily persuaded."

"What he means," says Scully, "is that I don't hear a story about a sea monster and automatically assume it's the Lord's gospel truth."

Dales shakes his head in disgust.

"Why did you bring her here?" he asks Mulder.

"She knows your reputation, your early work on the X-Files," Mulder replies. "That, and she has a knack for getting to the bottom of things."

Scully, who has been mopping her face with a paper towel, throws it into a trashcan—which is filled with empty liquor bottles.

"Apparently, so does Mr. Dales," she says, pointedly.

"It's a good thing I have a reputation," replies Dales. "Otherwise, how could it be impugned?"

Scully grudgingly admits to the retired agent that, having heard his phone message to Mulder, there's good reason for alarm.

Dales brings the agents up to date. He tells them that Sara Shipley phoned him in a panic, telling him that something with tentacles had grabbed her husband, Jack Shipley, while he was in the bathroom, and had choked him to death.

"And you have no reason to doubt Ms. Shipley's report?" says Scully.

"No. Both she and Jack are marine biologists," says Dale. "Or, at least, they were. I fear the worst."

"She's missing, too?" asks Mulder.

"Uh-huh. I got on the horn to the local constabulary, but they're about as helpful as a fart in a windstorm."

Mulder grins.

Dales tells the agents that he would have investigated himself, except for his bum hip, and adds that *someone* has to go out into the storm to get to the bottom of the mystery. Reluctantly, Mulder and Scully suit back up.

"What is it that brought you out here in the first place, Mr. Dales?" asks Scully.

"I came down for the weather," he replies.

Scully tries to suppress a grin.

"Don't sneer at the mysteries of the deep, young lady!" declaims Dale. "The bottom of the ocean is as deep and dark as the imagination."

At 9:14 that evening a waterlogged Mulder and Scully shove their way though the boarded-up front door of the Shipley residence. It is dark and deserted. Mulder sweeps his flashlight beam across the laundry room: There is a clear, slimy substance on the drainpipe of the washing machine. Mulder reaches out to feel it. It sticks to his hand and stretches out like bubble gum. Scully reports to her partner that she has seen no signs of life. He shows her the slimy substance. There is a clanging sound, and the lid of the washer is pushed up from inside, then dropped, by an unknown force.

Mulder picks up a mop handle and stabs tentatively at the machine.

"I don't know whether I'm going to need my gun or a harpoon here," he says.

He flips open the washer's lid with the long stick. There is a weird growl—and the Shipleys' cat jumps out of the tub and scoots through the door.

"How the hell did the cat get in the washing machine?" asks Scully.

"Maybe he was taking a dip," says Mulder. "After he finished boarding up the windows."

The agents continue their search. They stop at the boarded-up door to the bathroom and begin to pry it open.

"Well, howdy-do!" drawls a male voice behind them.

Mulder and Scully turn to face a heavyset deputy sheriff, gun in hand. He asks them what the hell they think they're doing. They tell him that they are FBI agents. He doesn't buy it.

"Don't all the nuts roll downhill to Florida!" says the deputy, keying his radio.

"This is Deputy Greer. Come on out to Sandspit Road. I got two suspects here at the Shipley residence. B and E, possibly foul play, over."

Despite their protests, he tells Mulder and Scully that they're under arrest and begins to read them their rights.

"Arthur Dales called us!" says Mulder. "Does that name mean anything to you?"

"I know Dales," says Greer. "I got a call from him, drunk as a skunk. What's new?"

"Well, what else would we be doing out on a night like this?" says Scully.

"You could be looters," says the deputy. "For all I know, you could be part of the Manson Family."

At that moment the Shipleys' cat races out of nowhere, heading toward the front door. Startled, Greer turns to look at it. Mulder steps forward, kicks the gun out of the deputy's hand, and picks it up. Greer sticks his hands in the air.

"Oh, no!" he says. "You're gonna kill me!"

"No," says Mulder. "But I'd like to."

Scully holds up her ID folder.

"The FBI? For real?" says Deputy Greer.

A few minutes later Mulder and a wet, exasperated Scully sit in their rental car. He briefs his partner on the search he and the deputy sheriff conducted: There was no one in the bathroom, but there was more strange slime in the bathtub and three inches of water on the bathroom floor. Supremely unimpressed, Scully suggests they drive to the airport before it closes for the storm's duration.

"Aren't you even curious what happened to these people?" asks Mulder.

"Yes, I'm curious," says Scully. "But I'm also suspi-

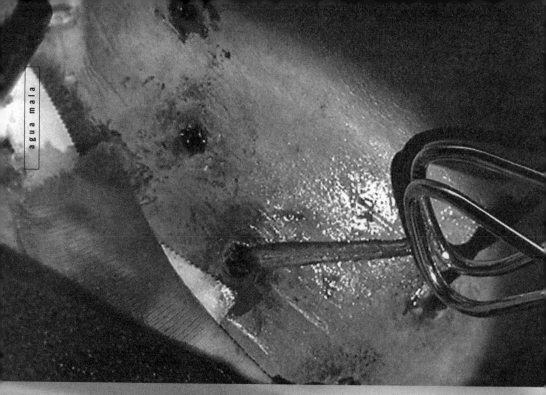

cious. I mean, I think that Mr. Dales's story is fueled by more than his imagination, and not much deeper than the bottom of a highball."

"Don't dismiss him so easily," says Mulder. "He discovered the X-Files forty years ago. He's seen things that I've only read about."

"Because sea monsters can only be read about, Mulder. Because they don't exist."

Mulder looks at Scully solemnly.

"If the sea is where life began," he intones, "where our ancestors walked ashore, then who's to say who knows what new life might be developing in its uncharted depths?"

Scully stares at Mulder for a moment, considering all this.

"You know what?" she says finally. "Maybe you are a member of the Manson Family."

She tells Mulder that there's nothing more for them to do in Florida; that they should leave the Shipley disappearances to local law enforcement; and that they've met their responsibilities to themselves and to Arthur Dales.

"Well," says Mulder, "we should at least tell him we're giving up."

Inside the Shipley house Deputy Greer—muttering about pesky FBI agents, imaginary sea monsters, and drunken informants—continues to search. As he enters the laundry room the floor drain bubbles up at his feet. He bends down to investigate, pries off the drain screen, reaches down into the drain, and pulls out the Miami Dolphins T-shirt that Evan Shipley was wearing when he disappeared.

Later that evening Mulder and Scully drive through the storm, down a road choked with fronds from windblasted palm trees. They stop at a police roadblock.

"Howdy-do," says an officer, peering though the driver's window.

He tells the agents the storm has closed the road, and that they'll have to turn around and find a safe place to spend the night.

"What about the airport?" asks Scully. "Is there an alternate route?"

"Airport? Not tonight," says the policeman. "This hurricane's really bearing down on us. We got trees, power lines down all over the place. Now, you folks really shouldn't be out here in this. I want you to drive to the first safe place you can find. Understand?"

Scully replies that she and Mulder are FBI agents and need to get through. The cop shakes his head.

"Don't all the nuts roll downhill to Florida!" he says.

Scully takes offense, but Mulder cuts her off. He throws the car into reverse, does a bootlegger's turn, and speeds off in the opposite direction.

"That was just one 'howdy-do' over the line," he says.

At 10:42 P.M. outside the Breakers Condominium Complex—a darkened low-end complex in Goodland— Deputy Greer parks his cruiser and radios to his dispatcher that he's stopped there to see if the stranded residents need help. The dispatcher acknowledges him, and adds that because of the storm there will be no backup help available. Greer enters the building. A few moments later, the Shipleys' cat drops from the cruiser's warm engine compartment and scampers away. Greer

"WHATEVER IT WAS, I THINK IT CAME THROUGH THE PLUMBING."
—Mulder

enters a long corridor, knocking on apartment doors and asking loudly if anyone needs assistance. There is no answer.

One of the apartment doors swings open at his knock. He shines his flashlight inside and enters cautiously. He draws his gun and kicks open the bathroom door. Seated on the toilet is a man—or what might have once been a man—completely encased in translucent slime.

Greer cautiously approaches. A slimy tendril shoots out and grabs the deputy around the neck. He struggles to free himself, but is unable to prevent himself from being slowly, painfully strangled.

Later that night Mulder and Scully drive on through the flailing rain. Unbelievably, the storm has intensified.

"You know the good thing about zero visibility, Scully?" says Mulder. "It can't get any worse."

Scully shouts into her cell phone above the storm noise and static, then turns to Mulder to tell him that the Collier County Sheriff's office will guide them to the nearest emergency shelter. At that moment, her line goes dead. Mulder shakes his head.

"You know, Scully," he says, "someday we're gonna look back on this and we're gonna laugh. We'll just think of it as man pitted against the forces of nature. Think of it as a test of our mettle."

"I don't need my mettle tested," says Scully.

Flying palm fronds begin to thump against the car. Alarmed, Scully tells Mulder to pull off the road to ride out the storm. Mulder sees something in the road ahead: the flashing lights of Greer's police cruiser.

"We're about to get directions," says Mulder. "Who says there's never a cop around when you need one?"

The agents get out of their car and shine their flashlights on the empty cruiser.

"Mulder, isn't that—?"

"Forrest Gump," says Mulder.

They enter the condo building, spot the open apartment door, and find Deputy Greer sprawled on his back outside the bathroom. Greer's eyes are open but unfocused; he is struggling very hard to breathe. There are numerous small puncture wounds on his neck and chin. Scully examines him.

"This man needs a trach or he's going to die real soon," she says.

Mulder enters the bathroom. The slime-covered man is no longer sitting on the slime-covered toilet; on the floor, however, is the man's clothing. Mulder reaches down into the slime-filled bowl and pulls out a man's wristwatch.

"I've heard of passing the time—ouch," he murmurs.

In the living room Scully performs an emergency tracheotomy with the deputy's pen knife. She forces the blade into his throat; it enters with a hissing noise and fine spray of blood, which flies onto Mulder's face as he watches. Scully sticks an emptied ball-point pen casing into the hole to serve as an airway.

"It looks like he was attacked or stung," says Mulder, nodding toward the strange set of wounds. "What are those?"

"I don't know," says Scully. "But he's having a

175

reaction which is affecting his autonomic responses."

Mulder glances toward the toilet.

"Whatever it was," he says, "I think it came through the plumbing."

"All I know," says Scully, "is that we have to get a medevac unit out here as soon as possible."

"Well, if it's in the plumbing," says Mulder, "we have to make sure there's no one else in this building."

Scully nods, then keys Greer's radio and calls for help.

"My name is Dana Scully," she says. "I'm a medical doctor—"

The transmission is picked up on Arthur Dales's scanner.

"Scully! Ha, ha!" says Dales, stiff drink in hand.

"—requesting a medevac unit. I have a deputy who's been injured—who's been attacked by something as-yet unidentified—"

"*Un*identified?" says Dales. "My ass!"

In the hallway of the condo Mulder continues knocking on doors and comes across a twentysomething guy awkwardly hefting a television complete with cable box.

"Excuse me, sir," says Mulder. "Everything okay in your apartment?"

"Uh, yeah," says the man—whose name is Dougie—nervously. "It's all good."

"Need some help with your television?" asks Mulder, suspiciously.

Dougie gulps. At this moment they're interrupted by a smallish, nebbish Hispanic man coming toward them. He seems to be on the edge of panic.

"I thought I heard a voice!" he says. "Thank God. We didn't think anybody was coming. Are you the doctors?"

"No," says Mulder. "Do you need medical help?"

The man nods his head.

"Yeah. We called 911. But no one came. And everyone else was already evacuated. But we don't have a car. And then the phone died. My wife is pregnant. A week past her due date. God, I hope one of you has a car!"

Mulder points to Dougie.

"You don't know this man, Mr.—"

"Uh, Suarez. Walter Suarez. Uh, no. He's not with you?"

"I'll put it back," says Dougie, sheepishly.

"Yeah, everything in your pockets, too," says Mulder.

Suarez leads Mulder to his second-floor apartment. The living room is illuminated only by candles. On the couch reclines an extremely pregnant Hispanic woman.

"Angela," says Walter, "this is Mr.—"

"Mulder," says the agent. "Stay there, Mrs.

"—REQUESTING A MEDEVAC UNIT. I HAVE A DEPUTY WHO'S BEEN INJURED—WHO'S BEEN ATTACKED BY SOMETHING AS-YET UNIDENTIFIED—"

—Scully

Suarez. We're going to make sure your baby makes it safely into the world."

Angela peers at Mulder, frowning skeptically.

"Well, thank you, but I'm not in labor," she says, with a pronounced Spanish accent. "And my name is *not* Suarez, it's Villareal. He tells people I'm his wife. Like he's *so* macho."

Mulder turns to Walter. He shrugs. The agent tells the pair politely that he'd like them to come downstairs with him.

"Why? You got a car?" asks Angela, sharply. "Oh! Walter here doesn't have a car. Not to mention a job!"

"Right now," says Mulder, "I just want to get you someplace I know you'll be safe."

"From what?" asks Angela.

"I don't know," says Mulder. "But whatever it is, it may have seriously injured a sheriff's deputy."

"Who? Where?" asks Walter.

"In the manager's apartment. It could be in the complex's plumbing right now."

"Great," says Angela, hauling herself to her feet. "I have to go to the bathroom about every ten seconds."

They head out of the apartment, Angela leading the way.

"Kid's gonna be a fighter," says Mulder. "Anybody else in the complex that you know of?"

"No. No one," says Walter. "Oh! There's George. George Vincent. He lives on the first floor. I went and asked him for help, but he just yelled, 'Go away!' He never listens to no one."

A few seconds later Mulder pounds on George Vincent's door. A bearded middle-aged man peers through the peephole.

"Quit bangin' on the damn door!" he says.

Mulder identifies himself as a federal agent, and asks him to open up.

"Go away!"

Mulder tells him that he may be in danger if he refuses to leave.

"You may be in danger if you refuse to quit harassing me! I'm armed in here, and I'm within my rights."

Mulder tells him that that's great, but he may not be armed against the danger he's talking about.

"It don't matter. I'm armed against the junta, Cuba, and Castro. I ain't gonna cede my home to no revolutionaries without a fight. You got anything else you want to throw at me? Bring it on!"

Vincent snaps shut the peephole. Mulder shakes his head.

"All the nuts roll down to Florida," he grumbles.

In the manager's unit Scully covers Greer with a blanket while Angela and Walter watch. She tells them that a foreign organism has been released into his body and his condition is worsening.

"I can see that!" says Angela, sarcastically. "What the hell was chewing on his neck?"

"I don't know," says Scully. "It may have been some kind of waterborne parasite."

Walter turns to Angela to ask if she's seen Harry— whom his girlfriend identifies to Scully as their paranoid, cheapskate slumlord.

"He may have evacuated," says Scully.

"Harry?" snorts Angela. "Right. And I'm gonna give birth to the Christ child."

Mulder enters, with Dougie.

"Who are you?" Angela asks.

"Nobody," says Dougie.

"Nobody?" says Angela, hands on hips. "Well, it's nice to be surrounded by so many great men!"

Mulder and Scully move to the hallway to talk privately. He tells her they need to evacuate the deputy as soon as possible. Scully counters that she's been on the deputy's radio and been told that the roads are impassable.

"You mean we're stuck here?" says Mulder.

"At least until the weather breaks," says Scully.

As they talk, they're being observed by George Vincent through his peephole. Vincent is armed to the teeth, and his apartment is a survivalist redoubt. Vincent slams a full clip into his automatic, muttering about federal conspiracies. Above him, an overhead light fixture is leaking. The ceiling-mounted globe is slowly filling with water—and a coil of slimy translucent tentacle.

In the manager's apartment Scully pulls a thermometer out of Greer's mouth. His temperature is 106. Scully orders him placed in the bathtub and the tub packed with ice.

"But that thing is in the plumbing," says Dougie.

"Yeah, it may be," says Scully. "But unless we get his temperature down, he's not going to survive this. Now, get moving!"

Dougie heads for the refrigerator. As he does so, Scully—using a pair of hotdog tongs—pulls a short length of tentacle out of one of the holes in Greer's neck.

"I need a container," she says.

Dougie, Walter, and Mulder get Greer into the tub, and iced. Scully shines her flashlight at the tentacle, which lies in a water-filled mason jar. There are several muffled gunshots and screams. Mulder draws his gun and runs to the door of Vincent's apartment. Inside, Vincent is firing a pump-action shotgun at the ceiling again and again.

The doorknob turns and the door opens. Vincent appears, grinning weirdly. Mulder shouts for the gunman—still holding the shotgun—to drop his weapon.

"It's gonna take a whole lot more than this," says Vincent, "to kill whatever it is I just saw."

Mulder, Scully, Walter, and Angela enter Vincent's apartment. The entire ceiling fixture, and everything around it, has been blasted away.

"You didn't see it?" says Mulder.

"I caught it out of the corner of my eye," says Vincent. "But it swooped down at me."

Scully frowns.

"All that happened here is that a sewage pipe burst," she says.

"It looks like the four-inch tie-in to the second floor," says Mulder. "Whatever it is didn't just rip through the ceiling. It looks like it ripped through the pipe. It must still be in the building. It's probably in the outflow system."

"Maybe it'll just float back out?" says Walter, nervously.

Vincent walks over to Walter.

"Maybe it'll come up outta the can and grab you by the nuts!" says Vincent.

Mulder turns to Scully.

"Somebody's already got him by the nuts," he murmurs.

Scully grimaces, turns to the others, and tells all of them to remain calm.

"Remain calm?" says Angela. "I gotta pee so bad my back teeth are swimming!"

In the manager's bathroom Greer lies, still unconscious, in his ice bath. Dougie takes a bar of soap, rubs it on the deputy's finger, and yanks off his gold wedding band.

"Victory," he mumbles.

He splits, but not before accidentally brushing a box of Epsom salts into the bathtub. As he exits the bathroom he runs into Mulder and Scully—and Angela, making a beeline for the toilet.

"Supertanker coming through!" she says.

Walter works up his courage and grabs her by the arm.

"Angela, you can't go in there!" he says.

"My bladder is pressing against your unborn child, Walter," she replies testily. "He's going to have a head like a tortilla."

"That thing's in the plumbing!" protests Walter.

"The volume alone," says Angela, "could push it right back out to sea."

Mulder listens to this exchange intently and something clicks. He turns to his partner.

"Scully, that's how this thing is here!" he says. "The hurricane is sitting offshore, dredging up God knows what, and this thing must have been driven into the city's reclamation system through some offshore outfall pipe. From there it gained access to the pipes in this building."

Scully is unconvinced. She hands Angela a plastic bucket, and tells her they'll be waiting right outside the door. Angela enters the bathroom, glances at the unconscious Greer in the tub, and moves behind the shower curtain to relieve herself. A tentacle threads its way out of the deputy's shirt pocket.

Outside the door, while Mulder and Scully argue about his theory, George Vincent steps past Dougie and enters the apartment. Screaming, Angela rushes from the bathroom.

"I saw it! I saw it! It's in the tub with the deputy! It has giant arms, like an octopus!"

Mulder cautiously enters the bathroom. Flashlight in hand, he grits his teeth, yanks back the shower curtain, and sees nothing. All that's left in the tub are Greer's clothes, the empty box of Epsom salts, and a few inches of water.

"He's gone," says Mulder. "I think the deputy went out with the bathwater."

"So he was in there with it?" asks Vincent.

"No. I don't think he was," says Mulder.

He turns to his partner.

"Look, Scully, I think I know why no one's ever seen this thing before. It just doesn't live in water; it *is* water, taking shape only when it attacks, like it did when the hurricane backed seawater into the plumbing. Virtually unseeable, until then."

Scully shakes her head and holds up a mason jar. Inside it is the tentacle.

"Mulder, if that were true, this wouldn't be visible, would it? I mean, what this is showing us is that water actually tends to kill it."

"Maybe you just impeded its reproductive process," says Mulder. "Maybe it just needs time to complete its cycle. Like it had with the Shipleys."

"Mulder, the Shipleys weren't even in their house."

"No. They were when they were attacked, just like the deputy was here. Using their bodies to lay its own spawn. Using the bodies' water content to reproduce itself, to make itself anew.

"We've got to get out of here—to get to another building. We can use the deputy's prowler—how many people? We got two, four—sonuvabitch!"

Mulder rushes from the room. Scully is puzzled.

"The looter," explains Walter.

Mulder runs to the building's front door. He dashes outside—and the police cruiser is indeed gone. He reenters the lobby and shines his flashlight onto an overhead fixture. A tentacle crashes through the glass and goes right for Mulder's throat.

A few seconds later Mulder staggers down the hallway toward Scully and the others. His neck is ringed with puncture wounds and he cannot speak.

Reacting to this, Vincent reaches out and grabs Scully by the back of the collar, a pistol to her head. He drags her back in the manager's apartment and slams the door.

"What are you doing?" says Scully.

"Saving our lives," says Vincent.

"That's my partner out there! We can't just leave him out there! He's going to die!"

"What are you going to do for him?" asks Walter.

"Well, at least I can keep him breathing. Look, at

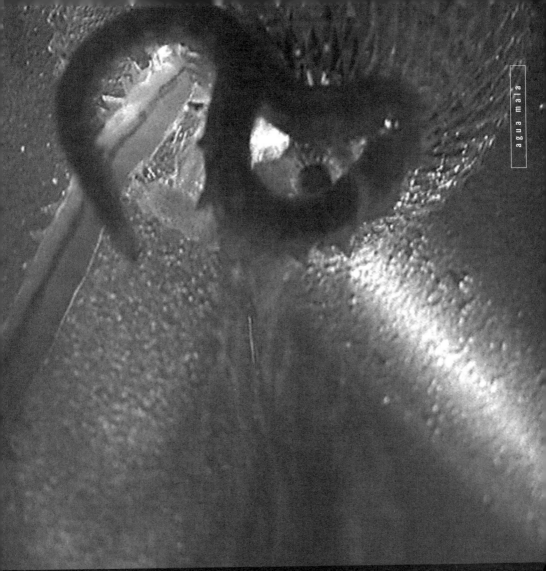

"THE GUN! PICK UP THE GUN! SHOOT OUT THE SPRINKLERS! JUST POINT AND SHOOT! SHOOT OUT THE SPRINKLERS!"

–Scully

least let me try! I'm a medical doctor."

"That's good," says Angela, standing in the bathroom door. "Because my water just broke."

A moment later Mulder sits slumped, struggling for breath, in the corridor. He shines his flashlight at an overhead fixture. It is swimming with water and curling tentacles.

Inside the apartment Angela is going into labor and Vincent is still aiming his pistol at Scully.

"It's not much of a choice, is it?" he snarls.

Scully stares at Vincent for a long second, then tells him she's going to deliver the baby. She orders him to

put down his gun and get her some clean water. Vincent looks at her suspiciously.

"How do I know you're really a doctor?" he asks.

"You don't," she snaps at him. "The truth is, I've never delivered a baby before. So stand back or make yourself useful, but stay out of my way."

In the hallway outside Mulder stumbles toward the building exit. He drops to the ground just short of the half-opened exit doors, straining for breath.

In the apartment Angela sits on the floor, straining mightily to push out her new baby. Scully urges her on, guiding the newborn with her gloved hands. An infant's cry is heard just as Vincent glances over his shoulder at an overhead light fixture. Water has begun to drip from the glass globe.

"I need some towels, damnit!" says Scully.

Vincent moves off to find some. At Scully's urging, Angela keeps pushing.

In the corridor Mulder lies faceup, gasping. There is a meowing sound: the Shipleys' cat, standing just outside, in the rain. Summoning up his strength, Mulder tries to crawl toward it.

In the apartment, tentacles are slithering in the light fixture. Angela gives another push. Realizing that the baby is on its way out, Scully rinses her hands in a pail of water and, momentarily distracted, stops.

"Hey, lady, what're you doin'?" says Vincent.

"It's the water!" says Scully.

"What?" says Vincent.

Scully looks up at the light fixture. Angela screams, and Scully glances down again to pull out the baby.

The light fixture bursts. A tentacle drops down and wraps around Vincent's neck. He drops his gun and struggles to free himself.

Scully, cradling the newborn, turns frantically to Walter.

"The gun! Pick up the gun! Shoot out the sprinklers! Just point and shoot! Shoot out the sprinklers!"

Vincent screams, tugging at the tentacles coiling around his neck. Trembling, Walter aims and fires.

The next morning dawns dry and warm. Outside Arthur Dales's trailer, Scully makes a call on her cell phone. Inside, the retired agent peels away a bandage and looks at the fading wounds on Mulder's neck.

"Yes. Ye gads, that's terrible," chuckles Dale.

Scully enters.

"Well, it's official," she says. "Ten pounds ten ounces of piss and vinegar. *El niño grande*—Leroy Walter Villareal Suarez, Jr."

"Oh, it's amazing!" says Dales. "Truly amazing!"

"What's that?" says Scully.

"That you could come here in the face of a hurricane, chasing a sea monster yet, and end up bringing a new life into the world. And then! Slay the monster and save this one's life as he was literally circling down the drain!"

Scully nods. Mulder frowns.

"She didn't save my life—"

"Oh, yes, she did. With a gun to her head, no less!"

"Well," says Scully, "you wouldn't have known to go out in the rain if I hadn't pointed it out to you that it was fresh water that killed the organism."

"No, no, no," says Mulder. "I saw the Shipley's cat, which had been saved, which had been in the washing machine. And the Shipleys had boarded up their house, which means that the only way they could have vanished was that the creature came up

through the plumbing in a backwash of seawater.

"And then there was the deputy, who vanished from a bathtub full of Epsom salts."

Dales is having none of this.

"If Agent Scully had not been there with you," he says, "I shudder to think what would have happened to you. I'd say you owe her your life. It takes a big man to admit this, but if I had someone as savvy as her by my side all those years ago on the X-Files, I might not have retired."

Mulder nods, albeit reluctantly. Dales hobbles to his kitchen cabinet and pulls out a bottle of booze.

"I suggest that we have a toast to your good fortune," he says. "I insist that we have it. So what'll it be?"

He pauses.

"Oh!" he adds. "Anyone for water?"

"*No!*" reply Mulder and Scully, in perfect sync.

BACK STORY/6X14

Very dark. Very wet. And that—in a nutshell—is just about every *X-Files* cast and crewmember's lasting impression of "Agua Mala."

"I mean, we just got *drenched*. It was like we were back in Vancouver!" says Gillian Anderson, laughing, when asked about her midseason encounter with 6X14's hurricane-borne sea creature.

"I don't think I shot anything for that episode during daylight, or with anything brighter than a flashlight or an emergency lamp in the hallway," says director Rob Bowman, shaking his head at the wonder of it all. "And dealing with all that water on a television production schedule? Unbelievable. Because every time somebody got wet we had to stop everything to dry them off.

"In particular, David and Gillian were constantly waterlogged. I have to hand it to them for working so well with us under such really terrible conditions."

Bowman adds that he himself shivered a bit when handed the script for 6X14.

"It had a couple of tricky elements in it," he says. "The first was the big squid. I didn't know if it was going to look scary or not. The second was the rest of the story. I didn't know if it would be compelling enough. But, in the end, we wiggled the camera and had the creature come in and out of the lights quickly to make it scarier. Then we played up the humor, to let the audience know that not all of this was supposed to be hard-edged drama—and I think it all came out very well; a hell of a lot better than I was afraid it might."

This came as pleasant news to executive story editor David Amann, for whom "Agua Mala" was only his second *X-Files* script. Several months after the fact, Amann confesses that he really had no idea what he was getting his coworkers into.

"I realized it a little bit," he says, "because I knew that when you type 'rain' you are causing everybody to get wet."

He adds, "But I did not fully appreciate what I'd done until I went on the set one night. They were shooting exterior stuff, and they had six or eight rain towers, and a rain bar hanging from a crane, and were showering everything in sight, with wind machines all over the place blowing water almost horizontally. It was truly a sight to behold. Awesome."

Ironically, says Amann, the first incarnation of what would eventually become "Agua Mala" was set far from the seashore—underground, in fact.

"They wanted me to come up with a story with Arthur Dales in it," he says. "So I thought about it and pitched Frank Spotnitz something about a monster loose in an abandoned cave with a gold mine inside it. It was not a great idea. But Frank responded to the idea of the monster being very creepy and shut up in an enclosed space. That's when we came up with the hurricane, and then the sea monster, and then a bunch of people shut up inside a building with it.

"After that, most of the rest of our work involved solving certain problems of logic. For instance, how do you get a sea monster onto land? There were early versions where the winds actually blew it onto the beach and it crawled up to the building and worked its way inside. But that gave way to it coming into the water pipes and through the light fixtures, which I think is subtler and ultimately more scary.

"Then we had to get Mulder and Scully into the building; the Shipleys' disappearance sprang from that. Then we came up with the subsidiary characters and their problems. And since nobody caught in this trap was really getting along with each other, this gave us various tensions we could bring to bear and work with, and some moments of humor when we needed it."

A prime need also, of course, was a Florida-style condominium complex that could be bombarded inside and out with thousands of gallons of water. The exterior scenes were shot at a surprisingly upscale apartment building at Belmont Shores, near Long Beach. Since nobody in their right mind would allow a film crew (or anyone else) to flood the floors and ceilings of their real building, all of the condo interiors—including an impressive 120-foot-long corridor—were built inside one of the X-Files sound stages. "I got the script for 'Agua Mala' in the middle of Christmas vacation, and realized we had to build everything from scratch—a huge project—so I'd better get the crew back early," says production designer Corey Kaplan.

"Yeah, that was a nice job," recalls construction coordinator Duke Tomasick. "But you sure wouldn't want to move into that place once we'd finished filming there. All those sets were pretty thrashed and waterlogged by the time we were done with them."

Also heavily absorbed in 6X14 was special effects makeup supervisor John Vulich—the man in charge of creating the translucent tentacles of the ravenous sea monster. "That was probably the single most difficult thing I did all season," says Vulich. "It's hard to make limbs that are both transparent and flexible, but we came up with a combination of silicon and urethane and some other kind of vinyl—the kind they use to make fishing lures. The tricky part was getting the mechanics inside invisibly. We painted the mechanics and wrapped them in rubber, and if we lit the tentacle just the right way, it sort of worked.

"We also used an old trick, quick and dirty, which is to take some hollow tentacles, wrap them around the actors, pull them away, then run the film in reverse to make it look like they're getting grabbed."

To keep Anderson, Duchovny, and the other actors from getting their skin completely dried out from constant exposure to water, makeup department head Cheri Montesanto-Medcalf sprayed their faces frequently with a special solution of Vitamin E. She also glued tiny rubber "octopus bite marks"—one hundred and thirty of them, a ninety-minute job, minimum—on Duchovny's face and neck. "We did that a couple of times," says Montesanto-Medcalf, laughing. "He seemed to like it."

And, finally, doing her own best to keep pneumonia at bay, costume designer Christine Peters brought to each set six dry copies (instead of the usual two or three) of every wardrobe item scheduled to be worn by a wet actor.

What little spare time she had, she spent talking to "the sweetest man in the world" seventy-seven-year-old Darren McGavin, the former star of Kolchak: The Night Stalker, who was making his first (and, unfortunately, last) Season Six appearance as retired FBI agent Arthur Dales.

Says Peters: "I'm a big fan of his and was pleased to meet him, but since to save his energies he doesn't like to come in for fittings, I had all kinds of pajamas and bathrobes for him to try on his first morning on the set. Well, we do all that, but about a half-hour before his first shot he's sitting there in his trailer with a shy little smile on his face. He says to me, 'You know what I'd really like? A seersucker bathrobe.'

"Well, thank God we were on the lot that day. We raced back to Main Wardrobe, dug through their vault of bathrobes, and came up with a seersucker bathrobe that fit him. And Darren was happy. So as far as I was concerned, the day was saved."

6X15

MONDAY

Trapped in an endless time loop, Mulder and Scully are fated to live the same day—the day that they die—over and over again.

EPISODE: 6X15
FIRST AIRED: February 28, 1999
EDITOR: Louise A. Innes
WRITTEN BY: Vince Gilligan & John Shiban
DIRECTED BY: Kim Manners

GUEST STARS:
Mitch Pileggi (AD Skinner)
Carrie Hamilton (Pam)
Darren Burrows (Bernard)
Monique Burrows (Head Teller)
Suanne Spoke (Woman Customer)
Arlene Pileggi (Skinner's Secretary)
Mik Scriba (Lieutenant Kraskow)
Wayne Alexander (Agent Arnold)
David Michael Mullins (Tour Guide)

PRINCIPAL SETTINGS:
Washington, D.C.; Arlington, Virginia

At the Cradock Marine Bank in Washington, D.C., a robbery is in progress. The streets surrounding the bank are blocked off with police cars; dozens of cops, using the cars as shields, stand ready with their guns drawn. A crowd of onlookers gathers beyond a cordon of crime scene tape. A man pushes his way through the crowd. A young, sloppily dressed woman at the edge of the crowd eyes him worriedly.

The man is Walter Skinner. He flashes his FBI ID and approaches a plainclothes detective.

"You in charge here?" he asks.

"Lieutenant Kraskow," the detective replies. "Is the Bureau taking over?"

Skinner shakes his head.

"You're welcome to any help I can give you," Skinner says. "But that's not why I'm here. What can you tell me?"

"Silent alarm tripped thirty minutes ago. We think there's one robber, armed, probably a handgun. Definitely no pro, or he would have been long gone. Single gunshot, about twenty minutes ago. Blinds are down, but we think we've got a body on the floor."

Skinner frowns worriedly.

"Two of my agents may be in there," he says.

At that moment there's a commotion behind the police line. A young woman—the same one glimpsed previously—is struggling to get out of the grip of a young cop.

"Skinner! Skinner!" she shouts. "Stop this! Don't let this happen!"

Skinner turns and looks at the woman, puzzled.

"Do I know you?" he says.

The young cop drags her away, still yelling.

In the lobby of the bank Scully crouches over Mulder, who has been shot in the chest. He is barely alive. Scully presses her hand to his gaping wound. Frightened patrons and bank employees lie sprawled on the floor. Some are crying. The rest are dead silent.

Scully looks up. Looming over her is the bank robber: a young, scraggly-haired, bearded man in an army surplus jacket. The jacket hangs open. Strapped to the man's chest is a homemade bomb—rows of blasting sticks taped together. From one of his hands dangles a .45. The other is poised over a switch attached to the bomb.

Scully fights to control her emotions.

"You're in charge here, you know." she says. "It doesn't have to end like this."

The robber pauses to think; at the same moment the lobby doors burst open. He knows what's coming next.

"Yeah, it does," he says.

A squadron of rifle-toting SWAT cops, perfectly choreographed, pours in.

"No!" shouts Scully, desperately.

The robber hits the bomb switch. The bank building explodes outward in a shower of flame, dust, flying glass, and masonry.

In the corridor of Mulder's apartment building a newspaper carrier tosses a fresh morning edition against his front door. In his bedroom, Mulder jerks awake at the sound. His waterbed—last seen in "Dreamland II" (6X05)—undulates beneath him. Mulder grimaces, sensing something amiss. He peels back the covers, swings his legs over the side, and steps onto carpeting so saturated with water that it squishes and puddles around his toes. He pulls back his sheet from the corner of the bed and sees a leaking seam spurting water.

"Sonuva—" he growls.

He glances at the alarm clock by his bedside. It's blank, shorted out by water from the leak spraying onto its wall outlet. He reaches for his wristwatch on the bedstand, and knocks his cell phone onto the wet carpet, getting it visibly soaked. Mulder tests it—it's dead. His wristwatch is working, however, it reads Monday, 7:16 A.M.

Mulder curses again, and squishes across the carpet to the kitchen. His bedroom phone begins to ring. Carrying a small pot, he hustles back to answer it, and trips over a pair of sneakers on the carpet. He bangs the pot on the floor in frustration, shoves it under the leak, and reaches up for the receiver.

"Hello?" he says. "It's coming through down there? It's my damn waterbed. My damn waterbed sprung a leak. Yeah, I know I'm not supposed to have a waterbed, but I don't know what to tell you. I think it was a gift. Yeah. All right."

He hangs up, stares at the leak, pokes at it with his finger, then tries to stop the flow by setting the pot down on the seam. It's hopeless.

At FBI headquarters later that morning Mulder stands at his office desk. He slits open an envelope, pulls out his federal paycheck, and tears the check from its payroll stub. He hastily scribbles his name on the back of the check, endorsing it. He hears footsteps approaching. He looks up to see Scully in the doorway, gazing at him sourly.

"I know," says Mulder. "I missed the meeting."

"No, you didn't miss the meeting," says Scully. "You're extraordinarily late for the meeting. It's still going on."

"What are you doing down here?" asks Mulder.

"We took a short break and I came looking for you. What are you doing here?"

"Having the best damn day of my life. Any moment I'm about to burst into song. 'Zippity Doo-Dah!'"

He gives his partner a short précis of the morning's disasters, adding that if he doesn't deposit his paycheck immediately, the check he wrote to cover the water damage will bounce.

"Ever have one of those days, Scully?" says Mulder.

"Since I've been working here? Yeah," says Scully. "When did you get a waterbed, Mulder?"

Already on his way out the door, Mulder doesn't seem exactly sure of the answer. He changes the subject.

"The bank's just down the street," he says. "I'll be back in ten. Cover for me, will you?"

He is gone in a flash.

"When do I not?" mutters Scully to herself.

At Eighth and E Streets a few moments later a rusted old 1970s hardtop pulls over to the curb, cutting off several angry motorists in the process. At the wheel is the bank robber we've seen earlier. Sitting beside him is the frantic woman who approached Skinner.

"We good?" asks the robber, turning to his companion. "Pam?"

"Go run your errand already," she says, tonelessly.

"Yeah. I just gotta pick something up. No biggie."

"Right, Bernard. No biggie."

"I'll be ten minutes. Wait here for me," he says, nervously.

No response. Bernard opens the door and gets out, nearly creaming a bicycle messenger scooting past.

"Hey, man! You need to watch it next time!" shouts the cyclist.

"You watch it!" shouts Bernard.

Pam looks straight ahead, mouthing the same words as Bernard and the cyclist as they argue.

Bernard half walks, half runs into the Cradock Marine Bank.

Pam looks into the rearview mirror and sees Mulder walking down the sidewalk toward her.

"Right on schedule, poor guy," she says.

Mulder passes her car. As he does so he slows and looks curiously into the passenger compartment, then moves on.

"You never did that before," says Pam, surprised.

Mulder hustles into the bank, pulls out his check and deposit slip, and stands impatiently at the end of a long line. At a courtesy desk nearby Bernard, agitated and sweating, scribbles something on a deposit envelope. Using the bank's clunky tethered pen he writes: THIS IS A ROBBERY.

At FBI headquarters at 10 A.M. Scully sits at a table in Skinner's office, with Skinner at the head and an empty seat next to her. Across from Scully sit several male agents. One of them reads from a file folder, reciting in a near-monotone the most boring set of crime statistics and projections imaginable. He drones on for what seems like several hours, then reaches his big finish.

"In any case," he says, "added variables make crime trends for the coming year particularly hard to predict."

Skinner sighs, then turns to Scully.

"The unpredictable future," he says. "Which brings us to Agent Mulder. Will he or will he not grace us with his report?"

Embarrassed, Scully gets up from her chair and leaves the room.

Inside the bank lobby an impatient Mulder is still mired in line. Bernard is still writing his holdup note. He crumples the note into a ball, then turns, pulls his .45 from his pocket, and points it toward the teller line.

**"CUSTOMERS, FACEDOWN!
YOU KNOW WHAT THIS IS!
ON THE FLOOR!"**
–Bernard

"I'M BLOWING THIS WHOLE FREAKIN' PLACE
RIGHT OFF THE MAP IF THEY COME IN HERE!"
—Bernard

"Customers, facedown! You know what this is!" he bellows. "On the floor!"

The customers and employees stand rooted in shock.

"Oh, God, don't shoot us!" cries the female customer standing next to Mulder.

"You're the boss," says Mulder, carefully, to the gunman.

He puts his hands up and, keeping his eyes on the gunman, slowly sinks to the floor. Alongside him, the female customer sobs hysterically. Mulder comforts her.

"All right! I'm the boss!" Bernard yells. "No silent alarms, no dye packs! Do it like the insurance company taught you!"

Bernard walks quickly to the head teller's window, thrusts the gun in her face, and hands her a plastic grocery bag.

"Start with the counter money—the quicker you go, the quicker I go. Everybody else out here on the floor!"

The teller begins pulling greenbacks out of her cash drawer. As she does so she surreptitiously presses a silent alarm button, out of sight beneath the counter, with her toe. The teller moves down the line to the next drawer. Lying on his belly, Mulder contemplates this latest bad twist in his workday.

"Zippity Doo-Dah," he says under his breath.

He swivels his head to peer through the bank's front door, and sees Scully crossing the busy street on her way inside. He looks up at Bernard, who has ordered the head teller to unlock the ATM and is shoving her toward it.

"Hey! Lock the doors!" shouts Mulder to Bernard. "You forgot to lock the front door!"

Bernard turns to look at Mulder, shoves the teller to the ground, and rushes to the door—too late.

Scully has already entered. He aims his .45 at her. Mulder stands and draws his gun. Bernard whirls and shoots him in the chest. Scully draws her own automatic.

"Drop it! Drop it now!" she yells.

Bernard turns back and aims at Scully.

"You drop it!" he shouts, shaking with crazed energy. It is a standoff, until Bernard opens his coat, revealing the bomb taped to his body. Seeing this, Scully thinks hard, then slowly lowers her weapon.

At FBI headquarters the meeting at Skinner's office is still droning on. The office door opens and his secretary walks in, her expression grave.

A few moments later the bank is cordoned off and surrounded by police. Pam still sits in the hardtop.

"Go, go, go," she murmurs.

A SWAT team leader pauses alongside her window.

"Go, go, go!" he shouts, waving the other SWAT cops ahead.

Pam gets out of the car and stands by the police line. Skinner runs past her, flashes his ID, and approaches a plainclothes cop.

"Who's in charge here?" he says.

"I am," says Lieutenant Kraskow. "Unless the Bureau's taking over."

There is a commotion behind them. Pam is struggling to get out of the grip of a young cop and past the police line.

"Skinner! Skinner!" she says. "Don't let them charge in there! Skinner!"

Skinner turns and looks at the woman, puzzled.

"Do I know you?" he says.

She is dragged away.

Inside the bank lobby Scully kneels over Mulder, pressing her hand against his wound to stanch the flow. She looks up at Bernard, his hand on the bomb switch.

"They're supposed to call, right?" he says.

"They're not going to call," says Scully, fighting for control.

"What's your name?" she asks.

"Yeah," says the robber with a smirk.

"Well, I've got to call you something, right? How about Steve? That's a nice, honest name. Steve?"

"Bernard," he says.

"Bernard," begs Scully. "I've got to get my partner out of here."

Bernard stares at Scully. Despite his best efforts he is starting to panic.

"I'm blowing this whole freakin' place right off the map if they come in here!" he shouts.

"Look, they don't know that!" says Scully, desperately. "Don't you realize that? They can't see you! They don't know what your plan is! Just walk out front of the door and show them!"

Bernard raises his gun and scowls.

"You want to get me killed!" he shouts.

Scully bows her head, looks at Mulder, who's slipping fast, then looks up to face Bernard again.

"I just want everybody to live. That's all," she says. "Just show them you have control over everything that happens here. You do. And it doesn't have to end this way."

Bernard smirks, then turns at the sound of the front door bursting open.

"Yeah, it does," he says.

A squadron of rifle-toting SWAT team members, perfectly choreographed, pours in.

"No!" shouts Scully.

Bernard hits the bomb switch. The bank building explodes outward in a shower of flame, dust, flying glass, and masonry.

In the corridor of Mulder's apartment building a newspaper carrier tosses a fresh morning edition against his front door. Inside, Mulder jerks awake at

the sound. Mulder grimaces, sensing something amiss. He peels back the covers, swings his legs over the side, and steps onto carpeting so saturated with water that it squishes and puddles around his toes. He pulls back his sheet from the corner of the bed and sees a leaking seam spurting water healthily.

"Sonuva—" he mutters.

He repeats the sequence we've seen before—with a few notable differences: Mulder's wristwatch now reads Monday 7:14; he manages to answer the phone call from his landlord and get the pot from the kitchen without tripping over his sneakers. Instead, he trips *backward* over his sneakers as he's scrambling to get another pot. As he lies on the floor, his phone begins to ring again.

In a low-budget Washington apartment Pam holds a telephone receiver to her ear. No answer. Bernard enters from an adjacent room, buttoning his coat tightly around him. Pam reluctantly hangs up.

"Who you calling?" says Bernard, suspiciously.

"Nobody," says Pam.

"What do you mean nobody? It's gotta be somebody."

"It's nobody you know, Bernard. Forget it."

Bernard shrugs and walks over to his girlfriend.

"There's something I gotta do," he says. "I want you to come."

"I'm not going with you," says Pam.

"Look, I'm not asking," says Bernard. "Pam? Don't go getting all weird on me."

Bernard moves to pick up his car keys. Pam steels herself to confront him.

"Look, Bernard, just go to work. It's not too late," she says.

"I'm not going to work today," says Bernard. "And don't say they're gonna fire me!"

"I wasn't going to say that," says Pam, sadly.

"'Cause you know what?" says Bernard. "Who cares. Like there's a big future in mopping floors. Like that's something to lose."

"We lose everything!" says Pam.

"No, no," says Bernard. "I got a plan. This time tomorrow, Pam—"

"Everything'll be roses," she says, finishing his sentence.

They exit. The table clock in their apartment flips from 7:16 to 7:17.

At FBI headquarters Mulder sits at his desk and yanks his paycheck from the envelope. It gets stuck, and a corner of the check rips.

"Oh, damnit!" he says.

He tears the check from the stub. Scully enters.

"I know," says Mulder. "I missed the meeting."

"Not yet," says Scully. "But only because it's the longest in FBI history."

"What are you doing down here, then?"

"Well, I came looking for you. We took a five-minute break three minutes ago. Mulder, your cell phone's not working. Did you oversleep?"

Mulder carefully tapes his check back together.

"Scully, did you ever have one of those days you wish you could rewind and start all over again from the beginning?"

"Yes. Frequently," says Scully. "But I mean, who's to say that if you did rewind it and start over again, that it wouldn't end up exactly the same way?"

"So you think it's all just fate?" says Mulder, endorsing the check. "We have no free will?"

"No, I think we're free to be the people we are: good, bad, or indifferent. I think it's our character that determines our fate."

"And all the rest is just preordained?" says Mulder. "I don't buy that. There's too many forks in the road."

To illustrate, Mulder recites the disastrous events of the morning; all of which, he contends, cascaded unpredictably from the fact that his waterbed sprang a leak. Scully listens incredulously.

"Since when did you get a waterbed?" she asks.

Mulder chuckles mirthlessly and ducks the question entirely.

"I might just as easily *not* have a waterbed," he says. "Then I'd be on time for this meeting," he says. "You might just as easily have stayed in medicine and not gone into the FBI. Then we'd never have met, blah, blah, blah."

"Fate," says Scully, skeptically.

"Free will," says Mulder. "With every choice you change your fate."

"Then let's change yours," says Scully. "I will deposit your check. You gather your files, go to Skinner's office, and give your report—before he takes it out on both of us."

A few minutes later Scully enters the bank lobby and gets on the end of a long line. Nearby, Bernard is writing his holdup note. Back at FBI headquarters, Mulder glances at his desk and sees his paycheck, unendorsed, on it.

"Endorsed my damn check stub," he mutters, disgusted.

A few moments later Mulder hurries down the sidewalk toward the bank. He passes Pam sitting in the car.

"Mulder!" she shouts, getting out and running after him. "Don't go in the bank today."

"Excuse me?"

"Bernard's in there. Please don't go in the bank."

"I'm sorry, do I know you?"

"You pass me every day on the street," says Pam, intensely. "Every single day! *This* day. On your way to the bank! And then you go inside and everybody gets killed: you, your partner, Bernard. Everybody."

Mulder studies the woman's face, trying to make sense of her.

"I pass you?" he says. "And we're dead?"

"Yes! Over and over! Only last time you looked at me like you knew me. Like you remembered. Please remember me!"

There is a muffled gunshot from inside the bank. Mulder turns, drawing his gun.

"Don't go," begs Pam, despondent.

Mulder crosses the street, enters the bank, and finds Scully and Bernard training their guns on each other. The female customer is at Scully's feet, wounded. He aims at the robber.

"Drop your weapon!" shouts Mulder.

"Drop it!" says Scully.

"I ain't dropping nothing!" says Bernard. "You put yours down!"

Gun outstretched, Mulder slowly approaches him. Bernard glances at the agent.

"I'll shoot her!" he says.

"What do you think I'll do then?" says Mulder.

Bernard opens his coat, revealing the bomb. Mulder freezes.

"Bernard? That's your name, right?" he says.

After a brief look of surprise—triggered by Mulder's knowledge of the gunman's identity—Scully kneels down and checks the wounded woman's pulse.

"Bernard, she's not dead," she says. "You're not a murderer yet."

"You could end this the right way!" says Mulder.

"Sir! Please!" says the head teller, trembling, to Bernard. "Listen to them. Don't hurt anybody else. A whole lot of police are coming!"

Bernard glances at her. Mulder and Scully are silent but apprehensive.

"You tripped the alarm," says Bernard, calmly.

He drops the gun to his side. Mulder and Scully take deep breaths. Bernard closes his eyes and reaches for the bomb switch.

"No!" shouts Mulder.

The bank explodes outward. On the street, Pam slumps behind her car, hands over her ears. She is unhurt, but crying, devastated as the echoes of the bomb blast fade away.

In the corridor of Mulder's apartment building a newspaper carrier tosses a fresh morning edition against his front door. Mulder jerks awake at the sound. This time he is curt with his landlord.

"Yeah, I know," he says. "I know. I know already. I'll pay for it!"

Mulder trips over his shoes on his way to get the pot.

His watch reads Monday 7:15 A.M.

At FBI headquarters later that morning Scully strides down a corridor, trying unsuccessfully to call Mulder's cell phone. As she waits for an elevator she hears a female voice behind her.

"Agent Scully," says Pam, an FBI tour pass clipped to her jacket.

"Yes?"

Pam begs her not to enter the Cradock Marine Bank, and not to let her partner enter either. Scully looks at her, puzzled. An FBI tour guide arrives and warns Pam that she's off-limits. She ignores him and gazes at Scully intently.

"If you walk into that bank, you'll die," she says. "Both of you."

She turns to leave.

A few minutes later Scully is in her office when Mulder rushes in.

"Oh, hey!" he says. "Did I miss the meeting?"

Scully tells him that she's on a break from the meeting he's missing. This time, however, Mulder pauses as he's opening his paycheck envelope.

"Wow, that is so strange," he says. "I just got the weirdest sensation of déjà vu. I've been having it all morning."

"Well, it's fairly common," says Scully.

"Yeah, but never to this degree. I mean I woke up, I opened my eyes, I was soaking wet—a long story—but I had the distinct sensation I had lived that moment before."

"Well, you may have," says Scully. "Did you do a lot of drinking in college?"

Mulder looks at Scully with a pained smile.

"You know," he says, "some Freudians believe the déjà vu phenomenon to be repressed memories escaping the unconscious. That it represents a desire to have a second chance, to set things right."

"Set what kind of things right?"

"Whatever's wrong."

"Mulder, it's more likely that we're talking about simple neurochemistry, a glitch in the brain's ability to process recognition and memory. It doesn't mean that the memory's authentic."

"Yeah, but what if it were?"

"What if you were living this moment before, and now you're living it again?"

"Yeah. So I could right some wrong, or change fate."

"Well, right now," says Scully, "I'd say you're fated to go to this meeting."

"No," says Mulder. "Actually I'm fated to go to the bank."

"Mulder, what bank?"

Mulder tells her. Looking troubled, Scully tells him of her strange encounter with Pam and Pam's prediction that she and her partner would die if they entered Cradock Marine. Mulder asks her for a description of Pam. Scully gives it to him; it seems to ring a faint bell. He thinks for a second or two.

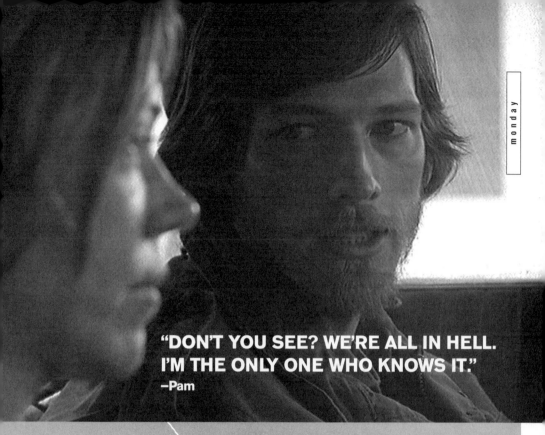

"DON'T YOU SEE? WE'RE ALL IN HELL. I'M THE ONLY ONE WHO KNOWS IT."
–Pam

"I'll use the ATM machine," he says, finally. "I won't tempt fate."

A few minutes later Scully sits in on the boring meeting in Skinner's office. Mulder's chair is empty.

Down the street Mulder pulls out his ATM card and sees that the machine is out of service. He looks across the street to see Pam, arms folded, staring at him. He stares back. After a few seconds, he crosses the street.

"Do you remember me?" asks Pam.

"You match a description," says Mulder. "You're the woman who gave a warning to my partner."

Pam nods.

"Have we met?" says Mulder.

"More times than I can count," says Pam, sadly. "Right here on this sidewalk. Usually, you'll walk right by. You'll pass a few minutes earlier, a few minutes later. Little details may change. But it always ends the same."

"What ends the same?"

Pam starts to cry.

"I keep having this conversation—" she says.

"We go inside the bank and we all die," says Mulder. "That's what you told my partner. Is there something going to happen inside the bank? Is there going to be a robbery?"

Pam nods tearfully.

"Every time I tell you there's going to be a robbery you run in there and try to stop it—and that's when things go bad.

"Don't you see? We're all in Hell. I'm the only one who knows it. Something went very wrong on this day the first time around. Something got screwed up. Things didn't end the way they were supposed to. And now it's like a needle stuck in a groove."

Mulder struggles to comprehend.

"You're saying this day repeats over and over again?"

"Until we get it right," says Pam. "Until my boyfriend doesn't blow up the bank. I have tried everything to stop him. I've hid his keys, I've drugged his coffee, I've even called the police on him myself. And he always gets here. He's meant to.

"It's you. It's you and your partner, every time. If it wasn't for you, nobody would die. *Please.* You can stop this. You're the variable. It has to be you! I've tried everyone else. All I'm asking is that you just walk away."

A few minutes later Mulder bursts through the door of Skinner's office. He asks the thoroughly annoyed Skinner where Scully is. Skinner tells him that she left to look for him. Mulder leaves immediately.

A few minutes later Scully enters the bank, passes Bernard writing his note, and looks for Mulder. Bernard draws his gun and yells for everybody to lie facedown. Bernard hands the bag to the head teller and demands she empty the till. The customers begin to sob and whimper. The woman customer begs him for her life. While Bernard points his gun at her, Scully—lying on the floor—makes a move for her gun. Bernard sees this. He's about to shoot her when Mulder bursts into the lobby, gun in hand.

"Drop your weapon!" shouts Mulder.

Bernard turns toward him and Mulder fires. Hit in the shoulder, Bernard falls. Scully gets up and takes his gun. With his good arm Bernard pulls his jacket open, and reaches for the bomb switch. Mulder stares at him—too late to do anything.

"He's got a bomb," he mutters, desperately trying to put the pieces together. "He's got a bomb. He's got a bomb. He's got a bomb. He's got a bomb—"

Bernard clicks the switch.

In the corridor of Mulder's apartment building a newspaper carrier tosses a fresh morning edition against his front door. Mulder jerks awake at the sound. Everything proceeds roughly as before. This time his wristwatch reads Monday 7:16 A.M.

At his office in the FBI building later that morning Mulder endorses his pay check, and asks Scully—on her break from the meeting—to cover for him as he ducks out to the bank.

Across from the bank Bernard pulls the hardtop to the curb. He turns to his girlfriend in the passenger seat.

"We good, Pam?" he says.

No answer.

"Pam?"

"I know," she says finally. "You just got to pick something up. No biggie."

Her shell-shocked demeanor angers Bernard.

"What is with you?" he says. "Why are you always in a mood?"

"Because nothing ever changes," she replies.

"Things are gonna change," he says. "You wait and see. I'll be ten minutes. Wait here for me."

Bernard exits the car, nearly collides with the bicycle messenger, argues with him, and enters the bank. Pam starts to cry.

Mulder walks past the hardtop. As he does so Pam rolls down her window. Mulder stops, and—with a look of unfocused curiosity—peers inside.

"Do I know you?" he says.

"Do you?" says Pam, choking back her tears.

"Yeah, you just look really familiar to me," says Mulder.

"Do I?"

"Yeah. I'm sorry to bother you."

A few moments later Mulder stands on line inside the bank. Still troubled by his encounter with Pam, he looks out the window and sees her still sitting in the car. His gaze falls on Bernard, writing his note at the courtesy desk. He stares at him for a few seconds. He mouths a single sentence, then begins reciting it, mantralike, under his breath.

"He's got a bomb," he says. "He's got a bomb. He's got a bomb. He's got a bomb. He's got a bomb—"

At the meeting in Skinner's office Scully sits next to an empty seat, struggling to concentrate. Skinner pointedly checks his watch. His secretary enters the room. She tells Scully that there's an urgent call from Mulder. She takes it in the outer office.

"Mulder, where are you?" she says impatiently.

"I'm at the bank," Mulder whispers into a phone at a loan officer's desk.

"Yeah, I know where you are," she says, "but what's taking you so long?"

"Scully, I need you to do something for me right now."

A few moments later still Pam sits—still in despair—in the car. There is a tap at her window. It is Scully, displaying her FBI ID. Pam rolls down the glass.

"Ma'am, will you come with me?" she says.

"Why?" says Pam, startled. "What's this about?"

"My partner said you'd know," says Scully.

Inside the bank lobby Bernard is finishing his holdup note. It reads: THIS IS A ROBBERY. PUT THE MONEY IN THE BAG. NO ALARMS. NO TR—

Before he can finish someone places an automatic pistol gently on top of it. He looks up to see Mulder standing at his side.

"Take it," says Mulder, softly. "I'm a federal agent. I don't want us all to die in here."

"What are you talking about?" says Bernard.

"You have a girlfriend outside in the car. And you've got a bomb. Something very bad is going to happen here today. And I want you to know that I'm not going to let it happen. But if you walk out that door right now, I'm not going to stop you. You're in charge here, Bernard."

"You're damn right," says Bernard.

"You can change your fate," says Mulder.

Bernard sighs, thinks, then grabs Mulder's gun, turns, and points it toward the teller line.

"Everybody down—now! You know what this is!" he yells.

The female customer screams. Bernard yells at her to get down. Mulder looks Bernard in the eye.

"If you don't believe me, ask her," he says.

Mulder nods toward the lobby door. Pam is entering the bank with Scully behind her. The instant Scully sees Bernard's gun, she draws hers and takes aim.

"Drop it!" she says.

Bernard yells at Pam for her to step away from Scully. Pam steps up and glares at Mulder.

"This isn't going to work," she says, angrily. "You can't be in here!"

Scully yells again for Bernard to drop his weapon. Bernard replies by demanding she drops hers.

"Listen to me, Bernard—" says Mulder.

"You get her out of here!" screams Bernard.

"You get her out of here!" says Mulder. "You're dooming her by doing this. You're making her live this day over and over again! Her, you, me—all of us!"

"What the hell are you talking about?"

"Every day you die in here and every day it starts all over again. You can't want this for her. It's hell!"

"Hell? I'm doing this for her!" says Bernard.

Pam shakes her head. She is crying.

"Listen to him, Bernard." she says.

Bernard shakes his head and turns to Scully.

"Put your damn gun down!" he screams.

"Put your gun down, Scully," says Mulder. "Trust me—it's the only way out of here. You've got to put your gun down and let them out. He's got a bomb."

Confused, Scully places her gun slowly on the floor.

"Come on, Bernard," says Pam. "Let's go."

Bernard slowly lowers his gun. A police siren sounds in the distance. It's getting closer.

"You sonuvabitch!" he yells.

Bernard raises his gun and aims it at Mulder. He pulls the trigger—just as Pam steps in front of him. She falls, badly wounded. Stunned, Bernard drops the gun. Mulder handcuffs him. Scully pulls out her cell phone, and calls for help. Mulder kneels over Pam.

"This never happened before," she whispers.

Mulder nods gravely. Her smile is one of relief, of coming peace. She draws her final breath.

In the corridor of Mulder's apartment building a newspaper carrier tosses a fresh morning edition against his front door. Inside, Mulder jerks awake at the sound. He sits up—on his familiar couch. His cordless phone rings. Mulder answers it.

"Mulder, it's me," says Scully, at her desk in FBI headquarters.

Mulder picks up his wristwatch. It reads Tuesday 7:16 A.M.

"I'm late again, aren't I, Scully?"

"Not yet," says Scully. "But Skinner wants to see us in his office as soon as possible. He's asking for our report on the robbery yesterday. I'd like to hear it, too."

Mulder trudges to the front door and retrieves his newspaper.

"You were there, Scully," he says.

"That's not what I mean," she replies. "You still won't explain what happened yesterday, how you knew that Bernard Oates was strapped with explosives."

"Call it a feeling," says Mulder.

"And it was also a 'feeling' that he had an accomplice in the car?"

"I don't think she was an accomplice," says Mulder. "I think she was just trying to get away."

Mulder tells his partner that he'll be in in an hour

193

and hangs up. He looks at the front page. A headline reads: WOMAN DIES IN ROBBERY ATTEMPT. Underneath is a photograph of Pam taken on a happier day.

BACK STORY/6X15

Bill Murray, eat your heart out.

According to co-executive producer Vince Gilligan and producer John Shiban, "Monday" was *not* a rip-off of the movie *Groundhog Day.* Or *Sliding Doors.* Or any other of the many recent treatments of the theme of alternate realities and/or desperate protagonists caught in closed time loops.

No.

"When we rip off something," jokes Gilligan, "we rip off only the very best. In actuality, we were ripping off an old episode of *The Twilight Zone.*"

Really?

"It was a wonderful episode called 'Shadow Play,'" explains Gilligan. "It starts with a man—played by Dennis Weaver—on trial for murder, standing in front of the judge. The judge declares him guilty and tells him that his penalty, death by electrocution, will be carried out within the week.

"It turns out that Dennis Weaver is having a terrible nightmare every single night, the same nightmare over and over and over again. He gets convicted of his crime and sent to death row—and the end of his dream, always, is him being electrocuted. He realizes it's a dream, and starts trying to tell that to the people around him: his lawyer and prosecutor and the prison guard and the prison chaplain. He says, 'Don't you understand? You people don't really exist. You exist only because I'm having this dream. And if you get me off, get me a reprieve from the governor, you'll continue to live a little longer. But the moment I die, you die also.'

"Now the really neat thing about this," continues the writer/producer, "is that the camera follows all these people home, and they're troubled enough by this weird conversation they've had with this crazy guy for some part of them to wonder: 'What if it *is* true?' And so they ask Dennis Weaver: 'Well, if you know it's only a dream, why are you so scared of being electrocuted? And Weaver says, 'Don't you understand! It's a nightmare! And in your nightmares everything is always scary—it doesn't matter if you've had it a thousand times!'"

Gilligan leans back in his chair, smiling happily. "It was brilliant," he says. "Every base was covered."

He adds that his and Shiban's *X-File*-ian variation on this theme—written under extreme time pressure after the Christmas hiatus—went faster than usual because many of its story elements were repeated, with slight but significant variations, over and over. Gilligan also says that he particularly liked how the episode turned out, as did his writing partner.

"To me," says John Shiban, "what makes it a change of pace from the usual episode is that Mulder's realization of the nature of the X-File he's trying to figure out comes from an intellectual place rather than an emotional place. Sure, there's emotion—he feels a lot of emotion for poor Pam's plight—but ultimately it's a complex mind puzzle, a sort of puzzle box, that he has to solve. And then we have some humor—Mulder's troubles with his waterbed—to help ease the viewer into repetitive scenes that might be monotonous otherwise."

Monotonous it was not. Indeed, numerous prominent members of the *X-Files* family—including Gillian Anderson and Frank Spotnitz—rate 6X15 as one of the best stand-alone episodes of this or any other season. One of the main reasons for this was the fact that many behind-the-scenes staffers were inspired to put in even more preproduction overtime than usual.

Director Kim Manners, for instance: Realizing that he would have to shoot what were essentially the same scenes up to five times, he diagrammed every camera angle and camera move in advance with an eye toward making each succeeding near-repetition somehow fresh and different. "It was a huge challenge," he says, "and there was a lot of pressure, which I seem to work best under."

For his part, first assistant director Bruce Carter took it upon himself to deconstruct, then reassemble, the entire complicated shooting script in terms of time, place, and continuity.

"I did a timeline—it was one of the things I was proudest of all year," Carter says.

He explains, "We needed it to keep track of what everybody is doing, and when they're doing it, each time the bank robbery repeats itself. For example, what's happening outside the bank? Where's Mulder now? Where's Scully? Where's Pam and her bank robber boyfriend? What's Skinner doing in his office? Who's in line at the bank, what are the tellers and head teller doing, and at what windows? Where's the SWAT team?

"It wasn't completely stipulated in the script, so it took me two weeks to figure out the exact time everything had to happen: when Mulder had to wake up; how long it took him to get to the office; what time the bank had to open, and so on and so on, for each slightly different version of the same morning event. When I finished this huge project I gave it to the script supervisor, and she always knew exactly where she was and how to set the on-screen clocks in whatever scene they were filming."

A bit less precise—but no less important—were several other contributions. Casting director Rick Millikan saw more than his usual quota of young actresses before casting the part of Pam. "It was a difficult part to cast," he says. "Because you had to feel sorry for this woman's terrible, unbelievable plight—basically she's trapped in a living hell—without at any time thinking she's insane.

Because Mulder would never believe this woman if there was even a hint of that."

Millikan and the producers' ultimate (and ultimately successful, it was unanimously believed) choice was Carrie Hamilton, comedienne/actress Carol Burnett's daughter, who has had extensive experience playing character roles in movies and on television. For the part of bank robber Bernard they picked Darren Burrows, formerly a regular (he played radio station employee Ed Chigliak) on *Northern Exposure.* "He did beautifully," says Millikan.

For the part of the "Craddock Marine Bank," Ilt Jones and his location department staff selected and secured an architecturally impressive ninety-six-year-old building, located at Fourth and Main Street in downtown Los Angeles, that had once indeed been a bank but was now a combination animation school/educational film production house. Under the supervision of production designer Corey Kaplan, the place was gutted and turned back into a financial institution: complete with double-glazed windows, faux marble columns, and fake ATMs, down to the check-writing desks and chained pens, procured from a standard bank-supply catalog by set decorator Tim Stepeck.

After a long, fruitless search in Los Angeles—apparently, the city's level of swinging bachelor hipness is lower than previously thought—Stepeck had to obtain the waterbed for Mulder's bedroom from a specialized San Francisco furniture store.

To give Pam the proper haunted look, makeup department head Cheri Montesanto-Medcalf applied plenty of mascara under Carrie Hamilton's eyes—then intentionally smudged it all badly. Pam's stringy, multi-hued hairstyle was Carrie Hamilton's own creation—but hair department head Dena Green had to recreate it precisely for the wig worn by the actress's stunt double.

Mulder's two-part paycheck and pay envelope—not exactly FBI issue, but as close to it as possible while satisfying the requirements of the plotline—was manufactured, after several phone calls to the J. Edgar Hoover Building, by the property master. The huge fleet of Washington, D.C., police cars—their roof lights powered by carefully concealed battery chargers, since keeping their engines running would create too much noise for filming—was assembled by picture car coordinator Danny Briggs.

But undoubtedly the most exciting moment of "Monday's" creation was the eleventh—and final—day of shooting at the downtown bank location. A four-block area was sealed off tightly. A total of eleven cameras—some running at regular speed; others cranked faster for ultra-slow motion—were trained on the building.

(Unavoidably, several of the cameras themselves were in other cameras' field of vision. They were painstakingly erased by special effects producer Bill Millar weeks afterward.)

The cameras rolled. Kim Manners yelled "action"—setting the complicated choreography in motion—and the *X-Files* special effects crew set off an impressive burst of fireball-producing explosives.

It had to be gotten right the first time, and it was. Enough footage was obtained for each of the "separate" conclusions to the bank holdup.

"I did my homework, and we were successful," says Manners. "I'm very proud of that."

The waterbed in Mulder's apartment first appeared in "Dreamland II" (6X05). While Morris Fletcher, Mulder and Scully's black-ops nemesis, will reappear later in the season, the waterbed now vanishes, presumably forever. "We figure Mulder's landlord made him get rid of it," cracks John Shiban.

Co-executive producer Vince Gilligan's references to his girlfriend in "Monday": Holly Rice grew up in Cradock, a suburb of Portsmouth, Virginia. Her mother's maiden name is Bernard.

Assistant director Bruce Carter is a former mineral geologist, who survived a plane crash in the Alaskan bush to get his first show business job in the 1986 Michael Keaton movie *Gung Ho.*

ALPHA

6X16

A **wolflike creature** from China—long thought extinct—is cutting a murderous swath through California. Aided by an animal behavior expert with suspicious motives, Mulder and Scully must somehow track it down.

EPISODE: 6X16
FIRST AIRED: March 28, 1999
EDITOR: Heather MacDougall
WRITTEN BY: Jeffrey Bell
DIRECTED BY: Peter Markle

GUEST STARS:
Andrew J. Robinson (Dr. Ian Detweiler)
Melinda Culea (Karin Berquist)
Jeffrey Cahn (Thomas Duffy)
James Micheal Connor (Jake Conroy)
Michael Mantell (Dr. James Riley)
David Starwalt (Frank Fiedler)

Tuan Tran (Fong)
Yau-Gene Chan (Woo)
Dana Lee (Yee)
Lisa Picotte (Stacey Muir)
Mandy Levin (Angie)
Treva Tegtmeier (Peggy)
Adrienne Wilde (Nurse)

PRINCIPAL SETTINGS:
San Pedro, Bellflower, and Signal Hill,
California; Washington, D.C.

alpha

The Chinese freighter *T'ien Kou* plows eastward across the Pacific. Two crewmen—their names are Woo and Fong—enter the cargo hold. They speak in Cantonese.

"Come on, Fong," says Woo. "Don't be scared!"

He leads his reluctant shipmate toward a large steel packing crate pierced with air holes.

"I saw them load it in Hong Kong," says Woo. "Tell me what you think it is. Yesterday I put my face up to the box. The thing inside tried to bite me."

"Maybe it's a tiger," says Fong, nervously.

"Maybe," says Woo.

Woo walks to one end of the crate to a narrow, covered viewing slot, slides it open, and shines his flashlight inside. The beam catches a pair of red, glowing, angry eyes.

Fong steps up to his friend and takes a look.

"With eyes like that," says Woo, "how can it be a tiger?"

The creature snarls and leaps toward the slot; the men jump back in fear. The creature inside gets even angrier; banging against the sides of its cage. Then nothing. After a few tense seconds Woo kicks the cage with his foot. No response.

"I think we killed it," says Woo.

He pulls a key out of his pocket and opens the padlock securing the crate. With Fong's help he lifts the heavy lid. Flashlight in hand, he peers inside.

Several days later the freighter is docked at San Pedro Harbor, near Los Angeles. The ship's captain, Yee, leads two port policemen into the hold and toward the metal crate. His expression is grave. He speaks excellent English.

"This hold was secured in Hong Kong," he says. "I don't know how this happened. It makes no sense. We found the cage still locked. Two of my men are missing."

The captain reaches the cage, the policemen close behind him. Kneeling beside it is a bearded man in his fifties, who looks at the captain with a mixture of contempt and tightly controlled anger.

"Who's in charge here? You?" he demands.

"Who are you?" replies Yee.

"My name is Detweiler. I'm the owner of this cargo. I was to be notified immediately of its arrival. There's an animal in here, damnit! It needs care."

He glances down. Blood has leaked from the cage and has pooled on the floor.

Captain Yee quickly opens the padlock. The policemen lift the lid and peer inside. At the bottom of the crate lie Woo and Fong, dead and horribly mauled.

At FBI headquarters at 7:10 that evening Mulder pins a photo of the dead crewmen on his office wall. Scully appears in the doorway.

"Aren't you going home?" she asks.

"I am home," says Mulder. "I'm just feathering the nest."

Scully asks him about the photo. Mulder recaps the incident in San Pedro.

"Mind if I ask the cause of death?" says Scully.

"In the crime report," says Mulder, "it says multiple bite wounds."

"From what?"

"Well, the Hong Kong manifest has the cargo listed as a dog."

"A dog? A *dog* dog?"

"*Yo quiero Taco Bell,*" cracks Mulder.

The joke gets the reception it deserves.

"That alone," adds Mulder, "is not what drew me to this case. The two men were found inside the container, which was locked from the outside."

"What happened to the dog?" asks Scully.

"Dog gone," says Mulder. "Doggone."

"Yeah, I got it," says Scully.

"Did anyone examine the victims, Mulder?"

Mulder shakes his head.

"Look," says Scully. "Bite wounds are rarely lethal in themselves. I mean, they are not the cause of death. They lead to it through the loss of blood. It makes me wonder how accurate this report is."

"Local PD wrote it up," says Mulder. "Department of Fish and Wildlife is on the case. I got an outside source who thinks it was a dog."

"Mulder, I don't have to tell you how absolutely and completely wrong that seems. I mean, they were found dead in a locked cage, right? Two grown men. You're not going to tell me that a dog did this."

Mulder looks at his partner, smiles, and shrugs.

"*Bad* dog," he says.

Later that night in the backyard of a small house in Bellflower, south of Los Angeles, a golden retriever barks excitedly at something. A uniformed U.S. Customs official named Jake Conroy steps onto his rear patio.

"WHAT HAPPENED TO THE DOG?"–Scully

"DOG GONE, DOGGONE."
—Mulder

"YEAH—I GOT IT."–Scully

"Shh! Quiet, JoJo!" he says. "C'mon. That's enough now."

He grabs the dog by the collar and begins to pull him inside—until he sees the silhouette of a large dog on his translucent back fence. JoJo continues to bark. Conroy yells for the strange dog to get out of his yard. The shadow does not move. Conroy locks his dog inside the house, then peers over the back fence. Nothing. He looks up and down the alley where the dog might have gone. Empty.

He reenters his house, walks through the kitchen, and calls for JoJo. She is lying motionless under a table in the foyer.

"There you are, girl," he says, affectionately. "Ya mutt! Big ol' lazybones!"

He walks over to his dog, kneels down, and gives her a scratch behind the ear. His hand comes away covered with blood. Conroy is horrified, and at that moment there is a savage growl from behind the Customs man. Conroy turns to see a snarling wolflike canine with bared teeth and glowing red eyes.

"Stay away!" shouts Conroy, fearfully. "Go on! Go!"

The slathering beast snarls again, and leaps. Conroy screams and tries to run for safety. He makes it as far as his screen door, which is spattered with his blood as the dog rips out his throat.

At the San Pedro docks the next day, a uniformed U.S. Fish and Wildlife officer—his name is Jeffrey Cahn—examines the bloody crate. Mulder and Scully arrive and introduce themselves to him. Cahn tells the agents that he and his men had a look around the ship. Scully asks him if they found anything.

"Nothing conclusive, really," says Cahn. "But I can tell you the dog is not likely still on the ship."

"How did you determine that?" asks Mulder.

"You ever owned a dog, sir?" says Cahn.

"Yeah," says Mulder.

"Had to clean up after it?"

Mulder smiles—he gets it.

Scully asks Cahn what type of dog they're looking for.

"I'm not really sure," he replies. "The man it was shipped to, his name is Detweiler. Dr. Ian Detweiler. He calls himself a cryptozoologist."

This gets Mulder's attention.

"Cryptozoologist?" he says.

"Yeah," says Cahn. "They deal with animals thought to be extinct, animals—"

"—that aren't supposed to exist," says Mulder, excitedly. "like Sasquatch, and the Ogopogo, and the Abominable Snowman, and—"

"Don't mind him," interrupts Scully. "He'll go on forever. Did you have a chance to talk to this Dr. Detweiler?"

"About five minutes ago," says Cahn, who at that moment is approached by the very man he's talking about.

"LOOSE? THIS
ANIMAL IS A
LITTLE BIT
MORE THAN
LOOSE.
IT SEEMS TO
HAVE KILLED
TWO PEOPLE."
—Mulder

"Officer Cahn, any progress?" asks Detweiler, impatiently.

In response, Cahn introduces him to Mulder and Scully. Detweiler turns to Mulder.

"Who should I be speaking to about the theft of this animal?" he says.

"Theft?" replies Mulder. "What do you mean theft?"

"This is a very valuable animal that's disappeared. A rare breed, and arguably a priceless specimen."

"A breed of what?" asks Scully, skeptically.

"Wanshang Dhole," says Cahn. "It's a canid."

"It's an Asian dog," says Mulder, quickly. "Supposed to have been extinct for the last one hundred and fifty years."

Detweiler turns to Mulder, surprised and pleased.

"Yes! That's right, actually," he says.

"And you have one of these?" asks Scully.

"I was on the expedition that caught it," says Detweiler.

Cahn looks at the scientist dubiously.

"Be that as it may," he says, "we now have an unquarantined animal loose."

"Loose?" says Mulder. "This animal is a little bit more than loose. It seems to have killed two people."

Detweiler smiles at Mulder reassuringly.

"No, no," he says. "This is not a predatory animal. Chinese folklore has imbued it with mythic qualities, but it doesn't even hunt. It scavenges."

At that moment another Fish and Game officer—whose name is Frank Fiedler—calls for Cahn from a nearby catwalk.

"I just got a report on the radio," he says. "Some kind of vicious dog attack in Bellflower."

At 9:32 that morning Jake Conroy's house is swarming with police. Mulder checks out the yard, then turns to his partner, who is approaching him.

"Watch your step!" he says, grinning.

Scully frowns worriedly, then delivers her report.

"Jake Conroy," she says. "Age thirty. He was employed as a Customs agent by the federal government. The bite marks match those of the victims on the Chinese freighter. In this case it bit off the man's hand. There's some talk in the house that he may have been involved in the theft of the animal, and it turned on him."

"Talk about biting the hand that feeds you," says Mulder.

"Well, it does make sense," says Scully. "The victim and his dog were attacked inside the house with all the doors shut. It couldn't have happened unless the dog was being kept inside."

"If all the doors were shut," replies Mulder, "then how did he get out?"

Scully has no answer.

"I think," says Mulder, "we're speaking in too-common terms about an animal we're calling a dog but which displays none of the behavior of man's best friend."

"You mean like covering up crime scenes?"

"You get a biscuit, Scully!"

"So you're talking about a dog that has human intelligence. Well, even if there were such an animal, where would we even begin to look for one?"

"With a human," replies Mulder, "who thinks like an animal."

Later that day Mulder and Scully drive through a rural area and enter Berquist Kennels, a large and well-kept compound. A fresh-scrubbed young woman is digging a fence post near a large wooden house. Mulder asks her if she's Karin Berquist.

"No. Stacey Muir," she says. "I'm just putting up this fence for her. She's been having some coyote problems. You two looking for Karin about boarding?"

"No," says Mulder. "It's actually more of a behavior problem."

"Yeah," says Scully. "He doesn't listen, and he chews on the furniture."

Mulder tells her they're with the FBI. Stacey leads them inside the house, to a dimly lit study crammed with books and pictures of dogs.

"You sure this woman's not an authority on bats?" asks Scully.

"Karin Berquist knows more about canine behaviorisms than anybody on the planet," says Mulder. "She's lived with wild canids and wolves in the wilderness on five different continents."

"How come you know so much about her and you don't know what she looks like?"

"I've never actually met her."

"Yet you assume she'll help us?"

"Well, no. Actually, it's not an assumption. She is the one who told me about this case."

"So, you two are chummy."

"I've read her books," says Mulder, a bit defensively.

On a nearby shelf are Berquist's books. They include *The Wolf Inside*, *Dogs Don't Lie*, and *Better than Human*. Scully shoots Mulder a suspicious look.

"She's not a real people person," says her partner.

Scully switches on a desk lamp, illuminating an I WANT TO BELIEVE poster, identical to the one Mulder used to have in his office.

"Well," says Scully, "she seems to have made a connection to you."

Karin Berquist enters. She is a fortyish woman dressed in dark, loose clothing. She wears no make-up, and her face is pale and drawn. She is followed by a pack of six or so small dogs who sit in place—instantly—at her command.

Mulder introduces himself and his partner. Berquist walks to the window, closes the blinds, and lowers herself slowly into a chair.

"I wish I'd known," says Karin, wearily. "I don't get many visitors. Stacey tells me you have a question about behaviorism."

"Yes, it's about the animal I'm tracking," says Mulder. "The one you mentioned in your e-mail. About its intelligence—"

"A canid's intelligence is far superior to ours, if that's what you want to know," says Berquist, frowning.

"Intelligent enough to murder?" asks Scully.

"Mulder? She's a friend of yours?" she sighs.

"We met online," says her partner.

Scully raises her eyebrows.

"Two professionals exchanging information," says Mulder.

In a dark alley in Signal Hill, just north of Long Beach, Frank Fiedler halts his truck in front of an overflowing Dumpster. The USF & W cop radios his dispatcher to report that he suspects something has

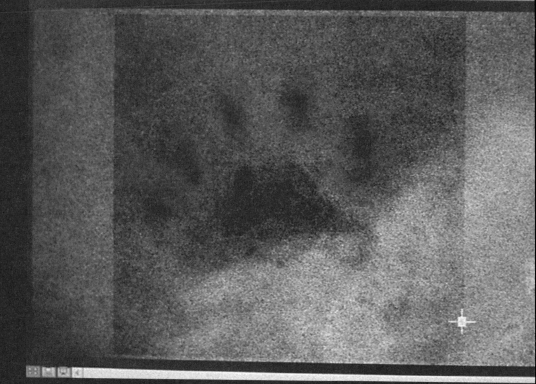

untitled 3

"Murder takes no intelligence," says Berquist."It's a human behaviorism."

"What about hunting?" asks Mulder.

"Coyotes use elaborate trickeries to draw out their prey. Many canids do. Alone or in packs."

"What about a Dhole?" asks Scully, arms folded.

"If you mean the Wanshang Dhole," says Berquist, staring glumly at the floor, "it's extinct."

She turns to Mulder.

"Is there any other reason you came here?" she asks.

"No. Thank you, Karin," he says.

Karin rises with some difficulty and heads abruptly out the door. The dogs follow her. Scully shoots Mulder a look.

been scavenging from it. Wielding a long catch pole, he sifts carefully through the garbage. He recoils— among the pieces of debris is a human hand, gnawed off at the wrist.

Something passes quickly behind him; he turns just in time to catch a glimpse of a doglike figure. He heads in the animal's direction, opens a large metal door, and steps down into a dark boiler room. He walks cautiously down a steam-filled corridor, and hears a noise behind him.

"Hey!" he shouts, turning.

He sees the silhouette of a man.

"Hello, sir!" says Fiedler, relieved. "I'm with U.S. Fish and Wildlife. Maybe you've seen a dog I'm looking for. Sir? Can you hear me?"

The shadowy figure does not reply. It walks slowly toward Fiedler, then seems to sink down to the ground, changing shape as it goes. It turns into a dog, emerging out of the mist toward the terrified Fiedler. It snarls—its eyes glowing red—and leaps for its human prey's throat.

At 8:34 the next morning the boiler room is a murder investigation site. Mulder and Scully join an angry Jeffrey Cahn.

"I'm joking. Sorry," says Karin, after an awkward pause. "Thought you might use some help."

Mulder looks Karin in the eye.

"You said that a dog, or a canid, hunts only what it needs. But I've got four bodies with bite marks on them from an animal that seems to kill for no other reasons."

Karin asks Mulder who the victims were. Mulder tells her, and that all of them came into contact with

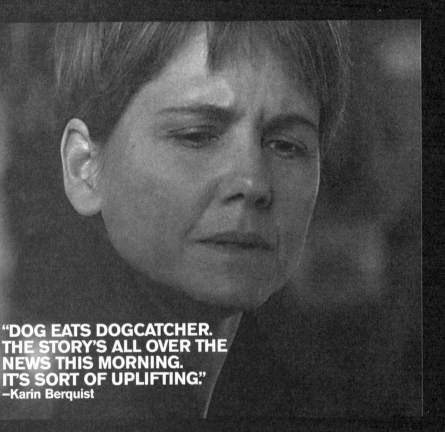

"DOG EATS DOGCATCHER. THE STORY'S ALL OVER THE NEWS THIS MORNING. IT'S SORT OF UPLIFTING."
–Karin Berquist

"You wanna catch a killer?" says the cop. "You arrest that cryptosonuvabitch who shipped that dog over here."

Scully asks him if it was the same dog. The question makes Cahn even angrier. Mulder tells him they're looking for his friend and colleague's killer, just like he is.

"You can catch it," says Cahn. "I'm gonna kill it."

Cahn stalks away. Karin Berquist arrives in the boiler room, and Scully frowns and tells Mulder she's going to examine the victim. Karin approaches Mulder, who tells her he hadn't expected to see her again.

"Dog eats dogcatcher," she says. "The story's all over the news this morning. It's sort of uplifting."

Mulder smiles embarrassingly, but says nothing.

the creature sometime before the attack.

"Classic dominant alpha territorial behavior," says Karin.

"No," says Mulder. "This animal seems to have ranged many miles to make its attacks. In each case it seems to have outsmarted, or at least tricked its victims."

"Unlike we *homo sapiens*," replies Karin, "canid motives are simple and direct. It would be an extraordinary case to find one who kills for sport. Likely we may never know. I'm sure someone will kill it first."

Mulder spots a familiar figure entering the room.

"This man over here claims to have caught it once," he says. "Maybe he can catch it again. It's Dr. Ian Detweiler. Do you know him?"

"COME ON, DOG. COME ON."
--Karin Berquist

"No," says Karin, "but I dislike him already."

Detweiler approaches Mulder and tells him—a little too vehemently—that he has examined the crime scene and there's no evidence his dog was involved.

"But it's still on the loose," says Mulder.

"How did you say you caught it originally?" asks Karin.

Suddenly defensive at this question, Detweiler says nothing. After an awkward silence, Mulder introduces him to Karin.

"We tranquilized it," says Detweiler, reluctantly. "After tracking it for two weeks."

"You admire it, don't you?" asks Karin.

"I admire its ability to survive," says Detweiler.

Karin turns to Mulder.

"I think I'll look around, too," she says.

Later that day Cahn stands by his truck, parked in the alley. He radios headquarters that he's leaving his tranquilizer gun in his car, and using live rounds from now on. He hears a sound somewhere behind him, turns suddenly, and is face-to-face with Detweiler.

"You scared me," says Cahn, relieved.

Detweiler's face is a mask of controlled fury.

"You kill that dog," he says, "and I'll kill you."

In Karin Berquist's darkened study she looks at a blown-up photograph of a paw print on her computer monitor. Mulder and Scully are also present.

"This man Detweiler said he found no evidence at the scene," says Karin. "With very little effort I was able to find several tracks on the floor of the building where the man was attacked."

"Do they tell you anything?" asks Scully.

"That this is a large, rangy animal," says Karin. "With primitive, even pre-evolutionary aspects. It isn't perfectly visible, but with the computer I can enhance the prints so you can see it: a fifth toe pad on the right paw. Canids only have four toes."

Mulder places his hand on Karin's and moves the cursor.

"Yeah, he's got a vestigial toe pad on his front paws—right there," he says.

Karin reacts slightly—but perceptibly—to his touch.

"The dewclaw," she says. "Serving no purpose now, though some believe it was once a prehensile thumb."

"And that's what you think the print indicates?" asks Scully.

"I'm told this animal went in and out of closed buildings," says Karin.

"Yesterday," replies Scully, "you dismissed the possibility outright that a dog—or a canid, as you call it—would behave like this."

"I dismissed the idea of murder."

"But you'll accept the idea that it behaves in every other way like Jack the Ripper."

"I'm just going by the facts," Karin replies. "In

Chinese myth, the Dhole can be evil, capable of opening doors, stealing wives, and disappearing into thin air. Maybe there is some basis in reality for this trickster myth."

"Oh, I'm fairly certain there is," says Scully.

A few minutes later Mulder joins Scully in their rental car. She is obviously troubled.

"How well do you know this woman, Mulder?" she asks.

"How well do you know anyone you meet on the Internet?" he replies. "She likes to talk."

"Well, I question her motives."

"Are you suggesting that this case was a way to get me out here? To meet me? I'm flattered, but no. I don't know this woman. But I'm gonna go out on a limb and say there's no way in hell she has anything to do with those four people being dead."

"She's enamored of you, Mulder," replies Scully. "Don't underestimate a woman. They can be tricksters, too."

At a veterinary clinic nearby later that day, a receptionist hands a prescription to a woman holding her St. Bernard on a leash. Detweiler enters and the dog barks furiously at him. The woman apologizes and takes the dog outside.

The proprietor of the clinic, Dr. James Riley, appears. Detweiler reminds him that he called earlier for an order of animal tranquilizer. Riley replies that he has very little on hand; Detweiler says he'll take anything he's got.

"Can I ask you what these tranqs are for?" says Riley.

"An animal that escaped from the port in San Pedro," says Detweiler.

"Not that dog that's been attacking people?" says Riley.

"Now, if you don't mind, I'm in a bit of a hurry," is his curt reply.

Riley fills out a charge slip for the drugs, runs it through his imprinter with Detweiler's credit card, and hands it to the scientist, who signs it.

"This dog you're looking for," says Riley. "You're not looking around here?"

"I'm afraid we are," says Detweiler, turning abruptly to leave.

Later that afternoon Dr. Riley walks back into the kennel area of his clinic, wishing a good night to his caged patients as he goes past. He clicks a padlock shut on the rear door. The caged dogs begin whimpering, then barking loudly. Riley turns to see the wild dog snarling at him, eyes glowing. He runs to the front door and escapes just ahead of it, locking the kennel securely behind him.

Shortly afterward the clinic is surrounded by police cars. Jeffrey Cahn—carrying a .45 pistol—enters the clinic with his men just behind him. Riley directs him to where the dog is trapped. He unlocks the door, gets a quick glimpse of the creature, and fires three times. Silence.

"Did you hit him?" asks Riley, nervously.

"I think so. He's down," says Cahn.

Lying on the floor, bleeding from a graze wound, is the St. Bernard.

"It's the wrong dog." says Riley, distressed.

A short time later Mulder and Scully arrive at the clinic. Cahn sheepishly tells Mulder what happened. Scully listens for a moment, then heads toward the front door.

Inside the kennel area the St. Bernard lies on an examination table, anesthetized, while Dr. Riley tends to his wounds.

"All done, pal," says the vet, stripping off his gloves. "You're gonna be all right. Now I've gotta find out how you got back in here, huh?"

Scully enters the clinic lobby and looks around. After a few moments she spots a framed photo on the wall of Karin Berquist with several of her dogs. The picture is inscribed: TO MY GOOD FRIEND JAMES RILEY—STAY WILD, KARIN. She is contemplating this when she hears a man's scream from the back room. She draws her gun and enters the kennel.

"If you can hear me, don't move!" she announces. "Just stay where you are and tell me you're okay!"

Silence. She walks to the examination table, on which the St. Bernard is lying perfectly still. On the floor nearby is the bloody corpse of Dr. Riley. The veterinarian's throat has been torn out. Scully kneels down, checks for a pulse, and calls out for Mulder.

Mulder approaches, takes in the grisly sight, draws his own gun, and leaves with his partner to call the paramedics. When the agents are out of sight, the St. Bernard slowly morphs into the killer dog and leaps off the table.

Late that night Karin Berquist sits in front of her computer monitor. Scully enters her study and sits across from her.

"Where's Fox?" asks Karin, expectantly.

"Continuing his investigation," says Scully, evenly.

"You're not working together?"

"No. This is my investigation."

"Of?"

"You," says Scully.

A moment of awkward silence.

"I thought at first that they were eccentricities," says Scully. "Or affectation. The dark, the clothes. But it's photosensitivity; your sleeves cover up the skin lesions. It's why you're here among the humans, instead of out in the field. Systemic lupus erythematosus."

Karin closes her eyes.

"Lupus. From the Latin for wolf," she says. "Ironic, isn't it?"

"Ironic? Or perverse?" asks Scully.

Karin sighs.

"I ignored the symptoms for years," she says. "I've always felt more like a wolf than a person."

"But not with Mulder," says Scully, softly. "With Mulder, you found somebody you could communicate with. Someone who challenged you. But that wasn't enough. You needed to lure him out here."

Karin is stung and angered.

"I lack your feminine wiles," she says, sarcastically.

Scully closes her eyes and turns away.

"You don't believe it, do you?" says the agent. "Not for a minute that there's an animal out there, killing."

"I don't believe that this man Dr. Detweiler ever caught it," replies Karin. "I lived in Asia. I know about the Wanshang Dhole. And if it survived for over a century it was because it was more cunning than man. More cunning than this man Detweiler ever dreamed of."

"More cunning than you?" asks Scully sharply, adding, "I'm watching you."

"You watch," says Karin, softly, "but you don't see."

In the kennel area at the veterinary clinic Mulder scrapes several drops of dried blood off the floor and places them in an evidence Baggie. He rummages through the receptionist's desk and comes across Detweiler's credit card receipt for the animal tranquilizers. He picks up the phone and begins to dial.

In the alley in Signal Hill Jeffrey Cahn's truck stands empty, its door open. A dispatcher comes on the radio, calling for Cahn with the news that there's an emergency phone call for him. Cahn is nowhere to be seen until, after several increasingly urgent calls, he races to the truck to pick up his microphone.

The dispatcher patches him through to Mulder, who tells him of Detweiler's drug purchase. The agent asks Cahn to come to the clinic and help him. Cahn tells Mulder he'll be there in fifteen minutes.

Cahn gets into the driver's seat and starts the engine. His eyes drift to the rearview mirror. He sees the killer dog, teeth bared and eyes glowing. It snarls, leaping forward onto its victim.

At Los Angeles County Hospital in Torrance the next morning, Cahn lies unconscious in intensive care. Mulder enters his room and sees Detweiler sitting in a chair next to his bed.

"What are you doing here?" demands Mulder.

"I heard what had happened," explains Detweiler. "I didn't know how bad he might be. I thought I might get a description of the animal."

"Who told you he'd been attacked?" asks Mulder.

"I've been in contact with Officer Cahn. I learned through his office."

"No, you didn't," says Mulder, sharply. "No, you hadn't. Officer Cahn wouldn't have anything to do with you."

"He was going to kill it," says Detweiler.

"Does that frighten you?" says Mulder, hauling Detweiler brusquely to his feet. "You aren't hunting this animal. You know very well it can't be caught."

"Then how could I have brought it here?" says Detweiler.

"That's what no one can figure out. Except for Karin Berquist. She knows what was in that cage, and she knows that it must be killed. And that's the thought that she can't bear, because she doesn't want this thing to be extinct anymore than you do."

"You're not making any sense!"

"I think I am," says Mulder, coolly. "You went to China looking for that animal. You may have tracked it, as you claim, but the rest is far from the truth. You found the Wanshang Dhole. But you never caught it, because it caught you.

"You may not have known what was happening to you at first, but you're well aware now. That when night comes you stop being yourself."

"That's insane!"

"No. *You* become the trickster. A shape-shifting man who becomes an animal. You killed because you could. You may have resisted it at first; you may have hated what you'd become. Eventually it took you over. That's where the tranquilizer came in. I found traces of etorphine in animal blood at the clinic. You injected yourself with the tranquilizers hoping to stop the killings. But they didn't, and they haven't, and they won't."

Detweiler exits the hospital room, stone-faced. The first person he sees is Karen Berquist.

"I protected you as long as I could," she says. "I won't any longer."

Later that day Mulder enters Karin Berquist's study. She is waiting there for him.

"I can usually get a sense of a person right away from the dogs," she says. "Dogs are the best judges of character I know."

"I'm sensing something myself here," says Mulder. "I'm thinking that maybe I've been misled. That you haven't been perfectly honest with me about this case."

"I've been honest with you. Though perhaps not with myself," says Karin. "I was looking forward to meeting you. I wouldn't admit how much."

"You might also have admitted what you knew about this animal. That it wasn't an animal at all."

"I heard the reports and called you out—if only so you could disprove them. What I knew was it couldn't be a dog responsible for those killings."

"It's Detweiler, isn't it?" says Mulder.

"Yes," says Karin. "I only realized it when I saw him.

"My failure was in thinking I was protecting the animal, that by deceiving you, it might be captured alive. He's got to be put down, Fox. That's the only way to stop him."

Mulder tells her that Scully is tailing him, watching Detweiler's every move.

"He'll elude her easily," she says.

"And go where?"

"To the man he only wounded," she replies. "To the hospital. To finish the kill."

At the hospital later that night Scully sits on a bench outside Cahn's room. Mulder arrives; his partner asks him why he pulled her away from Detweiler, who hasn't shown the slightest sign of returning for Cahn.

"It's not yet dark," replies Mulder. "You should take a load off. We might be here all night."

He tells her his theory about Detweiler being the killer dog, and the doglike behavior which would compel him to finish off Cahn. He adds that Karin Berquist confirmed it. Scully stares at her partner skeptically.

"Mulder, the only thing Karin Berquist is interested in is you," she says. "You're kidding yourself if you don't think she's manipulated this entire situation for her own purposes."

"He'll come here tonight, Scully," says Mulder. "You'll see."

That night Karin locks her dogs in the new gated run. She hobbles back to her house, then stops, hearing something in the distance.

At 2:02 A.M. Mulder sits in the hospital corridor. He

stands abruptly, wakes Scully—who has been sleeping on a bench beside him—and tells her that Detweiler isn't coming.

"You'll get no argument from me," says Scully, groggily.

"He's not coming here tonight," says Mulder. "Karin knew that. She lied to me."

At the kennel Karin enters her house and walks upstairs to her study. She pulls a tranquilizer pistol out of her desk drawer and loads it. A wolflike figure emerges from the woods and runs toward her house.

Karin's phone rings. She picks up the receiver and places it on the desk.

"Karin? Fox Mulder," says the faint voice at the other end. "I know what you're doing. If you can hear me, lock your doors. I'm on my way."

The killer dog enters the house through an unlocked door and, panting slightly, moves slowly up the stairs. Karin stands and cocks the pistol. The dog appears across the room from her and snarls. Karin stands her ground. She puts down the gun.

"Come on, dog," she says, softly. "Come on."

The creature leaps for Karin's throat and knocks her backward into a window. The glass shatters. Woman and dog fly outside the house, then plunge two stories to the ground.

The caged dogs start to bark furiously. Mulder and Scully arrive, and see a naked Detweiler impaled on a fence post, dead. Karin Berquist, covered with blood, lies a few feet away.

In his office at FBI headquarters the next day, Mulder sits slumped forward with his head in his hands. Scully stands in the doorway.

"You going home?" she says quietly.

"Yeah. Pretty soon," says Mulder.

"You think this was your fault," she says.

"I think," he says, "that I believed her very quickly. Maybe that was my fault, too."

"Why wouldn't you believe her?"

"I barely knew her."

"She had many secrets, that's for sure," says Scully. "I think that Karin Berquist lived by her instincts. That she sized people up pretty quickly, and I think she had you figured out to a *T*.

"I think she saw in you a kindred spirit, Mulder. I think she may not have been able to express that to you. Maybe what she did was the highest form of compliment."

Mulder sighs.

"You going to be okay?" asks Scully. "Oh—this came for you."

She hands her partner a large white tube, mailed from Berquist Kennels, and leaves. Mulder opens it. Inside is a large poster. He unrolls it and attaches it to his wall. It is the poster that hung in Karin's study. I WANT TO BELIEVE, it reads.

BACK STORY/6X16

"Scary Dogs in the City."

Thus read the index card hanging for several months in first-year staff writer Jeffrey Bell's office. By the late fall of 1998, however, these four little words were well on their way to becoming a fully formed *X-Files* stand-alone episode.

Explains Bell: "The whole thing started when I saw a pack of dogs hanging out near a freeway in downtown Los Angeles. I thought, *Nobody owns these dogs, yet these dogs are somehow surviving. How?*"

Having pitched this rather open-ended concept early in the season, Bell looked up from his computer one day to see that his embryonic idea was scheduled as the sixteenth episode of the season. He frantically began writing on several different story ideas that he pursued doggedly to dead ends.

"One of them," recalls Bell, "was a reversal of the movie *Incredible Journey,* in which a desperate family moves three thousand miles to get away from their killer pet—who's waiting for them at their new house, really pissed. Another one, which was a little like 'D.P.O' [3X03] and a little like 'The Rain King' [6X07], was about a kid who worked at the dog pound and who didn't get angry; the dogs got angry for him. The pack of dogs was his id. But neither one of these had enough really cool visuals. Then Frank Spotnitz came up with the idea of the dog escaping from the ship."

Spotnitz also came up with the idea of Mulder's online "romance" with the canine expert Karin Berquist. But by that time it was January 2, and preproduction on 6X16 was scheduled to begin January 21.

In a classic case of *X-File*-ian brinkmanship, Bell started writing the script from scratch, while just about every other member of the writing staff massaged his hastily produced pages at one time or another. Indeed, "Alpha" was still being rewritten right up to the start of shooting on February 2. And in the meantime, the rest of the behind-the-camera-staff was struggling to figure out how to transfer this rather hairy project to film.

"It was a nightmare," groans executive producer Michael Watkins, shuddering at the memory of auditioning dozens of supposedly "trained" German Shepherds, wolves, and wolf hybrids for the part of the killer Wanshang Dhole. One trainer, he remembers, demonstrated "control" of her beasts by pulling on their massively linked choke chains and brandishing an ax handle; another suggested seriously that the *X-Files* cast and crew members be wrapped with electrical wires—to be zapped with current when necessary—for their own safety while working around the animals. At virtually the last minute a skilled, humane trainer-handler named Clint Rowe—who, in his capacity as a breeder, had sold border collies to Frank Spotnitz and Chris Carter—was hired, along with his three wolf-Malamute hybrids Flame, Eli, and Ki-che. For several close-up scenes a puppet dog head was used; all of the animal sequences went safely and smoothly.

"We saw many, *many* women," sighs casting director Rick Millikan of his exhausting search for an actress to play the difficult role of the enigmatic, somewhat androgynous Karin Berquist. (The day before Karin's first scene the experienced actress Melinda Culea—wife of the episode's director, Peter Markle—was selected. Nepotism aside, she was deemed by all concerned to have done a fine job.)

"The script called for an actual freighter to be filmed. But on a television budget, how do you get one to film at sea *and* sit at the dock where and when you want to shoot it?" laments locations manager Ilt Jones. Early in the production process the decision was made to create the exterior freighter images digitally. For the opening shot of the ship at sea, special effects producer Bill Millar commissioned a matte painting of the vessel—based on a twenty dollar model obtained through mail order—and inserted it into a real-world ocean filmed separately. The shot of the freighter tied up at the wharf was even more complex. After shooting an empty berth at the Port of Long Beach, then, without moving the camera, filming separate images of police cars arriving, forklifts maneuvering, etc., Millar "docked" his virtual freighter via computer.

Thankfully, however, *some* aspects of "Alpha" proceeded relatively painlessly. In searching for a suitable residence for Karin Berquist, Ilt Jones lucked out and located an uncannily appropriate ranch-style residence in Calabasas, an affluent suburb less than an hour's drive northwest of Los Angeles.

Says Jones, "The place belonged to a lawyer and his wife, a special education teacher who'd traveled the world, mountaineering and doing all sorts of other outdoorsy things. They'd brought back all these cool shrunken heads from New Guinea and death masks from Angola, and we actually left a lot of the decor just as it was. There was also a glorious canopy of trees around the house, and it was in a beautiful rustic setting. I fell in love with the place."

Rick Millikan had no trouble at all casting the unfortunate Chinese sailors Woo and Yee; there are ample numbers of Mandarin-speaking Chinese immigrant actors waiting for their big break in Hollywood.

Costume designer Christine Peters found it an interesting challenge finding the right wardrobe for Karin Berquist. "To me, she was a cross between Margaret Mead and Georgia O'Keefe," and when it came time to find the light-sensitive character a hat, Christine discovered serendipitously that the wide-brimmed model she herself schlepped around in the back of her car did the trick perfectly. "And believe it or not, I even got it back afterwards," beams Peters.

alpha

Researcher Lee Smith, ranging even more widely than usual, provided some real-world underpinnings to the plotline by providing background data on ancient Chinese mythology; the disease lupus; the ethical use of animal tranquilizer guns; and, *apropos* of animal-related crimes detected in foreign-registered merchant vessels docked in the United States, the jurisdictional boundaries between the U.S. Coast Guard, FBI, L.A. Harbor Police, U.S. Customs Service, and U.S. Fish & Wildlife Service.

Special effects makeup supervisor John Vulich manufactured the latex appliance that enabled the kindly veterinarian Dr. Riley to have his throat bitten out. Composer Mark Snow, in creating the score for 6X16, made liberal use of the Shakahachi flute, an ancient Japanese musical instrument.

Among his many other duties, producer Paul Rabwin supervised the dubbing of animal sounds onto "Alpha's" soundtrack. On other episodes Rabwin has hired human voice actors to do the barking and growling, but this time it was deemed that the real thing was sufficient.

This is Peter Markle's second *X-Files* episode. He previously directed "Christmas Carol" (5X05).

Actress Melinda Culea (Karin Berquist) has been a regular on *Knots Landing* and *The A-Team*. She has also guest-starred on numerous other shows, including *St. Elsewhere*, *Civil Wars*, and *Star Trek: The Next Generation*.

Special effects producer Bill Millar is a native of England. One of his first jobs was on the animation staff of the film *Close Encounters of the Third Kind;* he has since supervised special effects for many television series, including *Blue Thunder, Dark Shadows,* and *Buffy, The Vampire Slayer.*

T'ien Kou, the name of the Chinese freighter, translates to "Heavenly Dog," a colloquial Chinese term for "shooting star."

6(X)17

TREVOR

A violent prisoner gains the ability to **walk through walls**—unleashing a series of horrifying murders.

EPISODE: 6X17
FIRST AIRED: April 11, 1999
EDITOR: Lynne Willingham
WRITTEN BY: Jim Guttridge & Ken Hawryliw
DIRECTED BY: Rob Bowman

GUEST STARS:
John Diehl (Pinker Rawls)
Catherine Dent (June Burdett/Gurwitch)
Tuesday Knight (Jackie Gurwitch)
Frank Novak (Superintendent Raybert Fellowes)
David Bowe (Robert Werther)
Lamont Johnson (Whaley)
Keith Brunsmann (Bo)
Jerry Giles (Security Guard)
Jeffrey Schoeny (Trevor)
Cary Pfeffer (Anchorman)
Terri Merryman (Newscaster)
Jerry Giles (Security Guard)
Lee Corbin (Guard)
Christopher Dahlberg (State Trooper)
Robert Peters (Sergeant)

PRINCIPAL SETTINGS:
Jasper County, Jackson, and Meridian, Mississippi

Whaley holds the plywood in place while Rawls, wielding a hammer, nails it to the window frame. The wind howls through the compound.

"Man, this little piece of wood ain't gonna hold no twister!" shouts Whaley. "We need to dig a hole, you know what I'm sayin'? Big hole! Man oughta be givin' us shovels! This whole damn place gonna blow away! Why we even bother?"

Rawls's response is no response. He just keeps hammering nails.

"Yo, boy! Back me up here!" shouts Whaley.

"Shut up and hold it still!" shouts Rawls.

Whaley does a double take, offended.

"I know you ain't talkin' to me!" he shouts.

No response.

"You a big man, huh? Is that right? Charley Potatoes, big-ass criminal! Are you a bad man?"

Rawls simply keeps hammering. This makes Whaley even angrier.

"You a little bitch! That's all you are! You ain't got no money, you ain't got nothin'! I hold it still."

Smiling evilly, Whaley rattles the plywood against the window. Then he laughs loudly in his work partner's face.

Calmly, Rawls takes a nail out of his mouth, then swings his hammer in a wide arc. In a flash Whaley's hand is nailed neatly to the plywood. The big man screams in high-pitched agony.

A few minutes later Rawls, heavily guarded, stands shackled hand and foot in the prison superintendent's office. The superintendent looks out the window at the approaching storm.

"Messed up ol' Whaley, did he?" asks the superintendent.

"Messed him up good," replies a guard.

The superintendent turns to Rawls.

"Now, what'd you go and do that for?" he asks.

"Man pissed me off, Boss," says Rawls.

"Who the hell doesn't?" replies the superintendent. He turns to the guard.

"Box him," he says.

This order rattles Rawls for the first time, as it does the guards, also.

"You can't put me in the box, Boss. Storm's coming," says Rawls.

"You shoulda thought of that before you messed up ol' Whaley," says the superintendent.

"The hell with Whaley! You can't put me in that box, Boss!"

The prisoner is dragged away yelling and screaming. The guard, looking worried, tells the superintendent that there are reports of tornado touchdowns all over the county. The superintendent shrugs.

"I can't be responsible for acts of God," he says.

Rawls is locked into the Box—an outhouse-sized structure standing exposed to the elements in the

At Road Farm #6, a rough-looking prison compound in Jasper County, Mississippi, a group of inmates, supervised by shotgun-toting guards, work frantically to ready their camp for an approaching storm. A rawboned white prisoner in his late thirties—his name is Rawls—totes a plywood 4-by-6 to a barracks window. Helping him is a bald black man—his name is Whaley—who is approximately twice the other prisoner's size.

middle of the compound. He screams to be let out while rattling the sheet metal walls furiously.

After the storm is over the guard walks slowly toward the Box; all that's left is a few jagged pieces of its foundation. Rawls is gone, too. The guard enters the superintendent's building, knocks on his office door, and calls his name. No response.

He unlocks the door and pushes it open. The superintendent lies on the floor, dead. The man's body has been severed in half at the waist; the ragged edges of his torso blackened with a soot-colored substance.

At the county morgue in Jackson, Mississippi, several days later Mulder and Scully examine the bifurcated corpse of the superintendent, Raybert Fellowes. Mulder reads aloud a preliminary report: There was not a drop of blood found in his office. With a latex-gloved hand Scully fingers the crumbling, blackened surface of the cut.

"Maybe he was killed elsewhere," says Scully.

Mulder shakes his head.

"I don't think so," he says. "Whoever did it took forty minutes to do it—in the middle of a tornado."

He points to the sooty area.

"What do you make of that?" he asks.

"I don't know," sighs Scully. "It's not a simple bisection; there's a considerable amount of his abdomen missing. It almost looks like a burning, but it's too localized. Maybe an industrial acid."

Mulder glimpses at the file. He tells Scully there was no acid found in the office. Scully thinks for a moment, then averts her eyes.

"Spontaneous human combustion?" she suggests sheepishly.

Mulder breaks into a delighted smile.

"Scully!" he says. "Dear Diary: today my heart leapt when Scully suggested spontaneous human combustion!"

"Mulder, there are one or two somewhat well-documented cases," says Scully, defensively.

Mulder says nothing, but gazes into the distance and nods with exaggerated solemnity.

"Mulder, shut up!" says Scully, annoyed. "Okay, what do you make of this?"

"I don't have a theory," replies her partner. "But I know someone who does."

At the prison compound later that day, the guard tells Mulder and Scully that he's sure Pinker Rawls committed the murder, but that he can't tell them how. Mulder explains to Scully that Rawls was killed—apparently—by the tornado that preceded the superintendent's murder.

"So we're looking for a dead man?" says Scully to her partner.

"I disagree," says Mulder. "I think this Pinker Rawls is very much alive. You know, they never found his body."

Mulder walks around the office, rapping walls and window frames with his knuckles. He reaches the wall behind the superintendent's desk, feels a slight irregularity, and pushes lightly with his finger. A small chunk of plaster falls out. He pushes slightly harder with his palm. A large section of the wall falls outward, letting in sunlight and a clear view of the woods outside.

"Termites?" he says.

A few minutes later the guard presents the agents with a cardboard box containing Rawls's earthly possessions. Mulder examines it while Scully reads from Rawls's file.

"Wilson Pinker Rawls, age thirty-four. Eight years into thirty for robbing a wire office in Bay Saint Louis. The ninety thousand dollars he stole was never recovered."

"It's not in here," says Mulder. "Ouch!"

He pulls out a blister roll of a dozen or so condoms and holds them up proudly. Scully frowns.

"His record dates to 1978," she says. "Mostly small time. History of violence throughout."

Mulder finds a color photograph of a younger Rawls, standing in front of a wood-frame house. Next to him, her arm around his neck, is a sexy young woman in biker chick garb. Mulder shows it to Scully.

"I wonder who she is?" he says.

Later that day, in a smallish but well-kept house in the middle-class neighborhood of Meridian, a smiling young woman—her name is June—pours coffee for her boyfriend, Robert. June is, in fact, the woman in Rawls's photo: cleaned up considerably and dressed conservatively. June takes a glossy bridal magazine from the coffee table.

"Hey, Robert, can I show you something?" she says, sweetly. "Just a little food for thought?"

"Wait, sweetie," says Robert. "They're talking about the tornado."

Robert turns to a nearby TV set, picks up the remote, and turns up the volume. On the screen a newscaster is announcing the tornado strike on the prison farm and the death of the superintendent.

Now June is interested, too.

"A second casualty was a prison inmate," says the newscaster. "Wilson P. Rawls, age thirty-four—"

Upset, June drops her coffee cup.

"You okay, June?" says Robert.

Trying hard to pull herself together, June excuses herself and leaves the room.

That night, at a nearby mini-mall, a security guard parks his subcompact patrol car and shines his flashlight through the window of a large, shuttered discount store. He detects movement inside, enters, and sees Pinker Rawls trying on a casual shirt and a pair of cheap jeans.

"DEAR DIARY: TODAY MY HEART LEAPT WHEN SCULLY SUGGESTED SPONTANEOUS HUMAN COMBUSTION!"–Mulder

"You got a gun pointed at you! Don't try to run!" says the guard.

"I ain't running," says Rawls, coolly.

He grabs a package of tube socks from a nearby display, rips it open, and—ignoring the guard's shouted instructions—calmly tries on a pair.

"Ooh!" he says, closing his eyes and smiling. "There's something so nice about puttin' on a brand-new pair of socks!"

"Take those off, boy!" orders the guard.

Instead, Rawls grabs a pair of sneakers and puts them on. The guard loses patience. He grabs Rawls by the collar, tells him to put his hands behind his back, and handcuffs him to a floor-to-ceiling pole. He turns his back and walks away to radio for backup—and as he does so, Rawls walks away from the pole. The handcuffs fall, unopened, to the floor. The security guard looks out the store window to see Rawls in the driver's seat of his patrol car, its roof lights flashing.

The escaped con merrily waves the stolen sneakers out his window, then drives away.

A short while later Mulder and Scully arrive at the store. Mulder shows a mug shot of Rawls to the guard; he tentatively identifies him.

"How'd he get away?" asks Mulder.

"You got me," says the guard. "Guy's like Houdini. Turned my back and he was gone. I had him right here."

He shows the agents the pole, still perfectly intact. Mulder examines it briefly.

"Can I see your handcuffs?" he asks.

The guard hands Mulder the cuffs. Mulder raps them against the pole, then twists them with very little force. They break off in his hand as if they were made of peanut brittle. He turns to Scully.

"Do we have a last known address for Pinker Rawls?" he asks.

A short while later the stolen patrol car—lights still flashing—sits empty outside a broken-down bungalow in a trashy neighborhood. Rawls crashes into the house, yanking out drawers and angrily pawing through piles of debris. A marginal-looking guy in his thirties, looking frightened, steps cautiously through the front door.

"Hey. Hello?" he says. "Rawls?"

The convict stops his search, recognizing the other man.

"What's up?" says Rawls.

"You're on the news, man. They're sayin' you got killed."

"Where is she?" asks Rawls.

"June?" says the man.

Rawls nods.

"She's gone. Long gone, man. She left me like four years ago. You mad 'cause her and me shacked up? I'm sorry, buddy."

Rawls's expression is unreadable.

"Bo, I just want what's mine," he says, evenly.

Bo swallows hard.

"I might have her address," he says, nervously.

Rawls turns his back and walks away. Bo walks directly to a nightstand and pulls open a drawer.

"You got nothing in there but your nine," says Rawls calmly.

The other man reaches in and pulls out a pistol, then whirls, aiming it directly at his old friend.

"Get the hell out of my house!" he shouts.

"You gonna shoot me?" says Rawls, mockingly. He smiles crookedly. He raises his hands as if he's giving up, then wriggles his fingers, voodoo-like. He hops a step and lets out a short yell.

Bo jumps back, frightened. Rawls hops and yells again. Frightened, Bo clicks back the hammer with his thumb.

"You gonna do something?" sneers Rawls.

Bo fires once, then twice, then empties the entire gun at the intruder. The bullets pass completely through Rawls's chest—but there is no blood. Seemingly unaffected, he advances slowly on the cringing, whimpering Bo.

The next morning Mulder and Scully arrive at Bo's house. They spot the security guard's car, draw their weapons, and kick open the door. Seated in a chair against the wall is Bo—dead, his entire face scooped away and ringed with black soot. There is no blood. The agents force back their revulsion. Scully glances down at the corpse.

"Pistol in his hand. Slide locked open. Shell casings everywhere," she says. "I don't see any bullet holes in him, Mulder."

Mulder pulls a wallet from the corpse's pocket and shows it to Scully.

"Don't recognize him from his driver's license, do you?" he says.

"Bo Merkle. This is his house," says Scully.

"Yeah, but Rawls used to live here. And he's come back looking for something."

Scully suggests that what he's searching for is the money from the wire office robbery, which Bo Merkle didn't have, judging from the house's decor. Mulder pulls out the photo of Rawls and his old girlfriend.

"Maybe she knows," says Mulder. "That's this house, isn't it?"

Scully nods.

"I bet Rawls is looking for her," says Mulder.

Scully clicks on her cell phone, reports the murder to the local police, and asks to be transferred to the records division. Mulder walks to the other end of the house, where there are seven BB-sized dimples in the wall.

He takes out a pen knife from his pocket and digs

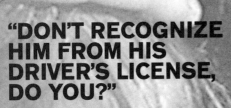

"DON'T RECOGNIZE
HIM FROM HIS
DRIVER'S LICENSE,
DO YOU?"

–Mulder

a flattened slug out of one of the holes. Mulder rubs it with his fingertip. It pulverizes into gray powder.

At the crime scene a few minutes later, policemen swarm over the house. Mulder looks at the crumbling slugs, contained in an evidence bag, intently. Scully joins him.

"Got a name to go with the face," she says. "June Gurwitch. There's no current address, though, and no record of her since 1996."

"Maybe she changed her name," says Mulder. "Maybe she was afraid she'd end up like that."

Scully nods, and tells Mulder that the state police just put out an APB on Rawls.

"You might warn them not to shoot to kill," says Mulder. "He seems to find that annoying."

Scully frowns.

"Look, Mulder, even if those were bullets—"

"They are," says Mulder. "It's just that their composition's been changed. Just like the handcuffs, and just like the prison wall."

"—even if these were bullets, there is no way they could pass through Rawls in the way you're describing. Not without leaving him sprawled dead on the ground for us to find."

"I think they just went right through him," says Mulder. "Like his wrists went through the handcuffs and he walked right through that prison wall."

Scully looks at Mulder skeptically.

"He walks through solid objects," she says.

Mulder nods.

"Changing their composition fundamentally," he says. "Making steel brittle, turning lead bullets into powder—"

"And flesh into carbon?"

"I don't know how else to explain what happened to that prison superintendent," says Mulder, "or to poor Mr. Merkle there, who's got no face anymore."

"But where's the science in all of this, Mulder? You're talking alchemy."

"I'm not saying that it can't be explained scientifically. Maybe it's the tornado."

He looks his partner in the eye.

"Okay, do we both agree on who he's looking for?"

"June Gurwitch," says Scully.

"And do we have any idea of how to find June Gurwitch?"

"She has a sister named Jackie," says Scully. "And I have the address."

That night the phone rings in the kitchen of June Gurwitch's house in Meridian. June answers it.

"Hey, it's me," says a female voice at the other end. "Is this a good time?"

"No, Jackie," says June, irritated. "It is never a good time."

Cigarette in hand, Jackie Gurwitch stands in her own

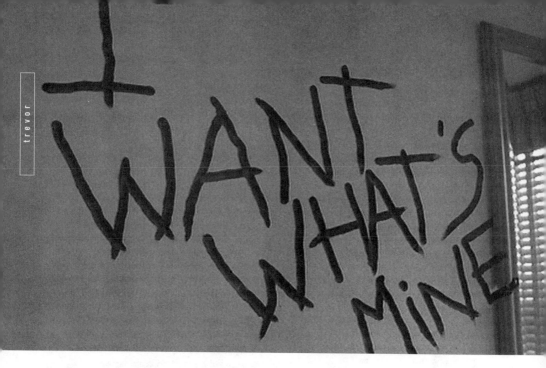

kitchen, which is considerably less upscale than her sister's.

"Look, the Jackson City police just called me," says Jackie nervously. "They're lookin' for you!"

"What'd you tell them?"

"Nothing. But they brought up Pinker. And they wanted to know what he might want with you."

"Pinker's dead," says June. "I heard it on the news today."

"Well," says Jackie, unconvinced, "maybe you'd better call 'em."

June's boyfriend, Robert, calls out to her from another room.

"I gotta go," says June, hanging up.

Upset, Jackie takes a drag on her cigarette. A door bangs open behind her. She cowers, then backs up to her kitchen counter, opens a drawer, and pulls out a large carving knife. Terrified, she moves slowly to the hallway and flips on a light. Rawls steps around a corner and stands directly in front of her. Trembling, Jackie brandishes the knife.

"Hey, Jackie," says Rawls, calmly.

Jackie flees to her bedroom and barricades the door with a heavy dresser. She locks the window, then turns. Rawls is in the room with her. He has stripped naked. Jackie gasps.

"Jackie, tell me where she is," says Rawls.

"I'm not tellin' you anything!" says Jackie.

Rawls walks past Jackie and looks out the window. Mulder and Scully are pulling up in their rental car. He backs Jackie—still holding the knife—into a wall.

Guns drawn, Mulder and Scully enter the front door. Scully calls out Jackie's name. No response. They search the silent house. Nothing—until Mulder reaches the bedroom. On the bedroom door, scrawled in strange

black lettering, are the words I WANT WHAT'S MINE.

Mulder kicks through the door, which gives way as easily as balsa wood. Jackie sits on the edge of her bed, in shock, but alone and unhurt.

"Where'd he go?" asks Mulder.

"He left," says Jackie, in a dazed voice.

A few minutes later the police are swarming over the house. Scully tells Mulder that Jackie will be staying with her son at a friend's house, and that she didn't tell Rawls where to find her sister.

"And, Mulder," adds Scully, sighing, "she said that he walked right through the wall."

Mulder nods solemnly.

"Bo Merkle's car is parked down the street. That's how he got here," he says. "But I don't know how he left."

"Maybe he left on foot, or he stole another car," says Scully.

"Why would he leave without getting the information he wanted?"

"Well, maybe he's still in the neighborhood. The local PD can search," says Scully. "In the meantime, you and I need to get going. To Meridian. That's where June Gurwitch lives. Or June Burdett, as she's now called."

The agents get into their car and back away. Lying inside the car's trunk, naked and crouched into a ball, is Pinker Rawls. He can hear everything the agents say.

At 6:12 that morning Mulder and Scully arrive at June Gurwitch's house. They are greeted on the front porch by Robert, still in his pajamas and bathrobe.

"Agents Mulder and Scully with the FBI," says

Scully. "We are looking for a June Gurwitch, also known as June Burdett."

"'Also known as'?" says Robert, confused. "Look, what's this all about?"

Scully tells him about Rawls's search for June Gurwitch. Her boyfriend still doesn't understand. Mulder spots someone standing silently behind Robert, watching.

"June?" he says.

"Pinker's alive, isn't he?" says June, sadly.

Robert stares at her, uncomprehending. June averts her eyes.

A few minutes later the agents and June sit in the living room. Robert stands in a doorway, apart.

"Jackie? She and her son?" June asks softly.

"They're both fine," says Scully.

June nods, relieved. After a moment or two of silence Mulder speaks up.

"Who is Rawls to you?" he asks.

"A mistake," says June. "Biggest one of many. We lived together."

The agents say nothing.

"Are you sure you know who you're looking for?" says June. "I remember one time, this guy cuts Pinker off on the highway—you know, just cut him off, the kind of thing that happens to everybody. But what does Pinker do? He followed this guy for over sixty-two miles, right over the state line, me pleading with him the whole way to stop. Follows the guy all the way to his house, guy gets out of his car smiling, doesn't know what's coming.

"Pinker pulls a picket off a white picket fence and cracks that guy's skull open with it. He's not gonna stop."

"What does Rawls want?" asks Mulder. "The money? The ninety thousand from the Bay Saint Louis robbery?"

"I didn't even know about that until they came to the door to arrest him, okay?" says June. "I mean, Pinker was already in prison before I found that money. By accident."

"So you took it?" says Scully.

"Eventually, yeah. I thought about it for about a week or two."

"And where's the money now?" says Mulder.

"Put a down payment on this place. Bought a couple of sofas. A PC for Robert."

June looks up at her boyfriend. He frowns, shakes his head, and exits. June watches him go, then turns back to the agents.

"I just wanted another chance," she says.

A few minutes later the police are at the house, ready to take June and Robert into protective custody. Robert walks away from June and buttonholes Scully.

"Look, I have a job," he says. "I have responsibilities. I can't just disappear like this."

"It's best you both stay under twenty-four-hour guard until Rawls is apprehended," says Scully. "It's for your protection."

"No—it's for *her* protection!" says Robert. "Let's be clear here. This guy Rawls or whatever, he's not looking for me. *She* took his money."

June reaches for his hand.

"Robert, I'm sorry—"

"Excuse me!" says Robert, pulling away. "I've got my own place. I promise to stay the hell away from here, okay? How about it? Look, I just want to get away from here. *I* didn't break any laws."

He stalks away. Scully looks at June sympathetically, then turns toward Robert.

"Don't discuss this with anyone, Mr. Werther," she says.

"I'm forgetting it ever happened," he says.

Mulder shakes his head, takes June's overnight bag, and places it in his car trunk. He closes it and notices a ragged crack in the trunk lid. Mulder pokes at the steel, which cracks like an eggshell. He looks at Scully, takes her car keys, and turns to a nearby trooper.

"Get her out of here," he says, motioning to June. "I want a guard on her at all times."

Scully looks at him, astonished.

"Rawls was in the trunk?" she asks.

"Yeah," says Mulder, drawing his gun. "And we took him right where he wanted to go."

Inside June's house a naked Rawls is rummaging through her papers. Mulder enters the room and Rawls is gone. He searches the rest of the house, and discovers that the bedroom has been ransacked.

Scully calls out to him from the living room, where Mulder had been just a moment or two before. Scorched crookedly onto the wall is—again—the phrase I WANT WHAT'S MINE. The final letter stops short of where it runs into a wall-mounted mirror.

"Think he's trying to tell us something?" asks Mulder.

Some time later the house is being combed by local cops and crime techs. Mulder traces Rawls's message with a latex-covered finger. Bits of charcoal dust coat his finger as he does so.

Scully enters from another room, carrying an official-looking document.

"Scully, look at this," says Mulder. "I'm assuming that Rawls used a finger to write this, just like the other one. But look here."

"He stopped at the mirror," says Scully.

"Or the mirror stopped him," Mulder replies. "And what makes an object solid, Scully? What prevents one solid object from passing through another solid object? Usually."

"Electrostatic repulsion," says Scully. "Individual electrons repelling one another like magnets."

"Electrons," says Mulder, quickly. "What if Rawls's ability somehow has to do with electricity? What could preclude it, or contain it?"

"Resistance against electrical current," says Scully. "A good insulator. Like rubber. Like glass."

"Exactly!" says Mulder. "Rawls couldn't pass through this."

Mulder points to the mirror. Scully turns all this over in her mind.

"Say that your theory is correct," she says. "That he can walk through walls. Why go through all this effort over an old robbery score? It's ninety thousand dollars. He could get that anywhere, right?"

Mulder nods, thinking.

"It's not about the money," he says. "It's never been about the money. Yet he turned this place upside down."

"Which means he was looking for something and I think it had to do with this."

Scully hands Mulder the document she's been carrying. It's a lien for an unpaid hospital bill: a C-section delivery for June Gurwitch in 1992—a few months after Rawls was sent to the state prison farm.

In a hotel room nearby a state trooper guards a despondent June Gurwitch. A TV newscaster is announcing the statewide manhunt for Rawls. The bored trooper reads a magazine.

"I'd like to call my sister," says June.

"Sorry, ma'am," says the trooper. "No calls."

June grabs her purse, pulls out a cigarette, and lights up.

"It's a nonsmoking room, ma'am," says the trooper.

June tosses away the cigarette disgustedly. Behind and above her, a small section of the ceiling bulges as if it were rubber. A hand appears, and then a face: Pinker Rawls.

In the hotel room that afternoon the state trooper lies dead, his severed arm still clutching his automatic. A state police sergeant, shaken, tells Mulder that the trooper put up a fight, but that Rawls overwhelmed him and kidnapped June.

"Where are they headed?" asks Mulder.

"He stole a station wagon," the cop replies. "Last seen headed south."

Scully enters the room and pulls Mulder aside.

"He has to intend for June to lead him to his child," she says.

"We've got to get there first," says Mulder.

"Yeah. But where?" says Scully.

She tells Mulder that their best bet would be to check state adoption records, which would take time. Mulder nods, weighing their options. He turns to the state police sergeant.

"I'm going to need some equipment—special issue," he says.

On a deserted stretch of rural highway the stolen station wagon is parked under an overpass. Rawls is in the driver's seat; a terrified June sits alongside him. Country music pours out of the car radio.

"Pinker, I apologize," says June. "Look, I'm just very scared right now, okay? Talk to me. Please, please say something. Anything."

Rawls is silent.

"Look, I'm sorry about the money—your money," says June. "I shouldn't have taken it. It was wrong. I was wrong! Pinker, I can pay you back."

Rawls finally stirs. He snaps off the radio and stares at June.

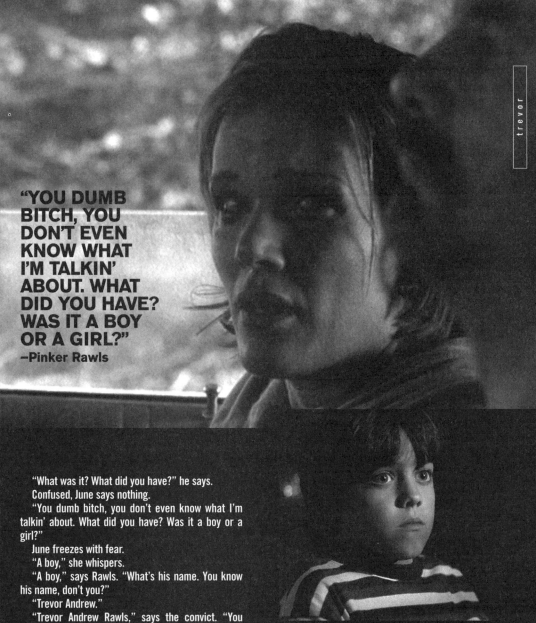

"YOU DUMB
BITCH, YOU
DON'T EVEN
KNOW WHAT
I'M TALKIN'
ABOUT. WHAT
DID YOU HAVE?
WAS IT A BOY
OR A GIRL?"
–Pinker Rawls

"What was it? What did you have?" he says.

Confused, June says nothing.

"You dumb bitch, you don't even know what I'm talkin' about. What did you have? Was it a boy or a girl?"

June freezes with fear.

"A boy," she whispers.

"A boy," says Rawls. "What's his name. You know his name, don't you?"

"Trevor Andrew."

"Trevor Andrew Rawls," says the convict. "You never were gonna tell me. I would have gone to my grave never knowing.

"Years later, million-to-one shot, I hear about it on the farm from a guy who knew a guy who knew a guy. You know what that means? That means God wanted me to know. He fixed it so I'd hear, then he fixed it so I'd have passage. And I'm here. God's will."

"What do you want with the boy?" whispers June.

"He's my son. Now you're gonna take me to him."

In the hotel room Mulder and Scully work the phones, trying to track down the whereabouts of June's child. The sergeant hands Mulder his special equipment: twelve-gauge shotgun shells that contain nonlethal slugs. Mulder tells Scully that all he could find out was that the child was a boy, and that there are no official adoption records.

"Well, maybe she didn't go through official channels," says Scully. "Maybe the kid's with a friend or a relative."

Silence for a moment. Then the agents look at each other, clearly thinking the same thing.

On the floor of Jackie Gurwitch's kitchen that night, a seven-year-old boy plays noisily with his toy cars. Jackie is nearby, stirring chicken noodle soup on the stove.

"Come on, Trevor," she says. "Put your toys away. Dinner's almost ready."

Trevor reluctantly complies. The kitchen phone rings. As Jackie moves to answer it, there's a knock on her front door. She walks to the foyer as her answering machine picks up the phone call. It's Mulder. Whatever he has to say, Jackie doesn't hear it. She opens her door to see her sister, alone, standing in front of her.

"I'm so sorry," says June.

Jackie steps back and Rawls steps forward.

"You could have saved me a trip," he says. "Where is he? My boy—where is he!"

He grabs June by the back of her neck and pushes her inside. He sees Trevor sitting at the kitchen table, takes a deep breath, and turns to Jackie.

"It's okay," whispers Jackie, terrified. "Mama's here."

Rawls pulls his son to his side.

"Come on, I'm not gonna hurt you. We'll have a man-to-man, just have a nice talk. You're Trevor, right? Trevor Andrew? My name is Pinker. But you can call me Pinky."

The frightened boy says nothing.

"But, anyway, you and me, we're gonna take a trip. You got some stuff you want to pack up?"

The boy is petrified. Jackie tells him to pack his things. He leaves. As Rawls watches him go, Jackie grabs the Pyrex soup pot off the stove and throws the hot liquid in his face—with no effect. Rawls

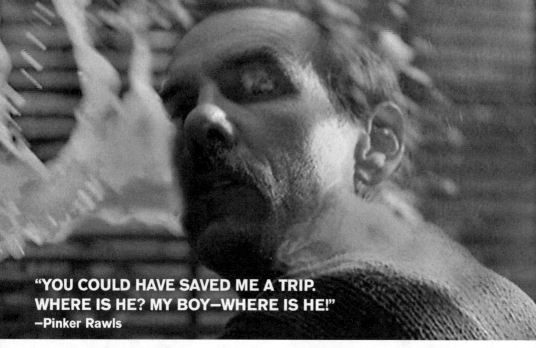

**"YOU COULD HAVE SAVED ME A TRIP.
WHERE IS HE? MY BOY—WHERE IS HE!"
–Pinker Rawls**

"I appreciate all you've done, taking care of him," he says, haltingly. "You're a good mother. Better'n some I could say."

Rawls walks slowly over to Trevor.

"Somethin' smells good in here," he says, smiling. "What're you gonna have?"

Trevor is confused by this.

"Hi, Aunt June," he says.

"Hey, baby," says June.

Rawls whirls, grabs June roughly, shoves her into a standup pantry, and closes the clasp. He orders Jackie to serve Trevor his supper, then—struggling for control—kneels down in front of the boy.

"It's all right, " he says. "It's gonna be all right. Don't be upset. I ain't gonna hurt nobody."

approaches her. She swings the glass pot and connects with his head. Rawls staggers, nearly falling.

"Run, Trevor! *Run!*" she shouts.

Trevor flees from the house. Jackie swings again, misses, and is dragged to the floor by Rawls. Rawls slugs the woman, then runs after Trevor. Inside the pantry, June bangs the door against the clasp.

Rawls runs outside, calling his son's name. He spots Trevor hiding behind a tree and pursues him through the large, debris-strewn backyard. Trevor runs around a corner—and runs into Mulder and Scully.

"Get him out of here, Scully," says Mulder, wielding a 12-gauge.

Rawls advances toward Mulder, who shoots a rubber slug into his chest. Rawls staggers, and takes three more slugs before running away and disappearing right through a solid wall. Amazed, Mulder watches the man's clothing fall in a heap next to the wall. Brandishing the shotgun, he runs to the back entrance, enters the kitchen, and comforts the injured Jackie.

In back of the house Scully leads Trevor quickly by the hand toward the abandoned gas station where her car is parked. She fumbles with her keys, hears something, turns—and sees Rawls, naked, advancing on them.

She takes Trevor's hand, thinks hard, and leads him as fast as they can run into a derelict glass-sided telephone booth about forty feet away. She slams the glass door shut, then jams her gun into the door's folding mechanism, immobilizing it. Rawls pounds his hands against the glass, howling in frustration.

Scully hugs Trevor protectively. Rawls reaches down to the ground, picks up a chunk of asphalt, and slams a hole in the glass. Then he peers in at his son—nearly comatose with fright—and hesitates, momentarily contrite.

He drops the asphalt chunk and walks away. At that moment he is illuminated by a pair of headlights: The stolen station wagon is bearing down at him. June is at the wheel.

Rawls stands his ground, passes through the car hood and engine block, and is gruesomely impacted on the wagon's glass windshield. Seeing this, Scully shields Trevor's eyes and leads him away. Mulder approaches the stopped car and the bloody body parts trailing behind it.

June sits at the wheel, in shock. Mulder reaches inside and switches off the engine.

"I had to do it!" says June, anguished. "He would've hurt Trevor and God only knows what he was thinking. What did he want?"

Shocked himself, Mulder looks down.

"Maybe another chance," he says, slowly.

The distraught woman lowers her head and weeps soundlessly.

BACK STORY/6X17

The name of Ken Hawryliw—unpronounceable and virtually unspellable—is well known to serious students of The X-Files. As the show's Vancouver-based property master from 1993 to 1998, he was responsible for many of the vital design details of the show, including such signature props as Mulder's and Scully's FBI ID documents and the Alien Bounty Hunter's retractable stiletto.

What only his close confidants knew, however, was that Hawryliw was also a screenwriter. "I'd had a couple of

scripts optioned up here in Canada before I went to work for the show," says Hawryliw from his home in Vancouver. "But when I started on The X-Files, I put my writing career temporarily on hold. First of all, I had a terrifically demanding full-time job. Secondly, I realized that just being around the show would be a great learning opportunity. The scripts were so good, and I was working so closely with such great story minds, that it couldn't help but make me—eventually—into a better writer."

Hawryliw made his first move in 1998, when The X-Files left for Los Angeles and he shifted to Millennium to supervise that show's prop department for its third and final season. He decided then to team up with Jim Guttridge, an L.A.-based composer/screenwriter whom he'd met through a mutual friend.

"Jim was a big fan of the show," recalls Hawryliw, "and he'd written an X-Files script that he asked me to help get to Chris. I read it, and though it really wasn't written like an X-Files script, I told him I thought the premise was really good. And Jim said: 'Why don't we make a deal? You help me rewrite it into an X-Files script and we can submit it together.'"

A couple of script submissions and a dozen pitches later "Trevor" was born. "When the idea for 'Trevor' arrived, it worked itself out fairly quickly," says Hawryliw. He adds, "The basic leap that we take—what Frank refers to as the 'beautiful idea,' which every X-Files has to have—is that there's this unique man who can walk through walls. Now, who would this ability best apply to? Well, a convict, obviously—a guy in prison who would want nothing more than to get out of prison. But then we had to give him an even stronger, more compelling reason to want his freedom, and that was where his son came in."

Hawryliw says that several intense conversations with a Canadian theoretical physicist convinced them that the emerging science of superconductivity could provide a useful explanation for Pinker Rawls's unusual abilities.

In the opinion of director Rob Bowman, however, the real key to the appeal of "Trevor" lies elsewhere: in the complicated psychology of Pinker Rawls and in the highly charged relationship between himself and June, his ex-girlfriend.

"Pinker is a crazed killer, but not a monster," says Bowman. "I think a monster is a guy who kills indiscriminately, without remorse. But although Pinker is mercurial and ultimately not fit to be on the loose, I think we gradually come to realize that his prime motivation is not all bad. I mean, in truth, the real villain of the piece is June—an upwardly mobile woman who basically sold out her boyfriend, then gave up her son so she would be more attractive as a single woman. I think she makes an interesting contrast to Pinker—a man who'd do anything to get out of prison and be with his son."

Bowman adds that he feels that several scenes in

"Trevor," including the one in which June tells Pinker their son's name, provided some of the best dramatic moments of the season. However, getting them up on the screen was—as usual—a more or less uncharted adventure.

After Hawryliw and Guttridge handed in their first draft, substantial changes were ordered. Originally set in Oklahoma's "tornado alley" and in a conventional state prison, Rawls's lockup was changed for budgetary reasons to a Mississippi work farm, and filmed at the Veluzat Ranch, a spaghetti Western-type set (highly modified by the X-Files crew for the occasion) in Canyon Country, north of Los Angeles.

Originally, too, the show included an effects-laden action sequence in which Mulder pursues Rawls from one end of a motel to the other; Rawls takes a short-cut by passing through the motel's interior walls. The scene was eliminated both to save money and to shift the episode's emphasis from the supernatural to the emotional.

In early February the script was given an intensive polish by co-executive producer Vince Gilligan and producer John Shiban, then released to a production staff rounding quickly into the final quarter of their shooting season.

To play the lead guest role of Pinker Rawls, casting director Rick Millikan read a number of actors without success. At the last minute, thankfully, he thought of calling John Diehl: a supporting player in many recent movies, including Nixon and Stargate, but perhaps best known as Crockett and Tubbs's fellow detective on the first three seasons of Miami Vice. "He'd been on my list to put into the show since Day One," says Millikan. "It turned out the producers liked him, too—he'd read for us a couple of times already—and we were able to get him in without even a reading."

After his first reading of the script, producer Paul Rabwin began thinking about a couple of interesting problems: How to film, without spending a fortune on special effects or post-production wizardry, (1) the sequences in which Rawls passes through walls, and (2) the follow-up shots where Mulder discovers that the substances Rawls has passed through are weakened and crumbling.

Good writing, clever camera angles, strategic use of breakaway cement, and—in the case of Mulder's trunk lid—the miracle auto-body repair substance Bondo erased many of the difficulties. Others presented themselves periodically.

"A really good one," says Rabwin, "was during the sequence where Mulder pushes on a wall and a big chunk in the shape of a man falls out. The first time we did it, all we got was a big square hole, which didn't work. But we didn't want it to look like Bugs Bunny with his ears sticking out, either. So we designed a phony wall with a breakaway section that suggested, rather than

outlined perfectly, a man's roundish head, shoulders and upper torso."

Visual effect supervisor Bill Millar augmented the mechanically produced wind and flying debris in the prison storm scene with some computerized effects; the later shot of Jackie Gurwitch tossing hot soup in Rawls's face was partly an electronic construct, also. The climactic scene of Rawls being trapped and killed against the glass windshield of June's speeding vehicle was aided greatly by the near-dismantling of a 1972 Ford Country Squire station wagon by picture car mechanic Kelly Padovich.

One memorable behind-the-scenes moment undoubtedly belongs to hair department head Dena Green, who was instructed by Rob Bowman to sweep John Diehl's hair toward the back of his head in any scene immediately following one in which his character passes through a solid object.

Ken Hawryliw and Jim Guttridge, on the first day of filming, stood happily on the X-Files set to see their first script pages go before the camera. "It was extremely surreal," says Hawryliw, "but very, very much worth it."

The character of Trevor Gurwitch—and in fact the entire episode—was named after Trevor Marquiss, a young nephew of producer John Shiban who lives in Las Vegas, Nevada.

Hair department head Dena Green is a California native in her early thirties. After honing her craft in a Los Angeles salon, she worked as Teri Hatcher's personal hairdresser on Lois and Clark and on the ABC series Brooklyn South.

After Millennium production ended in mid-1998, props master Ken Hawryliw decided to become a full-time screenwriter. He says, "I've been back and forth to L.A. every couple of weeks doing interviews for other shows and pitching feature ideas that Jim and I have worked on. 'Trevor' has opened a huge amount of doors for us."

MILAGRO

EPISODE:6X18
FIRST AIRED: April 18, 1999
EDITOR: Louise A. Innes
TELEPLAY BY: Chris Carter
STORY BY: John Shiban & Frank Spotnitz
DIRECTED BY: Kim Manners

GUEST STARS:
John Hawkes (Phillip Padgett)
Nestor Serrano (Ken Naciamento)
Angelo Vacco (Kevin)
Jillian Bach (Maggie)
Michael Bailey Smith (Guard)

PRINCIPAL SETTING:
Washington, D.C.

A struggling young writer,
obsessed with Scully, seemingly
has the power to make his grisliest fantasies
come true.

In a painfully bare living room, a thin, goateed man in his early thirties sits at his desk. A cigarette burns in an ashtray; a sheet of blank paper waits impassively in an old IBM typewriter. The man glances at a series of 3-by-5 index cards, filled with plot points, pushpinned to the wall. He thinks, paces, smokes, takes a drink, places his ear to the wall, and listens to the voices in the next apartment.

Hours pass with no results.

The man lights a cigarette, flips the butt into the toilet, and stares at himself in the mirror over his sink. He reaches through the buttons on his work shirt and digs his hand into his chest. Blood flows copiously down his hand and arm. He pulls out his heart, still beating, and contemplates it silently.

Some time later the man walks slowly down the stairway of his apartment building to the incinerator room. He is carrying a brown paper bag. He sees a heart suspended in the incinerator's flames. He then tosses the bag into the flames.

He rides the elevator back up to his apartment. It stops at the lobby; the doors open, and Scully gets on. She is carrying a file folder. The writer eyes her silently, but intently—enough so that it makes the agent more than slightly uncomfortable.

The elevator stops at the fourth floor. Scully gets out, followed by the writer, trailing a few yards behind her. Scully knocks on the door of Apartment 42. The man, still staring unblinkingly at Scully, unlocks and enters the apartment next door.

Mulder opens his door and invites his partner inside.

"I rode up on the elevator with someone," says Scully. "Someone from next door."

"Young guy?" asks Mulder.

"Yeah."

"New neighbor. Why?"

"You met him?"

"Briefly, yeah. He's a writer."

"What does he write?"

"He didn't say."

Scully nods, sits down on Mulder's couch, and shows Mulder the contents of her file folder: several official-looking documents, plus several photographs of a gruesomely murdered young woman.

"These are my autopsy reports from the second victim," she says.

In the apartment next door the writer rolls his desk chair to the wall, stands on it, and strains to hear Mulder's and Scully's words through a heating register.

"You'll see that the heart was removed in the same manner as the previous victim," says Scully. "No incisions, no scope marks, no cutting of any kind."

"And yet you still refuse to believe my theory?" says Mulder. "That what this is is psychic surgery?"

"Mulder, psychic surgery is some man dipping his hands in a bucket of chicken guts and pretending to remove tumors from the sick and gullible."

"Or," counters Mulder, "it's a grossly misunderstood area of alternative medicine."

"Well, 'medicine,' as you refer to it, is about keeping people alive." says Scully.

"Well, absent another theory," says Mulder, "how else do we account for the impossible extraction of a man's heart?"

The writer's ear is still pressed to the heat register. "I don't know, Mulder," says Scully.

"We have no evidence, no m.o. to speak of," says Mulder. "This could be the perfect crime."

"Well, a crime is only as perfect as the man or the mind that commits it," says Scully. "And even if it were perfect, if he made not one mistake, there is still his motive. Find the motive, find the murderer."

That night the writer lies in bed, smoking. His expression is troubled. He throws off his covers, sits up, and leaves the room.

In a wooded parkland near the District of Columbia, an old Jeep Cherokee is parked. In its front seat are two teenagers, Kevin and Maggie.

"That's why I didn't want to come here, Kevin," says Maggie.

"I'm not even doing anything!" says her boyfriend.

"Well, you're thinking about it!"

"There's a console between us. How much can I do?" whines the boy. "You make it sound like I'm an attacker."

"Well, we talked about this," says Maggie, uncertainly.

"I told you I loved you," says Kevin, softly.

Maggie leans in hesitantly. Somebody in a hooded sweatshirt is standing in front of the Jeep, watching them. The teenagers kiss and Maggie immediately pulls back.

"There you go again!" she says. "That thing you do! You know what I'm talking about!"

"That's the way I kiss, Maggie!"

"Well, I get the message."

Maggie opens her door, gets out, and walks quickly away. After a few seconds Kevin follows her. He calls for his girlfriend; she does not respond. Someone else emerges from the underbrush: the man in the hooded sweatshirt.

Startled and scared, Kevin turns and runs away. The hooded man chases after him, catches him, and throws him to the ground. His assailant reaches down to him and pulls his bloody heart from his body. Kevin screams in terror and pain.

In his apartment the writer types furiously. All that can be seen are his final two words: *beating heart*.

At FBI headquarters the next morning the phone rings in the X-Files office. Scully answers it. It is Mulder.

"Hey, Scully, glad I caught you. We got a third victim.

A sixteen-year-old kid out on Lover's Lane."

"Are you sure?" says Scully.

Mulder is at the crime scene, standing over Kevin's bloody corpse.

"Yeah," he says. "I'm sure many a person's had their heart broken out here, but not quite like this. I was hoping you'd be here to explain it in medical terms to the local PD."

"I'm not sure that I could," says Scully. "Did anybody see anything?"

"No. Nothing," says Mulder. "It's like there's nowhere to start on this case. Nothing to ask, nothing to say."

"Well, there's got to be something, Mulder. Something about his victims. Why he chooses them. A pattern."

"So far there's absolutely nothing, Scully," says

DNA that would begin his unraveling? She had a condign certainty that the killer was a male, and now, as she held the cold metal at her fingertips, she imagined him doing the same, trying to picture his face.

"It would be a plain face, an average face. A face people would be prone to trust. She knew this inherently, being naturally trusting herself. But the image she conjured up was no better than the useless sketch composites that littered her files. Presciously, she knew this wasn't her strength as an investigator. She was a marshal of cold facts, quick to organize, connect, shuffle, reorder, and synthesize their relative hard values into discrete categories. Imprecision would only ignite sexist criticism. That she was soft, malleable, not up to her male counterparts."

In her office Scully still stares at the pendant, phone cradled on her shoulder. Absentmindedly, she smoothes back her hair.

The writer continues:

"Even now as she pushes an errant strand of Titian hair behind her ear, she worried her partner would know instinctively what she could only guess. To be thought of as simply a beautiful woman was unthinkable.

"But she was beautiful. Fatally, stunningly prepossessing. Yet the compensatory respect she commanded only deepened the yearnings of her heart. To let it open. To let someone in."

In their office later that morning Scully shows Mulder the medal.

"It's called a *milagro*," she says. "It's the Spanish word for miracle. It's worn as a lucky charm. It was dropped off at reception by a man in his late twenties, early thirties. Average looking, average build. They weren't able to get a good ID. There are no fingerprints, and no DNA from his saliva."

"It came here for me?" says Mulder.

He flips the medal into the air, like a coin, and catches it.

"I don't think it's the killer, Scully," he says.

"Did you see that it's a burning heart?" says his partner.

"I see it's a burning heart," says Mulder. "But we're dealing with a killer who leaves absolutely no clues. Why would he do something as heavy-handed as this?"

"Well, maybe it has something to do with his next victim. Maybe he's taunting you."

"Maybe it's not me at all. Maybe he sent it to you. Maybe it's a secret admirer."

Scully blinks, then quickly shrugs off Mulder's taunt.

"I think I'll check it out," she says.

"Actually, let me," says Mulder. "You've got a 9 A.M. with the D.C. Medical Examiner. He's going to let you autopsy the latest victim."

IN HIS APARTMENT THE WRITER TYPES FURIOUSLY. ALL THAT CAN BE SEEN ARE HIS FINAL TWO WORDS: *BEATING HEART.*

Mulder. "It appears to be a series of random attacks."

Scully looks over her shoulder. Someone has slid an unmarked envelope under the office door. She walks a few feet to pick it up.

Scully tells Mulder about the envelope, and opens it. Inside is a small pendant. On it is the image of a burning heart. Scully examines the medallion, fascinated.

Inside his apartment the writer sits at his desk, still typing rapidly. The words run through his mind as he sets them down on paper. They are:

"Her prompt mind ran through the Golconda of possibilities: Was this trinket from the killer? Was there a message contained in its equivocal symbolism? Was he a religious fanatic who had in fervid haste licked the envelope, leaving the telltale

"YOU'LL SEE THAT THE HEART WAS REMOVED IN THE SAME MANNER AS THE PREVIOUS VICTIM. NO INCISIONS, NO SCOPE MARKS, NO CUTTING OF ANY KIND." –Scully

"AND YET YOU STILL REFUSE TO BELIEVE MY THEORY? THAT WHAT THIS IS IS PSYCHIC SURGERY?"–Mulder

"Thank you for making my schedule," says Scully, sarcastically. "But I'm going to have to be late for that appointment."

Later that morning Scully walks into the sanctuary of a large church and walks toward the pulpit. Near the altar is a large painting: a figurative representation of Christ. In his hand he holds his heart, which is burning. Someone comes up from behind and stands next to Scully.

It is the writer.

"I often come here to look at this painting," he says, staring straight ahead. "It's called 'My Divine Heart,' after the miracle of Saint Margaret Mary. Do you know the story? The revelation of the Sacred Heart? Christ came to Margaret Mary, his heart so inflamed with love that it was no longer able to contain its burning flames of charity.

"Margaret Mary, so filled with divine love herself, asked the Lord to take her heart, and so he did, placing it alongside his until it burned with the flames of his Passion, before he restored it to Margaret Mary, sealing her wound with a touch of his blessed hand."

Scully stares at the man for a few moments, struggling to recognize him.

"Why are you telling me this?" she asks.

The writer turns to face Scully.

"You came here specifically to see this painting, didn't you?"

"Yes. How did you know that?"

"I saw you enter. The way you knew right where it was."

Scully struggles to conceal her reaction.

"I know you," she says, finally. "You live next to someone I work with. Why are you following me?"

"I'm not. I only imagined that you'd come here today."

"You imagined it?" says Scully skeptically.

"Yes. I'm a writer. That's what I do. Imagine how people behave."

He adds, in a near monotone:

"I have to admit I've noticed you. I do that. Notice people. I saw that you wear a gold cross around your neck, so I was taking a chance with the painting, explaining something you may have already known. I saw Georgetown parking permits on your car dating from 1993, and a government exempt sticker that lets you park anywhere you like. You don't live in this area, but as a federal employee you have reason to frequent it.

"You're fit, with muscular calves, so you must exercise or run. There's a popular running route right nearby that you might use at lunch or after work. You'd have noticed this church in passing, and, though parking is always a problem in this part of town, your special privileges would make it easy to visit. Not as a place of worship, but because you have an appreciation for architecture and the arts.

"And while the grandeur is what you take away from your visit, this painting's religious symbolism would have left a subconscious impression, jogged by the gift you received this morning."

Scully is surprised—and appalled—by all of this.

"That was from you?" she says.

"I have to admit to a secret attraction," says the writer. "I'm sorry I didn't include a note explaining that, but you didn't know me then."

"Yeah. And I don't know you now," says Scully, with an angry grimace. "And I don't care to."

"I see this is making you uncomfortable. And I'm sorry," the writer replies. "It's just that I'm taken with you. That never happens to me. We're alike that way."

Without another word Scully turns and leaves the church.

Later that morning she enters the D.C. Morgue. Kevin's body lies on an examination table, covered by a white sheet. Mulder greets her and kids her about being late. Scully tells him that she was doing research—and learning that she owed him an apology.

"For what?"

"The *milagro* charm," says Scully. "You were right about its insignificance."

"No, I think I was wrong," says Mulder, quickly. "I think it's very significant. I think it may be a communication from the killer. Most of my research shows that most credible practitioners of psychic surgery believe themselves to be imbued with the Holy Spirit. Their hands become the miracle tools of God."

Scully smiles wryly and holds up the *milagro*.

"Mulder," she says, "this is nothing more than a tool, used by a lovelorn Romeo who just happens to be your next-door neighbor."

"Who? The writer?"

"My secret admirer, who claims to know the mysteries of my heart. He cornered me today and told me my life story. It was kind of frightening, actually."

"Is he our killer?" asks Mulder.

"No," says Scully. "'Frightening,' as in too much information and intimate detail. What kills you is his audacity."

"Did you get his name?" asks Mulder.

"No," says Scully. "But that shouldn't be too hard to find out, should it?"

Later that day Mulder stands in the lobby of his apartment building. He takes a lock pick out of his pocket, looks around, and opens the mailman's lock on the building's mailboxes. He reaches into the box next to his and pulls out several envelopes. One of them is a phone bill addressed to Phillip Padgett, 2630 Hegal Place, Apt. No. 44, Alexandria, Virginia 23242.

He glances down at a stack of giveaway community newspapers. He picks one up, scans it, and presses the button for the elevator. The front door opens and Padgett, in running shorts, enters. Mulder coolly slips the phone bill into his newspaper and rides up with Padgett. The two men size each other up.

"I'm sorry," says Mulder. "I forgot your name."

"Padgett. Phillip Padgett."

"You're a writer. Anything I'd know?"

"I don't think so," says Padgett.

The elevator reaches the fourth floor. The two men exit and fumble for their keys in front of their respective doors. Padgett turns toward Mulder.

"You're an FBI agent," he says. "Working on anything interesting?"

"A murder case," he replies.

"Anything I'd know?" says Padgett.

"Possibly," Mulder replies.

The two men enter their apartments. Still in his running clothes, Padgett sits at his desk on which there is a growing pile of neatly typed pages. He writes:

"The overture in the church had urged the beautiful agent's partner into an act of Hegelian self-justification. Expeditiously violating the Fourth Amendment against mail theft, he prepared to impudently infract the First."

Padgett glances up at the heating register. In his apartment Mulder has raised himself up and put his head next to his end of the vent, listening.

In the D.C. Morgue Scully, completing her autopsy, strips off her bloody gloves and throws them in the trash.

Padgett writes:

"But if she'd predictably aroused her sly partner's suspicions, Special Agent Dana Scully had herself become simply aroused.

"All morning, the stranger's unsolicited compliments had played on the dampened strings of her instrument, until the middle C of consciousness was struck square and resonant. She was flattered. His words had presented her a pretty picture of herself. Quite unlike the practiced mask of uprightness that mirrored back to her from the medical examiners and the investigators and all the lawmen who dared no such utterances. She felt an involuntary flush and rebuked herself for the girlish indulgence."

Scully removes her protective clothing. She reaches into her pocket, pulls out the *milagro*, looks at it, then pockets it again, embarrassed.

That night moonlight streams into Padgett's apartment. There are two steaming cups of coffee on a night table in his bedroom. He lies on his bed, fully clothed.

"But the images came perforce and she let them play. Let them flood in like savory, or more a sugary confection from her adolescence when her senses were new and ungoverned by fear and self-denial.

Now Padgett and Scully are entwined passionately on the bed. The writer's hands caress her legs. Slowly,

"YOU'RE CURIOUS ABOUT ME."
—Padgett

sensuously, he unbuttons her blouse, exposing her lacy black bra. Padgett kisses her powerfully on the lips. Aroused, Scully embraces him and kisses him unreservedly in return.

"Ache, pang, prick, twinge. How ironic the Victorian vocabulary of behavioral pathology now so perfectly described the palpitations of her own desire. The stranger had looked her in the eye and knew her more completely than she knew herself. She felt wild, feral, guilty as a criminal.

"Had the stranger unleashed in her what was already there? Or had he only helped her discover a landscape she'd by necessity blinded herself to? What would her partner think of her?"

On the other side of the apartment wall, Mulder opens and reads Padgett's phone bill. Apparently, the writer has made no phone calls whatsoever.

"Mr. Popularity," Mulder murmurs, glancing at the community newspaper on his coffee table.

A few minutes later the elevator in Mulder's building reaches the fourth floor. The doors open and Scully gets out. She walks to Mulder's door, raises her hand to knock, but stops herself. She looks at Padgett's door, behind which the sound of furious typing can be heard.

Inside his apartment Padgett types the words *the compulsion was overwhelming*. There is a knock on his door, and he rises to answer it.

It is Scully.

"Hi," she says, hesitantly. "I, um, was going next door and I thought that I'd return this."

She holds out the *milagro*. Padgett does not move to take it.

"Why?" he asks.

"Because I can't return the gesture," says Scully, plaintively. "I can't."

Padgett nods.

"You're curious about me," he says.

Scully nods in return. She lowers the *milagro* and peers past him into his apartment.

"You don't have any furniture," she says.

"I have what I need. I write at my desk. I sleep in my bed."

"You don't eat?"

"I live in my head."

"Writing your books?"

"Yes."

"Anything I'd know?"

"No. They're all failures. Except the one I'm working on now. I think I'm getting it right."

"Why now all of a sudden?" says Scully.

"Best not to question it. See, you *are* curious about me."

"Well, you lead a curious life."

"It's not so different from yours, I imagine. Lonely." Scully looks away nervously.

"Loneliness is a choice," she whispers.

"So how about a cup of coffee," says Padgett, with a slight smile.

In Mulder's apartment the agent looks through a stack of newspapers. He looks for older copies of the community newspaper he'd scanned earlier.

Next door Scully, alone in the living room, glances at Padgett's typewriter. The last sentence he has written is: "How will it end?"

Padgett enters carrying two steaming mugs of coffee. He hands one to Scully.

"My life's not so lonely, Mr. uh—" she says softly, raising the mug to her lips.

"Padgett."

"It's actually anything but. How is it you think you know me so well, Mr. Padgett?"

"I'm writing about you."

"Right," says Scully, evenly. "Since when?"

"Since I first noticed you. You live in my old neighborhood."

"And you moved into this building by coincidence?"

"No."

"You moved here because of me?"

"There wasn't anything available in your building. And it's not like you spend much time at home. I should have said something, but I just can't get it all down fast enough. To really write someone I have to be in their head; I have to know them more completely than they know themselves."

Scully's eyes drift to Padgett's manuscript.

"This is all about me?" she says.

"Well, you're an important part."

"May I read it?"

"It's not finished," he replies.

An awkward silence. Padgett smiles brightly.

"I can't tell you how helpful it is having you here," he says, "being able to talk to you like this. Would you sit and stay for a minute?"

"You don't have anywhere to sit," says Scully.

A few moments later Padgett walks into his bedroom and switches on his bedstand lamp. It doesn't work. Scully stands in the doorway.

"I'm due next door," she says.

"You haven't finished your coffee," says Padgett, checking the lamp's plug and switch.

"I'm very uncomfortable with this," says Scully, with a bit of melancholy.

"Why?" says Padgett. "You're armed, aren't you?"

Padgett finally gets the lamp lit, but the bulb burns out almost instantly. He leaves the bedroom to get a bulb. Scully walks slowly to the window. Moonlight floods in.

"A view only a writer can appreciate," says Padgett, returning.

"If you know me so well," asks Scully, "why am I standing here when my instincts tell me to go?"

"Motives are never easy," says Padgett, screwing in the new bulb. "Sometimes it occurs to one only later."

Scully sits on the edge of the bed, Padgett beside her. The lamp goes out.

"Imagine that," whispers Padgett.

They are together in the darkness. Padgett turns and looks at Scully. There is a sound of a door bursting open, followed by the sight of Mulder, gun drawn, in the doorway. He whirls to face her.

"Scully!" he says. "You all right?"

"Yes!" says Scully, indignantly.

Mulder enters the living room, moves quickly to Padgett's desk, and rummages through his manuscript.

"Mulder!" says Scully, Padgett standing behind her. "What are you doing?"

"Putting this man under arrest," he replies, shoving

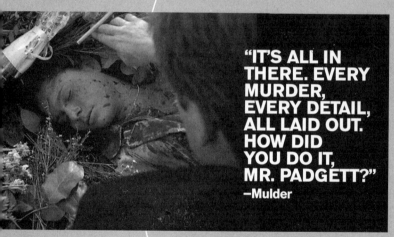

"IT'S ALL IN THERE. EVERY MURDER, EVERY DETAIL, ALL LAID OUT. HOW DID YOU DO IT, MR. PADGETT?"
—Mulder

a page into Scully's hand and hustling Padgett out the door.

Horrified, Scully glances down and reads five neatly typed words: *felt his warm beating heart.*

In a jail cell later that night Phillip Padgett sits and reads Mulder's community newspaper. Mulder stands over him.

"Yes, I've seen this paper," says Padgett, calmly.

"Yeah. It's where you found your victims," says Mulder. "In the personals. They'd all run personal ads."

"They were lovers," says Padgett.

"And you targeted them," says Mulder.

"I only write about them."

Scully enters the cell carrying a file folder.

Mulder tosses Padgett's manuscript, enclosed in a fat evidence bag, on Padgett's lap.

"This is your confession?" he says.

"No, that's my novel."

"It's all in there," says Mulder. "Every murder, every

detail, all laid out. How did you do it, Mr. Padgett?"

"If I sit long enough," says the writer, "it just comes to me."

"The murders!" says Mulder.

"I only knew what was in my mind and wished to express it clearly."

Mulder nods grimly.

"How about 'The Stranger'?" he asks. "Is that you? How about Ken Naciamento? The self-proclaimed Brazilian psychic surgeon. Is he your accomplice?"

"I guess you could say that. He's a central character."

"Did you direct him to do it?"

"Jungians would say," says Padgett, "that it's the characters who choose the writer, not the other way around. So I guess you could argue he directed me. By their nature, words are imprecise and layered with meaning—the signs of things, not the things themselves. It's difficult to say who's in charge."

Frustrated, Mulder moves toward Padgett. Scully puts her hand on his arm, stopping him.

"Why, Mr. Padgett?" asks Mulder. "Maybe that's a question that you can answer."

"That's the one question that I can't," he replies.

Mulder grabs the manuscript and turns to leave. Padgett becomes agitated.

"Agent Mulder," he says. "My book—did you like it?"

"Maybe if it were fiction," he says.

In the corridor Mulder tells Scully that they need to track down Ken Naciamento, Padgett's accomplice. Scully tells him that she already has, and that Naciamento, who came to the U.S. in 1996, has been dead for two years.

"Padgett couldn't have done it alone," says Mulder.

"Well, maybe he didn't do it at all," says Scully. "Maybe he imagined it, like he said. Like Shakespeare. Or Freud. Or Jung. Maybe he has some gift, a clear window into human nature."

"No one can predict human behavior," says Mulder. "No one can tell you what another person's going to do. If he imagines it, it's *a priori,* before the fact. I think that's pretty clear from what he wrote about you. You know you're in here, don't you?"

"I read a chapter. What does he say?"

"Well, let's just say it ends with you doing the naked pretzel with the Stranger on a bed in an unfurnished fourth floor apartment. I'll assume that's *a priori,* too?"

"I think you know me better than that, Mulder," says Scully.

Mulder hands her the manuscript.

"Maybe you want to finish it," he says.

Later that night, in another part of the prison, Scully reads Padgett's manuscript with dread and fascination. A guard enters, and hands her a piece of paper sent to her by Padgett.

"He says it's a statement," says the guard, "but I think he's putting somebody on."

The guard leaves. Scully reads:

"Grief squeezed at her eggshell heart like it might break into a thousand pieces, its contents running like broken promises into the hollow places his love used to fill. How could she know this pain would end? That love, unlike matter or energy, was in endless supply in the universe. A germ which grows from nothingness, which cannot be eradicated even from the darkest of hearts."

In a dark cemetery somewhere a young woman—it is Maggie—stands before a newly dug grave site, grieving. She looks up to see the hooded man—Ken Naciamento—standing in front of her. She tries to run away, but he catches up to her and throws her to the ground. He reaches down and pulls out her beating heart.

Inside the prison, Scully reads:

"If she had known this—and who could say she would believe it?—she would not have chanced to remain at his sad grave until such an hour. So that she might not have to learn the second truth before the first: that to have loved was to carry a vessel that could be lost or stolen. Or worse, spilled blood red on the ground. And that love was not immutable. It could become hate as day becomes night, as life becomes death."

Shocked, Scully rises quickly and leaves the room.

At a nearby cemetery the next morning, Scully tells Mulder that Maggie is missing. Her partner nods, and tells Scully that there are signs of a graveyard struggle, but that the area has been so trampled by a funeral that evidence collection will be impossible.

At this moment Mulder spots a man in a hooded sweatshirt near one of the cemetery maintenance trucks. He draws his gun, sprints after the man, and tackles him. He turns his quarry over and faces a terrified stranger.

"Mulder, that's not him," says Scully, who's sprinted after him. "Mulder—"

"The truck! Check the truck, Scully!" says Mulder.

"Mulder. He works here!" says Scully.

Mulder runs to the man's flatbed truck, reaches into a pile of plants and flowers, and uncovers Maggie's corpse.

Later that day the agents stride through the prison corridor.

"How did you know, Mulder, that the body would be in the truck?" asks Scully.

"I imagined it," says Mulder, curtly.

"It's still no evidence that Padgett directed the killer, Mulder."

"What do you need? A signed work order?" says Mulder. "Of course he directed him."

They stop in front of Padgett's cell. Scully lowers her voice.

"Mulder, you are making critical assumptions without any facts," she says, intensely. "What about time of death? What about—?"

Mulder grabs his partner by the shoulders, moves her to where he's been standing, and takes her former place.

"You're about to argue my usual side, aren't you?"

"Mulder, why couldn't he have imagined it?" whispers Scully. "Why couldn't he just be in the killer's book?"

"You read his book! You read what he wrote about you!" says Mulder, angrily. "Are you trying to tell me that he got inside your head? That what I read is true?"

"Mulder, of course not."

"I don't know how they communicate!" says Mulder. "This is the only way I can think to catch them."

Mulder turns, enters Padgett's cell, and calmly tells the writer that he's free to leave. He hands Padgett the manuscript, apologizes, and adds that he's free to finish his book.

"Thank you," says Padgett. "I made a mistake myself. In my book I'd written that Agent Scully falls in love. But that's obviously impossible. Agent Scully is already in love."

Later that day Padgett enters his apartment, sits down at his desk, and begins tearing up the final pages of his book. There is a noise behind him. He turns, and sees Ken Naciamento, in his hooded sweatshirt, watching him.

"You seem surprised to see me," says Naciamento.

"Yes. Completely," says Padgett, shaken.

"Why? I'm your character."

"What do you want?"

"I'm here to help you finish."

Padgett shakes his head.

"I can't figure out your motive," he says.

"You imagine me so perfectly in every way," says Naciamento. "So perfectly that you bring me to life. Why did you choose me?"

"I needed a perfect crime. And she's a doctor. She'd be horrified by what you do."

"*I'm* horrified. I just want to know why I'm doing it."

"So I could meet her," says Padgett, uneasily.

"That's not a reason," sneers Naciamento. "That's an excuse."

In Apartment 42 Mulder and Scully are watching Padgett via a tiny fiber optic camera inserted into the heat register. On Scully's monitor the writer is sitting quietly at his desk—alone.

In Padgett's apartment, Naciamento, looming over

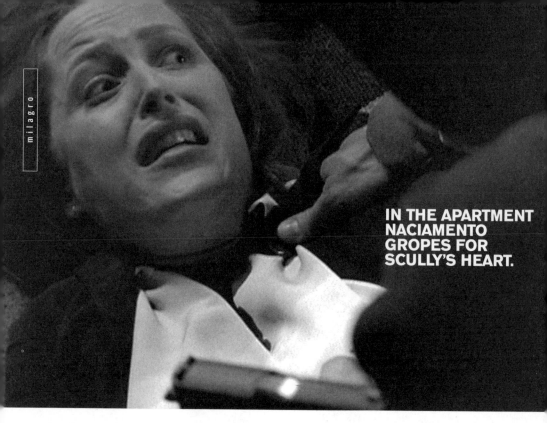

**IN THE APARTMENT
NACIAMENTO
GROPES FOR
SCULLY'S HEART.**

the writer, reads from the part of the manuscript that the writer was about to discard.

"Now, what is this?" he demands.

"A big mistake," says Padgett, embarrassed. "I misjudged her character. Her interest in me. She's only trying to get his attention but doesn't know it."

"Now we're on to something," says Naciamento. "The old unconscious at work."

"I wanted to love her," says the writer, plaintively.

"No wonder you can't finish your book, Padgett! Why do I want their hearts?"

"You tell me. Why do you do it?"

"I'm your character. You tell me. My reason is your reason."

"I want to feel love," says Padgett, softly.

Naciamento shakes his head.

"No. No. You had it right up to there. You were a tool of the truth. And when it finally arrives—when I arrive—you don't want to see it."

"But what is the truth?" says Padgett.

Naciamento closes his eyes.

"Man imagines," he says, "that he, too, can open his heart and expose the burning passion, the flames of Charity. Like the Creator himself. But this is not in his power."

"But I have love in my heart."

"Yes! As a thief has riches, a usurer money. You have it! But man's only power—only true power—is to destroy it."

"Then what's the end of my story?"

"There can only be one true ending, if it is to be perfect."

"She dies?" says Padgett, appalled.

"See?" says Naciamento, with a cruel smile. "It almost writes itself."

In Mulder's apartment late that night Scully monitors Padgett, who's sitting at his desk, typing. Mulder joins her. They watch him rise, gather up the manuscript, and leave the room. Mulder reaches up and swivels the camera—nothing. He rushes out of his apartment to see the elevator doors closing. He races down the stairs.

In the incinerator room Padgett, standing before the dancing flames, prepares to toss his book into the fire.

"Padgett! Freeze!" yells Mulder, gun drawn. "Step away from the incinerator!"

Padgett does so.

In Mulder's apartment Scully zips her boots up and quickly leaves the apartment—to face the hooded man, Naciamento, in the hallway. He grabs Scully by the neck and pushes her back into the apartment.

In the incinerator room Mulder has his gun trained on Padgett.

"What do you think you're doing?" demands the agent.

"Destroying my book." says Padgett.

"Destroying evidence, you mean," says Mulder. "Let me see what you wrote."

"I'll tell you," says Padgett. "He kills her."

In Mulder's apartment Scully has been forced to the floor on her back by the killer. She struggles desperately, but Naciamento is overpowering her. He reaches down into her chest. Blood flows onto on her blouse. Screaming in agony, she reaches for her gun.

In the incinerator room Mulder trains his gun on Padgett with one hand and pages through the manuscript with the other.

"You came down here to give these instructions to your accomplice?" he asks.

"No. He told me how it ends."

"Who?"

"My partner."

"You were alone up there."

Gunshots ring out from Mulder's apartment. Scully empties her gun into Naciamento with no effect.

In the basement Mulder drops the manuscript and sprints to the stairway. Padgett gathers the pages off the floor.

In the apartment Naciamento gropes for Scully's heart.

In the basement Padgett throws a handful of manuscript pages into the incinerator.

Mulder races through the fourth-floor corridor and flings open his front door. Scully lies on her back, unconscious, her chest covered with blood. She is alone.

Mulder peers down at her. She gasps with terror and opens her eyes wide. Sobbing uncontrollably, she pulls Mulder toward her. Mulder closes his eyes and hugs her tightly.

Inside the incinerator Padgett's manuscript burns brightly. Its creator lies in front of the fiery furnace—a bloody cavity where his heart once beat. His voice is heard for the last time:

"A story can have only one true ending. Even as the Stranger felt compelled to commit his final words to paper, he knew they must never be read. To see the sum of his work was to see inside his own emptiness—the heart of a destroyer, not a creator. And yet reflected back upon him, at last he could see his own ending. And in this final act of destruction, a chance to give what he could not receive."

BACK STORY/6X18

Where is the dividing line between artistic introspection and obsession? Between dedication and self-immolation? These are the provocative questions posed by three of the most senior X-File writer/producers in this highly disturbing—and disturbingly personal—episode.

Says executive producer Frank Spotnitz, who has been with the show since its second season: "You know, it's amazing how all-consuming a writer's life is. I mean when your job is to write, you're *always* writing. I find

myself thinking about scripts and plots and characters when I'm in traffic, when I'm on my way to the doctor's office, all the time. The real challenge, actually, is keeping it from crowding out your real life. Because it wants to."

Adds producer John Shiban, in his fourth year of intensive work on the series: "You know, all of us here spend a lot of long days and late nights trying to dig into the darker recesses of our imaginations. In many professions—not just writing—I think there is the big problem of getting so close to your work that it becomes more real to you than your family or home life. That possibility certainly scares me. And that's what *The X-Files* is all about, I think: finding the things that scare us. And the things that scare us the most are the things we know are really a part of us."

Shiban explains that the idea for "Milagro"— which he calls "a writer's horror story"—was born one day in January when he and Spotnitz were sitting and talking about the peculiar stresses and demands of their jobs.

He says, "It suddenly seemed an easy fit to do a story about someone who imagines things so well that they come to life, become real. I mean, the image of someone pulling out his own heart will be familiar to anyone who's ever agonized over a novel or a script.

"But what I think I'm most proud of is the fact that this is the first *X-Files* that actually tells the story from inside another character's—not Mulder's or Scully's—head. There's a voyeuristic quality to it, and because of that I think it's hard to look away when you watch it."

Because of complicated scheduling problems and Chris Carter's temporary unavailability—he was writing the pilot episode of his new series, *Harsh Realm*, early in the year—Spotnitz and Shiban plotted and boarded the bare bones of 6X18, then handed it over to the *X-Files*'s creator, who made his own additions and deletions while writing the teleplay. "Chris's great contributions," says Spotnitz, "were the gift of faith and healing coming from Christ, and also the beautiful turn at the end, where the writer, Padgett, proves he *does* have love in his heart by giving his own life to save Scully's."

Adds Carter, who when asked about the subject laughs and says he has "some familiarity" with writers' obsessive fantasizing and over-identification with their characters:

"'Milagro' was a really good idea that nearly drove me insane," he says. "For the longest time I tried to figure out what the character of Naciamento was trying to tell the writer, and what Padgett's own motive, which he didn't realize himself, was. This became the subject of great debate and I worked and worked on it, coming up with things, throwing them out, then repeating the process until we finally came up with something that made sense to Padgett, to the story, and to ourselves."

When the script was finished and distributed in

milagro

mid-February, long-term *X-Files* hands immediately recognized its distinctiveness.

"It was so intimate, so *quiet*," says director Kim Manners. "No big explosions or supernatural stuff, just two people looking into each other's eyes—and Scully being drawn toward this man like a moth toward a flame. A sexual excitement underneath everything. A psychodrama. Very cool."

Manners adds, however, that he immediately saw two potential problems in translating the script to the screen: that Scully, in being attracted to Padgett, would look merely like a sex-starved woman making an irresponsible choice; and that Padgett, in spinning out his tale of writerly obsession, would come off as an obviously unbalanced psychotic.

The first pitfall, says Manners, was solved by suggesting to Gillian Anderson that Scully, although somewhat attracted to Phillip Padgett as a man, was predominantly driven by an intellectual and professional curiosity about the writer's intense personality and bizarre pursuits.

The second problem was solved by choosing John Hawkes to play Padgett. The part, in fact, had been written expressly for the actor; some weeks earlier Hawkes had auditioned for the lead guest role—as Pinker Rawls, the man who could walk through walls—in the previous episode, "Trevor" (6X17).

While not deeming Hawkes right for that part, Chris Carter and Frank Spotnitz noticed a dignity and simplicity in his bearing that would prevent the protagonist of "Milagro" from becoming a caricature.

"And I think John pulled it off perfectly," says Manners. "His performance really balanced Gillian's character."

After that, says the director, the logistics of "Milagro"—a relatively (and helpfully) low-budget production because of its intimate and personality-driven nature—were "a piece of cake."

Well, not quite. Two carefully selected Los Angeles-area churches, selected to stand in for the one in which Scully encounters Padgett (and the painting of "The Divine Heart"—actually a new work commissioned by production designer Corey Kaplan) pulled out before filming began, and a frantic late search had to be launched for a replacement.

Similarly frustrating was a search for a suitable graveyard. Most Southern California "memorial parks" are of the Forest Lawn variety, with marker plaques sunk flush into the ground. It took locations manager Ilt Jones several days of hard scouting to find a serviceable cemetery—with old-fashioned vertical tombstones—in Altadena, a quiet suburb east of Los Angeles.

In his score for "Milagro," composer Mark Snow used the recorded sound of a human heartbeat several times as a percussive element.

Angelo Vacco, who played the murdered teenager Kevin, is a former *X-Files* production assistant. He previously appeared in "F. Emasculata" (2X22).

John Hawkes (Padgett) previously guest-starred in "The Judge," a first-season episode of *Millennium*. He also appeared in *Playing God,* the 1997 movie starring David Duchovny, and *Home Fries*, the 1998 film written by *X-Files* co-executive producer Vince Gilligan.

The index cards that Phillip Padgett pins to his wall in "Milagro" are covered with "plot points" from the T. S. Eliot poem "The Wasteland."

Although a tombstone in one of the cemetery scenes is inscribed with the name "Salinger," the reclusive novelist J. D. Salinger is still very much alive. "It was a joke of some kind by somebody in the props department," explains executive producer Frank Spotnitz.

THREE OF A KIND

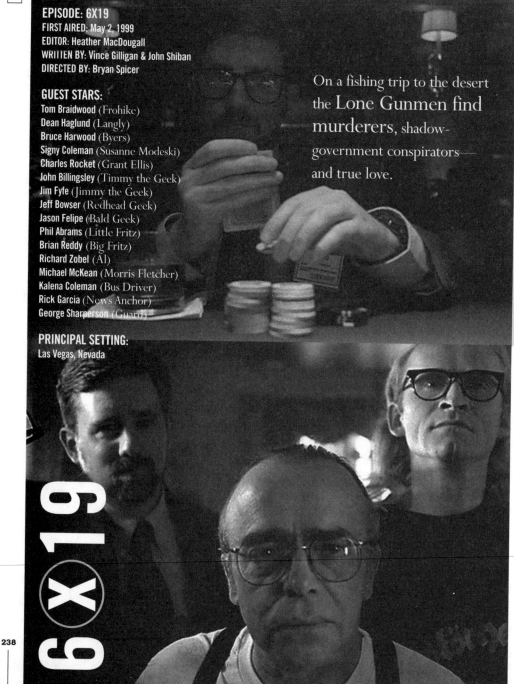

EPISODE: 6X19
FIRST AIRED: May 2, 1999
EDITOR: Heather MacDougall
WRITTEN BY: Vince Gilligan & John Shiban
DIRECTED BY: Bryan Spicer

GUEST STARS:
Tom Braidwood (Frohike)
Dean Haglund (Langly)
Bruce Harwood (Byers)
Signy Coleman (Susanne Modeski)
Charles Rocket (Grant Ellis)
John Billingsley (Timmy the Geek)
Jim Fyfe (Jimmy the Geek)
Jeff Bowser (Redhead Geek)
Jason Felipe (Bald Geek)
Phil Abrams (Little Fritz)
Brian Reddy (Big Fritz)
Richard Zobel (Al)
Michael McKean (Morris Fletcher)
Kalena Coleman (Bus Driver)
Rick Garcia (News Anchor)
George Sharperson (Guard)

PRINCIPAL SETTING:
Las Vegas, Nevada

On a fishing trip to the desert the Lone Gunmen find murderers, shadow-government conspirators— and true love.

238

6 X 19

On a lovely day in an immaculate suburb, a mild-mannered man in a dark suit climbs out of his car, walks to his picture-perfect house, enters its tasteful interior, and greets his two adorable toddlers. He narrates:

"My name is John Fitzgerald Byers. I was named after our thirty-fifth president. And I keep having this beautiful dream.

"In my dream, the events of November 22nd, 1963, never happened. In it, my namesake was never assassinated. Other things are different, too, in my dream. My country is hopeful and innocent, young again. My fellow citizens trust their elected officials, never once having been betrayed by them. My government is truly of the people, by the people, for the people. All my hopes for my country, for myself—all are fulfilled. I have everything a person could want. Home and family. And love."

Byers enters a lush, beautifully kept backyard. He bends down to pat his faithful dog. A pretty blonde woman—Susanne Modeski, last seen in "Unusual Suspects" (5X01)—turns from the lemon tree she's been tending, smiles warmly, and hugs Byers tightly. They kiss.

In the next instant Byers stands in a desert wasteland alone. He holds a man's wedding ring in his hand. He stares at it, despairing. He continues:

"Everything that counts for anything in life, I have. But the dream ends the same way every time. I lose it all."

At the Monte Carlo Hotel in Las Vegas a defense contractors' convention—Def-Con '99—is underway. In a private salon just off the casino floor, five conventioneers—including Byers, wearing a pair of black horn-rimmed glasses—play a high-stakes game of Texas Hold 'Em.

Three of Byers's fellow poker players are rumpled middle managers named Big Fritz, Little Fritz, and Al. The fourth, the dealer, is a good-looking man in a well-cut suit. He deals himself and each player two "hole" cards, then deals three community cards faceup on the table. Al looks up at Byers.

"Hey, what's your name again?" he says.

"Funsten. Stuart Funsten. Hi," Byers replies.

"You bring the little lady, Stuart?" asks Al.

"I'm not married," says Byers.

"Smart man. Hundred," says Little Fritz, tossing some chips into the pot.

Byers tosses his own ante into the pile.

"You guys come to this every year? Def-Con?" he says.

"Every year," says Little Fritz, tossing his cards to the table disgustedly. "Fold."

"Wouldn't miss it," says Big Fritz.

"Out," grunts Al.

"So," says Byers, tossing another chip. "You guys working on anything interesting these days?"

The dealer's eyes flicker briefly in Byers's direction.

"Aaagh, same old black-ops crapola," says Big Fritz. "You know what it's like."

Little Fritz pipes up.

"Hey! We're doing some neat stuff with neutron bombardment," he says. "Yeah! You can cook somebody's brain in their skull, like hardboiling an egg."

"Speaking of crapola," says Big Fritz. "Fold."

A hotel waiter—actually, Lone Gunman Melvin Frohike in a hotel waiter's outfit—sets down a drink at the dealer's elbow. Frohike's name tag reads FELIPE. The dealer hands him a $20 chip.

"Ah," says Frohike. "A man of distinction."

The dealer eyes Byers coldly, then deals another community card faceup.

"So, you in, Mr. Funsten?" he says.

"Yeah," says Byers, tossing two chips in the pot.

"It looks like it's just you and me," says the dealer.

The dealer slides in his chips and deals the last card to the table.

"Another two hundred," says Byers.

"I'll see you two hundred," says the dealer, "and raise you one thousand."

"Ho, *ho!*" chortles Little Fritz.

"He's buying the pot, Stu!" leers Al.

"Three clubs showing. Could be a flush!" says Big Fritz.

"One thousand and I'll raise you one thousand," says Byers.

"What stones he has!" says Little Fritz.

In the back of the salon Frohike clears his throat warningly. Byers doesn't look at him. The dealer smiles tightly and points to Byers's convention badge.

"I see you work for Conglomerated," he says. "You guys make a great AE135 unit."

Byers stares, at a loss for a reply. At the back of his right ear, attached to his eyeglasses, is a tiny flesh-colored speaker.

"Don't freak. Don't freak. I'm on it. AE135," says a small, tinny voice.

In another room in the hotel the third Gunman, Ringo Langly, sits at a table facing two glowing laptop computers. His hands fly over the keyboard. On one screen appears a long list of aircraft parts.

"Bingo!" says Langly. "442J-stroke-AE135. Air-conditioning unit for B-2 bombers. Talk air conditioners."

Langly glances at his other screen. On it is a video image of the poker match, broadcast from the table

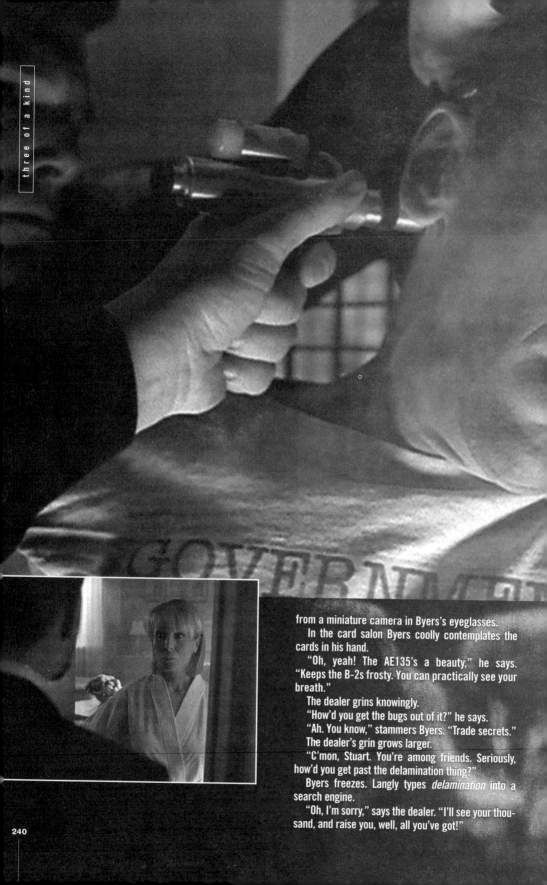

from a miniature camera in Byers's eyeglasses.

In the card salon Byers coolly contemplates the cards in his hand.

"Oh, yeah! The AE135's a beauty," he says. "Keeps the B-2s frosty. You can practically see your breath."

The dealer grins knowingly.

"How'd you get the bugs out of it?" he says.

"Ah. You know," stammers Byers. "Trade secrets." The dealer's grin grows larger.

"C'mon, Stuart. You're among friends. Seriously, how'd you get past the delamination thing?"

Byers freezes. Langly types *delamination* into a search engine.

"Oh, I'm sorry," says the dealer. "I'll see your thousand, and raise you, well, all you've got!"

The dealer's smile doesn't fade. He turns over his own cards.

"King high," he says.

He reaches over and rakes in the pot.

Langly flings himself backward in his chair, disgusted.

At the back of the room Frohike drops an ashtray with a loud bang.

The dealer turns to Al.

"Call security," he says. "Have them pick up 'Mr. Funsten' here. *And* his partner."

"Delamination," says Byers. "You made that up."

"My advice to you, Stuart or whatever your name really is?" says the dealer. "It's that poker's not your game."

Moments later a huge security guard flings Byers and Frohike bodily out of the salon. They rendezvous with Langly in their hotel room.

"Three thousand dollars!" says Langly. "I told you to fold!"

"Did you at least get any usable prints off the drink glasses?" asks Byers.

"Are you kidding?" says Frohike. "We had to leave them all behind. How are we going to salvage this?"

"We're not," says Langly, glaring at Byers. "This convention's a bust. Five days and three grand invested, and we've got *bupkes* to show for it."

Byers takes off his horn-rims wearily.

"Who was that player anyway?" he says. "The guy who made us—he wasn't wearing a convention badge. I think he's worth looking into."

There is a loud knock on their door. The Gunmen tense up, on the alert.

"CIA! Open up!" says a male voice.

Frohike peers through the peephole and is unimpressed. He unlocks the door and opens it.

"Hey, hey, hey! Jimmy and Timmy!" says Frohike with false bravado.

Two nerds stand before him. Timmy is clad in impeccable Advanced Placement Calculus Club attire. Jimmy's well-worn T-shirt is a blowup of Lee Harvey Oswald in mid-grimace as he's being shot by Jack Ruby. Red letters spell out the words GOVERNMENT PATSY.

"Hey! Where were you guys today?" asks Jimmy.

"Around," says Byers, defensively.

"Oh, yeah?" says Timmy, deadpan. "Maybe snooping for some hot 411?"

"On the sneak tip?" says Jimmy, sarcastically.

"Maybe," says Langly, sullenly.

"Oh, yeah? Maybe we were, too," says Timmy.

"And maybe we got some," says Jimmy.

"Well, maybe we did, too," says Frohike.

Members of the two camps eye each other, daring the other to speak first.

"Aw, we got *bubkes*," says Jimmy, finally. "Buncha tight-lipped defense contractors."

Panic begins to infiltrate Byers's expression. Langly gets no hits on his search query.

He glances at Langly's hole cards on the video screen.

"Stall him," he says to Byers. "And *fold!*"

Byers pulls himself together. The other players lean forward expectantly.

"You want to know how we fixed the delamination problem?" he says, smiling bravely. "We subcontracted the whole damn thing to the Japanese, and triple-billed the government. Same thing we always do."

The other players laugh merrily. Byers slides his entire bankroll into the pile, then lays his cards on the table.

"Queen-high flush," he says.

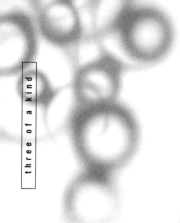

"I'm gonna go way out on a limb here," says Frohike, sarcastically, "and say it's your T-shirt."

"You just don't get it, man," says Jimmy. "This says that I'm on to them. This says I comprehend the military-industrial power dynamic. That's what this whole thing is about: wetworks, political assassination. That's their theme for this year."

"Where'd you hear that?" asks Byers.

"Oh, yeah! Like I'm gonna reveal my sources. Suffice it to say, there's some big new stealth assassination technology that's supposed to be unveiled. And I will be there, front row."

"In the meantime," says Timmy, "we're hitting the restaurant."

"All-you-can-eat lobster buffet!" says Jimmy.

"Free floor show. Plenty of boobage. You guys down?" says his partner.

Langly nods eagerly. Byers shrugs and turns his back. Frohike remains behind with him.

"You're one hell of a sad sack, Byers," he says. "You're the one who pushes the hardest for us to come to these conventions. Then you get all squirrely once we get here. You're still looking for her, aren't you? Susanne Modeski?"

"I met her at a convention," says Byers.

"Ten years ago," says Frohike. "In Baltimore. And we both know what happened to her. Most likely she's dead."

"No. She was a brilliant scientist. Too important to the government."

"Buddy, either way," says Frohike, "we're both hoping she's in a better place than Las Vegas. C'mon."

A few minutes later Byers and Frohike stroll through the casino. Frohike stops to play a slot machine. Byers glances across the casino floor and sees Susanne Modeski, strolling through the gambling area.

"It can't be," says Byers, not quite believing his eyes.

He takes off in pursuit, loses her, then spots her heading for the elevator bank. He runs in that direction—right into an elderly man clutching a bucket of quarters. The old man tumbles face first to the ground, spilling coins in all directions. Byers apologizes, looks up, and the woman of his dreams is gone.

At 2:34 A.M. in Washington a cell phone rings on the nightstand in Scully's bedroom. The agent rolls over in bed and answers it groggily.

"Hey, Scully, it's me," says Mulder. "Listen, Scully, I need you on the next flight to Las Vegas."

"Las Vegas? Why?" she says.

"It's the Lone Gunmen. They're on to something big."

"What exactly?

In his hotel room Byers sits at the laptop, synthesizing Mulder's voice and sending it down the phone

"WELL! I JUST CAN'T DECIDE
WHO LIGHTS MY FIRE!"
—Scully

line to Scully. Frohike and Langly watch approvingly.

"It's really important," types Langly. "Trust me."

"Yeah, I trust you," says Scully. "It's those three I'm not so sure about."

"Look," types Byers, "I can't talk over an unsecured line. Please just get here. It's an emergency."

Scully reluctantly agrees to make the trip, then hangs up.

In the hotel room Frohike chuckles.

"She's gonna kick our ass," he says. "What do you need Scully for, anyway?"

"We're up against agents of the government," says Byers. "We need our own government agent."

"And that would be Mulder?" says Langly, sarcastically. "Why do you want just Scully?"

"Mulder's too high a profile. He's virtually a household name to the black-ops who kidnapped Susanne in Baltimore," says Byers.

Langly shakes his head and tells him that he's hacked into the hotel computer, and that Susanne is not registered.

"It was *her*. She's *here*," says Byers, fervently. "I've got to find her!"

"You've gotta find some ice," says Frohike. "You need a drink."

A few minutes later Byers is filling a bucket at the ice machine in the corridor. He looks up and sees the dealer from the poker game—this time wearing a convention badge—exiting the elevator. The dealer rounds a corner, and Byers peers around it, watching him surreptitiously.

The dealer knocks on the door to Room 1066. Susanne Modeski opens it and greets him with a kiss. The dealer steps into the room, out of sight.

Susanne slips the "Privacy Please" tag on the knob before shutting the door. Byers hugs his ice bucket, eyes widening in shock and despair.

The next morning Byers dunks his face deep into the ice bucket, now filled with ice-cold water.

"Stop trying to kill yourself, Byers. It's not deep enough," say Frohike. "Come see what we've got."

Byers comes up for air and wanders over to his companions. Frohike taps the computer keyboard and pulls up some information: The poker dealer is named Grant Ellis; his car is registered to a Department of Defense motor pool in Whitestone, New Mexico—where Susanne once worked at the Army Advanced Weapons Facility—and his hotel bills go directly to its administrative offices.

"He's looking like some shadow-government poobah," says Langly.

"He brainwashed her!" exclaims Byers.

Langly and Frohike look at one another, not convinced.

"That's what they do there!" insists Byers. "The E-H gas she developed. Call it psychological warfare, behavior modification, but it's all about mind control.

And undoubtedly the process has been refined in the last decade.

"She ran from them, refused to take part in their tests, their crimes against the American people. There's no way she would choose to be working for them now. Working for that guy. Kissing him! Clearly, he brainwashed her."

His two companions are silent for a moment, letting this sink in.

"I know a way to find out," says Frohike, finally.

Later that morning, Frohike—clad in hotel maintenance worker coveralls—strolls down the corridor, flirts with a pretty hotel maid, and takes up a surveillance position across from Room 1066.

In the hotel lobby Byers stares at the entrance of the salon where a private Def-Con seminar is being held. He shakes his head in frustration, and joins up with Langly a few yards away.

"I can't get into the conference," he says. "The guard who threw him out of the card game is at the door."

"Let *me* go," says Langly.

Byers flicks a finger at Langly's long hair, makes a face, and shakes his head. Someone comes up from behind him and claps a hand on his shoulder.

"CIA! *Freeze!*" says Jimmy.

The geek laughs uproariously, slapping palms with two new geeky companions.

"That just keeps getting funnier," says Langly, sarcastically. "Where's your girlfriend Timmy?"

"Out in the desert," says Jimmy. "There's this naked chick who'll teach you to shoot machine guns. It cost two hundred beans, though. I told him he was a putz."

Jimmy notes Byers's distracted look. He asks him what's up. Reluctantly, Langly answers that they're trying to figure out how to get into the Saguaro Room.

"Good luck!" scoffs a redheaded geek. "That's the Holy Grail. Bug sweeps—"

"Casino security outside, government security inside," says the bald geek. "There's no way any of us are getting in."

"*I* can get in," says Jimmy, striking a jaw-jutting pose. "And I will, too. When the time is right."

This gets Byers's attention.

"I need to get in there, Jimmy," he says "I need to know what's happening in there *today.* If you can really get in there, prove it."

In a hotel heating duct later that day, Jimmy crawls stealthily until he reaches a louvered vent. He opens the vent and peers into the Saguaro Room. On the dais Grant Ellis is holding forth on weapons technology. Susanne is sitting nearby. Jimmy pulls out a tiny camcorder, points it through the vent, and starts recording the scene. He pans down and sees a familiar face in his viewscreen.

"Timmy?" he says. "Damn!"

Timmy looks up toward the vent. Frantically, Jimmy shinnies himself backward through the duct and kicks out a vent grill in a service hallway. He pushes himself backward through the vent, and is grabbed by two black-suited black-ops agents, who drag him from the duct and brace him against the wall. Another man swaggers into view. It is Timmy.

"You're one of them!" says Jimmy, terrified.

Timmy confiscates the camcorder and pats him down for wires.

"You really screwed things up, Jimmy," he sneers. "We had big plans for you."

"What big plans?" says Jimmy.

Timmy merely pokes at Jimmy's T-shirt.

"Political assassination!" says Jimmy. "I was right! I was right about the whole thing!"

Timmy sizes up his captive, blank-faced.

"Every good plan needs a patsy," he says matter-of-factly.

He reaches into his pocket, pulls out a high-tech medical injection gun, presses the nozzle behind Jimmy's ear, and pulls the trigger.

Later that morning Byers and Langly rendezvous with Scully as she is checking into the hotel. She asks them where Mulder is.

"He may be hard to reach for the next few hours," says Byers, smoothly. "He suggested we work with you. Bring you up to speed."

"By all means," says Scully, skeptically. "Bring me up to speed."

At that moment there is a commotion in the lobby. A hotel employee, walking quickly toward the hotel's service entrance, relays Jimmy's name into a walkie-talkie. Two paramedics follow her—as do Byers, Langly, and Scully. Outside the hotel a crowd is gathering around a parked tour bus.

"He just jumped! No warning, no nothing! He just dived right in front of me!" says the female bus driver, hysterically.

Jimmy lies dead—crushed and covered with blood—under one of the bus's front wheels.

"This wasn't a suicide," says Byers.

"You knew this man?" asks Scully.

Byers says nothing. He turns and heads back to the hotel. Scully looks at Langly.

"What is going on here?" she demands.

Inside the hotel Frohike watches a maid exit Room 1066. He walks to the door, holds some sort of high-tech gizmo to the door, and swipes a blank card key through the lock. The door clicks open.

Frohike enters the room and zips open a black bag he's been carrying. Inside is a small electric screwdriver. He pockets it. Next is a small camcorder. He pockets that, too.

He goes to a small air vent near the baseboard,

pulls it open, and finds a tiny camcorder, taping him. He pulls out the camera's tape cassette, puts the camcorder back in the duct, and replaces the grille. He hears the front door open; Susanne is entering the room.

Frohike grabs his black bag and cowers in the bathroom. Susanne enters the bedroom part of the suite. She takes off her shoes and blouse, wanders into another part of the dressing area, and returns to her bedroom. She walks to the bathroom, prepares to enter, and is interrupted by a knock on the door. She looks through the peephole and is stunned by what she sees. She opens the door. Byers stands in front of her.

"Susanne? Do you remember me?" he says, softly.

"John! What are you doing here?" she replies.

"I'm here to save you," he says.

"From what?"

"I don't think you're—you're yourself," Byers stammers. "I think you've been mistreated. And confused. And I'm afraid that your beliefs, your opinions, are no longer your own."

"As in, I've been brainwashed?"

Byers nods.

"I don't know what to tell you," she says. "I haven't been."

"Your life may be in danger, Susanne," says Byers. "A friend of mine has just been killed. Murdered. And that man that you're with—?"

"My fiancé?" says Susanne. "I'm sorry, John. I think you'd better go."

She tries to close the door in his face. Byers forces it open again.

"Wait! Wait!" he says, quickly. "Ten years ago I saw you thrown into a car. Kidnapped right in front of me. Did that not happen? Did I just dream all of that?"

Susanne stares at him for a moment, smiles sadly, and nods.

"It happened," she says. "But things got better."

She closes the door gently, enters the bathroom, and turns on bathtub taps. Above her head a small access panel in the ceiling slowly closes.

Byers trudges down the corridor. Something falls onto his head: Frohike's black bag. Frohike looks down at him from another open ceiling access panel.

"Ooops. Sorry, buddy," says Frohike, swinging himself down. "That Susanne's a popular girl."

At the Clark County Morgue a sheet-covered body lies on an examination table. Scully and Langly stand nearby.

"You're absolutely sure you want to be here for this?" asks Scully.

"Oh, yeah. I'm cool," says Langly, struggling to hide his uneasiness. "Let's just find out what killed him."

Scully pulls the sheet off Jimmy, causing Langly to

"POLITICAL ASSASSINATION! I WAS RIGHT! I WAS RIGHT ABOUT THE WHOLE THING." –Jimmy the Geek

"EVERY GOOD PLAN NEEDS A PATSY."–Timmy the Geek

cringe. She clicks on an overhead mike, begins her examination, and starts dictating her autopsy findings: all consistent with being run over by a bus.

Langly grows progressively greener. He averts his eyes.

"Uh, what if they did something to him?" he asks. "You know, to make him pancake himself?"

"Who's 'they'?" asks Scully.

Langly shrugs.

"You know—'them.'"

Scully nods dismissively.

"I'll begin with the Y incision," she says.

She picks up a scalpel and makes a long, deep cut across Jimmy's breastbone. Langly begins to lose it altogether.

"Langly, could you go over there and pass me the Stryker Saw, please?" says Scully. "It's over there by the counter."

Trembling, Langly retrieves the electric cutting instrument. He glances down into the gaping, bloody cavity of Jimmy's chest, and runs for the exit, dropping the saw on the floor. He barely makes it to the corridor before upchucking violently.

"You okay, Langly?" says Scully, mildly concerned.

No answer. Scully sighs, picks the saw off the floor, and, as she rises, notices something behind Jimmy's ear. It is a circular mark surrounding a tiny injection hole.

At that moment a man—Timmy—grabs Scully roughly from behind. He clamps a hand over her mouth, raises the injection gun to a spot behind her ear, and pulls the trigger.

In a nearby utility room Langly—in the midst of losing his last several meals—hears a clatter from the autopsy room. He runs back inside to see Scully lying unconscious next to the examination table. The Gunman grabs her by the shoulders and raises her to a sitting position. Scully opens her eyes.

"What happened?" she says.

"I'm thinking that you got a little queasy and took a header," says Langly. "You know, blood and guts—it can bother some people. You gonna be all right?"

Scully smiles goofily and turns to face Langly.

"Sure, cutie!" she says.

Langly is thunderstruck. He asks Scully if she's done with Jimmy's autopsy.

"Done, done, done!" she says.

Next, Scully tries unsuccessfully to roll away the autopsy table, but it is bolted securely to the floor. Langly looks at her, baffled, and asks her what killed Jimmy.

"In my medical opinion?" slurs Scully.

Langly nods. In reply, Scully imitates a tour bus blowing its horn, then claps her hands—once—to mime Jimmy getting splattered.

"And that's all you found?" says Langly, baffled.

"That's a-a-a-a-l-l I know," says Scully, collapsing to the floor once again.

Later that day in the hotel room Langly relays this non-news to Byers and Frohike.

"Man, she's seriously jet-lagged," he says, glancing at the laptop screen. "You got product already?"

Frohike plays the surveillance tape he stole from the duct in Susanne's hotel room. Susanne steps into view and sits on the bed. She speaks tensely to someone off screen.

"All this waiting," she says. "It's like they're always keeping tabs on us. Watching us."

"Honey, you worry too much," says Grant. "The plan is still on schedule. Everything's falling into place."

He sits on the bed next to her and gives her a kiss. Frohike clicks off the playback. Byers shakes his head.

"It's not her," he says. "They're making her do this somehow. She would not marry that man."

"You don't know him like I do," says a female voice behind him.

The three Gunmen turn, astonished. Susanne has unlocked their door—with the electronic gizmo that Frohike left behind in her room—and entered.

"Grant Ellis saved my life. He saved the lives of thousands," says Susanne, turning to Byers, "I need to talk to you. I can explain everything."

Frohike and Langly exit reluctantly. Susanne moves closer to Byers.

"You said something about a friend being murdered," she says.

"Not that I can prove it," says Byers. "But I think he saw something he was not supposed to see at your conference. You may be in danger."

"I am. Always. So is Grant," says Susanne.

"I've thought about this moment so many times. All the things I would say to you if I ever saw you again. And then there you were—at my door. And I—

"WE'VE GATHERED UP ENOUGH PROOF. THE PUBLIC IS READY TO BELIEVE, NOW MORE THAN EVER."—Susanne Modeski

"They took me, ten years ago. They did things to me. And it was like drowning every day—underwater, struggling to breathe. And one day a hand broke the surface, reached down, and pulled me up.

"I wanted it to be you, John. It was Grant. He worked for the Project. I didn't trust him, not for years. Not until I realized he was working against them in his own way. Stalling them, sabotaging their tests. He reminded me of you."

In the casino a few minutes later Langly and Frohike feed the slot machines. A downcast Timmy—back in geek disguise—approaches them, and invites Langly to a game of Dungeons & Dragons in memory of Jimmy.

"Lord Manhammer will be in attendance," says Langly, solemnly.

Langly departs.

Frohike cocks an ear toward the casino bar, from which a female giggling sound—somehow familiar, somehow not—is emanating. It is, in fact, Scully—glowing and bubbly, surrounded by an appreciative posse of male gamblers, conventioneers, and lounge lizards. Frohike approaches warily.

"Scully?" he says.

"Oh, Hickey! Long time no see!" she says, gleefully.

A silk-suited smoothie whispers something in her ear. She raises her hand in protest.

"No, that's not nice! I like Hickey! Ha ha ha!"

"Cigarette?" says a leering middle-aged man extending a pack of Morleys.

It is, in fact, Morris Fletcher, the Area 51 spook last seen in "Dreamland II" (6X05). Scully smiles invitingly and pulls out a cigarette, slowly, with her teeth.

"You don't smoke," says Frohike, appalled.

"But who's got a match?" says Scully, cigarette dangling from her lips.

In an instant Fletcher and the other hangers-on spring into action, each producing a flaming lighter or burning match. Scully milks the moment, looking from man to man.

"Well! I just can't decide who lights my fire!" she says, teasingly.

"That's it!" says Frohike, snatching the cigarette from the agent's mouth. "All right, you dandies, back off! This is Special Agent Dana Scully of the FBI. If you so much as touch her, you may be committing a federal offense!"

The men slowly disperse. Fletcher is the last to move away.

"It could have been . . . stardust," he says, suavely.

"Maybe next time," says Scully, as she gives him a slap on the behind.

"Ooh!" says Morris, pursing his lips in anticipation.

Upstairs in the hotel Langly swaggers into Timmy's room, ready for some D&D action. He is greeted by Timmy and a squad of stolid security men.

Langly's smirk fades slowly as he realizes he's trapped.

In the Gunmen's hotel room Byers plays Susanne the surveillance tape of her and Grant.

"You didn't tape this?" asks Susanne, anxiously.

Byers shakes his head.

"Which means they surveilled us," she says, fighting back tears. "They know our plan. They know everything. This conference was our chance. To slip out on the last day—go public with all our files, all our weapons research. We could finally make it happen this time. We've gathered up enough proof. The public is ready to believe, now more than ever. But now they know everything. They'll kill us, John—Grant and me both."

At this moment Frohike leads Scully—still on Cloud Nine—into the room.

"I found Agent Scully Golightly holding court in the bar," he says.

Byers is shocked. But Susanne moves quickly toward her, brushes the hair from her right ear, and finds the familiar mark.

"She's not drunk. Look at this," she says. "That's from an injector gun."

"What the hell was she injected with?" asks Frohike.

"A derivative of E-H gas," says Susanne. "A-H: anoetic histamine, my latest creation.

"I could have developed it years ago, but I held off. I wasn't about to let those bastards I work for get their hands on it. Grant thought that if we secretly developed a small batch, and then destroyed the notes, we would have the proof we needed to go public. We'd also have a weapon to use against them."

"Who else has access to this anoetic histamine?" asks Byers.

"Grant and I are the only two people who have the samples—" says Susanne—the realization of her fiancé's betrayal slowly dawning.

Later that evening Susanne prepares a hypodermic, then injects it into Scully's arm.

"This will counteract the anoetic effect," she says.

"Oww! Just a little prick!" says Scully, before fainting dead away.

Susanne reassures the Gunmen that Scully will be fine after she sleeps it off.

"I don't understand," says Frohike. "Why would the government want to turn Scully into a bimbo?"

"That's just a potential side effect. Anoetic histamine impedes higher brain functions. It promotes suggestibility."

"Mind control," adds Byers. "Brainwashing."

"That explains Jimmy," says Frohike. "They told him to commit suicide."

"And Scully," says Byers. "They made her forget her autopsy findings. But what's their larger purpose? What are they planning?"

Susanne shakes her head. Langly scratches a small circular mark behind his right ear.

Early the next day a tranced-out Langly enters Timmy's room. Timmy hands him a cheap automatic.

"This is your weapon," says the black-ops man. "All you do is pull the trigger. You will enter the Saguaro Room at 10:05 A.M. This badge will give you access. Take a seat toward the back and wait. At 10:15, a break will be called. Rise, approach the target, and fire three shots."

In the Saguaro Room later that morning Langly enters and takes a seat toward the back. A speaker—Al, from the poker game—drones on about some highly technical, undoubtedly sinister subject; Grant Ellis and Susanne sit next to each other on the dais.

Susanne checks her wristwatch. It's 10:14. Outside the conference room, Scully flashes her FBI ID to the guard at the door. He shakes his head.

"Authorized attendees only," he says.

Inside, Langly checks his watch. So does Ellis, who asks Al if it isn't a good time to call a five-minute break. Al agrees.

The attendees get up from the chairs and begin to mill around. Langly stands, approaches Ellis and Susanne, pulls the automatic from his waistband, and fires three shots into Susanne's torso.

"Oh, my God!" exclaims Ellis.

Langly calmly sheathes his weapon and walks away. Scully enters, followed by the security guard, and kneels over Susanne's bloody form.

"Call for help," Scully orders the guard.

Two uniformed EMTs—Frohike and Byers—intercept his walkie-talkie transmission and radio back that they're on their way.

Grant kneels next to Scully.

"Who did this? Who did this?" he demands.

Scully turns to the guard and orders him to detain Ellis immediately. The guard yanks the protesting man away. Frohike and Byers load Susanne, unconscious, onto their gurney.

"Good work, party girl," whispers Frohike.

Timmy watches curiously as Scully leads the procession out the door. He kneels down, dabs a finger in a wet puddle of blood, and tastes it.

Scully leads Ellis into Room 1066, where Byers, Frohike—and Susanne, perfectly healthy, though still covered with blood—are waiting.

"Could we have a moment alone, please?" Susanne says.

The others leave. Susanne looks at Ellis with sadness and anger.

"Big surprise, huh?" she says. "Since you programmed my friend to kill me?"

"No, Susanne. It wasn't my idea," says Ellis.

"You knew about it. You gave it to them, the A-H.

If I hadn't thought to check Langly, if I hadn't given him the antidote—"

Susanne rips open her blouse, revealing a camisole dotted with exploded squibs attached to a remote-control device.

"Why save me?" she says. "Why save my life just to take it away?"

"You know why," says Ellis, quietly.

"You were done with me," says Susanne, bitterly. "You had what they wanted."

"*They* had what they wanted," says Ellis. "The Project was over. Honest to God, it wasn't my idea."

"All those years gaining my trust!" says Susanne, crying now. "You pretended that you loved me. What could they possibly give you for

"Sure," says Timmy, preparing to administer the *coup de grace.*

Byers charges Timmy and is pistol-whipped to the floor. Timmy aims at Frohike and Langly, now huddled with Susanne.

"You know the best thing about killing you three?" he says. "Now I won't have to dress like you anymore!"

He prepares to fire, but Byers pops him in the ankle with a dose of A-H. He falls to the floor, right on top of the Gunman.

Frohike and Langly haul him off their friend.

"Hi, cutie!" says Timmy.

"What do we do with him?" asks Frohike.

On a hotel TV later that day an anchorman announces that a man named Timothy Landau has confessed to the murder of Grant Ellis and Susanne Modeski. A picture of Timmy flashes on the screen.

In her room Scully is on the phone with Mulder. The connection is very bad.

"I'm at the hotel. Where are you?" she shouts. "What do you mean 'What hotel'? Las Vegas. I'm in Las Vegas. Aren't you? You called me. What do you mean you didn't call me?"

She pauses for a moment as the truth sinks in.

"Oh, man!" she mutters. "I am gonna kick their asses!"

That night at the hotel entrance Frohike and Langly load Susanne's bags into a taxicab. Susanne and Byers stand apart.

"Susanne Modeski is dead," says Byers. "Every computer at every county, state, and federal office knows it. This is who you are now."

He hands her a slip of paper. Susanne reads it, then looks up.

"Come with me," she says.

Byers is silent for a long moment. He closes his eyes and swallows hard.

"You're safer without me," he says.

"It doesn't make a difference," she says. "I'm going public."

"No, you're not," says Langly. "You've done more than enough. Leave it to us now. It's what we do."

Susanne smiles, reaches into her coat pocket, and hands something to Byers.

"This was made for Grant," she says. "I want you to have it."

She kisses Byers lovingly.

"Some day," she says, turning to leave.

She enters the taxi. Byers looks at her gift: a gold wedding band. Susanne gazes at Byers through the taxi's rear window as it drives away.

Byers's two friends stand alongside him. There is an awkward silence.

"So, you wanna hit the slots?" says Frohike, finally.

that? What was it worth to you, Grant? What was your price? What did you get?"

"Life," says Ellis, quietly. "They'd kill me."

The front door opens and Timmy steps inside. He raises a silenced pistol and aims it.

"I'm sorry, Susanne," says Ellis.

Timmy fires twice—and Ellis falls dead. Timmy aims at Susanne.

In the Gunmen's hotel room Frohike and Byers kibitz while Langly frantically hacks new data into public records. There is a knock at their door. Frohike opens up. It is Susanne.

"CIA. Freeze!" says a pistol-wielding Timmy, stepping into view behind her.

"Let her go," says Byers, stepping forward.

"You know, Byers," says Langly, "growing old with us ain't so bad."

"Oh, shut up, Langly!" says Frohike. "You *really* want him to kill himself?"

BACK STORY/6X19

The Lone Gunmen's Year in Review:

—Tom Braidwood (Frohike): After *The X-Files* left Canada in the spring of 1998, Braidwood—for five intense seasons the show's Vancouver-based first assistant director—planned on taking "a bit of a break." No such luck. During the summer he got a desperate call from a friend who was supervising *DaVinci's Inquest*, a popular Canadian Broadcasting Company crime drama filmed near his home. Since then he's been helping out on a "crash and burn basis," writing and producing for the series and preparing to direct several episodes in the upcoming season. He also did some second unit directing on *Millennium* and had a guest shot on the syndicated show *Viper*.

—Bruce Harwood (Byers): The mild-mannered Canadian actor had good luck last season, winning a part opposite Bill Pullman in the feature film *The Guilty*; making a guest appearance on *The Outer Limits*; and recording the audio version of *Skin*, the latest *X-Files* novel. On the minus side: he reports that Vancouver was "even colder and wetter than usual" during 1998 to 1999.

—Dean Haglund (Langly): Last season the itinerant actor/standup comic divided his time between Vancouver and Los Angeles, settling definitively in Southern California in April. He spent the summer of 1998 on the North American comedy club circuit but since then has confined his live performances primarily to Los Angeles venues. He filmed a hilarious, nationally broadcast Budweiser commercial with Brian Thompson (The Alien Bounty Hunter on *The X-Files*); they play a pair of "importers of stale beer." He won a part as "a computer geek for the Mob" in *A Family Owned Business*, a comedy movie scheduled for release in 2000.

Of course, all of the above leaves out the most visible part of the three men's resumes: as actors portraying irrepressible conspiracy theorists on *The X-Files*. This is the second consecutive year the Lone Gunmen have had their "own" show: a development prompted in equal parts by the characters' popularity with longtime fans and by the temporary absence of the show's stars.

Last year, during the week that the Gunmen-heavy "Unusual Suspects" (5X01) was being filmed in Vancouver, David Duchovny and Gillian Anderson were in Southern California completing the *X-Files* movie.

This year, during the eight days 6X19 was scheduled for production, Duchovny was nearby but unavailable: prepping the episode that would serve as his directorial debut (see p.262).

Co-executive producer Vince Gilligan and producer John Shiban, given the late-season task to create a new adventure for the trio, elected to reintroduce main characters and several unresolved plotlines from 5X01. "I'd been thinking a lot about what happened to Susanne Modeski—what happened to her after she drove off with X in that mysterious car at the end of 'Unusual Suspects' and where she wound up," says Gilligan, who was the sole writer of that fifth-season opener.

Says Shiban: "Las Vegas just seemed a really good place to put these guys. First of all, because the idea of them running through a casino is instantly hilarious. But the other thing that struck us is that Las Vegas is in some ways the most watched city in the world: There are eyes in the sky everywhere in a casino, and that seemed to complement the themes of secrecy and observation. that we were working with."

Adds Gilligan: "We would never have entertained the thought while we were shooting in Vancouver, but now we're only a few hundred miles from Vegas. So we decided we *had* to do it, and so we pushed for it."

Despite the season's ever-present budget pressures, some quick figuring produced the positive result that filming in Las Vegas—the very first time that a city other than Vancouver has "played itself" on *The X-Files*—was feasible.

(Actually, only two days of second-unit filming were budgeted for Las Vegas. Although the entire show appears to be filmed on location, many of the episode's interior scenes were filmed at the Century Plaza and Park Hyatt, two large hotels no more than a stone's throw from the Fox studio. Gillian Anderson did not leave Los Angeles.)

Location manager Ilt Jones relished the change of scenery. He also appreciated the reception accorded *The X-Files* in Las Vegas. "There's something about that city that shifts your whole frame of reference—everything there seems to revolve around getting stuff for free," he says happily.

He adds, "There's a lot of filming in Vegas, and so we went down the list of the forty or fifty hotels known to be film-friendly, asking each of them what they could do for us. At first the reaction was sort of luke-warm, then all of a sudden someone realized that this was *The X-Files*, for heavens sake, seen by I-can't-tell-you-how-many millions of people around the world, and then this huge bidding war broke out. We narrowed it down to six or seven contenders, then basically chose the hotel that gave us the best deal and the best look."

The winner was the Monte Carlo, a three-year-old,

3,000-room hotel-casino located in the heart of the "Strip" on South Las Vegas Boulevard. In exchange for several on-screen glimpses of the hotel's name, plus a line reading "Production Assistance Provided by" in the closing credits, *The X-Files* got free accommodations for its entire cast and crew; fee-free permission to film in any part of the hotel during the daytime (most Vegas hotels restrict filming in their casinos to the hours between midnight and dawn); and use of the hotel's huge illuminated message board to flash the Def-Con convention logo.

Crew members also got the chance to partake of the Monte Carlo's world famous buffet meals (breakfast $6.99; lunch $7.25; dinner $9.99) and to answer questions from hotel guests and other interested bystanders, most of which consisted of "Where's Mulder and Scully?"

"Scully," for one, was back in Los Angeles, working on uncovering a hitherto unsuspected side of her personality. Gilligan and Shiban admit that they wrote the scenes where the normally dead-serious FBI agent becomes a scatterbrained Guy Magnet in part to reveal to the world Gillian Anderson's bright smile and unusual laugh, which is displayed so often to her coworkers on the *X-Files* set.

"Yeah, it was a lot of fun," says Anderson, of the experience. "The tricky part was walking the fine line between drunk and drugged; between a Marilyn Monroe–type of flirtatiousness and just plain goofiness. In the end, I think I leaned more towards goofy."

Many other, albeit less visible decisions were going on around her. To simulate the furnishings usually found in Las Vegas hotel bedrooms, set decorator Tim Stepeck went shopping for black lacquer bedframes, chairs, and dressers in Los Angeles's Koreatown.

To procure the eyeglass video camera and other spy devices used by the Lone Gunmen and others in 6X19, property master Tom Day contacted a security consultant named Richard DiSabatino, an interesting fellow Day has worked with often, who sometimes returns his calls via cell phone from jungle locations in South America.

And, finally, to make the most of their stay in Sin City, Tom Braidwood, Dean Haglund, and Bruce Harwood apparently decided to remain in character the whole time.

Says Haglund, "I think Bruce lost maybe ten dollars on the slots, and was so horrified that he didn't do anything crazy at all during our whole time in the hotel.

"Tom and I went in the exact opposite direction. One time we did a night on the town together. We closed down a bar in *Las Vegas*. Do you realize how hard that is to do?"

Bryan Spicer, who directed "Three of a Kind," was the second-unit director on the *X-Files* movie.

Actress Signy Coleman reprises her role of Susanne Modeski from "Unusual Suspects." Since filming 5X01 she has appeared in the offbeat documentary *20 Dates*—as one of the dates of filmmaker Myles Berkowitz—and as a regular in the soap opera *The Guiding Light.*

Charles Rocket is the fourth and last alumnus of *Saturday Night Live* to guest star on *The X-Files* during Season Six. He was an *SNL* cast member during the 1980–81 season. Both Michael McKean and Nora Dunn appeared in "Dreamland" (6X04) and "Dreamland II" (6X05) and Michael McKean made a cameo in "Three of a Kind" (6X19) later that season. Victoria Jackson appeared in "The Rain King" (6X07).

Area 51, home of government spook Morris Fletcher— see "Dreamland" (6X04) and "Dreamland II" (6X05)— is only ninety miles north of Las Vegas. Air travelers at that city's McCarran Airport can sometimes spot curiously unmarked, windowless Boeing 737s: the aircraft long suspected to be carrying personnel to and from the secret airbase.

As part of his work on this episode, researcher Lee Smith called several Las Vegas hotels to ask them about their eye-in-the-sky surveillance systems. "You wouldn't believe how not interested they are in talking about the subject," he says.

"Def-Con" is an actual convention that has been held in Las Vegas, but it is a gathering of computer hackers, not defense contractors.

6X20

THE UNNATURAL

A rabid baseball fan—Fox Mulder—makes a startling discovery: Something alien has infiltrated his beloved national pastime.

EPISODE: 6X20
FIRST AIRED: April 25, 1999
EDITOR: Lynne Willingham
WRITTEN BY: David Duchovny
DIRECTED BY: David Duchovny

GUEST STARS:
Jesse L. Martin (Josh Exley)
M. Emmet Walsh (Old Arthur Dales)
Fred Lane (Young Arthur Dales)
Jesse James (Poorboy)
Burnell Roques (Buck Johnson)
Lou Beatty, Jr. (Black Coach)
Lennie Loftin (Coranado)
Brian Thompson (The Bounty Hunter/Grand Dragon)
Al Kaplon (Ump)
Ken Medlock (White Coach)
Chris Kohn (Catcher)
Daniel Duchovny (Piney Bench Player)
Doug Jones (Alien)
Julie Griffith (Beautiful Woman)
Gabriel Clifton (Black Kid)
Paul Willson (Ted)
Robb Reesman (Macon Cop)
Vin Scully (TV Baseball Announcer)

PRINCIPAL SETTINGS:
Roswell, New Mexico; Washington, D.C.

Roswell, New Mexico; July 1947:

On a floodlit sandlot at the edge of the desert, two baseball teams clash in friendly combat. In the field are the Southwest All-Stars, comprised of white players. At bat are the Roswell Grays, black professionals from the Negro League.

The All Stars' pitcher, a lanky farm boy with Coke-bottle glasses, winds up and flings a high hard one—fifteen feet over the batter's head.

"Ball four!" hollers the ump.

The Roswell batter takes his base.

"Moose couldn't find the plate if you nailed it to his ass!" grouses a white player standing on the sidelines.

"Shut yer pie hole, Piney!" says his coach, standing next to him. "Kid's gotta learn."

The next batter—a superbly proportioned man named Josh Exley—advances to the plate. The catcher looks at him, shudders, and motions for his fielders to back up. Exley enters the batter's box, digs in, turns to the catcher, and grins broadly.

"You sure your boy has the right prescription in those spectacles?" he says.

"Aw, don't worry, Ex," says the catcher, good-naturedly. "See, I told him to throw it right at your big nappy home-run hitting head. So you can bet a hundred clams that ball's goin' anywhere but there."

Exley nods happily. Moose grooves one, and he smacks a towering blast to left—just foul. The left fielder gives futile chase, then stops and stares into the blackness. Out of the void, inexplicably, the baseball rolls back to him and comes to a slow stop at his feet. Baffled, he picks it up, throws it home, and trots back in, perhaps a little faster than usual.

On the mound Moose toes the rubber, squints at the catcher, and throws another wild pitch. Ball one. The catcher starts a friendly conversation with his opponent.

"Hey, Ex! I heard the Yankees been callin' ya," he says.

"I'm fine playin' here in the Cactus League," Exley replies. "Nice and quiet."

Moose uncorks another wild one. Ball two.

"I don't know, Ex," says the catcher. "Yanks could use those sixty home runs a year. Now that Jackie Robinson's up there in the bigs, people sayin' you gonna be next: the first black Negro man of color in the American League! You'll be famous, man."

"Don't wanna *be* no famous man," says Exley, his bat cocked and ready. "Just wanna be a man."

Moose throws a hanging curveball and Exley slugs it to center field so hard and so far it looks like a satellite being launched into orbit. The batter stands at home plate and watches it disappear into the darkness.

"Sixty-one," he says happily.

Exley's teammates mob him and lift him to their shoulders. From this high perch Exley looks out toward center field. His smile slowly fades; his expression changing to one of terror.

Out of the distance come three mounted, robed, and gun-toting Ku Klux Klansmen. They are followed by about twenty torch-carrying Klansmen on foot. Both teams turn to face the approaching night riders. The white coach steps forward.

"What you boys want?" he says defiantly. "We're playin' a baseball game here."

"We got no beef with you, sir," says a mounted Klansman. "It's that black Babe Ruth hidin' behind ya. Josh Exley. That's who we come for."

Now the Grays' coach steps forward.

"Well, you can't have him," he says, stepping protectively in front of Exley.

The mounted Klansman, pointedly ignoring the black man, braces his rifle on his hip and addresses the crowd.

"We heard the Yankees wanna let a nigger play ball!" he yells. "So we just figgered we oughta play with him a little bit some first! Now, all you other niggers and nigger lovers can go home! It's Ex we want!"

The lead Klansman aims his rifle at Exley. At that instant Moose flings a fastball at the crown of his hood-covered head. The baseball bounces off with a hollow thud and the bigot spills from his saddle. Moose's next pitch knocks the second mounted Klansman silly. Then the third. The players rush the Klansmen and disarm them, yanking their hoods off their heads.

"You boys ain't so tough without your shotguns, are ya, fellas?" yells the Grays' coach.

The white coach kneels over the lead Klansman.

"You ain't but nothin' but a coward, hidin' behind your mama's bedsheets," he says derisively.

He spits a healthy gob of tobacco juice at the Klansman's face, then unmasks him. His face freezes with terror.

"Holy Mother of God!" he exclaims.

Under the crudely sewn hood is the face of a gray space alien.

WASHINGTON, D.C., April 1999:

Inside the X-Files office at FBI headquarters, a major league baseball game plays on a portable television. Scully staggers in, carrying a gigantic volume of bound newspapers. Mulder looks up.

> ## "I DON'T CARE. MULDER, THIS IS A NEEDLE IN A HAYSTACK. THESE POOR SOULS HAVE BEEN DEAD FOR FIFTY YEARS. LET THEM REST IN PEACE. LET SLEEPING DOGS LIE."
> —Scully

He's been paging through a similar volume.

"Mulder, it is such a gorgeous day outside," says Scully. "Did you ever entertain the idea of trying to find life on this planet?"

"I've seen the life on this planet, Scully," replies Mulder, "and that is exactly why I am looking elsewhere."

Scully pulls a frosted treat out of a paper bag she's been carrying and begins licking it happily.

"Did you bring enough ice cream to share with the rest of the class?" says Mulder.

"It's not ice cream," says Scully. "It's a nonfat tofutti-rice dreamsicle."

"I bet the air in my mouth tastes better than that," scoffs Mulder. "You sure know how to live it up!"

Scully takes offense.

"Oh, *you're* Mr. Live-It-Up, Mulder," she says. "You're Mr. Squeeze-Every-Last-Drop-Out-of-This-Sweet-Life, aren't you? On a precious Saturday you've got us grabbing life by the testes, by sneaking reference books out of the FBI library in order to go through New Mexico newspaper obituaries for the years 1940 through 1949. For what joyful purpose?"

"Looking for anomalies, Scully. Do you know how many so-called 'flying disc' reports there were in New Mexico in the 1940s?"

"I don't care," says Scully. "Mulder, this is a needle in a haystack. These poor souls have been dead for fifty years. Let them rest in peace. Let sleeping dogs lie."

"Well, I won't sit idly by as you hurl clichés," says Mulder. "Preparation is the father of inspiration."

"Necessity is the mother of invention," counters Scully.

"The road of excess leads to the palace of wisdom," he says.

"Eat, drink, and be merry, for tomorrow you may die," she says.

He: "I scream, you scream, we all scream for nonfat tofutti-rice dreamsicle—"

Mulder lunges for the cone, grabs it from the laughing Scully, and pops it into his mouth. A white glob of whatever falls onto the open reference book, smearing over an old, yellowed sports page. Scully gazes down scornfully.

"Mulder! You cheat! You've been reading about baseball this whole time!"

At that moment something on the page catches Mulder's attention. It is an article headlined: LOCAL ROSWELL POLICE OFFICER ARTHUR DALES CHATS WITH DIAMOND STAR JOSH EXLEY.

"Arthur Dales?" says Mulder.

He sneezes loudly—to cover the sound of his next move—and rips the page from the reference book.

"You just defaced property of the U.S. government!" says Scully, indignantly.

Grabbing the purloined page, Mulder tears out of the office. Scully watches him leave.

"You rebel!" she says, tossing her head in annoyance and jealousy.

Later that day Mulder, sports page in hand, steps carefully over a bum sleeping in the hallway of a seedy tenement. He knocks on an apartment door. An older gentleman opens up, but keeps the safety chain engaged.

"What in hell took you so long?" he says, crankily.

"I'm sorry, sir," says Mulder, confused. "I'm looking for Arthur Dales—"

"I'm Arthur Dales!"

"No, you're not."

"Don't be a wiseass, son!"

"No, I'm sorry, sir," says Mulder. "I know Arthur Dales, and you're not Arthur Dales."

"Arthur Dales is my brother! My name also happens to be Arthur Dales. Same name, different guy. The other Arthur, he moved to Florida, the lucky bastard."

Mulder stares, dumbfounded.

"Our parents weren't exactly big in the imagination department when it came to names," explains Arthur Dales. "If it helps you wrap your head around this stupefying mystery, Agent Mulder, we had a sister named Arthur, too. And a goldfish."

"How do you know *my* name?" asks Mulder, still somewhat dazed.

"My brother told me all about you," replies Dales, scornfully. "He says you're the biggest jackass in the Bureau since he retired. Yeah, we're big fans! Sometimes we stayed awake for hours, just talking about you. Just fascinating. Now, unless you're hiding some Chinese food, let's call it a day."

Dales shuts the door in Mulder's face. The agent regroups, shouting through the closed door that he has an old picture of either him or his brother taken in Roswell.

"Roswell—that's me," Dales shouts back. "I was a cop once in Roswell."

"Okay!" shouts Mulder. "And you're standing with 'Negro League legend Josh Exley, who disappeared without a trace during a season in which he reportedly hit sixty home runs—'"

"Sixty-one!"

"Sixty-one home runs in 1948—"

"Forty-seven!"

"Forty-seven, whatever. I don't really care about the baseball so much, sir. What I care about is this man with you in the picture who I believe to be an alien Bounty Hunter—"

The door opens a few inches. Dales shoves his angry face into the crack.

"Of course you don't care about baseball, Mr. Mulder," he says. "You only bother my brother about the important things like government conspiracies and alien Bounty Hunters and the truth with a capital *T*—"

"Wait a minute," interrupts Mulder. "I like baseball."

"You like baseball, huh? How many home runs did Mickey Mantel hit?"

Mulder thinks for a second.

"A hundred and sixty-three—" he says.

Dales looks disgusted and starts to slam the door. Mulder's hand shoots into the gap.

"—righty. Three hundred seventy-three lefty. Five hundred thirty-six total."

Dales smiles slowly, perhaps even invitingly.

Some time later Mulder sits in Dales's musty and cluttered apartment. The older man rummages through a box of knickknacks.

"What you fail to understand," says Dales, "is that baseball is the key to life—the Rosetta Stone, if you will. If you just understood baseball better, all your other questions—the aliens, the conspiracies—they would all, in their way, be answered by the baseball gods."

"Yes, sir, that may be true," says Mulder. "I'm thinking your experience in Roswell could be germane to a conspiracy between men in our government and these shape-shifting alien beings."

"Don't bore me, son," says Dales. "My brother Arthur started the X-Files over at the Federal Bureau of Obfuscation before you were born. He was working for the FBI and hunting for aliens when you were watching *My Best Friend's Martians*.

"You say 'shape-shifting.' Agent Mulder, do you believe love can make a man shape-shift?"

Mulder knots his brows in puzzlement.

"I guess women change men all the time—"

"I'm not talking about women! I'm talking about love!" says Dales. "Passion, like the passion you have for proving extraterrestrial life. Do you believe that passion has changed your very nature? Can it make you shape-shift from a man into something other than a man?

"Mr. Mulder, maybe you'd better start paying a little less attention to the heart of the mystery and a little more attention to the mystery of the heart. You got a dime?"

Dales hands Mulder a toy: a mechanical bank in the shape of a kneeling baseball pitcher.

"This little fella goes by the name of Pete Rosebud. If you keep pumping coffee money into him, he'll tell you a story about baseball and aliens and bounty hunters."

"You make me feel like a child," grouses Mulder.

Sheepishly, he places a dime in the pitcher's hand, pulls a lever. Pete throws the coin into a hole under his doffed cap.

"Perfect!" says Dales. "That's exactly the right place to start from then, isn't it? Now, the first thing you've got to know about baseball is that it keeps you forever young—"

Roswell, New Mexico; On June 25, 1947:

A young policeman stands outside Roswell Municipal Ballfield, squinting at a crudely printed racist handbill. It reads: KEEP BASEBALL PURE/KEEP BASEBALL WHITE/$500.00 REWARD/FOR KILLING JOSH EXLEY.

Exley and his Roswell Grays teammate, Buck Johnson, emerge from the small wooden stadium.

"Mr. Exley?" he says. "My name is Arthur Dales. I'm an employee of the Roswell police department."

"Have I broken a law, sir?" says Exley politely.

"You *stole*!" says Johnson, turning to his friend. "Second base in the third inning.

"I'm a witness, officer. I've seen Ex steal at least fifty bases this year!"

Exley laughs, shakes his head, and walks toward the team bus, parked nearby. Dales follows him.

"Sir, you haven't broken any laws. Not that I'm aware of," Dale says nervously. "I've been assigned by my superiors to protect you from certain parties."

"I'm the one who needs protection from certain parties!" says Buck. "Ex here's in bed by eight every night!"

Exley tells Dales that he appreciates the offer, but that he can protect himself. He reaches out to shake hands good-bye, but Dales doesn't let go.

"Now, I'm not a big sports hero myself," says the policeman, "and I don't have an opinion on Negroes— or on Jews, Communists, or even vegetarians for that matter. But I cannot stomach the murder of a man of any persuasion or color being flaunted in my town. Not on my watch. So you can be safe with me down in a cell at the precinct, or you can be safe with me on the bus. Seeing how this is still America, you're free to choose."

That night the Grays' team bus rolls toward another town. Dales sits uncomfortably in the front passenger seat, a lone white man in uniform amidst the drinking, card-playing, and singing players. Exley walks to the front of the bus and leans toward him.

"The fellas think that the umps would treat us better," jokes the baseball star, "if you could get us eight more of those uniforms to play in."

"Yeah!" says Dales, laughing. "You could change your name from the Roswell Grays to the Roswell Black and Blues!"

Silence.

Everybody has heard this crack, apparently, and nobody thinks its funny. Dales bows his head, deeply embarrassed.

After several tense seconds, Exley smiles. The other players laugh, then pounce. They grab at his police hat and uniform. Finally, he's swarmed under.

This is his team initiation.

Much later that night one of the sleeping baseball players is wearing Dales's uniform. Dales himself awakes—wearing the clothing of the sleeping player. Lighting flashes outside, and rain streaks down the bus windows.

Dales glances back to where Exley is sleeping, grins, and freezes. Reflected in the darkened window near Exley's head is the face of a gray alien. Dales makes his way down the aisle to Exley's seat. The reflection is still there. Frightened, he places his hand on the ballplayer's shoulder and shakes him awake. Exley opens his eyes.

"What's the matter, Arthur?" he says slowly. "You look like you ain't never seen a black man before."

In Arthur Dales's apartment in 1999 Mulder grabs a squeeze bottle of mustard from the refrigerator and applies a liberal amount to a hotdog.

"I gotta give it to you, Arthur," he says. "Calling a Negro league team from Roswell the 'Grays' is pretty clever. 'E.T. steal home! E.T. steal home!' You seriously want me to believe that Josh Exley, maybe one of the greatest baseball players of all time, was an alien?"

"They're all aliens, Agent Mulder," replies Dales. "All the great ones."

"Babe Ruth was an alien?" asks Mulder.

"Yeah."

"Joe DiMaggio?"

"Sure."

"Willie Mays?"

"Well, obviously."

"Mantle? Koufax? Gibson?"

"Bob or Kirk?" he says impatiently.

There's a knock on the back door. Dales moves toward it.

"See, Mulder, none of the great ones fit in," he says. "Not in this world, not in any other world. They're all aliens until they step between the white chalk lines. Until they step on the outfield grass."

"DON'T BORE ME, SON. MY BROTHER ARTHUR STARTED THE X-FILES OVER AT THE FEDERAL BUREAU OF OBFUSCATION BEFORE YOU WERE BORN. HE WAS WORKING FOR THE FBI AND HUNTING FOR ALIENS WHEN YOU WERE WATCHING *MY BEST FRIEND'S MARTIANS*."
—Arthur Dales

Dales opens his door, and is delighted to see a small boy of nine, wearing an old-fashioned poorboy cap, carrying a tall bottle nestled in a brown paper bag.

"Like clockwork! Poorboy with my medicine!" he says. "Give the kid a tip, will ya?"

Mulder gives Dales a dirty look, fishes out a dollar bill, and hands it to Poorboy.

"You're a regular Rockefeller, ain't ya?" says the kid.

It is 1947 again. Poorboy—wearing the same clothes and same cap—runs through the gate to Roswell Municipal Ballfield. In the grandstand, he meets up with his buddy, a black kid. Poorboy tells him that if Josh Exley hits a homer today, it'll be his sixtieth of the season, tying Babe Ruth's record. His friend replies that since Exley isn't a big leaguer, the record doesn't count.

"Does too!"

"Does not!"

"Does too!"

"Does not!"

"Does!"

"Not!"

They walk to their seats over the Grays' dugout. Arthur Dales, back in uniform, is stationed in the dugout as Exley's bodyguard. Just before the game begins, five players stand on the dugout steps, each placing chaws of tobacco in their mouths. Exley passes the tobacco pouch to Dales, who gamely bites off a hunk. The next moment he gags, bends over, and starts to retch violently.

"Perfect day for a ball game," says Buck Johnson, grinning slyly.

Seven innings and change later the Grays are locked in a tight battle with a visiting Negro league team, the Elysians. Josh Exley kneels in the on-deck circle.

Dales scans the crowd; he spots two tough-looking white men reaching into their shirts, pulling out their guns, and standing. Dales races toward Exley, knocks him to the ground, and shields him with his body. In the stands, the toughs are merrily squirting their water pistols at two friends sitting in front of them. Seeing this, Dales hauls Exley to his feet.

"There was a bee on you," he says, sheepishly.

"Must have been a real big 'un," says Exley.

"Coulda ripped your head off," says Dales.

Dales makes his way to the dugout. The rest of the Grays laugh hysterically. Exley turns and smiles.

"Hey, Arthur," he says. "Thanks."

Exley enters the batter's box. The Elysians' pitcher winds up and throws a pitch directly at the batter's head. There is no time for Exley to get out of the way; he topples forward, unconscious, across home plate. The catcher places his mitt under his head. His coach, his teammates, and Dales lean over him anxiously.

"Do you know your name, son?" says the coach. "Josh, do you know where you are?"

Exley's eyes roll around into focus. He starts speaking very quickly, in a strange, indecipherable language.

"Josh, man, wake up!" says Buck.

Exley keeps talking in the same eerie manner.

"Do you know where you're from?" asks the coach.

Exley raises his head.

"Macon. Macon, Georgia," he says in a normal voice.

Relieved, his teammates brush him off, haul him to his feet, and lead him to the dugout. The crowd cheers. Dales stays behind to pick up the catcher's mitt. The glove is hot to the touch, smoking. A glob of bright green ooze lies where Exley's head rested.

Later that day Dales phones the Macon police department and asks for background information on Josh Exley. He's told that Josh Exley is the name of a six-year-old black boy from the area who disappeared about five years ago. Dales is interrupted by a stocky police chemist. He hands him the baseball mitt for analysis.

The Macon cop asks Dales where he's calling from.

"Roswell. Roswell, New Mexico," he replies.

"Roswell," repeats the cop—who is in fact the alien Bounty Hunter—thoughtfully.

At the next Grays home game Poorboy dangles upside down over the dugout entrance and tells Exley, excitedly, that the Yankee scouts have arrived. He points out three middle-aged, clipboard-carrying white men.

"I'll be damned," says Exley, not thrilled.

Later in the game Poorboy and his pal shake their heads sadly at the terrible day Exley is having. In the batter's box, the slugger watches a meaty fastball whiz by

"BABE RUTH WAS AN ALIEN?"–Mulder

him for a called strike. In the stands the Yankee scouts shake their heads, stand, and leave the stadium. The pitcher delivers and Exley drives it over the center-field fence.

On the team bus that night Dales and Exley are the only passengers awake. The policeman approaches the ballplayer.

"Ex, why'd you tank that game today?" says Dales.

"I won that game today," says Exley.

"You tanked the game today. Want me to tell you why? Because your name isn't Josh Exley. Josh Exley is a six-year-old kid who disappeared from Macon, Georgia, about the same time you showed up in Roswell."

"I ain't never been to Macon," says Exley.

"When you got beaned, you said you were from Macon."

"Well, I also spoke in tongues, like I did when I was a little boy in church."

"You're hiding something," says Dales, not buying it. "That's why you don't dare get into the major leagues, because the sportswriters and everybody would be digging around. And they'd find out what it is, right? So you tank the game in front of those scouts today. Disappointing those kids. Disappointing your

teammates. Disappointing your race—"

"Don't go talkin' about my race!" says Exley, angrily. "You don't know *nothin'* about my race."

"I know that liars come in all colors," says Dales. "You got a secret? Famous or not, I'm gonna find out what it is."

Exley looks Dales in the eye.

"While you're out chasing secrets," he says, slowly, "you better make sure you're chasing the right ones."

Later that night the team bus is parked in front of a "colored only" motel. In his room, Dales awakes with a start; a muffled banging is coming from the next room. He switches on his lamp, grabs his revolver, walks to a connecting door, and peers through the keyhole. There is just enough moonlight to see that a tall man in a batting stance is practicing his swing.

"Ex," says Dales, relieved.

Dales smiles mischievously, reaches into his pants pocket, and pulls out a pocket knife. He jimmies open the lock, enters the room stealthily, and snaps on the light. In front of him is a gray alien—wearing men's underwear and a baseball cap—swinging a baseball bat. Dales screams, brandishing his tiny knife. The alien screams, also, in an eerie, high-pitched wail.

Dales immediately faints dead away.

At daybreak Dales is still unconscious. An alien hand gently taps his cheek. He opens his eyes and slowly focuses on the concerned alien in front of him. He faints again. The alien reaches for a glass of water and gets Dales to take a few sips. The policeman's eyes open and he faints yet again.

"This is ridiculous," says the alien, who has the same voice as Exley. "You're supposed to be a big bad policeman. Now, hold up, Arthur. Before you faint again, listen to me. It's me, Arthur. It's Ex."

"This is an interesting dream," murmurs Dales. "Wake up. C'mon, Artie—"

"Man, you're not dreamin'," says the alien. "This is what I really look like! This is the real me."

Dales reaches out to poke the alien's face.

"That's really you under there, Ex?" he says.

The alien pokes Dales—much harder—right back.

"I ain't under anything, Arthur! And I'm trying not to be insulted by your reaction to my true face. Look, would it be easier if I looked like this?"

The alien morphs into a beautiful woman, who takes off her cap and lets her long blonde hair fall down. She walks over and sits on Dale's lap.

"No, that's even weirder," says Dales, thoroughly spooked.

The door to the room opens, revealing the Grays' coach, who's come to tell Ex the bus is leaving. He peers in at Dales and his bombshell, averts his eyes in embarrassment, and quickly closes the door.

Later that morning, with the team bus on its way, Exley and Dales are huddled in a whispered conversation.

"So why did you leave your, uh, family in Georgia?" asks Dales.

"My people guard their privacy zealously," says Exley. "They don't ever want us to intermingle with your people. Their philosophy is we stick to ourselves, you stick to yourselves, everybody's happy."

"What happened?" asks Dales.

"You know what happened," says Exley, grinning.

"You fell in love with an earth woman?"

Exley laughs.

"No! I saw a baseball game!" he says.

"See, there's something you gotta understand about our race: We don't have a word for laughter. We don't laugh. I don't know if you noticed in between all that fainting you was doing, but we have very tiny mouths, so no smiling even.

"But I tell you, when I saw that baseball game being played, the laughter just rolls up out of me. You know the sound the ball makes when it hits the bat? That was like music to me. You know, the smell of the grass and the leather mitt—it was the first unnecessary thing I ever done in my life.

"And I fell in love. I didn't know the unnecessary

could feel so good. And the game was meaningless, but it seemed to mean everything to me. It was useless but perfect."

"Yeah, like a rose," says Dales.

"Yeah, like a rose!" says Exley, smiling broadly. "See, Arthur, you get it, you're a fan. From that moment on, I just couldn't fix myself to go home."

Buck calls Exley to the front of the bus, where some of the team members are singing a Negro spiritual. Exley joins in joyously.

In 1999 Arthur Dales and Mulder are sitting on the living room couch. On the coffee table are the remains of a Chinese takeout dinner, and many empty beer cans. Mulder asks whether the baseball-playing alien is somehow connected to the famous Roswell UFO crash in July 1947.

"You're just dying to connect the dots, aren't you, son?" says Dales. "Look, I give you some wood and ask for a cabinet, you build me a cathedral! But I don't want a cathedral, I like where I live. I just want a place to put my TV. Understand my drift?"

"Drift it is, sir," says Mulder.

"Trust the tale, Agent MacGyver, not the teller. That which fascinates us is, by definition, true. Speaking metaphorically, of course."

"Okay," says Mulder, frustrated. "Was Ex an alien who was metaphorically a man or a man who was metaphorically an alien, or something in between that was literally an alien-human hybrid?"

Dales looks blankly at Mulder, then hands him a bottle of whiskey.

"It's official," says Mulder, taking a swig. "I am a horse's ass."

Dales drinks to that.

"What is it to be human, Fox?" he says. "Is it to have the chemistry of a man? Now, in the universal scheme of things, a dog's chemistry is nearly identical to that of a man. But is a dog like a man?

"To be a man is to have the heart of a man," he says. "Integrity, decency, sympathy—these are the things that make a man a man. And Ex had them all. Had them all more than you or I."

It is 1947. The Alien Bounty Hunter walks down the street adjoining the Roswell ballpark. The Grays' team bus, returning the team from its road trip, pulls to a stop nearby. Exley is one of the first players off the bus. He spots the Bounty Hunter and freezes.

Later that day the police chemist calls Dales at his desk in the police station. He is visibly upset.

"This goo on the glove you gave me—is this a joke?" he says. "It's not like any chemical compound I've ever seen. It's from a life form which doesn't seem to be carbon-based—which, by the way, is impossible. This is way out of my league! I called the

FBI, and the Communicable Disease Center in Washington—"

"Washington? Oh, no, Ted!" says Dales. "Nobody was supposed to know about this. Can you get the glove back to me?"

"Sure. As soon as I finish up here," says the chemist.

In his laboratory the chemist finishes his analysis. His door opens, and Josh Exley steps into the room. The chemist turns to greet him, delighted.

"I know who you are—only the best damn ballplayer this side of the Bronx," he says.

"Well, thank you, sir. Arthur sent me down here to explain to you about this substance. That's my mitt it ruined."

"What *is* this stuff? Where did you get it?" asks the chemist.

"Mars," says Exley.

The chemist laughs.

"Actually, just to the left of Mars," adds the ballplayer.

Exley flings the chemist's lab equipment to the floor, then grabs the chemist by the neck, lifts him off his feet, and tosses him through a glass door. The chemist lies still, impaled with jagged shards. His murderer morphs back into the alien Bounty Hunter.

Late that day Exley does wind sprints at the ballpark. Dales approaches him, and tells him that he's wanted for the murder of the chemist.

"I'm not sure what's going on here," he adds, "but I do know that you're no murderer. You're gonna have to get out of town, Ex."

Exley picks up a pair of baseball gloves and tosses one to Dales. They play catch as they talk.

"Life ain't like baseball, is it?" says Exley. "I had a talk with my relative. A good talk. He made me understand reason, Arthur. Family's more important than a game. So, I gotta go home."

"You still consider them your family?"

"Of course I do. Who do you think my family is?"

"I don't know," says Dales. "Your team?"

Exley shakes his head, grinning.

"Don't get cornball on me, man. Next thing you're gonna be tellin' me is that I owe it to all the little kids to break the home run record, or that I owe it to the black folks who think I'm one of them to make it to the majors, or I should just keep playing out of some meaningless human concept of pride or loyalty.

"We don't think like that, man. We may be able to look like y'all, but we ain't y'all. You know the big thing that really separates us from you?"

"What's that?" says Dales.

"We got rhythm," says Exley.

Both men break into delighted laughter. Sirens sound in the distance. Exley walks quickly over to Dales.

"I'd better go," he says. "Hey, would you do me a favor? Would you tell people what I did on the field? Will you tell your kids how I played the game?"

That night Dale sits in the Roswell Grays dugout, confronting a squad of G-men led by an FBI agent named Coranado.

"This is no minor league New Mexico cowboy cop crap," says Coranado, scornfully. "If I told you what was really going on, you'd just stare at me in wild-eyed wonder and pee your pants like a baby. Now, tell me what I want to know. Where's Exley?"

"I told you," says Dales. "He told me he was going home."

At the desert sandlot Exley digs in against the Southwest All-Stars' pitcher and sends a homer rocketing into the night sky. Exley's teammates raise him to their shoulders. He sees the Ku Klux Klansmen approaching.

In the Grays' dugout Coranado is still in Dales's face. He says he has a witness who puts Exley at the chemist's murder scene.

"Now, I know they have a tendency to look alike," says Coranado, "but unless he's got a guy running around looking identical to him, he's a murderer, and you could be an accomplice, and the two of you are fast sliding down a giant razor blade into a big ol' glass of lemonade. But you can hand him over," says Coranado, "and you can wear your big hat and that pretty badge as long as you want."

"Are we finished?" says Dales, defiantly.

"No, Mr. Dales," says the FBI agent. "You are."

The G-men leave. Dales spots a catcher's mitt, picks it up, and notices a map of Roswell folded inside. On it, someone has drawn a baseball diamond. Home plate is over Bottomless State Park, just outside town.

At the ballfield the unmasked gray alien lies on the ground. All of the Klansmen and ballplayers—all but Exley—run away in fright. The alien comes to, then morphs into the Bounty Hunter.

The Bounty Hunter staggers to his feet, faces Exley, and unsheathes his stiletto.

"It's over," he says grimly.

"I know," says Exley, softly.

The Bounty Hunter walks toward Exley.

"I warned you. You didn't listen. Now you die."

"It's the right thing to do," says Exley, bravely.

"What do you know of the right thing to do? You who would risk exposing the entire Project for a game. A game!"

"I hit a home run tonight. Number sixty-one. A record."

The Bounty Hunter sneers, disgusted.

"Show me your true face so you can die with dignity," he says.

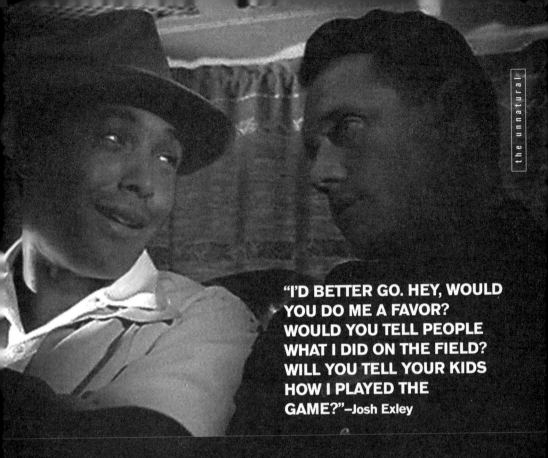

**"I'D BETTER GO. HEY, WOULD
YOU DO ME A FAVOR?
WOULD YOU TELL PEOPLE
WHAT I DID ON THE FIELD?
WILL YOU TELL YOUR KIDS
HOW I PLAYED THE
GAME?"**–Josh Exley

Exley does not respond.

"As your executioner, I show you my true face before I kill you."

The Bounty Hunter morphs into a gray alien.

"Show me your true face, or you will die without honor!"

Exley is terrified. But he fights back his fear.

"This is my true face," he says.

"So be it," says the alien.

Exley turns around slowly. The alien plunges the stiletto into the back of his neck just as Dales drives onto the ballfield.

"No! Stop!" yells Dales.

The Bounty Hunter mounts his horse and rides away. Dales runs to the fallen ballplayer and cradles Ex's head in his arms.

"No, let me be!" says Exley. "Get off of me! Our blood is like acid to you people! Arthur, get away. Don't touch it!"

Arthur looks at his hands. They are covered with red liquid.

"It's just blood, Ex. Look—just blood."

Exley gazes at Dales's hands, then smears some blood on his finger.

"Wow," says the alien, softly.

His face is a mask of anguish, but he is laughing also, as he dies.

In 1999, on his living room couch, Arthur Dales looks skyward and holds his hand to his heart, remembering.

At a public park in Washington that night Mulder stands in a batting cage, taking his cuts. Scully arrives and watches her partner for a moment, arms folded.

"So," she says finally. "I get this message marked 'urgent' from my answering service from one 'Fox Mantle' telling me to come down to the park for a very early or very late birthday present.

"And, Mulder, I don't see any nicely wrapped presents lying around."

Mulder steps back slightly from the batter's box.

"You've never hit a baseball, have you, Scully?" says Mulder.

"No," says Scully. "I guess I have found more necessary things to do with my time than slap a piece of horsehide with a stick."

"Get over here, Scully," says Mulder.

And, of course, she does.

From shortly after the Civil War to the early 1950s—when Jackie Robinson and his successors bravely integrated Major League Baseball—the United States was graced with a loose collection of players, teams, and leagues that are now categorized as Negro League Baseball. Largely ignored by the white press and public, the Negro Leagues were manned by extraordinarily talented African-American athletes, including black superstars such as Satchel Paige, Cool Papa Bell, Buck O'Neil, and Josh Gibson. Well-established teams like the Newark Eagles, Pittsburgh Crawfords, New York Black Yankees, and Homestead Grays battled against each other. They also barnstormed across the country, playing white and black squads made up of everyone from local farmhands to moonlighting white major league ballplayers.

In the past twenty years or so—partly as a reaction to the increasing commercialization of professional sports—there has been a revival of interest in the Negro Leagues' history, and a sincere appreciation of how its players defied racism simply by playing the game they loved so well. The topic has been frequently addressed by many contemporary sports writers, novelists, social commentators, documentarians, and screenwriters.

Including David Duchovny.

In the fall of 1998 the X-Files star met with executive producer and series creator Chris Carter, and the two quickly agreed that Duchovny would write a late-season episode: his first solo writing job on this or any other series. As he told a reporter last April, the actor—a serious baseball fan from way back—found his inspiration for what would become "The Unnatural" from the true story of a New Mexico minor leaguer named Joe Bauman.

Playing for a team called the Roswell Rockets—Roswell, New Mexico, of course, being the site of the 1947 "UFO crash" that kick-started America's obsession with the possibility of extraterrestrial visitors—Bauman, who never made it to the major leagues, set a record by hitting 72 home runs during the 1954 season.

"I thought, 'Roswell, that's weird,'" said Duchovny. "What if he [the home-run hitter] was an alien?"

As Duchovny's script took shape, Bauman turned into Negro League star Josh Exley (introducing the major theme of the "alienating" force of racism); mythological elements like the presence of the Alien Bounty Hunter were introduced; and, most importantly, retired FBI agent Arthur Dales became a major protagonist of the story both as an idealistic young man and as a crusty-but-sentimental old codger, to be played as always by Darren McGavin.

After he finished writing 6X20—over the course of several months, with feedback from Chris Carter and executive producer Frank Spotnitz—Duchovny decided to make "The Unnatural" his directorial debut as well.

Which was fine with Chris Carter. "David wrote a great script," he said at the time. "And it's always better when you direct your own script if you've got the ability and the desire."

By mid-March of 1999, Duchovny—whose wife, actress Téa Leoni, was seven months pregnant with their first child—was well into the intensive work of preproduction. He had already made his major casting decision, choosing Jessie L. Martin to play Josh Exley, and had convinced the critically praised actor to squeeze in 6X20 around his then-role as Calista Flockhart's love interest on the Fox series Ally McBeal.

Just as crucially, perhaps, Duchovny had also convinced much of the X-Files crew—a bit apprehensive, understandably, about working with their star in a vastly different capacity—that they had nothing to fear on several important fronts.

"It was nice to see how truly humble he was," recalls locations manager Ilt Jones. "You know, I've worked with first-time directors before, and sometimes they try to bullshit you, to fake you into thinking that they know more than they actually do. Not David. Having been in the business, he obviously knew a lot about filmmaking, but he was never afraid to let on when he was doing something for the very first time.

"What was also interesting," adds Jones, "was to see how truly sponge-like this guy was. I remember hearing him talk on the first day of the eight-day prep period, then again on the last day of the prep period, and realizing that there's been this radical metamorphosis into somebody who suddenly understood the dynamics of directing. He is clearly a very bright guy."

Unfortunately, Duchovny's intelligence and flexibility soon had to be brought to bear on a problem that proved to be the sixth season's saddest. After two days of filming his role as Arthur Dales, Darren McGavin suffered a stroke serious enough to prevent him from completing his role on 6X20. While necessarily scrapping McGavin's footage (and replacing him with veteran character actor M. Emmet Walsh), the writer-director wrote new scenes for the "other" Arthur Dales, which in no way precluded McGavin's eventual return to The X-Files.

The rest of the episode, happily, contained only the usual quota of improvisation and inspiration. The episode's major scenic casting coup was the rental of Littleton Ballfield, a jewel-like all-wood stadium in Ontario, California, to stand in for Roswell's baseball stadium. Located fifty miles east of Los Angeles, it was formerly know as Ontario Ball Park and was used in past years as a venue for semipro games and as the spring training home of the minor league Los Angeles Angels. It looks much the same as when it opened on March 14, 1937. To fill the stands with spectators, The X-Files advertised in local newspapers and on local radio stations for fans to come to their "baseball game" dressed in 1940s clothing.

"When they arrived we did a whole bunch of giveaways, and David gave autographs and mingled with the crowd," says Ilt Jones. "The first day was a little slow but on the second day there were mobs of people. It was great."

To outfit all of the baseball teams in 6X20—the 1940s were definitely the pre–double-knit era—costume designer Christine Peters journeyed to Sports Robe, a specialized Hollywood costume house, and brought back numerous period designs to director Duchovny for his final selection.

To complete the on-field picture, hair department head Dena Green—equipped with photographs of 1940s ballplayers to let the baseball-playing extras know exactly what they were getting into—set up a Truman-era haircut assembly line outside the ballpark.

To provide the Roswell Grays with transportation, picture car coordinator Kelly Padovich rented two identical antique buses—1947 model Flexibles—and used one (in the Grays' team colors and logo and with each hubcap painted to look like a baseball) for exterior shots and the other for interior filming. A number of 1930s and 1940s passenger autos were rented as well; Duchovny himself designed the Roswell police logo on the side of young Arthur Dales's squad car.

Coming up with a "Pete Rosebud" bank—the cast-iron mechanical toy that old Arthur Dales shows proudly to Mulder—proved surprisingly challenging to property Tom Day. "I really don't know why," he says, "but nothing we saw in prop houses, on the antique market, or in reproduction catalogs came anything close to what we were looking for. Finally, I had to have an artist sculpt it, then get other people to mold it and pour it and paint it and rig it to work. I think it was actually one of the most expensive props we built the entire season. If not *the* most expensive."

Also a little higher-budget than usual: Mark Snow's twangy, Ry Cooder-esque score for "The Unnatural," which was the first *X-Files* score in the series' entire history to be recorded with actual musicians, rather than synthesizers. The two musicians involved were virtuoso slide guitar player Nick Kirgo (a cousin of Mark Snow and a friend of David Duchovny) and legendary harmonica player Tommy Morgan (who performed the harmonica solo on the theme song of the movie *Midnight Cowboy).*

To play Josh Exley in his alien incarnation, special effects makeup supervisor John Vulich dressed two very spindly actors—Walt Phelan and Doug Jones—in body suits, long prosthetic fingers, and a friendly looking mechanical alien mask. Special effects producer Bill Millar performed his usual magic to morph Josh into a beautiful woman and back again, as well as producing the ghostly alien head on the bus window and propelling several digital baseballs into the heavens.

And, finally, to confirm the baseball history and statistics used in the script, researcher Lee Smith called the Baseball Hall of Fame in Cooperstown, New York—right in the middle of the wildest snowstorm that upstate town had seen in decades.

"I tried to reach the research library," says Smith, "but the only person in the entire place that day was the director. The top man. I guess he was the only one who could make it in through the storm. He picked up the phone and explained what was happening, and when I told him I'd call back when everybody was back at work, he said, 'No, no. Hang on!' And then he was gone for a long time, and when he came back on the line he had all the information I needed. And then some."

Indeed, propelled by their love of the game and/or for David Duchovny, just about everybody involved in "The Unnatural" seems to have gone out of his or her way to help out or to offer praise.

Says Chris Carter: "I think that David, a person who has a very intimate understanding of the show, made the best of his opportunity to tell a very different kind of *X-File*, and expand the elastic show that it is."

Says Gillian Anderson: "I was proud of David for writing the script. I thought it was wonderful. He was kind and gentle and respectful and humble, and always tried to do his best."

6X20's title is a play on "The Natural," the acclaimed 1952 baseball novel by author Bernard Malamud (turned into a movie starring Robert Redford in 1984).

Daniel Duchovny, who plays the bench jockey Piney, is David Duchovny's older brother.

M. Emmett Walsh (old Arthur Dales) has been a familiar face in films and on television for more than thirty years. His credits include *Little Big Man; Escape from the Planet of the Apes; The Jerk; Blade Runner;* and *The Milagro Beanfield War.*

Although budget problems initially prevented Vin Scully from being hired as the baseball announcer on "The Unnatural," the famed sportscaster—who is the original inspiration for the name of Gillian Anderson's character—agreed to meet an *X-Files* sound crew in his Dodger Stadium broadcast booth and record the part for free.

The baseball jersey Mulder wears in the episode's final scene honors Josh Gibson, the legendary Negro League slugger. Gibson spent much of his career playing for the Homestead [Pennsylvania] Grays.

The tagline for this episode is "In The Big Inning."

6(X)21

FIELD TRIP

After being exposed to a hallucinogenic, Mulder and Scully are trapped inside a subterranean cave—and the dark recesses of their own minds.

EPISODE: 6X21
FIRST AIRED: May 9, 1999
EDITOR: Louise A. Innes
TELEPLAY BY: Vince Gilligan and John Shiban
STORY BY: Frank Spotnitz
DIRECTED BY: Kim Manners

GUEST STARS:
Mitch Pileggi (AD Walter Skinner)
Robyn Lively (Angela Schiff)
David Denman (Wallace Schiff)
Jim Beaver (Coroner)
Tom Braidwood (Frohike)
Dean Haglund (Langly)
Bruce Harwood (Byers)

PRINCIPAL SETTINGS:
Washington, D.C.; Brown Mountain and Asheville, North Carolina

"I've got mosquito bites, I've got blisters. I hate those new boots," complains Angie.

"Honey, why so p.o.'ed? I thought we had a good time?" says Wallace.

"You had a good time," his wife replies. "You had a fine time tromping around and leaving me a mile behind."

Wallace apologizes. The couple kiss and make up, after which Angie presses her hands to her temples, tells Wallace she has a headache, and goes into the bathroom.

In the shower she wets her hair, applies shampoo, and has a strange vision: rivulets of viscous yellow goo oozing down the shower stall wall. In a moment the image is gone, but Angie, shaken, is almost immediately terrified by another one. She is in a tight dark spot; the water coursing over her is transformed into yellow goo.

Later that night Angie is in her bathrobe, her head still throbbing. In their motel room, Wallace sits on the bed next to her.

"You still mad at me?" he asks.

"No, I'm not mad," she says, still shaken by what she's seen.

"So, I guess we're never going hiking again," says Wallace. "It's indoors forever from now on."

They snuggle up on the bed together. Angie, in great pain, is silent.

"Angie, honey, what's up?" asks her husband.

"Just hold me," she says.

Some time afterward two human skeletons—stripped of all flesh—lie in a slight depression in a dark field. They are in the identical position as the young couple.

At FBI headquarters several days later Mulder projects a slide of the entwined skeletons on his office wall. He identifies the remains as the Schiffs, who were last seen in the vicinity of Brown Mountain, North Carolina. Mulder adds that they were discovered after they'd been missing only three days—in temperatures which never exceeded seventy degrees.

"Which rules out decomposition," says Scully, who'd been watching this. "I'd say predation, but the bones would be scattered."

"Not to mention that these skeletons are not wearing any clothes," says Mulder.

"Right," says Scully, nodding. "Well, I'd say it looks like a double murder, possibly one with ritualistic overtones."

Mulder does not appear convinced. Scully presses on.

"The bodies may have been stripped, then skeletonized, possibly by boiling, or by the use of some kind of acid solution," she says. "Maybe the arrangement of the bodies has some meaning for the killer, or killers. At any rate, I'd term it 'ritualistic.'"

At a mid-priced motel an attractive young couple—Angie and Wallace Schiff—enter their room. They are sweaty and dirty from a day spent outdoors.

"UNLIKE EVERYTHING
ELSE. I'M NOT SURE WHAT
TO MAKE OF IT, GIVEN THE
SHORT TIME FRAME."
—The Coroner

"That's a pretty big operation you're describing," counters Mulder. "There was no evidence found at the scene. No tire tracks, no footprints."

"Well, what do you think this is?" says Scully.

"Brown Mountain," says Mulder instantly. "It doesn't ring a bell?"

Scully shrugs and shakes her head.

"Brown Mountain lights?"

His partner is still baffled.

"It's a famous atmospheric phenomenon dating back nearly seven hundred years. Witnessed by thousands of people, back to the Cherokee Indians. Strange multicolored lights are seen to dance above the peak of the mountain. There's been no geological explanation, no scientific credible explanation at all. But there are those of us who believe that these strange multicolored lights are really—"

"UFOs," says Scully, sarcastically. "Extraterrestrial visitors from beyond, who apparently have nothing better to do than buzz one mountain over and over again for seven hundred years."

Mulder pushes out his lower lip in a mock pout.

"Sounds like crap when you say it," he says.

"I'm just wondering if there's a connection, Scully," he adds. "I mean, the conditions of these bodies is reminiscent of certain Southwest cattle mutilations. Those are cases where there is no physical evidence, and they've long been associated with UFO activity."

Scully smiles wearily.

"Mulder, can't you just for once—just for the novelty of it—come up with the simplest explanation? The most logical one? Instead of automatically jumping to UFOs, or Bigfoot, or—"

"Scully, in six years how often have I been wrong?" says Mulder, interrupting her impatiently.

"No, seriously," he quickly adds. "I mean, every time I bring in a new case we go through this perfunctory dance. You tell me I'm not being scientifically rigorous, that I'm off my nut. And in the end, who turns out to be right? Like ninety-eight point nine percent of the time?"

Scully says nothing.

"I just think," says Mulder, "that I've earned the benefit of the doubt here."

At the Boone County Morgue in Asheville, North Carolina, the agents watch as a coroner pulls the two skeletons out of cold storage. Scully dons a pair of latex gloves and leans in for a closer look.

"The connective tissue is more or less intact," she says.

"Unlike everything else," says the coroner. "I'm not sure what to make of it, given the short time frame."

"If you'll pardon an obvious question," says Scully, "are you sure that these are the right two bodies, and not two others that have lain out six months?"

The coroner replies that he's triple-checked the dental records. He hands Scully a file, which includes color photographs of Angie and Wallace Schiff.

Mulder peers into the file and examines the pictures closely.

"And they were both found near Brown Mountain, right? Where, exactly?" he asks.

The coroner offers to write him directions. While he's doing this, Scully rubs her gloved fingertips on the bottom of one on the skeleton's ribs. It comes away covered with a familiar-looking yellow goo. Scully shows it to the coroner.

"Would you happen to know what this is?" asks Scully.

"Well, the remains were found in a swampy area—it's some sort of organic material related to that. Bog sludge," says the coroner.

For his part Mulder doesn't seem all that interested. He turns to his partner.

"I'm going to check out where the bodies were found," he says. "You coming?"

"No," says Scully, lost in thought. "You go ahead."

At Brown Mountain later that day a blue SUV comes to a halt in a boggy, grass-covered field, but not before running over a clump of puffball mushrooms. The mushrooms emit a small white cloud of spores as they are crushed.

Mulder gets out of the SUV, looks around, and bends down to examine a patch of dark earth. He pushes his finger into the ground. It comes up coated with yellow goo. He straightens up and catches sight of a man scurrying through the underbrush. The man freezes and stares back.

Mulder, startled, can barely believe his eyes.

"Wallace Schiff?" he shouts.

The man bolts. Mulder pursues him up a rocky hillside and watches him crawl into the manhole-sized opening of a small cave. Mulder pulls out his flashlight and shines it into the cave mouth, calling Schiff's name.

At noon at the coroner's office Scully examines a drop of the yellow goo under a microscope. The coroner enters, carrying a computer printout.

"We've got your gas spectrometer results," says the coroner. "That stuff on the bones that I said was bog sludge? It isn't."

Scully scans the printout.

"Water, hydrochloric acid, electrolytes, pepsins, and trypsins," she reads aloud.

Surprised, she looks up.

"It's a digestive secretion."

"Stomach juices, pretty much," says the coroner, nodding. "Pretty damn close to it. Except for this."

"Chitinase?" says Scully.

"It's a digestive enzyme as well. But it's strictly plant. Not animal."

At Brown Mountain Mulder squeezes through the entrance to the cave, then stands upright as the chamber grows larger a few feet inside.

"Hello?" he shouts.

No response.

At the morgue the coroner shows Scully files on two similar cases: bodies of hikers, found after months or years, which were found as skeletal remains. Scully notes that the bodies were all found not far from where the Schiffs turned up. Alarmed, she pulls out her cell phone and calls Mulder. He does not answer.

"Do me a favor," says Scully to the coroner, urgently. "Forward a sample of that secretion to the FBI lab in Quantico. I want them to run a complete analysis. And in the meantime, can I borrow your truck?"

Inside the Brown Mountain cave, Mulder shines his flashlight on the granite walls. Yellow goo oozes down to the floor. He hears a noise behind him, whirls, and sees Wallace Schiff, cowering behind a boulder.

"Please! Don't take me!" says Wallace, terrified.

"Hey, come out here!" says Mulder. "Step closer. I won't hurt you."

Wallace reluctantly moves out from cover.

"You're not one of them?" he quavers.

"One of who?" says Mulder. "Are you Wallace Schiff?"

Schiff manages a nod.

"Well, I hate to tell you this, Wallace, but you're supposed to be dead. They found your skeleton not two hundred yards from here."

"It's a fake," says Wallace. "They put it there."

"Who put it there?" asks Mulder.

"You know who."

"The Brown Mountain lights," says Mulder.

Wallace nods.

"They abducted us. Me and my wife Angela. They took us aboard their—oh, God!"

"Wallace," says Mulder, carefully. "They found your wife Angela, too. Lying right alongside your skeleton."

"No!" shouts Wallace. "Don't you get it? They faked our deaths! They have that kind of technology! Who the hell would be looking for us if they thought they already had our bodies? You see? They returned me, but Angela, she's still up there! Being experimented on! And I don't know what—what do I do?"

Later that day Scully, at the wheel of the coroner's truck, pulls up next to Mulder's parked SUV. She gets out and calls his name.

Nothing.

She notices a man's footprints stamped into the soggy ground. They lead toward the hillside. As she follows them, Scully steps on a clump of puffball mushrooms. They emit a cloud of spores; Scully notices this.

Inside the cave Mulder shines his flashlight around the cave walls.

"First thing first. We've got to find a way out of here," he says.

"Right behind you," says Wallace, pointing.

Mulder turns and sees a faint aura of sunlight filtering down a tight passage.

"What the hell is going on?" he says, baffled and a little angry. "That was solid rock a minute ago. Now there's nothing there."

"Oh, God!" says Wallace, agitated again. "It's them. They're affecting your head. Maybe mine, too! What if I can't even tell what's real?"

Mulder's heard enough. He tells Wallace to follow him out of the cave. Wallace shakes his head, petrified.

"They're out there, man!" he says.

Before Mulder can respond a deep rumble shakes the cave. A brilliant blue-white light thrusts through the cave entrance. Wallace runs deeper into the cave. Mulder follows him. The white light probes after them.

Outside the cave entrance, Scully shines her flashlight inside. She sees nothing. She calls her partner's name, hears nothing, then walks slowly back toward her truck.

"A LIGHT. A BRIGHT LIGHT. OVER BROWN MOUNTAIN. STRANGE LIGHTS, DANCING OVER THE PEAK. THEY TOOK ME. AND WALLACE, TOO!"
—Angela Schiff

Deeper into the cave, still lit by the probing light, Wallace huddles behind Mulder.

"Don't let them see you!" he hisses.

The light fades.

"They're gone," says Mulder.

"Yeah. For now," says Wallace.

Wallace holds a glowing Coleman camping lantern. At his feet is a pile of brand-new hiking and camping gear.

"Thank God they didn't find us," says Wallace.

"They should have," says Mulder, eyeing his companion with suspicion. "Maybe they came here for something else."

Mulder leads Schiff through a thicket of stalactites. They enter another large chamber and see Angie Wallace lying on the ground. Wallace kneels down to hug his semiconscious wife.

"Oh, my God! Angie—they brought her back!" he says.

"Angie, can you talk to me?" says Mulder. Do you remember what happened? Can you tell me?"

Angie struggles to remember.

"A light. A bright light," she says. "Over Brown Mountain. Strange lights, dancing over the peak. They took me. And Wallace, too!"

"And then what happened?"

"It all went black. And when I woke up I didn't know where I was. I couldn't see Wallace anymore."

"This place they took you to," says Mulder. "Can you describe it to me? Tell me what it looked like?"

"It was white. A white place. It was featureless. I was lying on a table. I couldn't get up. Nothing was holding me down, but I couldn't move."

"Were there men there?"

"Yes. There were men. Standing over me. But I couldn't see their faces."

"Did they perform tests on you?" asks Mulder, gently.

"Yes, they did tests," says Angie, sobbing. "Terrible tests!"

Mulder places a hand on Angie's shoulder, aiming his flashlight at a fresh scar on the back of her neck.

"What is that?" asks Wallace.

"It's an implant," says Mulder. "I've seen this before."

Almost hysterical now, Angie recalls the placement of the implant: a spinning drill, she says, came out of a bright light and bored directly into her. Not much more calmly, Wallace asks Mulder if there's an implant in him, too.

"No," says Mulder. "Male abductees don't usually report this. And so far, everything you've both described is textbook down to the last detail, except for one. The two skeletons that were found: yours and Angie's. I've never heard that before. It doesn't really make sense."

Wallace turns to his wife, then shrugs.

"Maybe they're like those cattle mutilations you hear about," he says. "Maybe they're somehow related. Maybe they're part of their tests."

"I had that thought," says Mulder. "But there's no precedent for it. It's in none of the literature."

"They didn't want anybody to find us. I guess they didn't want you to know the truth," says Wallace.

Mulder considers the man's odd statement carefully, then insists that the couple leave the cave with him. The Schiffs refuse, telling Mulder that the aliens are watching them from outside. Angie stands and looks with horror toward the cave entrance.

"They're coming. I can feel it," she says.

The light blooms again and the rumbling resumes.

"They're here!" Angie shouts.

Wallace screams at Mulder that they've got to hide. Mulder refuses, and heads toward the light. He is swallowed up by the blinding illumination.

That night the elevator in Mulder's apartment building stops at the fourth floor. Scully gets out, walks down the corridor, and knocks on Mulder's door. Her partner, looking tired and nervous, opens up.

"Mulder, why the hell did you leave North Carolina without telling me?" she asks. "You disappear and then I get a furtive call that you're back here in D.C.!"

"Sorry," says Mulder quietly. "Does anyone know you're here?"

Scully shakes her head, annoyed. Mulder lets her in. She walks to the living room, and to her astonishment, sees Angie and Wallace Schiff. Mulder introduces them to her.

Warily, Scully keeps her eye on the couple while she talks in low tones to her partner.

"Mulder, I ID'd their remains myself," she says.

"Yeah, I think you were meant to," whispers Mulder.

"Agent Scully?" says Angie, from across the room. "The aliens planted decoys so you would think we were dead."

"The aliens," says Scully, skeptically.

In the back of the room a small alien emerges, peeking out shyly from behind a pile of cardboard boxes. Scully is stunned.

"I abducted *him*," says Mulder. "It's a gray. It speaks to me. We communicate telepathically. He told me everything."

"I-I can hear him," says Scully, astonished. "Oh, my God!"

Later that night Scully stands, still stunned, in the living room with Mulder and the Schiffs.

"I ABDUCTED *HIM*. IT'S A GRAY. IT SPEAKS TO ME. WE COMMUNICATE TELEPATHICALLY. HE TOLD ME EVERYTHING." —Mulder

Mulder takes Scully aside, and speaks with quiet urgency.

"Scully, I need you to put aside your scientific bias for a moment. Because what I'm about to tell you is going to change your life forever. Your life, my life, the life of everybody on this planet."

"Mulder—"

"It's out there. I've found it. The truth. This couple—they were abducted by a UFO. Brown Mountain lights."

A few moments later Angie tells Scully the story of how she received her alien implant.

"Just like what happened to you," says Mulder.

Scully winces, and shakes her head.

"Mulder, from what very little I understand about this case, this is not what happened to me."

"There's more," says Mulder, taking her by the hand and leading her into his darkened bedroom.

"It doesn't like the light," he says softly.

"Who?" says Scully, puzzled.

"I, uh, I don't even know what to say, Mulder. Where to begin. I mean, you were right. All these years you were right."

"You think so?" says Mulder, with a slight smile. "What about the skeletons?"

"They were faked. They were decoys."

"You're buying that decoy theory?" asks Mulder, softly. "What about that organic substance we found on the skeletons, that goo you were so interested in?"

"It was nothing. It was bog sludge."

Mulder winces, as if he's suffering a piercing headache, and rubs his temple with his fingers.

"That doesn't sound like you, Scully," he says haltingly. "It, uh—I can't believe you're buying this."

"Mulder, I'm admitting that I was *wrong*. Are you all right?"

At his kitchen sink Mulder splashes cold water on his face. He glances down, and sees that the tap is spewing yellow goo. A moment later the tap is running clear again. In a cold sweat, obviously ill, he turns off the tap and walks into the living room.

"This doesn't make any sense," he tells Scully. "These two. Their stories. The skeletons."

"Mulder, if I of all people can believe this, why can't you?"

Mulder's vision blurs bright yellow for a moment. Then, for another few seconds, everything is back to normal.

He turns to the Schiffs, who are melting away into a yellow ooze. Scully looks at her partner, gravely concerned. The entire room undulates around him. Then Scully melts away.

At that moment Mulder—eyes half-closed, twitching and dripping yellow ooze—is jammed inside a strange, latticelike underground cocoon.

That day Scully returns to the cave entrance, the Asheville coroner behind her. She tells him that Mulder seems to have vanished. The coroner assures her they'll catch up to him eventually.

Scully kneels down over a footprint and swipes it with a latex glove. The white latex becomes stained yellow.

"It's more of that digestive material," she says. "It looks like it's coming up out of the ground."

They examine the area around the cave mouth. The coroner points out footprints going in and out of the cave.

"They were only going in before," says Scully, baffled.

"I guess you missed him," says the coroner.

"How?" says Scully. "This cave's not much more than a hole in the rock."

Scully peers into the tiny cave. She turns as she hears the coroner call her, then walks to the spot where he's standing. At his feet, lying in the weeds, are the bleached bones of a human skeleton.

Later that day the skeleton lies on an examining table in the coroner's office. In shock and hollow-eyed, Scully stares down at it. The coroner enters.

"The courier just arrived," he says. "They brought your partner's charts."

Scully opens a large FBI envelope, pulls out a set of dental X-rays, and slaps them onto a light box. An adjacent light box hold another set. There is a prominent filled molar—the same tooth on the upper left—on each film. The X-rays are identical. Scully realizes the truth.

"I'm sorry," says the coroner, sympathetically. "I know it's difficult."

Scully struggles for control. Fighting back tears, she walks slowly back to the skeleton.

"That, um, that digestive secretion we keep finding. Could it have done this to him?"

"I'm not sure I follow," says the puzzled coroner.

"Well, it's chemically similar to gastric juices, right? I mean, maybe he fell in it. Or maybe it's a product of a particular vegetation that grows in the area."

The coroner considers this for a second. He is sympathetic but not swayed.

"That all sounds plausible, I guess," he says. "Except for one thing. There's no sign of it on these remains."

Scully checks. The skeleton is dry.

"It was on the Schiffs," she says, at a loss.

The coroner speaks to her gently.

"I just think we need to look for the simplest explanation," he says. "The most logical."

Scully is startled to recognize her own words to Mulder.

"What is the most logical explanation?" she asks carefully.

"I'd say we're looking at a murder. One with ritualistic overtones. I think his body was stripped, and then skeletonized, possibly by boiling, or the use of an acid solution."

Scully stares at the coroner but says nothing.

"Don't worry, Agent," he says. "We'll take care of the arrangements. We'll have the remains sent to Washington."

At FBI headquarters several days later a depressed Scully, wearing black, sits across from Walter Skinner. The AD is reading an X-File: Scully's report on the death of her partner. Skinner thanks her sympathetically for her efforts, and advises her to take a short leave of absence. Scully does not respond.

"Agent?" says Skinner.

"Sir," asks Scully, in a strained voice, "you're satisfied with my conclusions in this case?"

"I take it you're not?"

"I was unable to determine a clear cause of death," says Scully. "Nor was I able to fully account for the condition of Agent Mulder's body."

"You concluded he was a victim of a ritual killing."

"No! I mean, that was one possible scenario that I mentioned, but in my mind it was the least plausible."

"Not only is it plausible, it's likely," says Skinner. "Why are you questioning your own findings?"

"My role on the X-Files," says Scully, "has always been to provide a rational, scientific perspective in cases that would seem to defy explanation. A counterpoint to Agent Mulder."

"And you have done that!" says Skinner, with feeling. "You have performed admirably."

"Have I?" says Scully. "How many X-Files have my scientific approach fully and satisfactorily explained?"

Scully adds that Mulder's death makes no sense to her scientifically. Skinner answers her gently.

"Given Mulder's life work," he says, "it's tempting to attribute his death to the paranormal, the unexplained, the unknown. But that's simply not the case. We need to see this for what it is and, given that, I promise you we'll get the bastard who did this."

Later that day Scully knocks on the door of Mulder's apartment. It is opened by Frohike, who admits her into a small crowd of mourners, friends, and FBI colleagues. This apparently is Mulder's wake.

"I'm sorry," whispers Skinner, moving past her.

Scully looks into Mulder's bedroom. Inside is Mulder's coffin. Byers approaches Scully and asks her how she's holding up.

"I still can't believe it," she whispers.

"Neither can we," says Langly, also present. "I half expect Mulder to come knocking at that door—surprise!"

Frohike steps up and offers Scully a glass of wine. "This'll dull the pain," he says.

Scully turns him down. Frohike takes a swig from the glass himself. Byers confides to Scully that the Gunmen have launched their own investigation. Scully seems a bit relieved.

"I was starting to think I was the only one who was at all suspicious," she says.

"We'll find him!" says Frohike, forcefully. "We'll find him and make him pay!"

"Find who?" asks Scully.

"The sonuvabitch who killed Mulder!"

Scully looks confused and disappointed. Byers compliments her on her report, and says that the Gunmen concur that it was a ritualistic murder.

Scully eyes them incredulously.

"Those are not my findings!" she says. "You guys believe that, too, that Mulder was murdered?"

"It's the obvious answer," says Langly.

"No! It is *not* the obvious answer!"

"We believe," says Byers, "his body was stripped, then skeletonized, possibly by boiling, or the use of an acid solution."

Scully stares at the three men, sickened.

"What the hell is wrong with everybody?" she says angrily. "There are unanswered questions here. Am I the only one that's asking them?"

"You three, of all people. You should be all over this, not buying the party line. Look, something else is going on here. Am I the only one who knows it?"

In sudden pain, Scully puts a hand to her temple. Her vision is tinged with yellow, and for a second or two she sees a wall of goo cascading in front of her. Her vision clears.

Skinner walks over to Scully and advises her to go home and get some rest. Scully frowns at him, angry.

"What have you done with him?" she says.

"Scully, you're emotionally distraught. You need to calm down—"

"Where is Mulder?! Where is he? *What have you done with him?*"

Skinner grabs Scully by the shoulder, and tells her forcefully that she must now accept the fact that Mulder is gone. She pulls loose.

"Look!" shouts Scully. "Something else is going on here! Where is he! Where's Mulder?"

Skinner does not respond. There is a knock on the apartment door. Scully turns and opens it.

Mulder enters, very much alive.

"Scully?" he nods, greeting her.

All the other mourners in Mulder's apartment have vanished. Mulder's coffin is also gone—as is, indeed, the entire bedroom.

Mulder sits on his couch, hunched forward, and speaks softly—almost hypnotically—to Scully.

"We were in the cave when the light came," he says. "It was a blinding blue-white light. And then they took me. I was abducted.

"I found myself in some kind of medical bay. It was white, featureless. It was just as the Schiffs had described it—"

"Mulder, the Schiffs are dead," says Scully.

"No. Actually they're not."

"Mulder, their remains were discovered in a field. That's what brought us to this case in the first place. I found your remains in that same field."

"Me? I'm here," says Mulder.

"How did you get here?" says Scully.

"The aliens brought me back here."

"From North Carolina direct to your apartment door? Mulder, you don't remember getting here, do you? Neither do I."

Mulder shrugs, unconcerned.

"It doesn't change what happened," he says.

Scully looks at him suspiciously.

"Mulder, why did you knock? This is your apartment. You don't seem the least bit surprised to find me here. And what about the Schiffs? I mean, if they're alive, as you say, then where are they? Where did they go?

"Mulder, five minutes ago this room was filled with people attending your wake."

"Well, what can I say, Scully? I'm here. I'm real."

"Mulder, this is not reality. This is a hallucination. It has to be. And either I am having it, or you are having it, or we are having it together."

"Brought on by what?" says Mulder, skeptically.

"Something that we found in that field, Mulder, because that's where it began."

She thinks for a moment and has a flash of insight.

"Mushrooms!" she whispers. "Wild mushrooms, Mulder! They were growing there. I stepped on one and it gave off spores. Several varieties of wild mushrooms are known for their hallucinogenic properties. If we inhaled it—"

"Whatever happened to 'the most logical explanation'?" asks Mulder.

"This is it!" she says. "What if we're still there? If we're still in that cave in North Carolina? That we're not in this apartment right now? I think that Angela and Wallace Schiff were digested by that substance I found

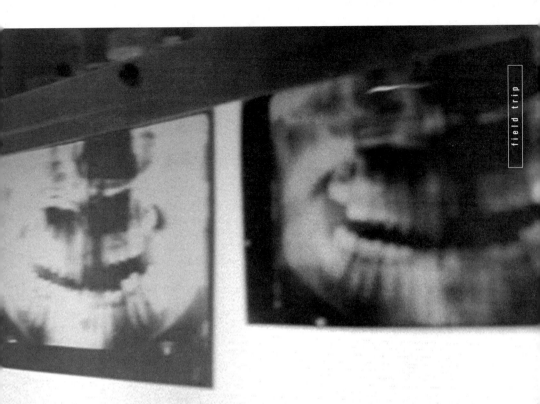

"NEITHER CAN WE. I HALF EXPECT MULDER TO COME KNOCKING AT THAT DOOR—SURPRISE!"–Langly

CASE #: X-751483

PERTAINING TO THE DEATH OF SPECIAL AGENT FOX MULDER

AGENTS OF RECORD: Dana Scully

TO: Assistant Director Walter S. Skinner

CC: Senior ASAC

The following report pertains to the death of Special Agent Fox M

The exact cause of Agent Mulder's death is not and cannot cle in this record. Nor can the condition of his body be fully explained. Th real physical evidence other than the state of Agent Mulder's body le unanswered questions to come to a definite conclusion. This report offer several possible scenarios with varying degrees of plausibility.

Torture, alien mutilation, ritual killing, vengeance murder, a

273

all over that field. That they were dissolved and then expelled out of the ground. What if that substance and this hallucinogen are from one and the same organism?"

"A giant mushroom," says Mulder.

"A giant fungal organism, Mulder! We already know that they exist. Biologists have found specimens ranging dozens of acres, that weigh hundreds of tons. And what if this one needs to feed on living tissue, Mulder? There is carnivorous plant life. There's the Venus flytrap, and the Pitcher plant. Mulder, what if this one puts off a hallucinogen—"

"To lure its prey into the cave," says Mulder.

"To make it complacent," says Scully. "To keep it still while it devours it."

Mulder puts his hands to his temples, in pain again. He has a momentary flash: He is trapped in the cocoon, covered with viscous slime. The vision ends.

"What if we're still underground, Mulder?" says Scully. "What if we're moving deeper into the cave or being moved? Mulder, what if we're being digested? Right now?"

Scully melts into a yellow ooze. The room behind her dissolves.

In the mushroom field at Brown Mountain a dirt- and goo-caked hand erupts from the earth. It is followed by Mulder, who slowly and painfully drags himself out of the wet earth. He reaches back into the ground, gropes for something, and pulls Scully—semiconscious and also covered with goo—onto the earth's surface beside him.

Several days later Mulder and Scully sit facing Skinner in his FBI office. Scully tells the AD that the exact size of the giant underground organism has yet to be determined. Mulder adds that they've contacted several government agencies, asking them to come up with a way to safely destroy it. Scully hands Skinner a computer printout.

"The lab results determined that the spores we were exposed to have a chemical structure similar to LSD," she says. "They also contain an alkaloid which induces a state of narcosis."

Skinner glances down at a file folder.

"It's a rare day when both of you sign off on the same report," he says.

At this Mulder becomes distracted.

"I was just thinking," he says slowly, turning to his partner. "I'm not exactly clear on how we escaped. Once you recognized we were under a chemical influence, then we simply kind of broke its spell?"

"That's right," says Scully.

"Scully, how could we simply will ourselves out of the chemical hallucination? Can you name me one drug that loses its effect once the user realizes it's in the system?"

Scully cannot.

"I assume the effects wore off to the point where you both were able to make your escape," says Skinner.

This satisfies neither of the agents.

"Scully, how long were we underground?" says Mulder. "Hours? Half a day? How come our bodies don't show any effects of being burned by digestive fluids? We were covered in hydrochloric acid, yet look at our skin. Nothing."

"Mulder, where are you going with this?" asks Skinner impatiently.

"Scully, *we never escaped*," says Mulder. "We're still trapped underground."

"Mulder, we did escape," says Scully, calmly. "I think you're suffering from post-traumatic stress."

"No, I'm not!" insists Mulder. "This is not real. You, you're not real. I'll prove it, Scully."

He stands, draws his gun, and aims it at Skinner.

"Mulder!" shouts Scully.

Mulder fires once, twice, three times. Skinner's torso is pierced with smoking holes, which begin to ooze yellow goo. Scully watches, astonished, as Mulder melts into yellow ooze.

Deep underground at Brown Mountain, Mulder and Scully are cocooned side by side. Mulder thrusts his hand out of the dark earth and is spotted by a team of searchers.

Skinner and the coroner—wearing respirators—are the first to the scene. They reach down and frantically dig toward the two agents. They are joined by other rescuers, who pull Mulder and Scully from the earth and wheel them to a waiting ambulance.

Regaining partial consciousness, they are loaded into the ambulance side by side. The vehicle pulls away. Mulder stretches out his hand to his partner. She clasps it as tightly as she can.

BACK STORY/6X21

Serious fans who missed this late-season standalone—perhaps conserving their brain cells for the following week's mythological season-ender—may have made a serious error.

"Field Trip" is an extraordinary episode for several distinct reasons: among them a subtle, convoluted, but ultimately crystal-clear, powerful plotline; an epochal Mulder-Scully confrontation on the very nature of the science/passion schism that separates the two main characters; and a serious meditation—within a prime-time entertainment show, no less—on the very nature of human perception and reality.

"It was quite an experience," recalls Frank Spotnitz, who is credited with the story for 6X21.

Explains the *X-Files* executive producer: "As I remember it, it went through a lot of permutations. Originally, it was about Mulder trapped in a cave with a monster. Then both Mulder and Scully were trapped

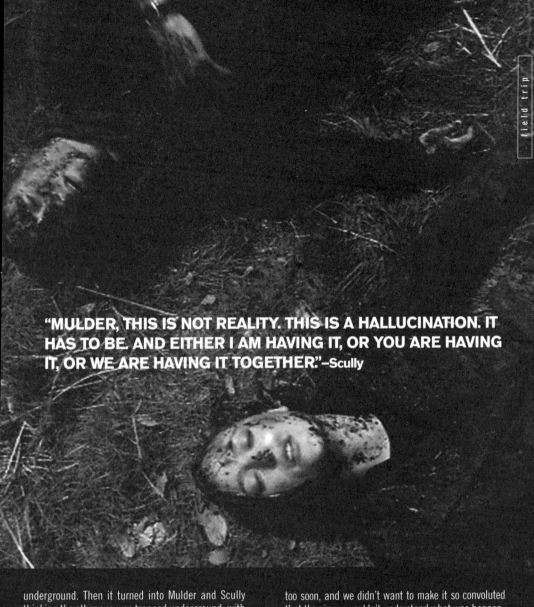

"MULDER, THIS IS NOT REALITY. THIS IS A HALLUCINATION. IT HAS TO BE. AND EITHER I AM HAVING IT, OR YOU ARE HAVING IT, OR WE ARE HAVING IT TOGETHER."–Scully

underground. Then it turned into Mulder and Scully thinking the other one was trapped underground, with only Mulder gradually realizing what was really happening. And then suddenly everyone became *very* excited. Because we'd never really done an *X-File* like this. We could explore Mulder's and Scully's differences by seeing the extremes of their two hallucinations—a serious version of what we did comically last season in 'Bad Blood' [5X12].

"It was then that we knew we could do a scene were Mulder says to his partner, 'You tell me you need scientific proof. But aren't I right ninety-nine percent of the time?' And where else could we play a scene where Scully sees a gray alien and says, 'You were right, Mulder. All these years you were right!'?

"The whole story was a wonderful mind game. But we didn't want to cheat, and we didn't want to tip our hands

too soon, and we didn't want to make it so convoluted that the viewer wouldn't understand what was happening. Frankly, I was a little worried."

Spotnitz's worries were assuaged when the teleplay—assigned to co-executive producer Vince Gilligan and producer John Shiban—was turned in. Spotnitz felt that the script's early clues, particularly Mulder's and Scully's respective triggering of the puffball mushrooms, were perfectly placed.

"Another really important thing we did," says Vince Gilligan, "was making sure that the audience didn't think that Mulder and Scully weren't really in jeopardy—that it was all just a dream, like that whole season on *Dallas* a few years back. That's why we made sure they realized that the goo from the mushroom would kill them if they didn't figure out what was going on."

Meanwhile, further behind the scenes, researcher

Lee Smith was having a busy week consulting with botanists and mycologists (mushroom experts), and learning more than most of us will ever need to know about a giant five hundred–acre fungus known to live underground in rural Wisconsin. He also spent many interesting hours on the telephone with experts from "The Body Farm": a thirty-acre facility of the University of Tennessee's Department of Forensic Anthropology, where human body parts from donated cadavers are buried underground in different ways and under different conditions—the better to monitor their decomposition and provide baseline information for crime investigators. And others.

At his shop on Los Angeles's northern fringe, special effects makeup coordinator John Vulich—working slightly outside of his specialty—was turning several art department designs into the spidery, eight-foot tall fiberglass pods ("Corey Kaplan told me she wanted them to look organic and earthbound, not alien," says Vulich), that imprisoned the hallucinating Mulder and Scully underground.

In sharp contrast to this traditionalist approach were the methods used by special effects producer Bill Millar. In order to "melt" Mulder and Scully on screen, he had to capture their bodies digitally in high resolution and in three dimensions. To do this he took David Duchovny and Gillian Anderson to a special facility in Glendale, where an advanced laser device scanned their (fully clothed) bodies and in fifteen or twenty minutes turned their complicated surfaces and curves into easily manipulated computer data.

Well, not so easily manipulated.

"When we looked at our first tests," says Millar, "we realized we couldn't melt Mulder and Scully without some degree of difficulty, because David and Gillian couldn't just melt. They had to melt like movies stars—without looking grotesque, without looking comical, without turning Gillian temporarily into Margaret Thatcher or David into John Hurt as the Elephant Man.

"So we went back in and, utilizing the same data, did a leading edge melt where parts of them melted and turned into the goop that was underground, and the goop would work its way down their bodies so that their facial features would remain intact until the goop overtook them."

Alas, outside of the digital realm the goop—actually, a vegetable-derived food thickener with yellow food coloring added—overtook them frequently.

"I mean, jeez! They spent hours and hours covered with this stuff, all over their eyes and ears and hair!" says second-unit production manager Harry Bring, who marveled at Duchovny's and Anderson's stolid acceptance of these working conditions.

So did most of those present at the Ventura Farms movie ranch, north of Los Angeles, where all of the scenes outside the cave mouth were filmed. To shoot the sequences where Mulder and Scully claw their way or are pulled to the surface, large pits were dug, scaffolding was constructed inside them, and the actors—wearing wet suits under their costumes and covered with dirt and goop—spent hours between shots crouching beneath the cold earth.

"I have to tell you," says Vince Gilligan, "that I *really* was afraid when we turned this episode in that we'd get a call from David or Gillian saying, 'What the hell is this? You think I'm gonna get covered in goo and lie down in a hole in a field somewhere?'

"Well, we heard back there was some good-natured griping, but on the day they shot it, they didn't complain at all."

The part of the small gray alien in "Field Trip" was played—in body suit, mask and gloves—by seven-year-old Cody Weselis, son of X-Files stunt coordinator Danny Weselis.

The pods were moved to the Fox Studio's sound stage, where the scenes involving them—and the goo-drenched David Duchovny and Gillian Anderson—were filmed by the show's second unit. Vulich also worked with the special effects department to manufacture the tiny exploding mushrooms—which spewed Fuller's Earth on cue via squeeze bulbs and plastic tubing—and, of course, the various complete and partial skeletons that were so important to the plot.

At production designer Corey Kaplan's direction, numerous members of the art department thumbed through old geology textbooks and adventure magazines to get the correct look and feel for the dozens of stalactites (the ones that point downward) and stalagmites (the ones that point upward) that her department manufactured.

These were temporarily installed—at location manager Ilt Jones's strong recommendation—inside the Bronson Caves, an easily accessible network of underground chambers located in Los Angeles's Griffith Park. Perhaps best remembered as the entrance to Bruce Wayne's *sanctum sanctorum* in the old *Batman* TV series, it is one of the most frequently filmed natural phenomena in the Hollywood area—which means, of course, that it's one of the most frequently filmed natural phenomena anywhere. In fact, when the *X-Files* cast and crew spent several days working there last April, they joined a list of hundreds of television shows and movies reaching back to the Silent Era.

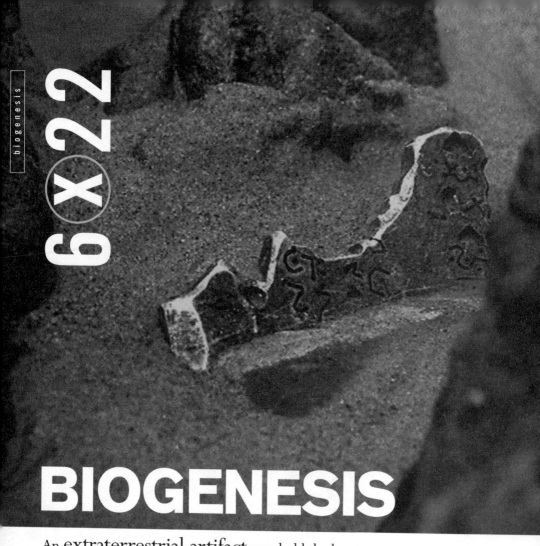

6X22

BIOGENESIS

An **extraterrestrial artifact** may hold the key to
the origins of life on Earth. Fox Mulder must decipher
its mysteries, before it destroys him.

EPISODE: 6X22
FIRST AIRED: May 16, 1999
EDITOR: Heather MacDougall
WRITTEN BY: Chris Carter & Frank Spotnitz
DIRECTED BY: Rob Bowman

GUEST STARS:
Mitch Pileggi (AD Walter Skinner)
Nicholas Lea (Alex Krycek)
William B. Davis (The Cigarette-Smoking Man)
Mimi Rogers (Agent Diana Fowley)
Michael Chinyamurinidi (Dr. Merkmallen)
Murray Rubinstein (Dr. Sandoz)
Michael Ensign (Dr. Barnes)

Floyd Red Crow Westerman (Albert Hosteen)
Bill Dow (Chuck Burks)
Chet Grissom (Detective)
Sheila Tousey (Native American Nurse)
Warren Sweeney (Dr. Harriman)
Samuel Kwaku Minta (Yelling Man)
Ayo Adeyemi (African Man)
Benjamin Ochieng (Second African Man)
Marty Zagon (Landlord)

PRINCIPAL SETTINGS:
Ivory Coast, West Africa; Washington, D.C.;
Silver Springs, Maryland; Gallup, New Mexico

278

The Earth is a precious blue-white gem, suspended in blackness. We hear the voice of Dana Scully. She says:

"From space, it seems an abstraction, a magician's trick on a darkened stage. And from this distance one might never imagine that it is alive."

Waves crash on a deserted, far-off shore. Then a rapid series of images, comprising the varied and complex elements of physical, natural, cultural, and scientific evolution. Scully continues her narration:

"It first appeared in the sea, almost four billion years ago, in the form of single-celled life. In an explosion of life spanning millions of years, nature's first multicellular organisms began to multiply. And then it stopped. Four hundred and forty million years ago, a great mass extinction would kill off nearly every species on the planet, leaving the vast oceans decimated and empty.

"Slowly, plants began to evolve, then insects, only to be wiped out in the second great mass extinction upon the Earth. The cycle repeated again, and again: Reptiles emerging independent of the sea, only to be killed off. Then, dinosaurs struggling to life, along with the first birds, fish, and flowering plants. Their decimations were Earth's fourth and fifth great extinctions.

"Only one hundred thousand years ago, *homo sapiens* appeared. From cave painting to the Bible, to Columbus and *Apollo 11*, we have been a tireless force, upon the Earth and off, cataloguing the natural world as it unfolds to us. Rising to a world population of over five billion people, all descended from that original single cell, that first spark of life.

"But for all our knowledge, what no one can say for certain is what—or who—ignited that original spark. Is there a plan? A purpose or a reason to our existence? Will we pass, as those before us, into oblivion? Into the sixth extinction that scientists warn is already in progress?

"Or will the mystery be revealed through a sign, a symbol? A revelation?"

On a beach in modern-day West Africa—on the Ivory Coast—a man yells excitedly in Swahili. His fellow fisherman quickly surround him. He points to his feet: In the sand, partially buried, is a flat metallic object about the size of small handgun. It is covered with strange and unrecognizable symbols.

Some time afterward, a distinguished older man,

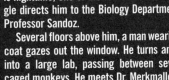

Dr. Solomon Merkmallen, sits writing at a portable desk on the same African beach. He hears a frantic call and runs with surprising speed toward the water. The fishermen point out the metallic object. He is surprised and more than a little apprehensive.

Later that day the object sits on Merkmallen's desk at the Universite Cote D'Ivoire. Merkmallen opens a locked cabinet and takes out a soft felt envelope. He gently unwraps another object: a matching metallic artifact inscribed with the same kind of iconic writing. The jagged edges of the two objects seem to match. He fits the pieces together, and they fly from his fingers, landing at the other end of the large room. The artifact impales itself in a well-worn leatherbound book: the Bible.

Apprehensively, Merkmallen walks over to retrieve it. The scientist removes the shard and holds it up, marveling. The two pieces have been fused into one. He places it back on the table; the artifact begins to spin around its own axis. It quickly picks up speed until the frightened man grabs it and wraps it again in the felt envelope.

Merkmallen walks to another desk to make an international phone call. The Bible lays open where he has left it. The rip caused by the artifact has underlined one passage.

It is Genesis 1:28: *"And God blessed them, and God said unto them, Be fruitful and multiply, and replenish the earth and subdue it: and have dominion over the fish of the sea, and over the fowl of the air, and over every living thing that moveth upon the earth."*

Three days later Merkmallen, carrying a worn leather satchel, walks hesitantly across the campus of American University in Washington, D.C. It is nighttime; one of the few students on the quadrangle directs him to the Biology Department office of a Professor Sandoz.

Several floors above him, a man wearing a white lab coat gazes out the window. He turns and walks back into a large lab, passing between several rows of caged monkeys. He meets Dr. Merkmallen at the front door.

"Dr. Sandoz?" says the African.

The other man grasps his hand warmly.

"Dr. Merkmallen! My God, I thought something had happened to you!"

"Oh?" says Merkmallen. "Did you not get my message? We were delayed in Frankfurt."

"Well, the important thing is that you're here now, and you're safe. You've brought me something, this discovery of yours. I'm quite anxious to see it."

The two men sit at a desk.

Merkmallen clutches his satchel tightly in his lap.

"I was concerned I might be relieved of it in customs," says Merkmallen. "There was some trouble with the X-ray machine in Germany."

"What kind of trouble did you have?"

In response to this, Merkmallen looks at the other man, puzzled.

"I told you of its power," he says. "My credentials were the only thing that prevented me from being further detained."

Merkmallen takes the felt envelope out of his satchel. The caged monkeys become agitated and begin to howl. He unwraps the artifact, uncovering its strange markings.

"I can't explain how it is," says Merkmallen, leaning forward, "but the two pieces have become one. I was hoping that it might match the piece that you found, so that you might see for itself its magic."

The other man takes the artifact and turns it over in his hands.

"Have you had any luck reading it?" he asks.

Alarmed, Merkmallen stares at him.

"You're not Dr. Sandoz, are you?" he says.

Shortly afterward another professorial-looking man makes his way up an American University stairwell, and hears the shrill cacophony of the agitated lab monkeys. Moving quickly, he enters the biology lab. The lab-coated scientist is gone, as is the artifact. Sprawled on the floor, head lying in a pool of blood, is Merkmallen.

At FBI headquarters the next day Skinner is at his desk. Mulder and Scully sit across from him.

"A case like this, Dr. Merkmallen's views and theories being what they were," says Skinner, "I of course thought of your obvious interest. I believe Agent Mulder is familiar with his work. He flew in yesterday from Africa. Two hours later he's apparently murdered at American University.

"His body is missing, but there was enough blood on the floor to make a fair assumption. A couple of students also confirmed they spoke to him when he asked them for directions to find a Dr. Steven Sandoz—also a professor of biology."

Mulder hands Scully a file folder. Inside are photos of Merkmallen and Sandoz, who is in fact the second academic; the man who discovered Merkmallen's body.

"Both men espouse a theory called 'Panspermia,'" says Mulder. "It's the idea that life originated—"

"—elsewhere in this universe," says Scully.

"BOTH MEN ESPOUSE A THEORY CALLED 'PANSPERMIA.' IT'S THE IDEA THAT LIFE ORIGINATED—" –Mulder

"—ELSEWHERE IN THIS UNIVERSE." –Scully

"You've heard of this?" says Skinner, surprised.

"Yeah," says Scully. "It's the idea that Mars or other planets were habitable long before Earth. And that cosmic collisions on these planets blasted microbes into our solar system, some of which landed and flourished here."

"You'd accept that as plausible?" says Skinner.

"Well, almost any scientist would, theoretically," says Scully. "I mean, it's a theory; that's about it, though. You don't think it has anything to do with his death, do you?"

Skinner hands Scully a piece of paper.

"Dr. Merkmallen found an artifact in his country. This is a rubbing of the artifact. He claimed it contains a message, not only of his Mars theories, but the very meaning of human existence."

"Much less plausible," says Scully, frowning.

Mulder doesn't rise to the bait.

"Dr. Sandoz, the man he'd come to meet," he says, "made a similar claim in a science journal. He said he'd found an artifact that was almost identical to that one, with similar writings on it."

"And what was it supposed to say?" says Scully.

"Well, we'd have to ask Dr. Sandoz that," says Mulder.

"Well, why don't we?" asks Scully.

"We can't," says Mulder. "He's missing."

A few minutes later the agents enter the FBI elevator. It starts down toward their basement office.

"What are we doing, Mulder?" says Scully. "This is a police matter at best."

"Skinner wants us on the case," says Mulder.

"And you're going to try to convince me that you have no personal interest in this case?" says Scully.

"I am just a hired gun for the FBI," says Mulder, examining the rubbing.

Scully looks at him, annoyed.

"Two men suggesting that we are all Martians," she says. "Why would they possibly come to foul play?"

"Well, that's what we're being asked to figure out," he says.

"Mulder, I don't understand you—" she says.

As the elevator continues downward Scully argues quietly but intensely with Mulder. But her partner does not hear her; her words are drowned out by a cacophony of indistinct voices and a high-pitched tone, apparently inside Mulder's head. After twenty seconds or so, these voices fade.

"—this endless pursuit of the truth, Mulder, it just doesn't make any sense to me now. Mulder? Did you hear a word of what I just said?"

"No," says Mulder softly.

"No? Well, maybe you didn't want to hear it."

"No," says Mulder. "I couldn't hear it."

The elevator reaches the basement. Mulder hands Scully the rubbing and walks toward his office.

Scully calls after him. He stops and turns.

"Look," she says, "after all you've done, after all you've uncovered: a conspiracy of men doing human experiments. Men who are all now dead, you exposed their secrets. I mean, you've won. What more could you possibly hope to do or to find?"

"My sister," says Mulder, turning again to leave.

At American University later that morning policemen and forensic techs swarm over the lab where Solomon Merkmallen was murdered. A blood-covered blunt instrument, bagged as evidence, lies on the table where the scientists sat. Mulder and Scully enter. On the other side of the room is the academic whom Merkmallen mistook for Dr. Sandoz. His eyes catch Mulder's, and then turn away.

Scully shows her credentials to a D.C. plainclothesman. He tells her they've found blood, hair, and fingerprints on the murder weapon.

"Any word on this Dr. Sandoz?" asks Scully.

"No. But we're being told the prints are very likely his."

"Told by whom?"

"The man your partner is speaking with."

Across the lab Mulder is shaking hands with the academic.

"I'm Dr. Barnes, head of the department," he tells Mulder. "They've asked me to suspend classes and organize interviews with the faculty."

"Any ideas yourself about what happened here? About the missing Dr. Sandoz?"

"There's plenty of speculation here," says Barnes. "Apart from his laughable ideas, my colleague was capable of almost anything to advance his rather questionable reputation."

Scully walks toward the two men.

"Capable of murder?" she asks.

"Dr. Sandoz's notes," says Barnes contemptuously, "are full of talk about an artifact coming over from West Africa, but, like the man who was bringing it, that artifact has yet to be located."

"You're speaking of this," says Scully, handing Barnes the rubbing.

The scientist unfolds the paper and examines it. At the same moment Mulder cups his hand to his ear. The voices and the tone are starting up again—higher-pitched and louder this time. His face registers both distraction and pain. Despite Scully's concerned expression he walks away quickly, without explanation.

"Did you know that Dr. Sandoz believed this writing was from aliens?" says Barnes, smugly. "These are trivial men. They have no patience for the scientific process. They're happy to read their names in the tabloids. Pseudoscientists. Beyond embarrassment."

At a water fountain in the corridor a few moments later Mulder splashes water on his face.

"BUT, MULDER. IF IT WERE REAL, THEN WHY WOULD AN AMERICAN INDIAN ARTIFACT BE FUSED IN ROCK ON THE WEST COAST OF THE AFRICAN CONTINENT?"
—Scully

Scully approaches and asks him, worriedly, what's the matter.

"I don't know," he says tiredly. "Hollow noise. Same thing that happened to me at work in the elevator this morning."

"Do you have a fever?" asks Scully.

"No," says Mulder, glancing down at the rubbing in his partner's hand. "It sounds weird, but I think it's that thing."

"You're not kidding?" says Scully. "It's just a piece of paper."

She looks up at her partner. His expression is gravely serious.

Later that day an enlarged image of the rubbing is projected on the wall of the X-Files office. Scully is studying it, as is Chuck Burks, the University of Maryland investigator last seen in "Leonard Betts" (4X14). Mulder enters the room. He and Mulder shake hands warmly.

"I called Chuck, as I knew you would, for authentication," says Scully. "And to get his professional opinion on how you say it's affecting you."

"You know me," says Burks, smiling. "This is right up my twisted little alley. So, what exactly are you experiencing?"

"Noise. Aural dissonance. It comes and it goes," says Mulder.

"Is it happening right now?" asks Scully.

"No. But it was happening a few minutes ago."

"And it's only happening to you triggered by the rubbing," says Burks. "Wow! That blows me away."

"Why?" asks Mulder.

"Because the rubbing is a fake," says Scully, arms crossed. "And I'm not the first one to say so."

Burks shrugs.

"The writing is Cree. Phonetic Navajo," says Burks. "But no literal interpretation makes any sense."

"And the fact that it was found in Africa," adds Scully, "makes it all the more suspicious as a fabrication."

Once again, Burks is not so certain.

"Do you know what a magic square is?" he says.

"It has to do with the occult," says Mulder.

"Right. Very cool," says Burks. "They first appear in history around the ninth century."

Burks removes the rubbing from the overhead projector and substitutes a page from a magazine article. It has the same rubbing on it, but the writing has been divided into a grid with nine squares.

"As the story goes," continues Burks, "God himself instructed Adam in their use, and then handed down the secret to all his saints and prophets and wise men as a way of trapping and storing potential power to the person whose name or numerical correlative exercises that power."

Scully is less than overwhelmed. She puts her own

sheet of paper into the projector. It is the first page of the same magazine article, with a photo of its author—Dr. Barnes. The head and subhead read: GOD SPELLED BACKWARD: MANUFACTURING RELIGIOUS ARTIFACTS FOR FUN AND PROFIT.

"If he was blunt about his colleague when we met him," says Scully, "here he's just downright brutal."

"Does he back any of that up?" asks Mulder.

"It's quite scholarly, actually," says Scully.

Burks adds that Barnes has made a career out of exposing scientific and religious frauds.

"But wouldn't it be in his great interest," says Mulder, "to hide something that he couldn't disprove with his scholarship?"

"But, Mulder," says Scully, "if it were real, then why would an American Indian artifact be fused in rock on the west coast of the African continent?"

"Well, in 1996 a rock from Mars was found in Antarctica. How did it get there?"

"It was from outer space!" says Scully.

Mulder smiles, then raises his arms in triumph.

"Begs the question, doesn't it?" adds Burks. "Why produce a fraud with Navajo writing in Africa?"

Scully struggles to come up with an answer. But before she can, she follows Burks's worried gaze to Mulder. He holds his hands to his head, doubled over in great pain. The scrambled voices boom in his head.

"Let's go outside," she says quickly.

In the corridor the high-pitched noises in Mulder's head subside. Scully says she's going to schedule him for an imaging scan, or at the very least recommend that he go home to bed. Mulder shakes his head impatiently.

"I'm not going home to bed, Scully," he says. "I think I know what's causing this. I know what happened to those two professors and that artifact. I had a sense of it yesterday, when we met this man Barnes. This man Solomon Merkmallen is dead. Barnes knows it. He killed him. He killed him in that lab."

Scully frowns.

"Well, I hope you're not going to suggest that we arrest him on that rather baseless assumption."

"No, no," says Mulder. "Not until after I show you what he did with the body."

Later that day the landlord grumpily admits Mulder and Scully to Dr. Sandoz's Silver Springs apartment. Mulder searches the bedroom and closet; he finds a large empty suitcase with several baggage tags with the airline code for Gallup, New Mexico. He shows this to Scully, who has been examining a number of framed photographs hanging on Sandoz's living room wall.

"Well, I think I know who he was going to see," says Scully.

She points to a photo of a smiling Sandoz with

"I FOUND HIM IN A UNIVERSITY STAIRWELL. HE COULD HARDLY SPEAK. HE SAID I WAS THE ONLY ONE WHO WOULD BELIEVE HIM . . . ABOUT AN ARTIFACT."–Diana Fowley

"YOU'RE A LIAR."–Scully

Albert Hosteen—the Navajo World War II code talker last seen in "Paper Clip" (3X02).

"Maybe he's been using him to read the symbols on the artifact," says Mulder.

"Or write them," says Scully. "Mulder, you also said that we'd find a body. Care to make good on that prediction?"

Mulder smiles, walks into the kitchen, and holds his fingers to his nose.

"Scully, you packing any latex?" he says.

"No. Why?" she says.

"Smells like somebody forgot to take out the garbage."

He walks to the sink, wraps a dish towel around his hand, and pulls open the trash compactor. The stench is overwhelming and a swarm of flies emerge from the machine. Inside is the flattened, partially decomposed head of Solomon Merkmallen.

At FBI headquarters Skinner faces Mulder and Scully across a conference table.

"So you think this man Sandoz is innocent," says the AD.

"He's afraid for his life because of what he knows and what he has," says Mulder.

Skinner places the rubbing in front of Mulder. He doesn't seem to be physically affected, only very intense and concentrated.

"A genuine artifact," he says. "One of several pieces of an unknown whole. Dr. Barnes has one now, too. That's why he killed Solomon Merkmallen."

"The way his body was disposed of—" says Skinner.

"—was to incriminate Sandoz," says Mulder. "To make him look like the killer. It's also to hide something. Something no one would think to look for.

"Scully, could you please tell what your medical exam found, and the lab report."

Scully stares at Mulder with concern.

"Parts of his body were missing," she says. "His arms, his hands, parts of his vital organs and his thyroid."

"All of which would retain the telltale traces of radiation," says Mulder.

"Radiation from what?" asks Skinner.

"The artifact!" says Mulder, impatiently.

"On Agent Mulder's urging," says Scully, with deliberate calm, "I ran tissue samples through what's called a Charged Particle Directional Spectrometer. There was a trace of a kind of radiation called CGR—"

"—Cosmic Galactic Radiation," says Mulder, thickly. "It's a type of radiation only found outside our solar system."

Scully looks at Skinner.

"I don't know how to explain it," she says. "But I feel we can make an arrest—"

"Forget the arrest! We need to find these artifacts!" says Mulder.

He grabs his temples, as he is obviously having another episode. Abruptly, he looks up.

"Is there someone else on this case, sir?" he says.

"Excuse me?"

"There's someone else on this case. You're not telling me!"

Skinner looks at Mulder, nonplussed, and turns to Scully.

"What the hell's he talking about?" he says.

"I hear it. In my head."

Scully rises and takes Mulder's arm.

"Mulder, let's go," she whispers, leading him out of the office.

They walk a few yards away from Skinner's door.

"You're losing it, Mulder," says Scully.

"I am not. Listen to me—he's not telling the truth. I'm hearing people. He's spying on us."

"Mulder, you need to see a doctor," says Scully.

"I need to find those artifacts."

"*I'll* find the artifact. You need to go home right now. Mulder?"

Through his office door, opened slightly, Skinner watches the agents depart, still arguing. He shuts the door, pulls a key from his pocket, and walks toward a locked credenza. Through a peephole in its cabinet a black-and-white video camera is sighted on him. Unlocking the cabinet, he pulls a tape out of the VCR also nestled inside.

Skinner hears a slight noise behind him, and turns. Standing next to the conference table is Alex Krycek. With defiant obedience Skinner slides the tape across the table. With a small, cruel smile on his face, Krycek pockets the offering, turns, and departs.

At Southwestern General Hospital in Gallup the next day, Scully walks down a corridor. She sees a medical team emerge from Albert Hosteen's room, rushing the gravely ill man to emergency treatment. Scully enters his empty room; on a bedside table is a rubbing of the artifact. On the reverse side of the paper, in Albert's handwriting, is written a familiar biblical quotation: Genesis 1:28.

Scully's thoughts are interrupted by a Native American nurse, who enters the room to tell her that Albert is too sick to accept visitors. The nurse is reticent when asked what Albert is suffering from. Scully flashes her FBI ID.

"I know him," says the agent. "He's helped me in the past. I'm sure that he wouldn't mind you telling me."

"Albert has cancer," says the nurse, sadly. "He's suffering from its effects. He's dying."

At American University at 4:58 P.M. a small crowd of students enter a biology department classroom. Dr. Barnes, their instructor, follows them.

Watching from the other end of the hall is a casually dressed Mulder. He walks quickly past the classroom and into Barnes's faculty office. He searches through the professor's bookcase, desk, and filing cabinet, and freezes when he hears a noise behind him.

Barnes enters the office, walks to his desk, and senses something amiss. On full alert, he exits and enters the biology lab. Mulder watches him from behind one of the monkey cages. At that moment the noises in his head—very intense and painful this time—resume.

They subside when Barnes leaves the lab. Still in pain, though, Mulder shadows him through the university corridors. Barnes enters a stairwell and heads upward. The voices in Mulder's head become more intense. He can only manage to stagger up one flight before collapsing in agony.

At the hospital in Gallup the semiconscious Albert Hosteen is wheeled back into his room. This wakens Scully, who has been dozing in a bedside chair waiting for him. As the doctors and nurses tend to their patient, Scully's eyes open and they drift to the door of the room, through which Dr. Sandoz is entering.

He sees her and bolts back into the corridor. Scully runs from the room in pursuit.

Sandoz turns a corner and disappears from Scully's view. She stands in a deserted corridor, listening, then draws her gun and runs for the stairwell. She spots Sandoz just as he's about to push open the emergency door to the roof. He turns and faces her, raising his hands in the air.

"Okay," she says, still breathing hard. "I need answers from you."

At American University Mulder lies helpless in the stairwell. A stone-faced man—Krycek—walks up to him, looks down expressionlessly, and keeps climbing. Krycek emerges onto the roof of the biology building and walks slowly toward worried-looking Dr. Barnes.

"Are you the man who called?" says the biologist.

"Dr. Barnes, you and I are destined to be great friends," says Krycek, with a smirk.

He holds up the videocassette from Skinner's office. Barnes eyes it warily.

In Albert Hosteen's room in Gallup, New Mexico, Scully and Sandoz stand at the unconscious Navajo's bedside. Scully holds the rubbing in her hands.

"When I showed him the original artifact," whispers Sandoz, "he immediately recognized its power and importance. The trouble was, it was only one fragment. Not enough to read."

"But then other pieces surfaced?" asks Scully.

"Dr. Merkmallen found two more in the tidal shallows. He sent me a rubbing. Suddenly Albert was able to make a real translation."

"A passage from the Bible on an artifact that you're saying is extraterrestrial," says Scully, skeptically. "And how did the aliens get it?"

"They gave it to us. The text came from *them*. I can prove it," says Sandoz, forcefully. "It's written here. I'm sure of it."

Sandoz reaches into his pocket and pulls out a felt envelope. Inside it is a small artifact fragment. He places it on the bedside table.

"Albert was working to translate another section when his health turned," he says.

"And this was going to tell us what?" says Scully.

"I don't know yet. Albert said it just seemed to be random letters."

Scully looks down at the fragment. It has begun to spin slowly—then more quickly—around its axis. Scully slams her hand upon it. It stops.

Later that night a phone rings in Mulder's bedroom. The agent is in his bed, sleeping, obviously much-less-than-completely recovered. On the other end of the line is Scully, holding her cell phone. A woman's voice answers. Puzzled, she asks to speak to her partner.

"Hello?" says Mulder, weakly.

"Mulder, where are you?" asks Scully.

"I'm here, resting."

"Where? Who answered the phone?"

"I'm home. It's okay. Where are you?"

"New Mexico," says Scully. "With Dr. Sandoz."

"Does he have the artifact?" asks Mulder.

Scully hesitates a moment before she answers.

"Mulder, this artifact," she says hesitantly. "If I'm to believe what I'm being told about it, it has a passage on it from Genesis."

"Scully, that artifact is extraterrestrial. Did you know what that would mean?"

"No. It would mean nothing, Mulder."

"No!" he replies. "It would mean that our progenitors were alien. That our genesis was alien. That we are here because of them. That they put us here."

"Mulder, that is science fiction! It doesn't hold a drop of water!"

"You're wrong. It holds everything. Don't you see? All the mysteries of science, everything we can't understand or won't explain. Every human behaviorism. Cosmology, psychology, everything in the X-Files—it all owes to them. It's from *them.*"

"Mulder, I will not accept that. It's just not possible!" says Scully, forcefully.

"Then you go ahead and prove me wrong, Scully," says Mulder.

His partner hangs up. Mulder hands the phone to the woman at his bedside: Diana Fowley. Exhausted by his effort, Mulder falls back and lies still on his bed. Diana walks into the living room, dials the phone, and begins to undress. Her call goes through.

"I received a call from Agent Mulder this evening. He was in a particular state of distress," she says. "I

286

don't know why. But I'm going to stay here until I find out." She removes her blouse and walks quickly back into the bedroom.

Sitting at a conference table at a high-level government meeting the Cigarette-Smoking Man takes a long drag on his cigarette and smiles thinly.

Under the nighttime New Mexico sky a ring of pickup trucks, their headlights shining, illuminate a large open field. Two young Native American men carry Albert Hosteen on a stretcher toward a Navajo hogan—a place of healing, worship, and sacred rites. Scully and Dr. Sandoz follow at a respectful distance. Scully narrates:

"It began with an act of supreme violence: a Big Bang expanding ever outward; cosmos born of matter and gas. Matter and gas. Ten billion years ago. Whose idea was this? Who had the audacity for such invention? And the reason? Were we part of that plan? Ten billion years ago?

"Are we born only to die? To be fruitful and multiply and replenish the Earth before giving way to our generations? If there is a beginning, must there be an end?

"We burn like fires in our time, only to be extinguished. To surrender to the elements' eternal reclaim. Matter and gas. Will this all end one day? Life no longer passing to life? The Earth left barren like the stars above. Like the cosmos.

"Will the hand that lit the flame let it burn down? Let it burn out? Could we too become extinct? Or, if this fire of life living inside us is meant to go on, who decides? Who tends the flames? Can He reignite the spark even as it grows cold and weak?"

Inside the hogan Albert lies on a blanket on the ground, next to the fire. The other Navajos, including a medicine man, sit in a circle around him. Sandoz tells Scully that the healing ceremony is about to begin, and invites her inside.

"No. I don't think that's right," she says. "I don't share in their faith."

"The medical doctors say they've done everything they could," says Sandoz.

"I know," says Scully, sadly. "I think they have."

Her cell phone rings. It's Skinner, calling from a hospital in Georgetown.

He tells her that Mulder is in serious condition—for reasons the doctors cannot fathom—and that she should return to Washington right away. He hangs up. Scully turns to Sandoz.

"I have to go. I have to leave," she says, distressed by the news.

"Please," says Sandoz, showing her his artifact fragment, "don't let anybody know where I am until we know for sure."

Scully nods quickly and hurries off.

At Georgetown Memorial Hospital later that night Skinner sits, tired and despondent, on a bench in a corridor. Scully arrives.

"They just told me that he's in the special psychiatric unit!" she says angrily.

"I don't know what to do, Dana," says Skinner. "No one else does either. I knew you'd want to be here to see him. To talk to the doctors."

Skinner takes Scully's hand. Her anger dissipates.

"What? What is it?" she asks apprehensively.

In a nearby room at the hospital Diana Fowley watches a video monitor on which an image of Mulder, wearing a hospital gown in a padded room, paces while jabbering incoherently. Scully and Skinner enter—Scully noting Fowley's presence with alarm.

"Thank you for coming," says Fowley. "He was asking for you last night."

Scully gazes at the monitor, greatly distressed by what she sees. A physician—Dr. Geoff Harriman—enters and tells her she isn't authorized to be there. Scully cuts him off.

"What's wrong with him?" she demands. "This man right here, Fox Mulder."

In his cell Mulder lets out a blood-curdling scream.

"I'm not sure what's wrong with him," admits Harriman. "And we don't know what to do for him. He's got extremely abnormal brain function, but there's no signs of stroke. We're waiting to run some more tests."

"He's extremely violent. With what we've given him he should be in a barbiturate coma, but there's brain activity in areas we've never seen before."

"I want to talk to him," says Scully.

"No. He's a danger to anyone—" says Harriman.

"Not to me," insists Scully.

Harriman stands his ground. Fowley interrupts, asking if she could talk to Scully in the hall.

"About what?" asks Scully, contemptuously.

Skinner motions for her to go outside.

In the corridor Fowley asks Scully when Mulder's physical difficulties began. Scully replies that it started when Skinner assigned them their case: the murder of Solomon Merkmallen.

"This case has nothing to do with what happened to him," insists Skinner.

"Agent Scully says it does," says Fowley. "And you know my background, my previous work on the X-Files. If I can help on this case—"

"The X-File here is a fraud," says Skinner. "Scully has ample proof of that, evidence authenticated by a scholar and authority."

Scully is surprised—and somewhat appalled—by his statement.

"I never sent you that research," she says.

"Anyway," says Skinner, with irritation and a trace of embarrassment, "that case is being resolved."

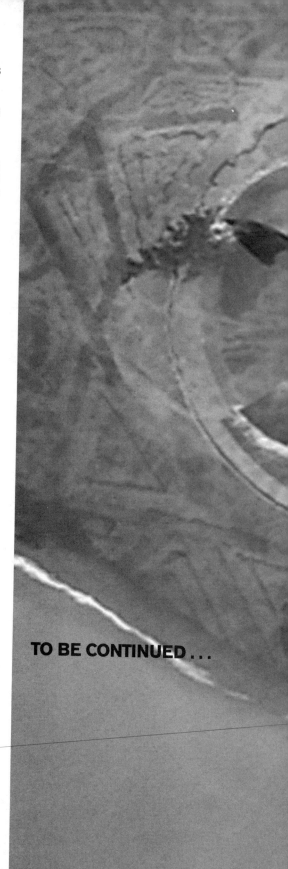

"Not as far as it affects Agent Mulder," says Fowley.

She turns to Scully.

"If you know what's causing this, why won't you tell me?"

Scully looks at Fowley, equally suspicious.

"Why were you with him last night?" she asks.

"He called me," Fowley replies. "I found him in a university stairwell. He could hardly speak. He said I was the only one who would believe him . . . about an artifact."

Scully's eyes are locked on Fowley.

"You're a liar," she whispers.

She turns on her heel to exit. Skinner grabs her arm to stop her.

"Scully—"he says.

"You're both liars," she says curtly, pulling away.

At the hogan in New Mexico the Navajo ceremony is well underway. Albert Hosteen lies unconscious. Dr. Sandoz stands and leaves.

At FBI headquarters Scully storms into the X-Files office. She scans the room, looking for something. Her eyes lock on a ceiling-mounted smoke detector, from which a black-and-white camera is surveilling her. Scully stands on a chair and reaches toward it, and is interrupted by her phone ringing. It is Sandoz, speaking on his cell phone beside his car parked near the hogan.

"Agent Scully, I'm sorry, I didn't know how to reach you. There's something—"

"Dr. Sandoz, I don't know if this is a secure line."

"Yes, all right," he says. "But I realize something. The letters that Albert translated on the artifact: I know what they are. Yes. They're coordinates, Agent Scully."

"For what?"

"For genes. They're symbols for gene clusters. The human genome. I think it's all here. The map to our human genetic makeup. Every gene on every chromosome! Proof of what I've been saying. If we could only find more pieces."

Sandoz stops and looks up; something has spooked a group of horses tethered nearby.

"Dr. Sandoz?" says Scully.

A shadow passes over the biologist's face.

"Hello?" says Scully.

There is no answer—only the sound of a single gunshot. A gloved hand snatches up Sandoz's cell phone from the ground. Sandoz himself lies dead; a bullet through his eye. Alex Krycek looks carefully around him, then leaves.

On the Ivory Coast thirty-six hours later, an African man holds up the rubbing of the artifact to a group of fisherman. They nod excitedly. The man walks over to Scully.

TO BE CONTINUED . . .

"It is the same," he says. "I'll take you, but they are afraid."

He leads Scully along the shoreline, through crashing waves to a rocky tide pool. Scully kneels and wipes away a thin layer of sand, exposing a metallic surface. She stops suddenly, then rises slowly and gazes ahead several yards ahead.

The metallic surface she's uncovered is only a small part of an immense object. She is standing on the hull of a triangular spacecraft—a vessel obviously not of this Earth.

To be continued . . .

BACK STORY/6X22

"Biogenesis," the 139th *X-Files* episode, completes the first full season of filming in Los Angeles. It reestablishes several characters—the Cigarette-Smoking Man, Alex Krycek, and Diana Fowley—left in post-apocalyptic limbo after "Two Fathers"/"One Son" (6X11 and 6X12).

It also marks the beginning of a new mythology for the series, one that goes beyond exploring the presence or absence of alien invaders and their human allies on earth and toward questioning the basis of human life itself.

In brief: Did *Homo sapiens*—emerging into the light one hundred thousand years ago, after the most recent of the five massive ecological catastrophes to afflict our planet—evolve "naturally?" Or was our genetic make-up, our planetary ascendance, our very human nature somehow affected by otherworldly influences?

"I've been interested in this subject for a while," says Chris Carter, citing recent scientific research on the five "great extinctions," plus other speculation—some emanating from legitimate scientific circles, some not—that extraterrestrial forces were present at mankind's creation.

What if, he asks rhetorically, hard evidence of all of this begins to turn up at the same time as indications of an imminent *sixth* great extinction?

"That would mean," says Carter, smiling, "that there would be a scientific basis to the search for extraterrestrials. Which plays perfectly into both Scully's scientific bias *and* Mulder's willingness to believe in the supernatural. Which means that Mulder's and Scully's belief systems will finally begin to come together—which is where we're going to go in Season Seven."

Alert viewers will note that the idea of alien genetic influence—in various forms from black oil to deadly bees to the mind-reader Gibson Praise's genetic abnormalities to the transformation of Cassandra Spender into a human-alien hybrid—has been a more or less constant theme in the recent mythological content of the series and the *X-Files* movie.

But "Biogenesis," explains executive producer Frank Spotnitz, takes this to a much higher level. "A lot of the major ideas in the episode are ones that Chris and I have been talking about for two or three years now," he says. "And so it actually became easier to visit those ideas once we'd cleared away the conspiracy [in 6X11 and 6X12]."

Not easy at all, unsurprisingly, was the transformation of "Biogenesis'" darkly complex script—much of which was written by Chris Carter while he was in Vancouver working on the pilot for *Harsh Realm* and faxed page-by-page to a nail-biting production staff—into a properly riveting season-ender.

"What Chris does," says Rob Bowman, 6X22's director, "is write down the side of the page. He never writes right to the point, he writes around it. And he trusts you to fill in the blanks, which is good writing but of course more of a challenge. And I wasn't sure while I was shooting it that it would all work, but I did believe in Chris's writing, and deep down I felt 'This is good.'"

According to Bowman, David Duchovny's real-life state of anxiety at the imminent arrival of his first child distracted the actor somewhat from his task, but not so that anyone would notice, since his character was also being distracted (albeit in a much more insidious way) by the cacophony of voices inside his head.

For the vital part of Dr. Solomon Merkmallen, director Rick Millikan called in Michael Chinyamurinidi, an actor who had moved to Los Angeles from his native Zimbabwe ten years ago and had tried out previously for the African-themed episode "Teliko" (4X04).

To cast the fisherman at the seaside African village where the extraterrestrial artifact is found, Millikan dipped into the surprisingly large pool of L.A.–based African immigrants available as extras and day players (including one extra-talented Nigerian-born extra, Ayo Adeyami, who serenaded the cast and crew with bracing sets of vigorous Yoruba drumming between shots).

To serve as the location for the seaside village itself, the producers rented Leo Carillo State Beach, a popular windsurfers' hangout about thirty minutes up the Pacific Coast Highway (Highway One), north of Malibu. Tidal conditions on the beach meant that director Rob Bowman had as little as forty-seven minutes per day to film certain scenes involving Scully's discovery of the artifact fragments at the waterline.

The portion of the beach used for filming was bisected by a rocky outcropping. On top of that point—in a miracle of eco-friendly rigging using no drills or screws or anything that would leave a permanent mark on the rock—key grip Tom Doherty and his crew erected a stable wooden platform (at times, the wind roaring in from the ocean sometimes reached forty mph) upon which they installed a forty-foot long camera crane with a computer-controlled camera at its end.

By floating large "green screens" in the surf, then

combining the shots filmed by the crane camera with a digital spaceship created by special effects producer Bill Millar, the alien craft was placed in the surf for Scully's final-scene discovery. All in all, this feat took twenty-five straight hours of high-speed computer time; Millar estimates its total cost at about $150,000.

To come up with appropriate lettering for the alleged extraterrestrial artifacts (the Navajo language being completely verbal, without any written notation or alphabet whatsoever), researcher Lee Smith dredged up articles about and photographs from the so-called "Kecksburg Incident," in which an alleged extraterrestrial object dropped in on a small town in Pennsylvania on December 9, 1965.

"I sent pictures of the weird writing on this bell-shaped article to the art department, and they did the rest," says Smith.

To obtain the requisite cloud of black flies for the scene in which Mulder and Scully discover Merkmallen's body in the trash compactor, property master Tom Day contracted with a Pasadena-based "fly wrangler," and prayed that the weather would be warm enough for this guy to corral a big enough crop at a local dairy to make it to the set with enough of the disgusting day players still alive. Day's prayers were answered.

On a much more serious level was the concerted effort by *The X-Files* to guarantee the accuracy and propriety of the Navajo symbols and religious ceremonies used in "Biogenesis." Hired to oversee it all—and to consult with his tribal elders back in New Mexico—was Hosteen Etsitty, a Navajo artist and lecturer who had previously created the Navajo sand paintings in "The Blessing Way" (3X01).

There were some inaccuracies in 3X01, including a Navajo ceremony combined with a Northern Plains Indian song; and for "Biogenesis" Etsitty recruited an apprentice Navajo medicine man, Thomas Goodluck, to conduct part of the Emergence Way, the proper Navajo ceremony for a dying man such as Albert Hosteen. Etsitty also approved the ceremonial Navajo garments, which the wardrobe and prop departments produced after much research and which amazed him with their authenticity and accuracy.

And, lastly, but perhaps prophetically, in filming the important scenes at Dr. Barnes's lab at American University, *The X-Files* facilitated an interesting convergence of science and what lies just beyond. To secure the appropriate academic environment locations manager Ilt Jones approached the Chemistry and Biochemistry Department at the University of California at Los Angeles, just a few miles from the Fox Studios.

"It's tough to get permission to shoot at UCLA," says Jones. "Which is a shame because they have many beautiful buildings but, obviously, they see their primary charter as education and research, not entertaining the viewers at home."

He adds, "So finally I had to meet with the chairman of the department, a very taciturn Polish-born chemist who looked like he had hydrochloric acid running through his veins. He really put me through the wringer. The first words out of this mouth were, 'Why on earth should we do this?'

"Which is a hard question to answer in under seven seconds. And which we eventually did answer in, I think, a very effective way: We gave the department twenty thousand dollars, to be used to pay for the education of a graduate student from overseas."

Will it be called "*The X-Files* Scholarship"? "The Mulder–Scully Student Fund"? "The Chris Carter Postgraduate Speculative Science Award"?

"You know," says Jones, smiling sheepishly, "I think they're still working on it."

Although *X-Files* management was prepared to suspend filming to accommodate the birth of David Duchovny's first child, it proved to be unnecessary. Thanks to good luck and some adroit scheduling, Madelaine West Duchovny—daughter of David Duchovny and Téa Leoni—was born on April 24, 1999; two days after the filming of Fox Mulder's final scene in "Biogenesis."

AWARDS
AND HONORS
1998–99

Prime-Time Emmy Awards
—Winner, Outstanding Makeup for a Series—Cheri Montesanto-Medcalf, Laverne Basham,
  John Vulich, Kevin Westmore, Greg Funk, John Wheaton, Mark Shostrom, Rick Stratton,
  Jake Garber, Craig Reardon, Fionagh Cush, Steve LaPorte, Kevin Haney, Jane Aull, Peri Sorel,
  Jeanne Van Phue and Julie Socash for "Two Fathers"/"One Son"
—Nominee, Outstanding Lead Actress in a Drama Series—Gillian Anderson
—Nominee, Outstanding Art Direction for a Series—Corey Kaplan, Lauren Polizzi,
  Sandy Getzler and Tim Stepeck for "One Son"
—Nominee, Outstanding Cinematography for a Series—Bill Roe for "The Unnatural"
—Nominee, Outstanding Single-Camera Picture Editing for a Series—Heather MacDougall for "S.R. 819"
—Nominee, Outstanding Music Composition for a Series (Dramatic Underscore)—Mark Snow for "S.R. 819"
—Nominee, Outstanding Guest Actress in a Drama Series—Veronica Cartwright as Cassandra
  Spender in "Two Fathers" and "One Son"
—Nominee, Outstanding Sound Editing for a Series—Thierry J. Couturier, Stuart Calderon,
  Michael Goodman, Jay Levine, Maciek Malish, George Nemzer, Cecilia Perna, Chris Reeves,
  Gabrielle Reeves, Jeff Charbonneau, Gary Marullo, and Mike Salvetta for "Triangle."

Golden Globe Awards
—Nominee, Best Television Series, Drama
—Nominee, Best Actress in a Drama Series—Gillian Anderson
—Nominee, Best Actor in a Drama Series—David Duchovny

Directors' Guild of America Awards (Golden Laurel Awards)
—Nominee, Outstanding Directing—Chris Carter for "Triangle"

Screen Actors Guild Awards
—Nominee, Best Performance by an Ensemble in a Dramatic Series
—Nominee, Best Actor in a Dramatic Series—David Duchovny
—Nominee, Best Performance by an Actress in a Dramatic Series—Gillian Anderson

Viewers For Quality Television
—Best Actress in a Quality Drama—Gillian Anderson

WORLDWIDE BROADCAST OUTLETS
During the 1998–99 season

The X-Files was licensed for broadcast in the following countries:*

1.	Afghanistan	42.	Guadeloupe	83.	Pakistan
2.	Algeria	43.	Guatemala	84.	Panama
3.	Argentina	44.	Guyana	85.	Paraguay
4.	Armenia	45.	Honduras	86.	Peru
5.	Aruba	46.	Hong Kong	87.	Philippines
6.	Australia	47.	Hungary	88.	Poland
7.	Bahrain	48.	Iceland	89.	Portugal
8.	Bangladesh	49.	India	90.	Puerto Rico
9.	Barbados	50.	Indonesia	91.	Qatar
10.	Belarus	51.	Iran	92.	Romania
11.	Belgium	52.	Iraq	93.	Russia
12.	Belize	53.	Ireland (Eire)	94.	Singapore
13.	Bhutan	54.	Israel	95.	Slovak Republic
14.	Bolivia	55.	Italy	96.	Slovenia
15.	Bosnia/Herzegovina	56.	Jamaica	97.	South Africa
16.	Brazil	57.	Japan	98.	South Korea
17.	Brunei	58.	Jordan	99.	Spain
18.	Bulgaria	59.	Kazakhstan	100.	Sri Lanka
19.	Cambodia	60.	Kenya	101.	Sweden
20.	Canada (English)	61.	Kuwait	102.	Switzerland
21.	Canada (French)	62.	Kyrgyzstan	103.	Syria
22.	Chile	63.	Laos	104.	Taiwan
23.	China	64.	Latvia	105.	Tajikistan
24.	Colombia	65.	Lebanon	106.	Tanzania
25.	Costa Rica	66.	Lithuania	107.	Thailand
26.	Croatia	67.	Luxembourg	108.	Trinidad & Tobago
27.	Cyprus	68.	Macao	109.	Turkey
28.	Czech Republic	69.	Malaysia	110.	Turkmenistan
29.	Denmark	70.	Malta	111.	Ukraine
30.	Dominican Republic	71.	Mauritius	112.	United Arab Emirates
31.	Dubai	72.	Mexico	113.	United Kingdom
32.	Ecuador	73.	Mongolia	114.	United States
33.	Egypt	74.	Morocco	115.	Uruguay
34.	El Salvador	75.	Myanmar (Burma)	116.	Uzbekistan
35.	Estonia	76.	Namibia	117.	Venezuela
36.	Fiji	77.	Nepal	118.	Vietnam
37.	Finland	78.	Netherlands	119.	West Samoa
38.	France	79.	New Zealand	120.	Yemen
39.	Germany	80.	Nicaragua		
40.	Ghana	81.	Norway		
41.	Greece	82.	Oman		

*Broadcast license windows last up to two years; the series may or may not be on the air at any given time.

RATINGS
SEASON SIX

AIRDATE	EPISODE	RATINGS/SHARE	VIEWERS (in millions)
11/08/98	The Beginning	11.9/17	20.34
11/15/98	Drive	11.0/16	18.50
11/22/98	Triangle	10.8/16	18.20
11/29/98	Dreamland	10.1/15	17.48
12/06/98	Dreamland II	10.0/15	17.01
12/13/98	How the Ghosts Stole Christmas	10.6/16	17.31
01/03/99	Terms of Endearment	10.5/15	18.69
01/10/99	The Rain King	12.5/18	21.24
01/17/99	S.R. 819	9.1/14	15.65
01/24/99	Tithonus	9.2/13	15.83
02/07/99	Two Fathers	11.5/16	18.81
02/14/99	One Son	10.1/16	16.57
02/21/99	Agua Mala	10.1/15	16.91
02/28/99	Monday	10.2/15	16.74
03/07/99	Arcadia	10.5/16	17.91
03/28/99	Alpha	10.1/15	17.67
04/11/99	Trevor	10.4/16	17.65
04/18/99	Milagro	9.0/14	15.20
04/25/99	The Unnatural	10.1/15	16.88
05/02/99	Three of a Kind	8.2/12	12.94
05/09/99	Field Trip	9.5/15	15.38
05/16/99	Biogenesis	9.4/14	15.86

Each rating point equals 980,000 homes, or 1 percent of all households in the United States. Share is based upon the percentage of TV sets in use within the time period. Total viewers for each episode is measured by Nielsen's people-meter service, which draws its figures from a small sample designed to represent all television viewers in the United States.
Source: Nielsen Media Research

SEASON ONE

PILOT 1X79
FBI Agent Dana Scully is paired with maverick agent Fox Mulder, who has made it his life's work to explore unexplained phenomena. The two are dispatched to investigate the mysterious deaths of a number of high school classmates.

DEEP THROAT 1X01
Acting on a tip from an inside source (Deep Throat), Mulder and Scully travel to Idaho to investigate unusual disappearances of army test pilots.

SQUEEZE 1X02
Mulder and Scully try to stop a mutant killer, Eugene Tooms, who can gain access through even the smallest spaces and awakens from hibernation every 30 years to commit murder.

CONDUIT 1X03
A teenage girl is abducted by aliens, compelling Mulder to confront his feelings about his own sister's disappearance.

THE JERSEY DEVIL 1X04
Scully and Mulder investigate murders thought to be the work of the legendary man-beast living in the New Jersey woods.

SHADOWS 1X05
Mulder and Scully investigate unusual murders committed by an unseen force protecting a young woman.

GHOST IN THE MACHINE 1X06
A computer with artificial intelligence begins killing in order to preserve its existence.

ICE 1X07
Mulder and Scully and a small party in the Arctic are trapped after the unexplained deaths of a research team on assignment there.

SPACE 1X08
A mysterious force is sabotaging the United States space shuttle program and Scully and Mulder must stop it before the next launch.

FALLEN ANGEL 1X09
Scully and Mulder investigate a possible UFO crash site, which Mulder believes the government is covering up.

EVE 1X10
Two bizarre, identical murders occur simultaneously on different coasts, each involving a strange young girl.

FIRE 1X11
Mulder and Scully encounter an assassin who can start fires with the touch of his hand.

BEYOND THE SEA 1X12
Scully and Mulder seek the aid of a death row inmate, Luther Lee Boggs, who claims to have psychic abilities, to help them stop a killer who is on the loose.

GENDERBENDER 1X13
Scully and Mulder seek answers to a bizarre series of murders committed by one person who kills as both a male and a female.

LAZARUS 1X14
When an FBI agent and a bank robber are both shot during a bank heist, the robber is killed but the agent begins to take on the criminal's persona.

YOUNG AT HEART 1X15
Mulder finds that a criminal he put away who was supposed to have died in prison has returned, taunting him as he commits a new spree of crimes.

E.B.E 1X16
Scully and Mulder discover evidence of a government cover-up when they learn that a UFO shot down in Iraq has been secretly transported to the United States.

MIRACLE MAN 1X17
The agents investigate a young faith healer who seems to use his powers for both good and evil.

SHAPES 1X18
Mulder and Scully travel to an Indian reservation to examine deaths caused by a beastlike creature.

DARKNESS FALLS 1X19
Mulder and Scully are called in when loggers in a remote Pacific Northwest forest mysteriously disappear.

TOOMS 1X20
Mulder becomes personally involved when Eugene Tooms, the serial killer who extracts and eats human livers, is released from prison.

BORN AGAIN 1X21
A series of murders is linked to a little girl who may be the reincarnated spirit of a murdered policeman.

ROLAND 1X22
Mulder and Scully investigate the murders of two rocket scientists apparently linked to a retarded janitor.

THE ERLENMEYER FLASK 1X23
Working on a tip from Deep Throat, Mulder and Scully discover that the government has been testing alien DNA on humans with disastrous results.

LITTLE GREEN MEN 2X01
With the X-Files shut down, Mulder secretly journeys to a possible alien contact site in Puerto Rico while Scully tries to help him escape detection.

THE HOST 2X02
Mulder stumbles upon a genetic mutation, the Flukeman, while investigating a murder in the New Jersey sewer system.

BLOOD 2X03
Several residents of a small suburban farming community suddenly turn violent and dangerous, prompted by digital readouts in appliances telling them to kill.

SLEEPLESS 2X04
Mulder is assigned a new partner, Alex Krycek, and they investigate a secret Vietnam-era experiment on sleep deprivation that is having deadly effects on surviving participants.

DUANE BARRY (PART 1 OF 2) 2X05
Mulder negotiates a hostage situation involving a man, Duane Barry, who claims to be a victim of alien experimentation.

ASCENSION (PART 2 OF 2) 2X06
Mulder pursues Duane Barry in a desperate search for Scully.

3 2X07
Mulder investigates a series of vampiresque murders in Hollywood and finds himself falling for a mysterious woman who is a prime suspect.

ONE BREATH 2X08
Scully is found alive but in a coma, and Mulder must fight to save her life.

FIREWALKER 2X09
Mulder and Scully stumble upon a deadly life form while investigating the death of a scientist studying an active volcano.

RED MUSEUM 2X10
Mulder and Scully investigate a possible connection between a rural religious cult and the disappearance of several teenagers.

EXCELSIUS DEI 2X11
Mulder and Scully uncover strange goings-on in a nursing home after a nurse is attacked by an unseen force.

AUBREY 2X12
Mulder and Scully investigate the possibility of genetic transferring of personality from one generation to another in connection with a serial killer.

IRRESISTIBLE 2X13
A psycho who collects hair and fingernails from the dead steps up his obsession to killing his soon-to-be collectibles himself.

DIE HAND DIE VERLETZT 2X14
Mulder and Scully journey to a small town to investigate a boy's murder and are caught between the town's secret occult religion and a woman with strange powers.

FRESH BONES 2X15
Mulder and Scully journey to a Haitian refugee camp after a series of deaths, finding themselves caught in a secret war between the camp commander and a voodoo priest.

COLONY (PART 1 OF 2) 2X16
Mulder and Scully track an alien bounty hunter, who is killing medical doctors who have something strange in common.

END GAME (PART 2 OF 2) 2X17
Mulder tracks an alien bounty hunter who has taken Scully prisoner while discovering that his sister may not be who she seems.

FEARFUL SYMMETRY 2X18
Mulder and Scully investigate animal abductions from a zoo near a known UFO hot spot.

DOD KALM 2X19
Mulder and Scully fall victim to a mysterious force aboard a navy destroyer that causes rapid aging.

HUMBUG 2X20
Mulder and Scully investigate the bizarre death of a retired escape artist in a town populated by former circus and sideshow acts.

THE CALUSARI 2X21
A young boy's unusual death leads Mulder and Scully to a superstitious old woman and her grandson, who may be possessed by evil.

F. EMASCULATA 2X22
When a plaguellke illness kills ten men inside a prison facility, Scully is called to the quarantine area while Mulder tracks two escapees.

SOFT LIGHT 2X23
An experiment in dark matter turns a scientist's shadow into a form of instant death.

OUR TOWN 2X24
Mulder and Scully investigate a murder in a small Southern town and its strange secrets surrounding a chicken processing plant.

ANASAZI 2X25
Mulder's and Scully's lives are jeopardized when an amateur computer hacker gains access to secret government files providing evidence of UFOs.

SEASON THREE

THE BLESSING WAY 3X01
With the Cigarette-Smoking Man pursuing the secret files that prove the existence of alien visitation and experimentation, and Mulder still missing, Scully finds her own life and career in jeopardy.

PAPER CLIP 3X02
Mulder and Scully seek evidence of alien experimentation by Nazi war criminals while Skinner tries to bargain with the Cigarette-Smoking Man for their lives.

D.P.O. 3X03
Mulder and Scully investigate a series of deaths related to a teenage boy who can control lightning.

CLYDE BRUCKMAN'S FINAL REPOSE 3X04
Mulder and Scully enlist the help of a man who can see when people will die while searching for a serial killer who prays upon fortunetellers.

THE LIST 3X05
A death row inmate makes good on his promise to return from the dead and kill five people who wronged him.

2SHY 3X06
Mulder and Scully track a serial killer who preys on lonely, overweight women via the Internet.

THE WALK 3X07
A suicide attempt and subsequent murders at a military hospital bring Mulder and Scully into contact with a quadruple amputee veteran who may have the power of astral projection.

OUBLIETTE 3X08
The abduction of a young girl prompts Mulder to seek the help of a woman who was kidnapped by the same man years earlier and who has the ability to feel what the victim feels.

NISEI 3X09
Video of an alien autopsy puts Mulder and Scully on the trail of a conspiracy involving Japanese scientists that may shed light on Scully's abduction.

731 3x10
Mulder is caught on board a speeding train with what might be alien cargo and a government killer while Scully seeks her own solution to the conspiracy.

REVELATIONS 3X11
Mulder and Scully seek to protect a young boy who displays wounds of religious significance from a killer, causing Scully to question her own faith while being cast in the role of the boy's protector.

WAR OF THE COPROPHAGES 3X12
A number of deaths seemingly linked to cockroaches cause widespread panic in a small town.

SYZYGY 3X13
Two high school girls born on the same day are involved in a series of deaths thanks to an odd alignment of planets that causes strange behavior in all the townspeople, as well as Mulder and Scully.

GROTESQUE 3X14
A serial killer maintains that an evil spirit was responsible for his actions, as Mulder's own sanity comes into question when the murders persist.

PIPER MARU 3X15
A French salvage ship finds mysterious wreckage from World War II that unleashes a strange force causing radiation sickness and leading Mulder into a web of intrigue.

APOCRYPHA 3X16
Mulder pursues Krycek and the mystery of the sunken World War II wreckage, while the shooting of Skinner brings Scully new clues to her sister's murder.

PUSHER 3X17
Mulder and Scully investigate a man possessing the power to bend people to his will who engages Mulder in a scary battle of wits.

TESO DOS BICHOS 3X18
The unearthing of an ancient Ecuadorian artifact results in a series of deaths potentially linked to a shaman spirit.

HELL MONEY 3X19
The deaths of several Chinese immigrants missing internal organs leads Mulder and Scully to a mysterious game with potentially fatal consequences.

JOSE CHUNG'S *FROM OUTER SPACE* 3X20
A novelist interviews Scully about a rumored UFO abduction of two teenagers that seems open to a number of different interpretations.

AVATAR 3X21
In the midst of a marital breakup Skinner becomes a murder suspect, while a clue to the case may lie in the form of a strange woman who appears to him in dreams.

QUAGMIRE 3X22
Mulder and Scully investigate a series of deaths that may be linked to a lake monster known by the locals as Big Blue.

WETWIRED 3X23
Mulder and Scully discover a conspiracy involving mind control through television signals that's responsible for a series of murders in a small town and begins causing Scully herself to behave strangely.

TALITHA CUMI 3X24
Mulder and Scully search for a mysterious man with the power to heal, whose existence risks exposing a conspiracy involving the presence of aliens on Earth, while various forces seek a strange weapon that comes into Mulder's possession.

SEASON FOUR

HERRENVOLK 4X01

As Mulder's mother lies dying, he and Scully are given tantalizing glimpses of a plan to secretly catalog—and clone—human beings. Only by putting the pieces together can they hope to save Mrs. Mulder's life.

UNRUHE 4X02

Someone is abducting, mutilating, and murdering the inhabitants of a small town. The primary evidence is a series of photographs depicting the killer's psychotic fantasies.

HOME 4X03

While investigating the death of an infant in a close-knit rural community, Mulder and Scully uncover an even darker family secret.

TELIKO 4X04

African-American men are disappearing. Their bodies, when found, are dead white—drained of pigment. Were they killed by a virulent new disease? Were they murdered? Or does the answer lie elsewhere?

THE FIELD WHERE I DIED 4X05

In an effort to prevent a mass suicide at a fanatical religious cult, Mulder and Scully interrogate one of the wives of the polygamous cult leader. Under hypnosis, her accounts of her past lives—and deaths—are inexplicably tied to the agents' own.

SANGUINARIUM 4X06

At a busy—and lucrative—cosmetic surgery clinic, doctors are murdering patients with the tools of their trade. Several clues point toward demonic possession.

MUSINGS OF A CIGARETTE-SMOKING MAN (4X07)

The secret biography of a sinister, all-powerful conspirator. Some old mysteries are cleared up—and some new ones are created.

PAPER HEARTS 4X08

Prompted by a series of prophetic dreams, Mulder reopens the case of a convicted child killer. The murderer claims to know the circumstances of Samantha Mulder's abduction.

TUNGUSKA 4X09

Diplomatic couriers are bringing a lethal alien life form into the United States. Mulder and Scully's investigation points to a high-level international conspiracy beyond even their comprehension.

TERMA 4X10

Stranded in the gulag, Mulder discovers the effects of the alien toxin—firsthand. In Washington, Scully battles a corrupt United States senator to keep their investigation alive.

EL MUNDO GIRA 4X11

Fear, jealousy, superstition, and prejudice converge when a young female migrant worker is killed by a mysterious yellow rain.

KADDISH 4X12

Someone—or something—is killing the members of an anti-Semitic gang. To find the truth, Mulder and Scully delve into the ancient canons of Jewish mysticism.

NEVER AGAIN 4X13

On a solo assignment out of town, a lonely Scully meets Mr. Wrong—a single guy who thinks his new tattoo is talking to him.

LEONARD BETTS 4X14

A headless corpse escapes from a hospital morgue. Mulder and Scully investigate; what they find leads them to the jagged dividing line between life and death.

MEMENTO MORI 4X15

Scully learns she has inoperable cancer—of the same type that killed nearly a dozen female UFO abductees. While she undergoes radical treatment, Mulder works desperately to unravel the conspiracy behind her disease.

UNREQUITED 4X16

A Marine Corps prisoner of war, abandoned in Vietnam by his superiors, returns to the United States with a vengeance—and a special talent for hiding in plain sight.

TEMPUS FUGIT 4X17

A former UFO abductee is killed in a catastrophic plane crash. Mulder suspects a conspiracy—and a cover-up.

MAX 4X18

Mulder and Scully get close to proving alien involvement in the crash of Flight 549. As they do so, they trigger a massive military disinformation campaign—and the deaths of several friends and colleagues.

SYNCHRONY 4X19

For centuries, scientists have debated whether time travel is possible—and if it ever will be. For Mulder and Scully, this age-old conundrum is the key to solving several baffling murders.

SMALL POTATOES 4X20

Mulder and Scully investigate several not-so-blessed events in a small southern town.

ZERO SUM 4X21

Walter Skinner makes a deal with the devil—a.k.a. the Cigarette-Smoking Man—in an effort to prevent Scully from dying of cancer.

ELEGY 4X22

Several young women have been murdered on Mulder and Scully's home turf. Their prime suspect is a mentally disabled man, Harold Spüller, who has been beset by a series of frightening apparitions.

DEMONS 4X23

After experiencing a series of blackouts and seizures—and what might be the recovery of repressed memories—Mulder gains new insights into his younger sister's abduction. However, while taking his inner journey, he may also have murdered two people.

GETHSEMANE 4X24

When a controversial scientist claims to have discovered evidence of extraterrestrial life, Mulder and Scully find their lives—and belief systems—in grave peril.

SEASON FIVE

UNUSUAL SUSPECTS 5X01
In an important chunk of X-Files pre-history, up-and-coming FBI agent Mulder crosses paths with an unlikely trio of eccentrics; pursues a beautiful alleged terrorist; and gets a searing glimpse into his own future.

REDUX 5X02
After faking his own suicide to shake off Syndicate and FBI surveillance, Mulder secretly searches for the cause of—and cure for—Scully's terminal cancer.

REDUX II 5X03
While Scully, dying from cancer, undergoes the desperate treatment her partner has stolen for her, Mulder penetrates the inner circle of the Syndicate-FBI conspiracy. He finds many of the truths that have long eluded him—as well as disillusionment, despair, and danger.

DETOUR 5X04
A primeval forest is threatened by encroaching civilization. Its secret inhabitants—fierce predators with glowing red eyes—fight back.

CHRISTMAS CAROL 5X05
While spending the Christmas holiday with her family, Scully receives a mysterious phone call. She is summoned to help a desperately ill child, whose tragic history is inexplicably linked to her own.

THE POST-MODERN PROMETHEUS 5X06
Deep in the American heartland, Mulder and Scully encounter—then attempt to unravel—the twisted schemes of a modern-day Victor Frankenstein.

EMILY 5X07
Scully's biological daughter is dying. Mulder uncovers the little girl's role in the alien conspiracy—while Scully fights to save her only child.

KITSUNEGARI 5X09
The serial killer known as "The Pusher"—a man with the inexplicable ability to impose his own will on others—escapes from a maximum security prison. He immediately pursues the man who captured him: Mulder.

SCHIZOGENY 5X09
In a blight-stricken farm town, a series of murders is attributed to child abuse. The real cause, however, lies deeper.

CHINGA 5X10
With the help of an eerie playmate, an autistic child is able to express her innermost feelings—and terrorize an entire New England village.

KILL SWITCH 5X11
A dying computer genius creates a murderous cybernetic life form. Mulder and Scully—aided only by the dead man's disciple—must somehow purge this predator from the Internet.

BAD BLOOD 5X12
Mulder sticks his neck out—and then some—to capture a small-town serial killer.

PATIENT X 5X13
As a disillusioned Mulder denies all evidence of extraterrestrial visitors, Scully—along with thousands of other abductees—is drawn toward a final confrontation.

THE RED AND THE BLACK 5X14
The world turned upside down: Recovering from a near-death experience, Scully is convinced that her memories of alien encounters are true. For his part Mulder clings to skepticism and science and uncovers new, even more dangerous, conspiracies.

TRAVELERS 5X15
One year before reopening the X-Files, young Agent Mulder investigates a bizarre murder. The answers he seeks lie in the not-so-distant past: during the Red Scare of the 1950s.

MIND'S EYE 5X16
A sadistic murderer is on the loose. The only witness to his crimes: a totally blind young woman, who somehow "sees" through the killer's eyes.

ALL SOULS 5X17
After a handicapped young woman is killed in the act of prayer, Scully is pulled into the case and forced to search her own soul for answers.

THE PINE BLUFF VARIANT 5X18
Playing a dangerous double game, Mulder infiltrates a gang of domestic terrorists.

FOLIE À DEUX 5X19
A giant buglike creature is sucking the life out of humans. Or so says one gun-toting, apparently mentally ill man, who holds a group of his coworkers, plus Mulder, hostage.

THE END 5X20
A child chess prodigy has the ability to read minds. If Mulder and Scully can protect him, he could be the answer to the mysteries they've long been exploring. If the rulers of the Syndicate capture him, he could be the key to world hegemony and the final destruction of the X-Files.